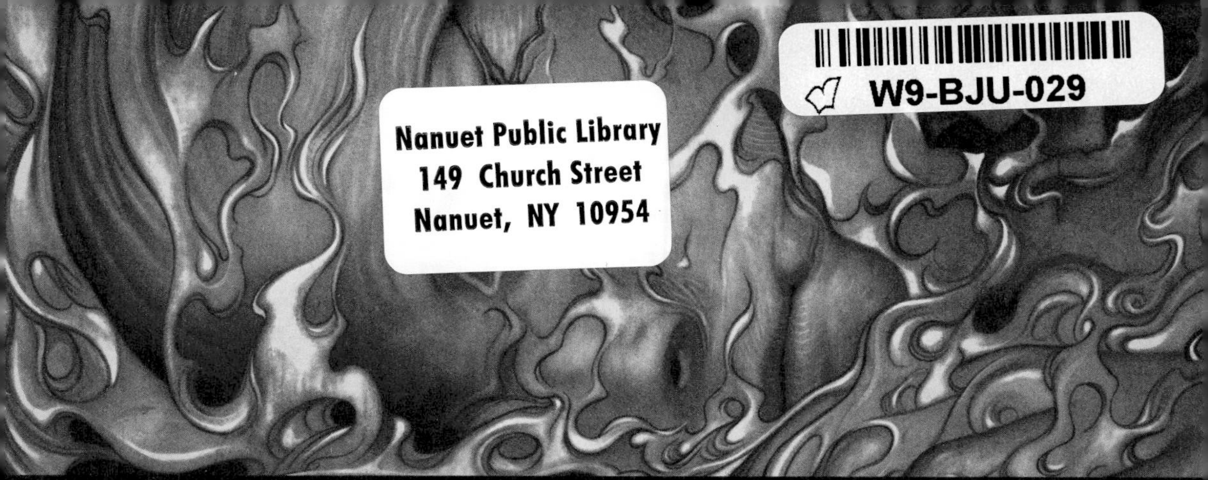

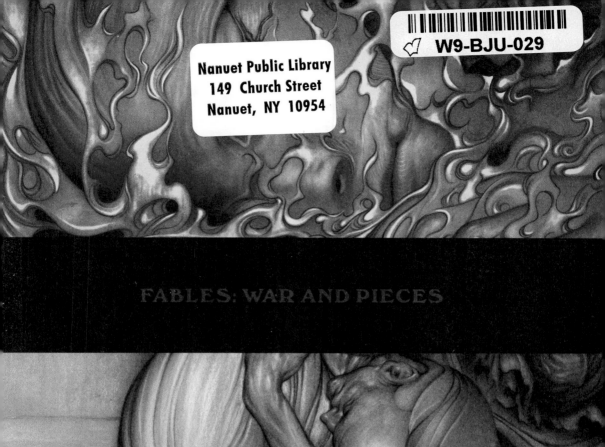

FABLES: WAR AND PIECES

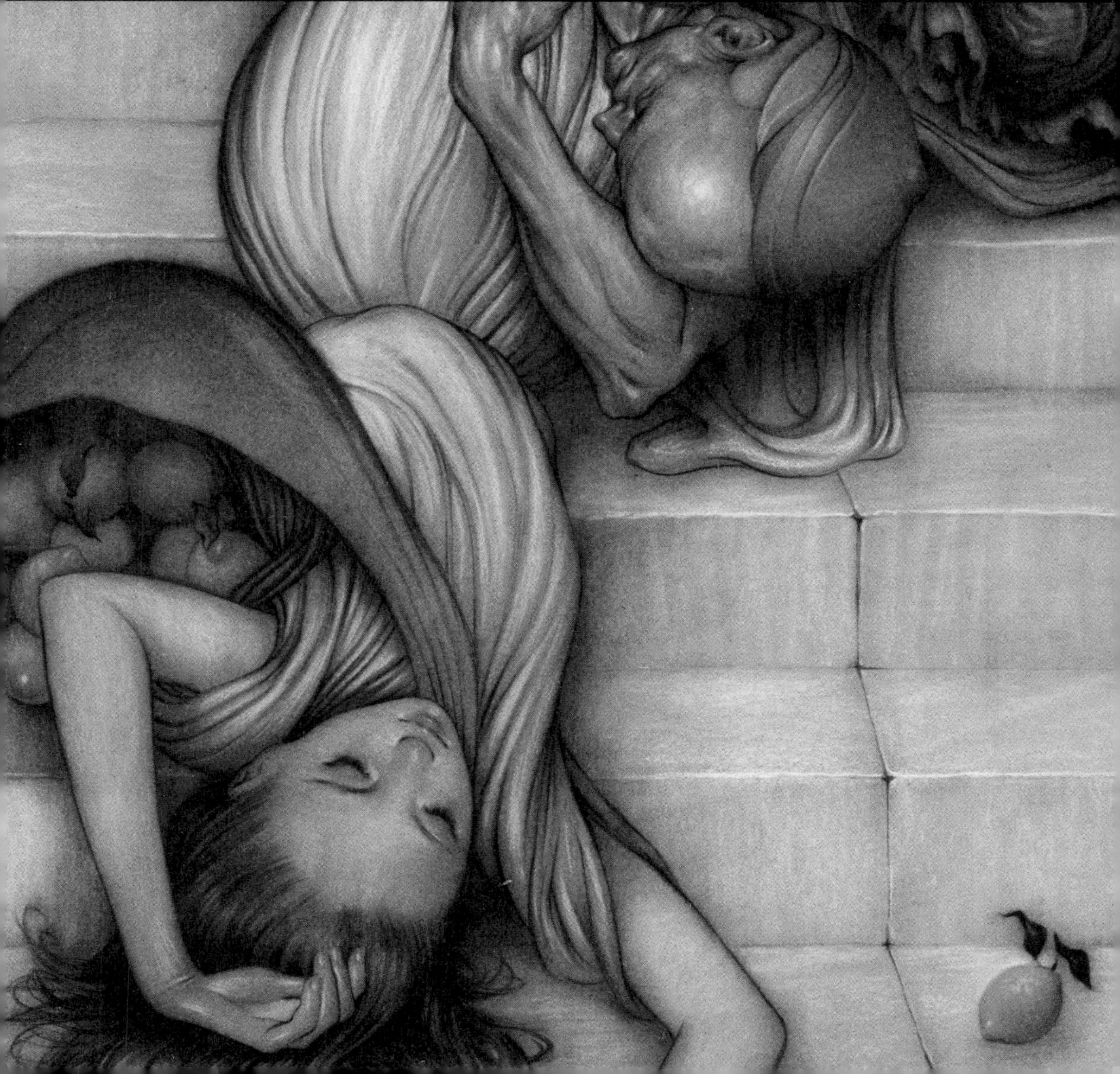

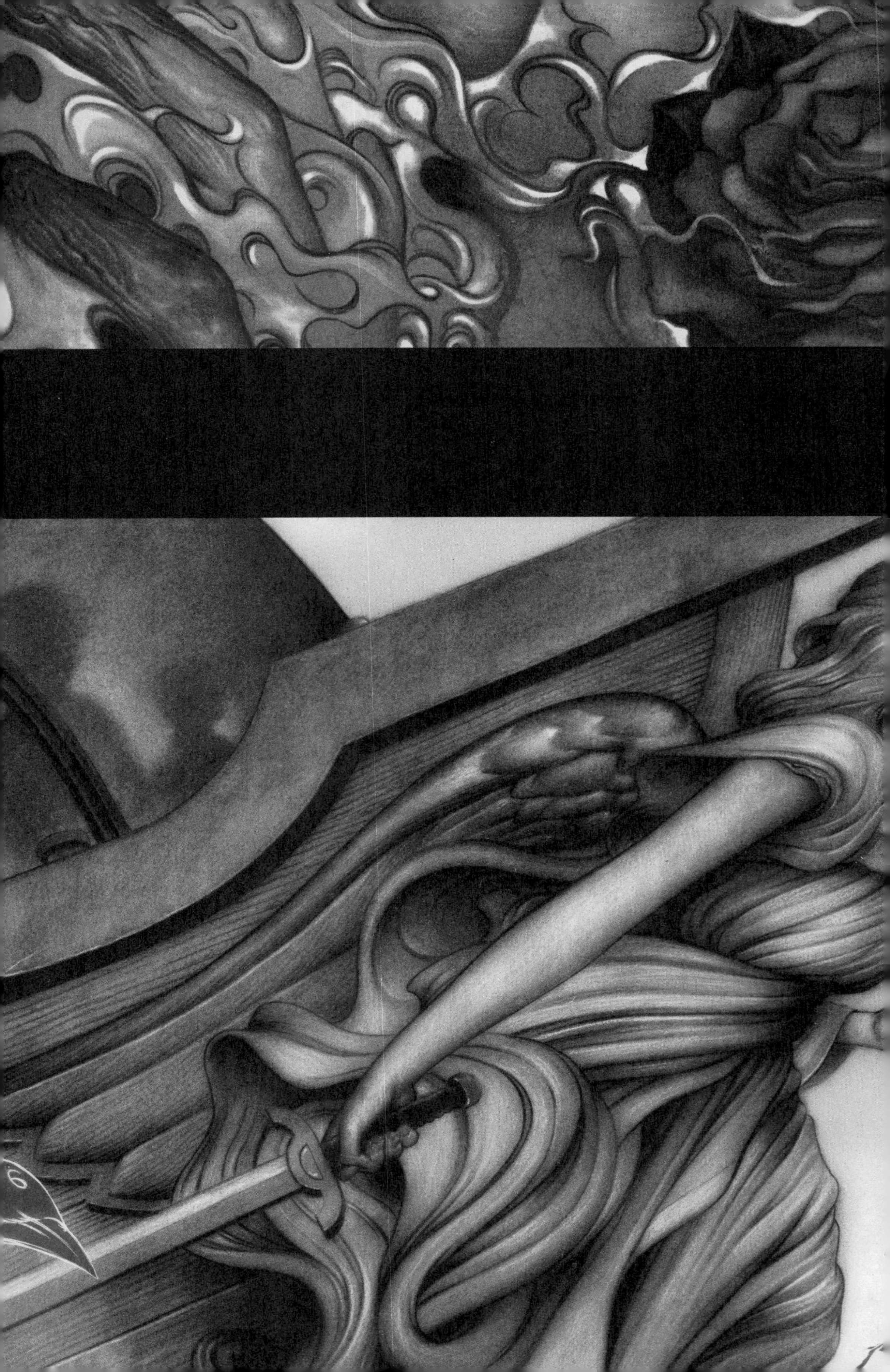

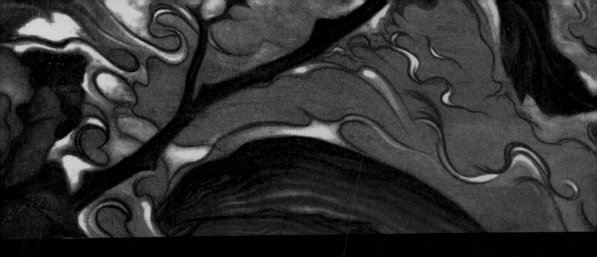

FABLES: WAR AND PIECES

FABLES CREATED BY BILL WILLINGHAM

Bill Willingham
writer

Mark Buckingham
Steve Leialoha
Niko Henrichon
Andrew Pepoy
artists

Lee Loughridge
Niko Henrichon
colorists

Todd Klein
letterer

James Jean
original series covers

WHO'S WHO IN FABLETOWN

BRIAR ROSE

She's the Sleeping Beauty, still suffering from the old curse: prick her finger and she falls into an endless sleep, along with everyone unfortunate enough to be near her.

PRINCE CHARMING

He's the Mayor of Fabletown and still an unrepentant rog

SINBAD

The former Arabian Fables envoy to Fabletown and one of the leaders of ancient Baghdad — the magical version.

BOY BLUE

A heroic war veteran who would much prefer to be nothing more than a dull clerk leading an uneventful and ordinary life.

BIGBY WOLF

A monster and a brute, but a reformed one, now on the side of the angels.

SNOW WHITE

Bigby's wife and mother of their seven children, and the one you want to turn to wher the chips are down.

FRAU TOTENKINDER

Leader of the 13th floor sorcerers, a pretty good witch with a pretty bad past.

KING COLE

The former mayor and current ambassador to the Arabian Fables.

THE STORY SO FAR

It's been building up for years, and now it looks like the full-scale shooting is about to begin. Fabletown and the Empire are poised on the brink of all-out war. Fabletown wants complete freedom, even if they have to utterly destroy the Empire to achieve it, and the Empire's given up on coaxing the rebellious Fabletown back into the fold — now they want nothing

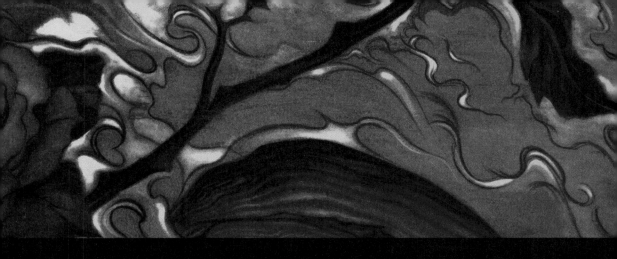

FABLES: WAR AND PIECES

FABLES CREATED BY BILL WILLINGHAM

Bill Willingham
writer

Mark Buckingham
Steve Leialoha
Niko Henrichon
Andrew Pepoy
artists

Lee Loughridge
Niko Henrichon
colorists

Todd Klein
letterer

James Jean
original series covers

Shelly Bond
Executive Editor – Vertigo and
Editor – Original Series

Angela Rufino
Assistant Editor – Original Series

Scott Nybakken
Editor

Robbin Brosterman
Design Director – Books

Hank Kanalz
Senior VP – Vertigo & Integrated Publishing

Diane Nelson
President

Dan DiDio and Jim Lee
Co-Publishers

Geoff Johns
Chief Creative Officer

Amit Desai
Senior VP – Marketing & Franchise
Management

Amy Genkins
Senior VP – Business & Legal Affairs

Nairi Gardiner
Senior VP – Finance

Jeff Boison
VP – Publishing Planning

Mark Chiarello
VP – Art Direction & Design

John Cunningham
VP – Marketing

Terri Cunningham
VP – Editorial Administration

Larry Ganem
VP – Talent Relations & Services

Alison Gill
Senior VP – Manufacturing & Operations

Jay Kogan
VP – Business & Legal Affairs, Publishing

Jack Mahan
VP – Business Affairs, Talent

Nick Napolitano
VP – Manufacturing Administration

Sue Pohja
VP – Book Sales

Fred Ruiz
VP – Manufacturing Operations

Courtney Simmons
Senior VP – Publicity

Bob Wayne
Senior VP – Sales

*Thank you to Duncan Fegredo,
Mike Oeming, Charlie Adlard,
Matt Brooker, Chris Opperman and
Scott Peterson who all gave good advice
and lots of support as I experimented
with art styles and page proportions
on the Cindy Arc... and an even bigger
thank-you to the whole creative and
editorial team on FABLES for being so
patient with me, so versatile, and
ensuring that FABLES looks so good.*

*Special thanks also to my family, friends
and my lovely wife Irma for forgiving the
long hours invested in this volume...
and to my friend Bill for creating such
a wonderful world for this lucky artist
to play in.*

*Dedicated to the memory of
Steve Whitaker and Phil Gascoine.*

— Mark Buckingham

*This collection is respectfully dedicated
to the wonderfully restless shade of
Edgar Rice Burroughs, who was the first,
in my encounters, to put great and
ponderous wooden fighting ships in the
sky. His were held aloft by the mysterious
Eighth Ray of Barsoom, while ours are
lifted by artful carpets, but it's the same
primal force at work in both cases.
Thank you, old ghost, for a lifetime of
inspiration.*

— Bill Willingham

Cover illustrations by James Jean
Logo design by Brainchild Studios/NYC

FABLES: WAR AND PIECES

Published by DC Comics. Cover, afterword,
sketchbook and compilation Copyright © 2008
DC Comics. All Rights Reserved.

Originally published in single magazine form as
FABLES 70-75. Copyright © 2008 Bill Willingham
and DC Comics. All Rights Reserved.
All characters, their distinctive likenesses and
related elements featured in this publication
are trademarks of Bill Willingham. VERTIGO is a
trademark of DC Comics. The stories, characters
and incidents featured in this publication are
entirely fictional. DC Comics does not read or
accept unsolicited submissions of ideas, stories
or artwork.

DC Comics, 1700 Broadway, New York, NY 10019
A Warner Bros. Entertainment Company.
Printed in Canada. Fifth Printing.
ISBN: 978-1-4012-1913-0

SUSTAINABLE FORESTRY INITIATIVE

Certified Chain of Custody
Promoting Sustainable Forestry
www.sfiprogram.org
SFI-00507
This label only applies to the text section.

Library of Congress Cataloging-in-Publication
Data

Willingham, Bill.
  Fables. Vol. 11, War and pieces / Bill
Willingham, Mark Buckingham, Steve Leialoha,
Niko Henrichon, Andrew Pepoy.
      p. cm.
  "Originally published in single magazine form
as Fables 70-75."
  ISBN 978-1-4012-1913-0 (alk. paper)
  1. Legends—Adaptations--Comic books, strips,
etc. 2. Graphic novels. I. Buckingham, Mark. II.
Leialoha, Steve. III. Henrichon, Niko. IV. Pepoy,
Andrew. V. Title. VI. Title: War and pieces.
  PN6727.W52F394 2012
  741.5'973—dc23
                                      2012038987

Table of Contents

WHO'S WHO IN FABLETOWN

BRIAR ROSE

She's the Sleeping Beauty, still suffering from the old curse: prick her finger and she falls into an endless sleep, along with everyone unfortunate enough to be near her.

PRINCE CHARMING

He's the Mayor of Fabletown, and still an unrepentant rogue.

SINBAD

The former Arabian Fables envoy to Fabletown and one of the leaders of ancient Baghdad — the magical version.

BOY BLUE

A heroic war veteran who would much prefer to be nothing more than a dull clerk leading an uneventful and ordinary life.

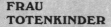

BIGBY WOLF

A monster and a brute, but a reformed one, now on the side of the angels.

SNOW WHITE

Bigby's wife and mother of their seven children, and the one you want to turn to when the chips are down.

FRAU TOTENKINDER

Leader of the 13th floor sorcerers, a pretty good witch with a pretty bad past.

KING COLE

The former mayor and current ambassador to the Arabian Fables.

THE STORY SO FAR

It's been building up for years, and now it looks like the full-scale shooting is about to begin. Fabletown and the Empire are poised on the brink of all-out war. Fabletown wants complete freedom, even if they have to utterly destroy the Empire to achieve it, and the Empire's given up on coaxing the rebellious Fabletown back into the fold — now they want nothing less than its total annihilation...

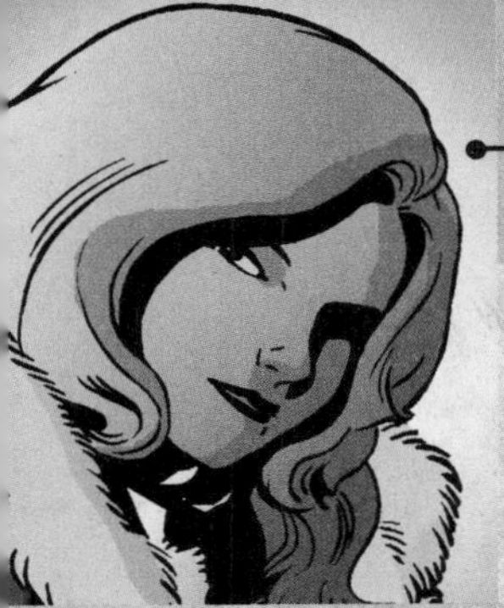

CINDERELLA

An intrepid off-the-books spy and troubleshooter, working clandestinely for the Fabletown leadership.

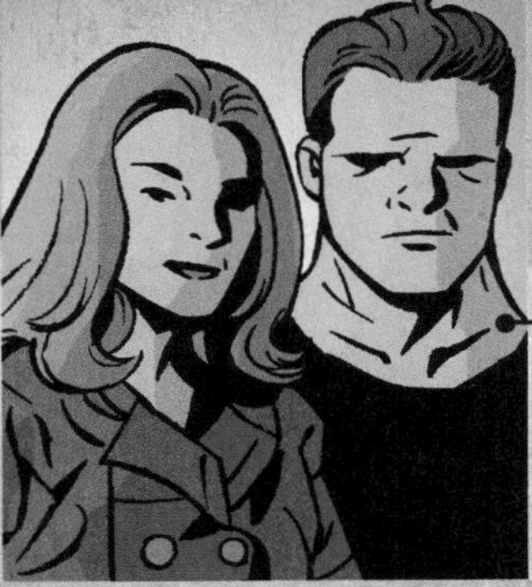

BEAUTY AND THE BEAST

She's the current deputy mayor and he's the sheriff.

RODNEY AND JUNE

Not members of Fabletown, but they live close by as spies for the evil Empire.

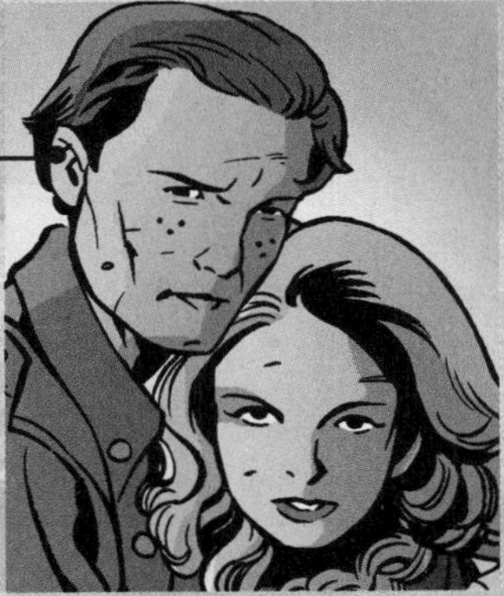

ROSE RED

Snow White's twin sister and administrator of the Farm.

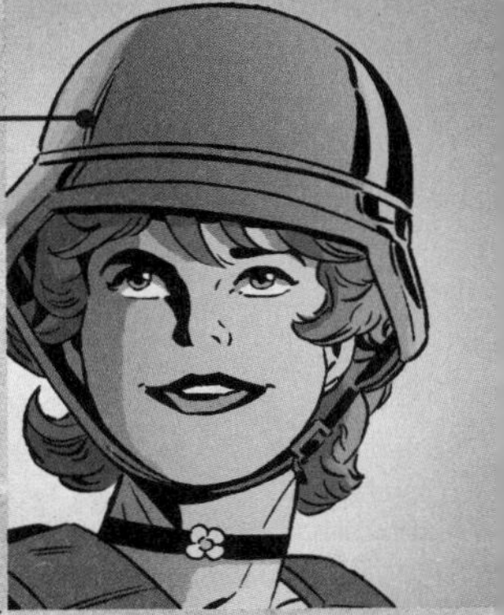

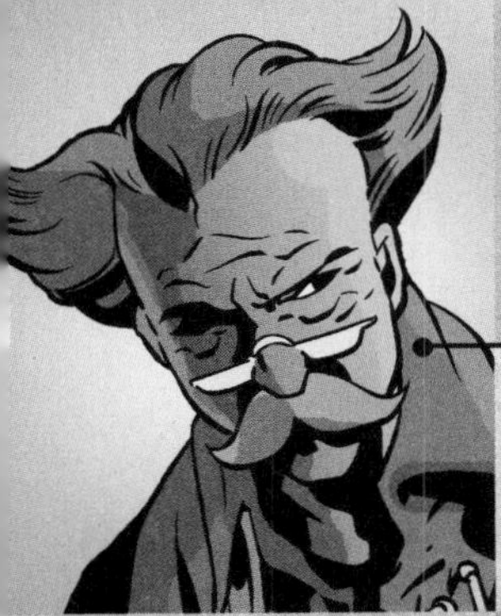

WHO'S WHO IN THE EMPIRE

GEPPETTO

He's the wicked Adversary, the man pulling the strings of the Empire, and he's bedeviled the refugees of Fabletown for centuries.

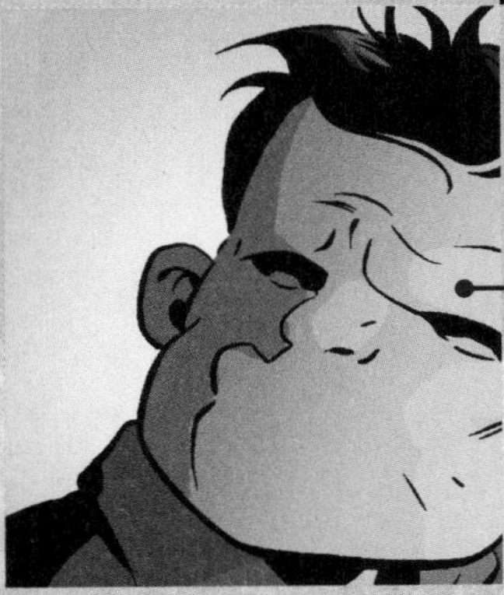

PINOCCHIO

Geppetto's first-carved son. He was back at home with his father for several years, until an argument sent him running away again.

THE EMPEROR

A figurehead, but a powerful one. He's really a big puppet, but lately there've been hints and indications that he wouldn't mind pulling his own strings.

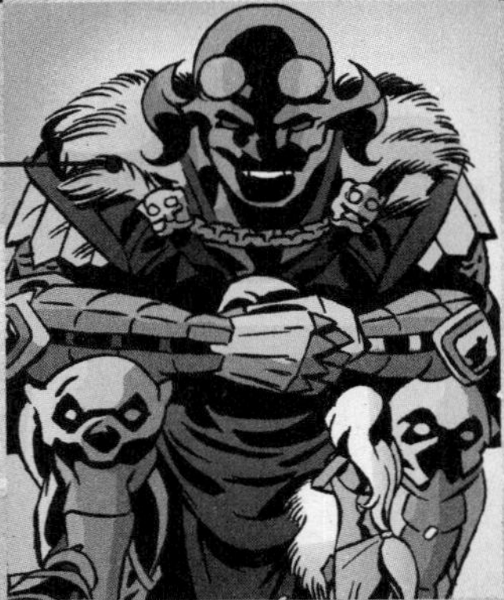

THE SNOW QUEEN

Geppetto's most powerful subject, and one of his most trusted advisors.

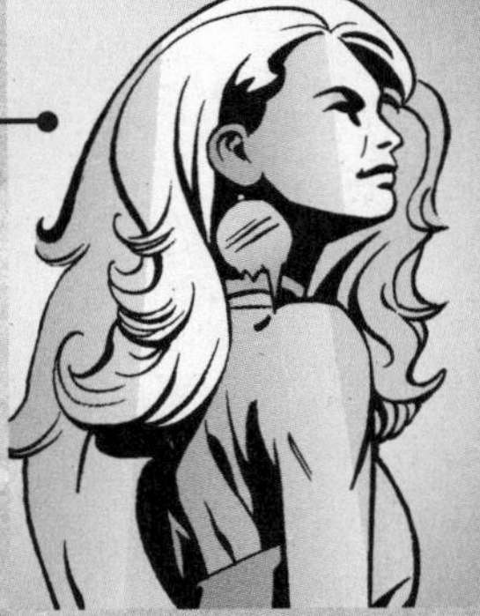

HANSEL

Burner of the Empire's unauthorized witches, he's lately undertaken some secret missions in the mundy world.

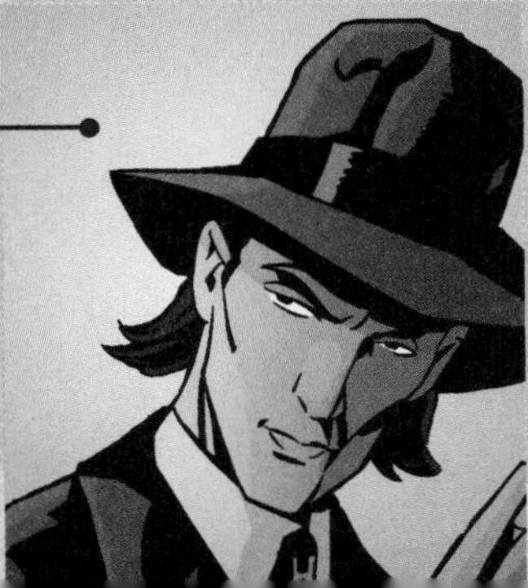

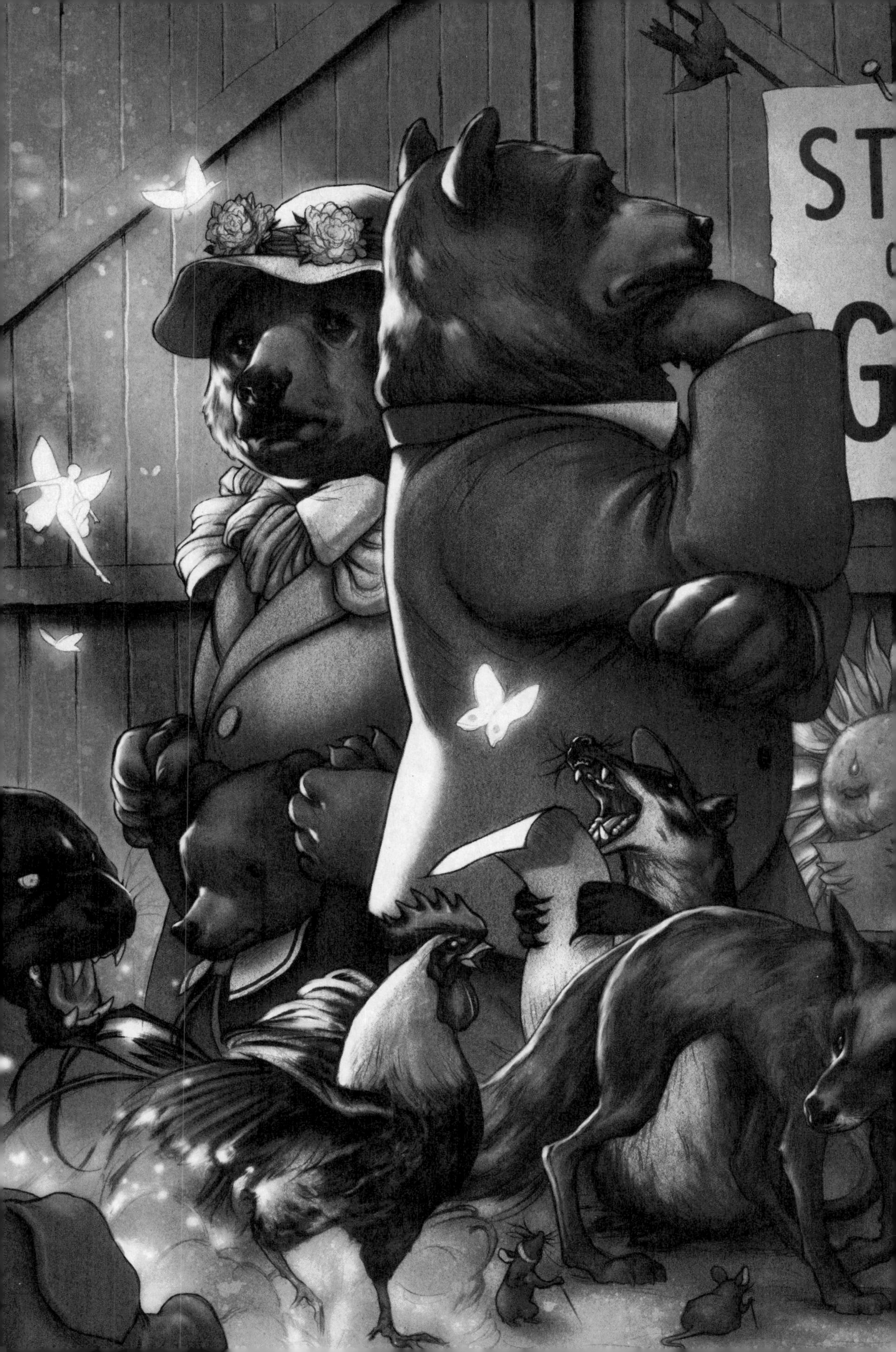
ST
G

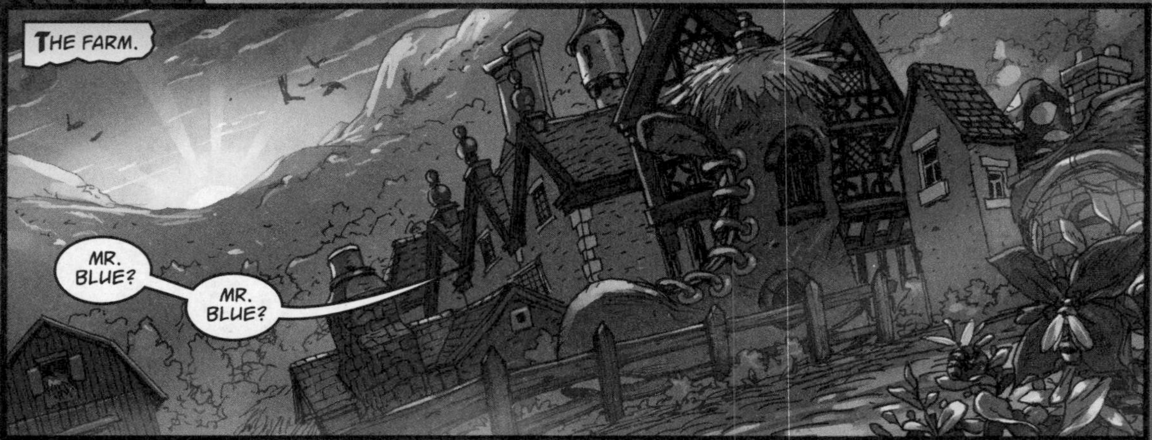
THE FARM.
MR. BLUE?
MR. BLUE?

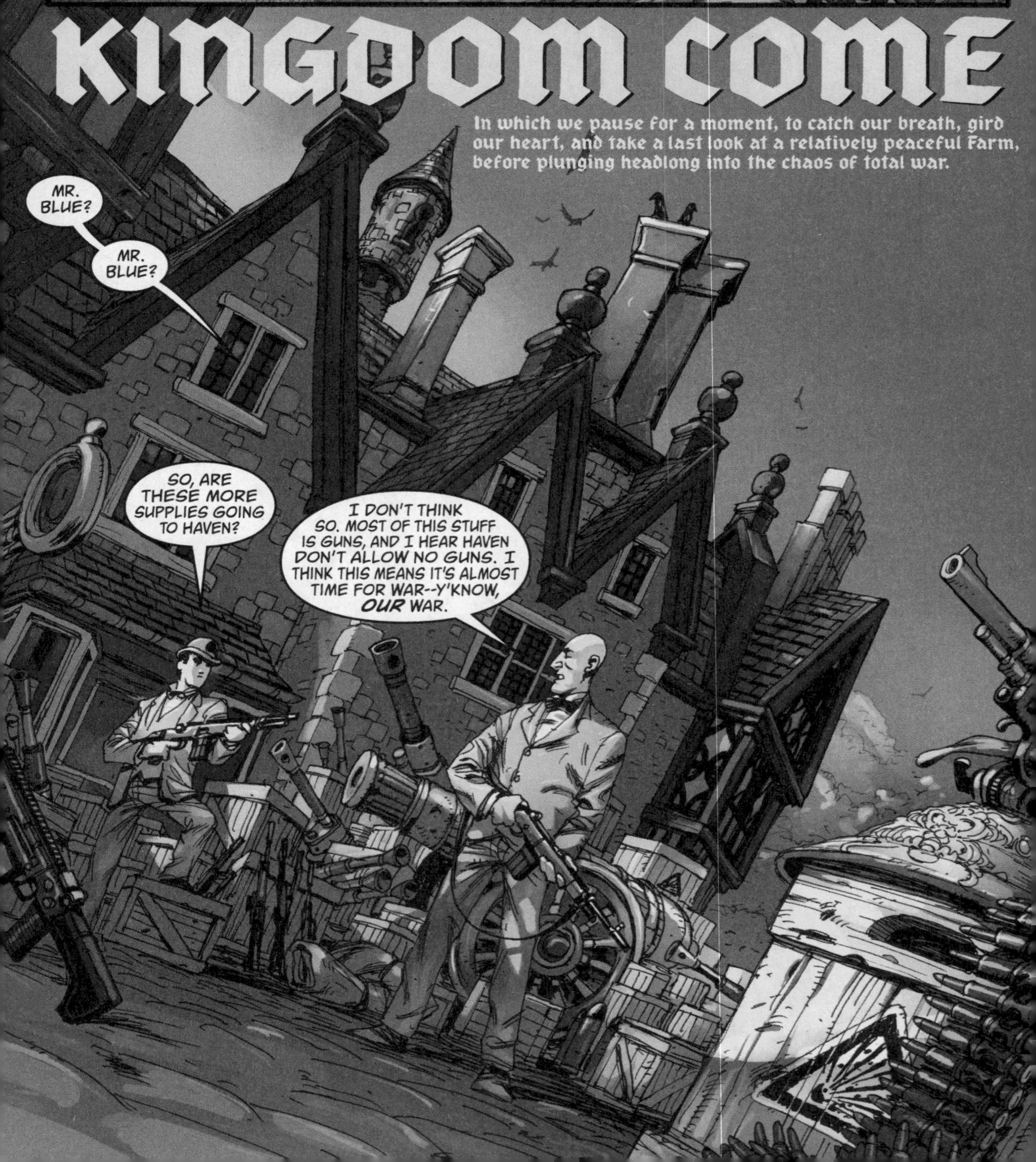
KINGDOM COME
In which we pause for a moment, to catch our breath, gird our heart, and take a last look at a relatively peaceful Farm, before plunging headlong into the chaos of total war.
MR. BLUE?
MR. BLUE?
SO, ARE THESE MORE SUPPLIES GOING TO HAVEN?
I DON'T THINK SO. MOST OF THIS STUFF IS GUNS, AND I HEAR HAVEN DON'T ALLOW NO GUNS. I THINK THIS MEANS IT'S ALMOST TIME FOR WAR--Y'KNOW, *OUR* WAR.

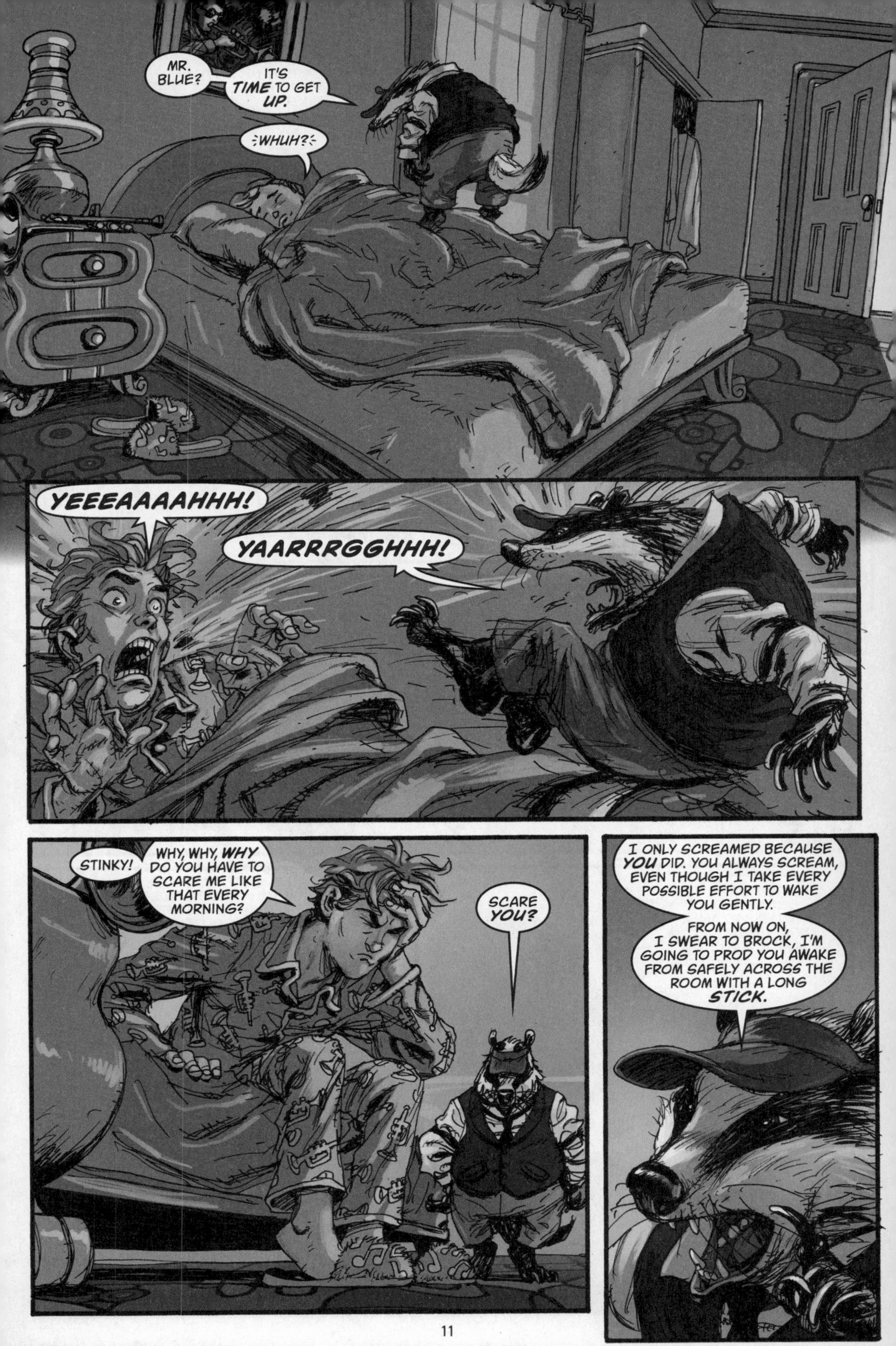

MR. BLUE?
IT'S TIME TO GET UP.
WHUH?
YEEEAAAAHHH!
YAARRRGGHHH!
STINKY!
WHY, WHY, WHY DO YOU HAVE TO SCARE ME LIKE THAT EVERY MORNING?
SCARE YOU?
I ONLY SCREAMED BECAUSE YOU DID. YOU ALWAYS SCREAM, EVEN THOUGH I TAKE EVERY POSSIBLE EFFORT TO WAKE YOU GENTLY.
FROM NOW ON, I SWEAR TO BROCK, I'M GOING TO PROD YOU AWAKE FROM SAFELY ACROSS THE ROOM WITH A LONG STICK.

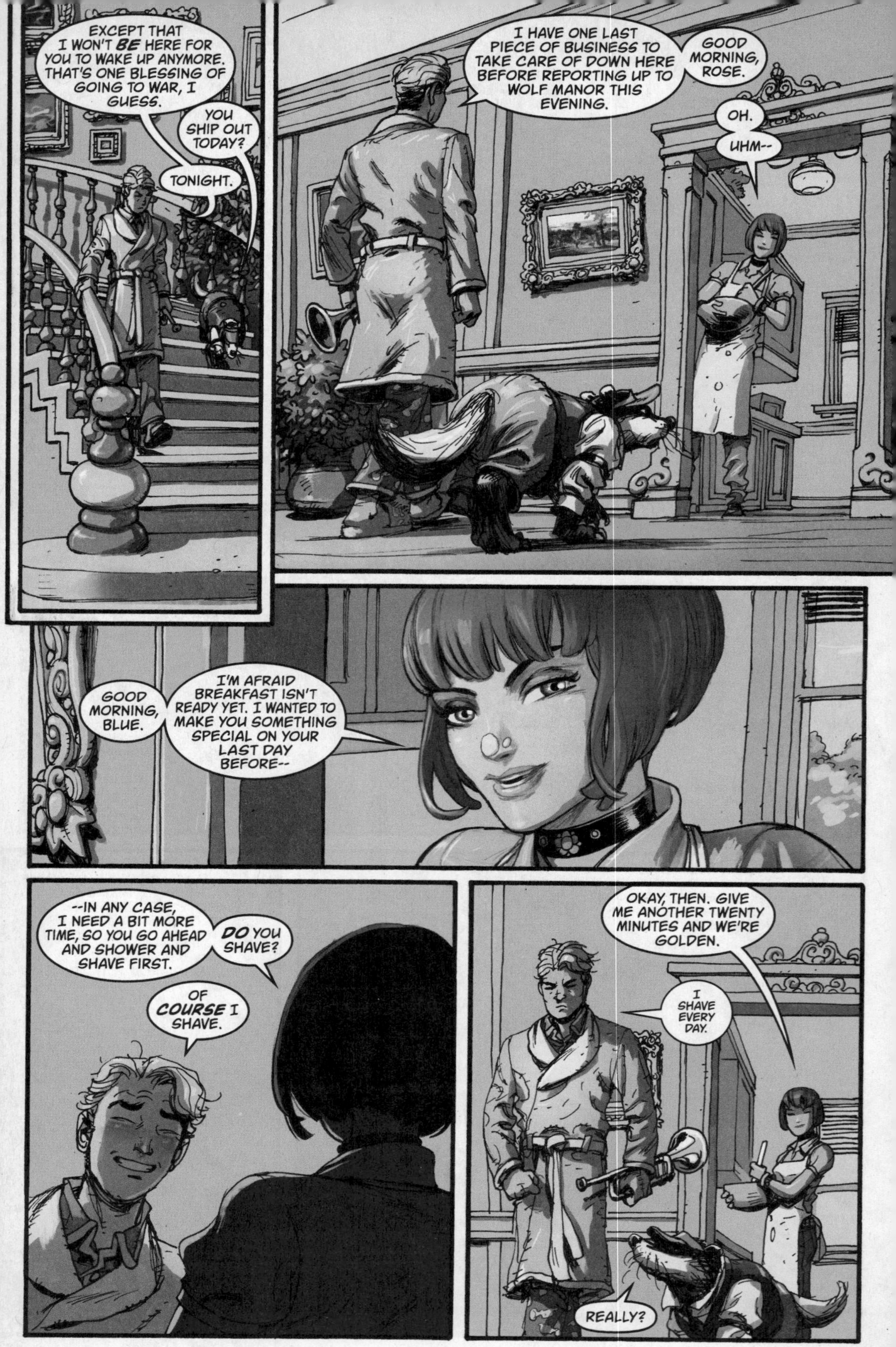
EXCEPT THAT I WON'T BE HERE FOR YOU TO WAKE UP ANYMORE. THAT'S ONE BLESSING OF GOING TO WAR, I GUESS.
YOU SHIP OUT TODAY?
TONIGHT.
I HAVE ONE LAST PIECE OF BUSINESS TO TAKE CARE OF DOWN HERE BEFORE REPORTING UP TO WOLF MANOR THIS EVENING.
GOOD MORNING, ROSE.
OH.
UHM--
GOOD MORNING, BLUE.
I'M AFRAID BREAKFAST ISN'T READY YET. I WANTED TO MAKE YOU SOMETHING SPECIAL ON YOUR LAST DAY BEFORE--
--IN ANY CASE, I NEED A BIT MORE TIME, SO YOU GO AHEAD AND SHOWER AND SHAVE FIRST.
DO YOU SHAVE?
OF COURSE I SHAVE.
OKAY, THEN. GIVE ME ANOTHER TWENTY MINUTES AND WE'RE GOLDEN.
I SHAVE EVERY DAY.
REALLY?

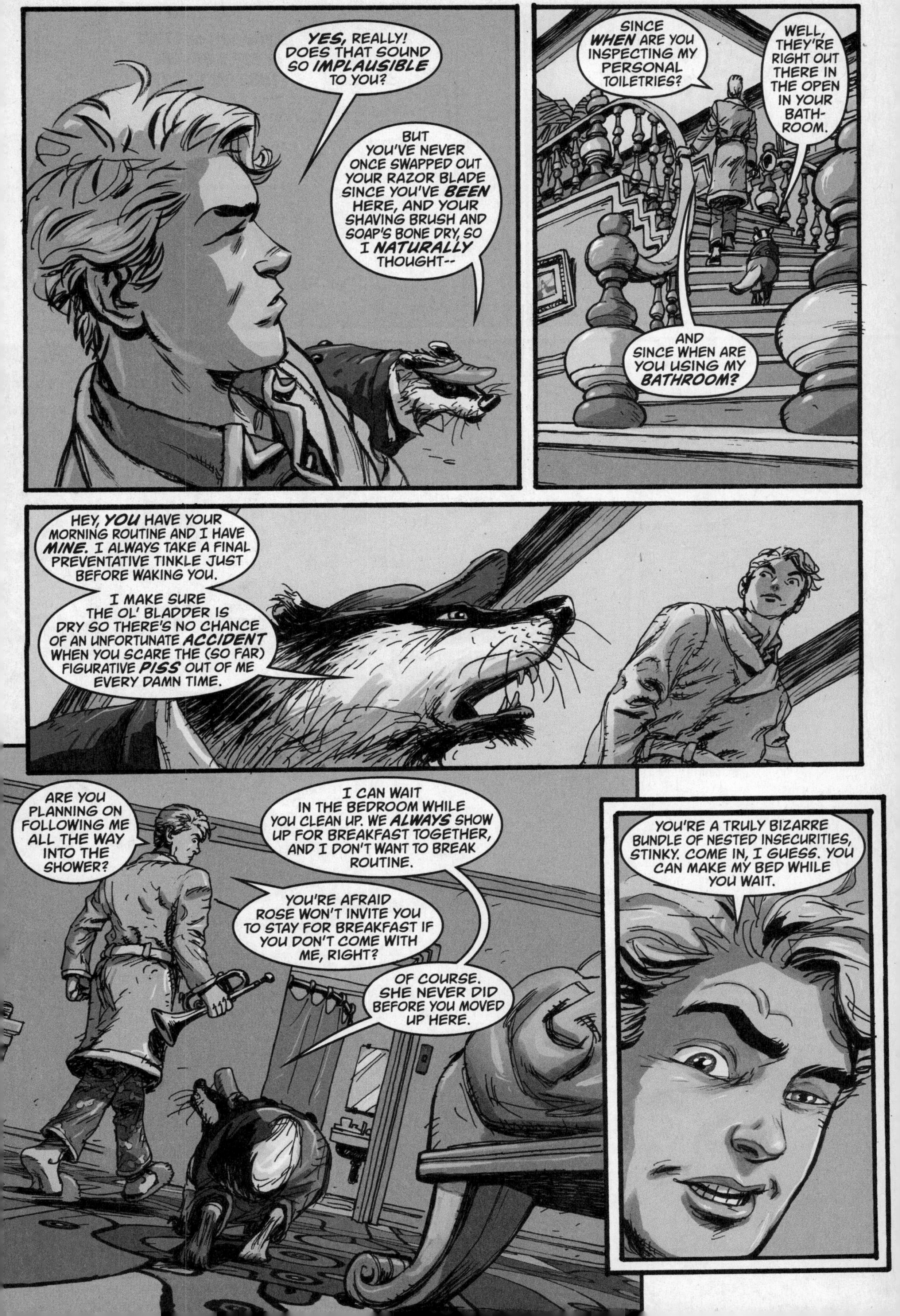
YES, REALLY! DOES THAT SOUND SO IMPLAUSIBLE TO YOU?
BUT YOU'VE NEVER ONCE SWAPPED OUT YOUR RAZOR BLADE SINCE YOU'VE BEEN HERE, AND YOUR SHAVING BRUSH AND SOAP'S BONE DRY, SO I NATURALLY THOUGHT--
SINCE WHEN ARE YOU INSPECTING MY PERSONAL TOILETRIES?
WELL, THEY'RE RIGHT OUT THERE IN THE OPEN IN YOUR BATH-ROOM.
AND SINCE WHEN ARE YOU USING MY BATHROOM?
HEY, YOU HAVE YOUR MORNING ROUTINE AND I HAVE MINE. I ALWAYS TAKE A FINAL PREVENTATIVE TINKLE JUST BEFORE WAKING YOU.
I MAKE SURE THE OL' BLADDER IS DRY SO THERE'S NO CHANCE OF AN UNFORTUNATE ACCIDENT WHEN YOU SCARE THE (SO FAR) FIGURATIVE PISS OUT OF ME EVERY DAMN TIME.
ARE YOU PLANNING ON FOLLOWING ME ALL THE WAY INTO THE SHOWER?
I CAN WAIT IN THE BEDROOM WHILE YOU CLEAN UP. WE ALWAYS SHOW UP FOR BREAKFAST TOGETHER, AND I DON'T WANT TO BREAK ROUTINE.
YOU'RE AFRAID ROSE WON'T INVITE YOU TO STAY FOR BREAKFAST IF YOU DON'T COME WITH ME, RIGHT?
OF COURSE. SHE NEVER DID BEFORE YOU MOVED UP HERE.
YOU'RE A TRULY BIZARRE BUNDLE OF NESTED INSECURITIES, STINKY. COME IN, I GUESS. YOU CAN MAKE MY BED WHILE YOU WAIT.

ATTENTION ALL
FARM ANIMAL
FABLES!

IMPORTANT MEETING
IN TOWN SQUARE
TODAY AT NOON!

PLEASE SPREAD THE WORD
TO THOSE WHO CAN'T READ
OR LIVE OUT IN THE FARM'S
MORE REMOTE CORNERS.

WHAT DO YOU SUPPOSE *THIS* IS ALL ABOUT?

MORE WAR GAMES, I'LL BET.

FABLES!

IMPORTANT MEETING
IN TOWN SQUARE
TODAY AT NOON!

PLEASE SPREAD THE WORD
TO THOSE WHO CAN'T READ
OR LIVE OUT IN THE FARM'S
MORE REMOTE CORNERS.

I DON'T THINK SO. IT SAYS JUST THE ANIMAL FABLES, NOT THE NEWCOMER HUMAN FABLES THAT LIVE IN THE TENTS.

WELL, IT'S GOING TO BE SOME SORT OF *BAD NEWS!* THEY DON'T PUT UP OFFICIAL NOTICES UNLESS IT'S BAD NEWS!

ATTENTION ALL
FARM ANIMAL
FABLES!

IMPORTANT MEETING
IN TOWN SQUARE
TODAY AT NOON!

PLEASE SPREAD THE WORD
TO THOSE WHO CAN'T READ
OR LIVE OUT IN THE FARM'S
MORE REMOTE CORNERS.

THE SKY'S *ALWAYS* FALLING FOR YOU, ISN'T IT?

ONLY BECAUSE THE SKY *IS* ALWAYS FALLING. TERRIBLE DISASTER'S ALWAYS JUST AROUND THE CORNER.

I BET THEY'VE RUN OUT OF *MUNDY* CHICKENS AND PIGS AND COWS--

--AND THIS MEETING IS TO INFORM US THAT THEY'VE DECIDED *FABLE* CHICKENS AND PIGS AND COWS ARE NOW APPROVED FOOD ITEMS FOR ALL THESE NEW HUMAN FABLES!

IT'S GOOD TO START PANICKING EARLY EVERY DAY. SAVES SO MUCH TIME.

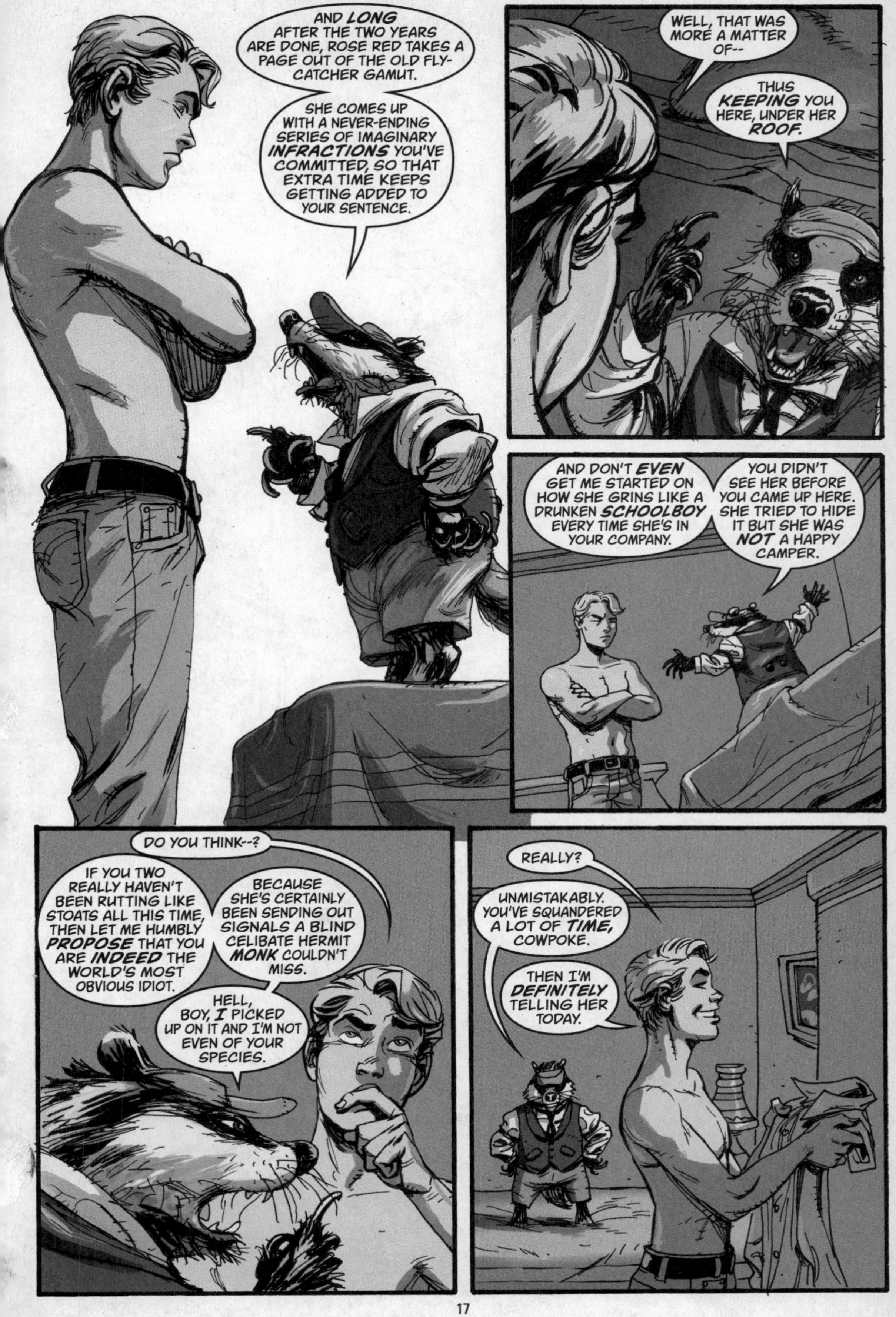
AND LONG AFTER THE TWO YEARS ARE DONE, ROSE RED TAKES A PAGE OUT OF THE OLD FLY-CATCHER GAMUT.
SHE COMES UP WITH A NEVER-ENDING SERIES OF IMAGINARY INFRACTIONS YOU'VE COMMITTED, SO THAT EXTRA TIME KEEPS GETTING ADDED TO YOUR SENTENCE.
WELL, THAT WAS MORE A MATTER OF--
THUS KEEPING YOU HERE, UNDER HER ROOF.
AND DON'T EVEN GET ME STARTED ON HOW SHE GRINS LIKE A DRUNKEN SCHOOLBOY EVERY TIME SHE'S IN YOUR COMPANY.
YOU DIDN'T SEE HER BEFORE YOU CAME UP HERE. SHE TRIED TO HIDE IT BUT SHE WAS NOT A HAPPY CAMPER.
DO YOU THINK--?
IF YOU TWO REALLY HAVEN'T BEEN RUTTING LIKE STOATS ALL THIS TIME, THEN LET ME HUMBLY PROPOSE THAT YOU ARE INDEED THE WORLD'S MOST OBVIOUS IDIOT.
BECAUSE SHE'S CERTAINLY BEEN SENDING OUT SIGNALS A BLIND CELIBATE HERMIT MONK COULDN'T MISS.
HELL, BOY, I PICKED UP ON IT AND I'M NOT EVEN OF YOUR SPECIES.
REALLY?
UNMISTAKABLY. YOU'VE SQUANDERED A LOT OF TIME, COWPOKE.
THEN I'M DEFINITELY TELLING HER TODAY.

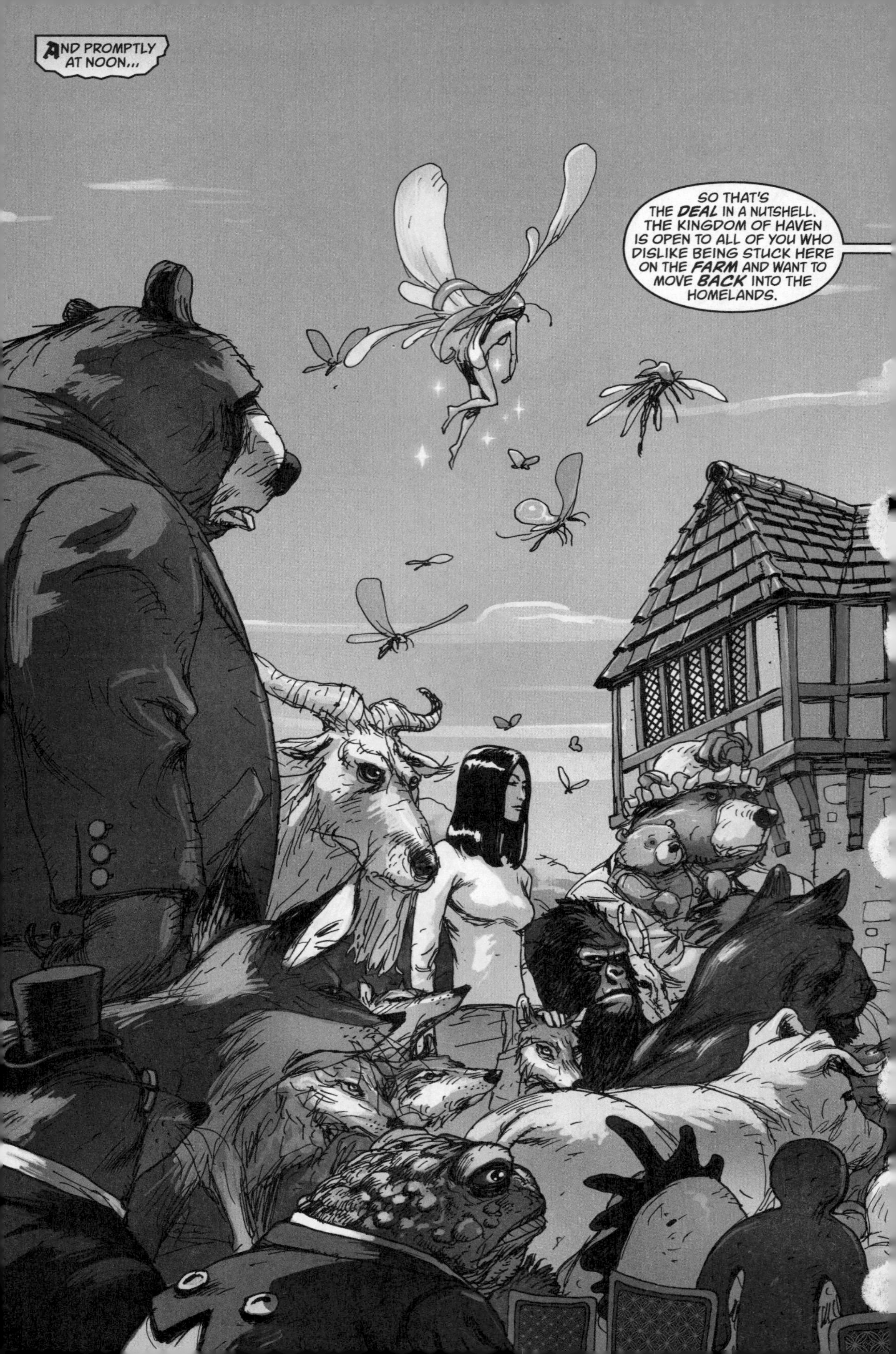
AND PROMPTLY AT NOON...
SO THAT'S THE DEAL IN A NUTSHELL. THE KINGDOM OF HAVEN IS OPEN TO ALL OF YOU WHO DISLIKE BEING STUCK HERE ON THE FARM AND WANT TO MOVE BACK INTO THE HOMELANDS.

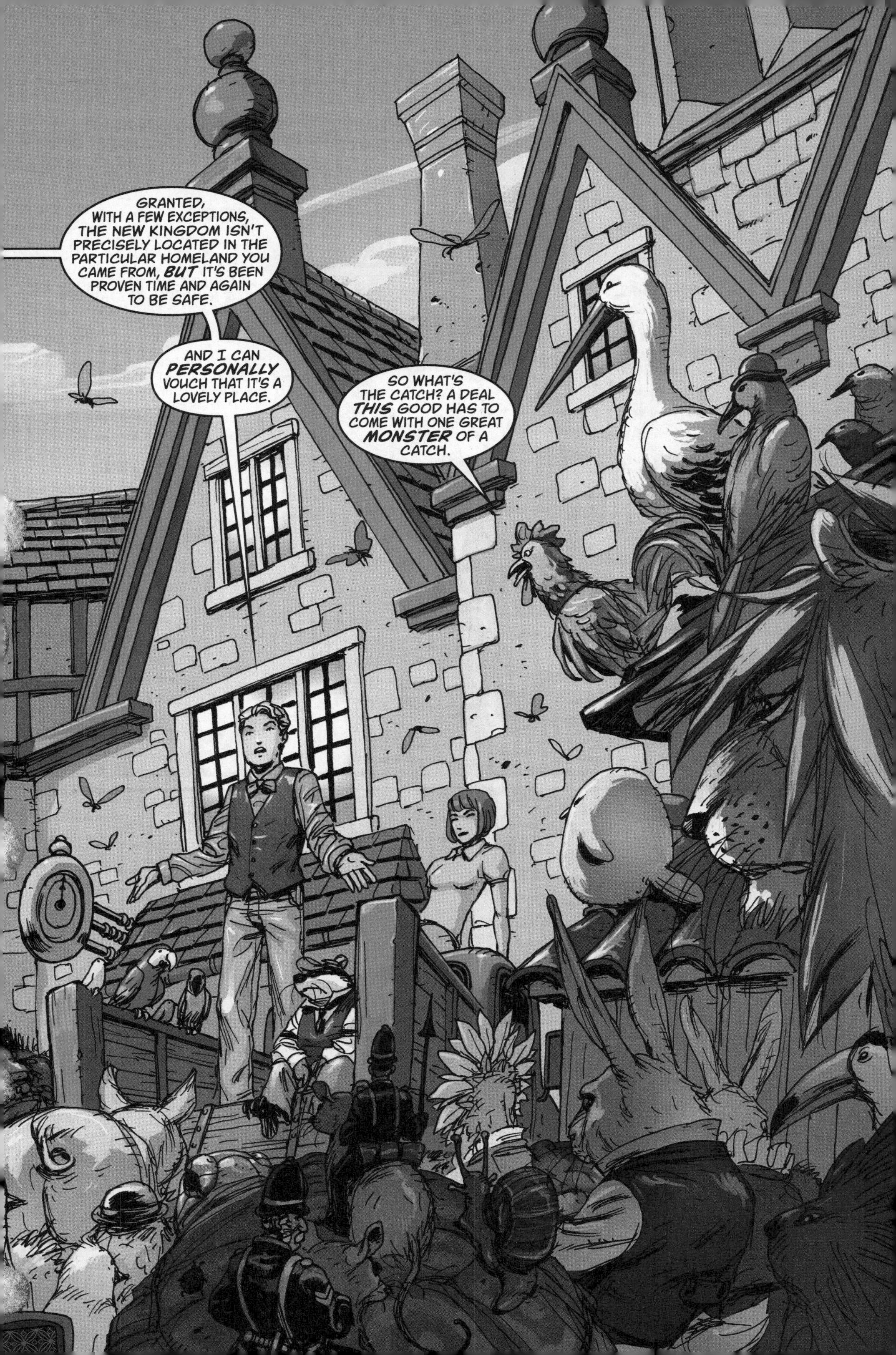
GRANTED, WITH A FEW EXCEPTIONS, THE NEW KINGDOM ISN'T PRECISELY LOCATED IN THE PARTICULAR HOMELAND YOU CAME FROM, BUT IT'S BEEN PROVEN TIME AND AGAIN TO BE SAFE.
AND I CAN PERSONALLY VOUCH THAT IT'S A LOVELY PLACE.
SO WHAT'S THE CATCH? A DEAL THIS GOOD HAS TO COME WITH ONE GREAT MONSTER OF A CATCH.

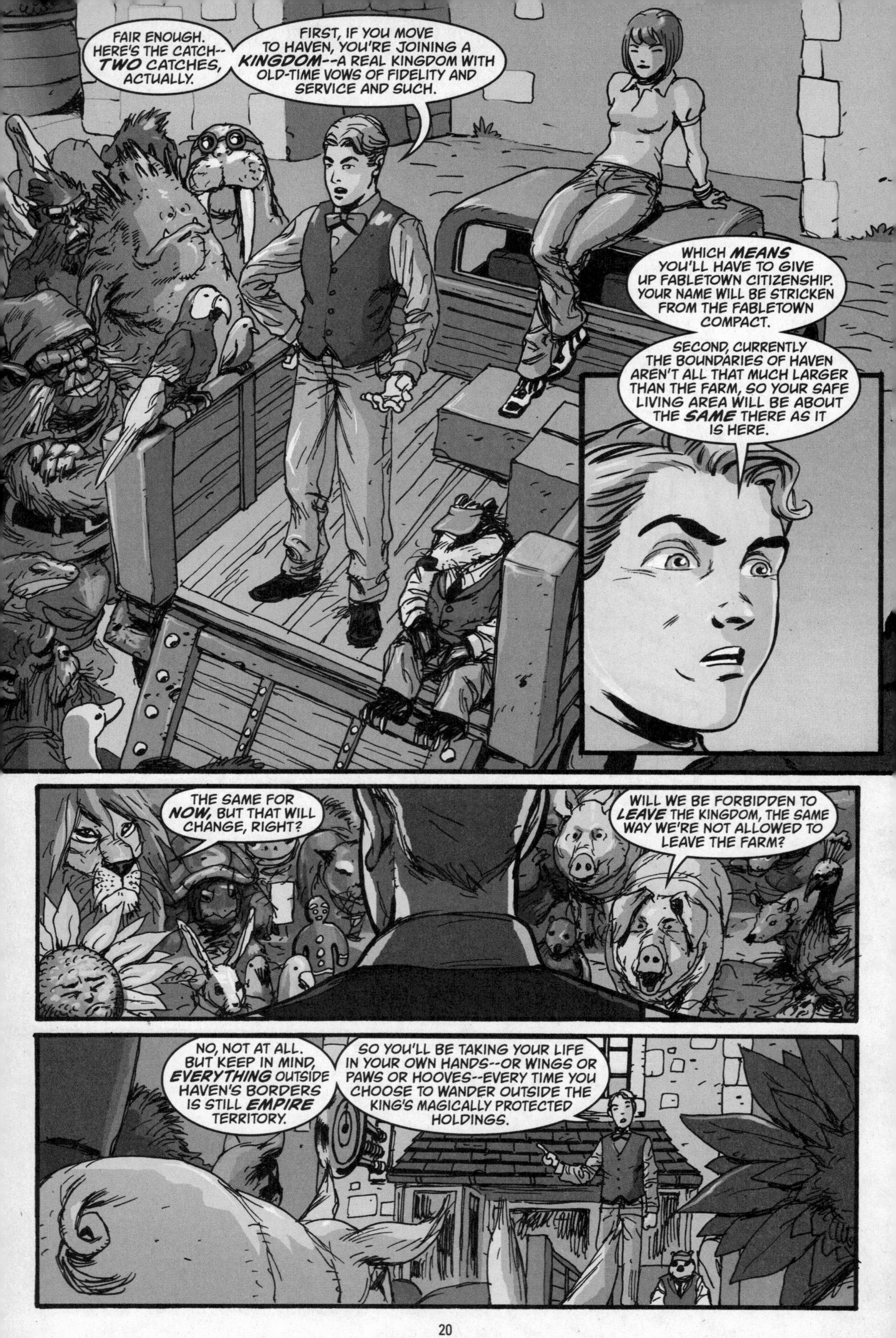
FAIR ENOUGH. HERE'S THE CATCH-- TWO CATCHES, ACTUALLY.
FIRST, IF YOU MOVE TO HAVEN, YOU'RE JOINING A KINGDOM--A REAL KINGDOM WITH OLD-TIME VOWS OF FIDELITY AND SERVICE AND SUCH.
WHICH MEANS YOU'LL HAVE TO GIVE UP FABLETOWN CITIZENSHIP. YOUR NAME WILL BE STRICKEN FROM THE FABLETOWN COMPACT.
SECOND, CURRENTLY THE BOUNDARIES OF HAVEN AREN'T ALL THAT MUCH LARGER THAN THE FARM, SO YOUR SAFE LIVING AREA WILL BE ABOUT THE SAME THERE AS IT IS HERE.
THE SAME FOR NOW, BUT THAT WILL CHANGE, RIGHT?
WILL WE BE FORBIDDEN TO LEAVE THE KINGDOM, THE SAME WAY WE'RE NOT ALLOWED TO LEAVE THE FARM?
NO, NOT AT ALL. BUT KEEP IN MIND, EVERYTHING OUTSIDE HAVEN'S BORDERS IS STILL EMPIRE TERRITORY.
SO YOU'LL BE TAKING YOUR LIFE IN YOUR OWN HANDS--OR WINGS OR PAWS OR HOOVES--EVERY TIME YOU CHOOSE TO WANDER OUTSIDE THE KING'S MAGICALLY PROTECTED HOLDINGS.

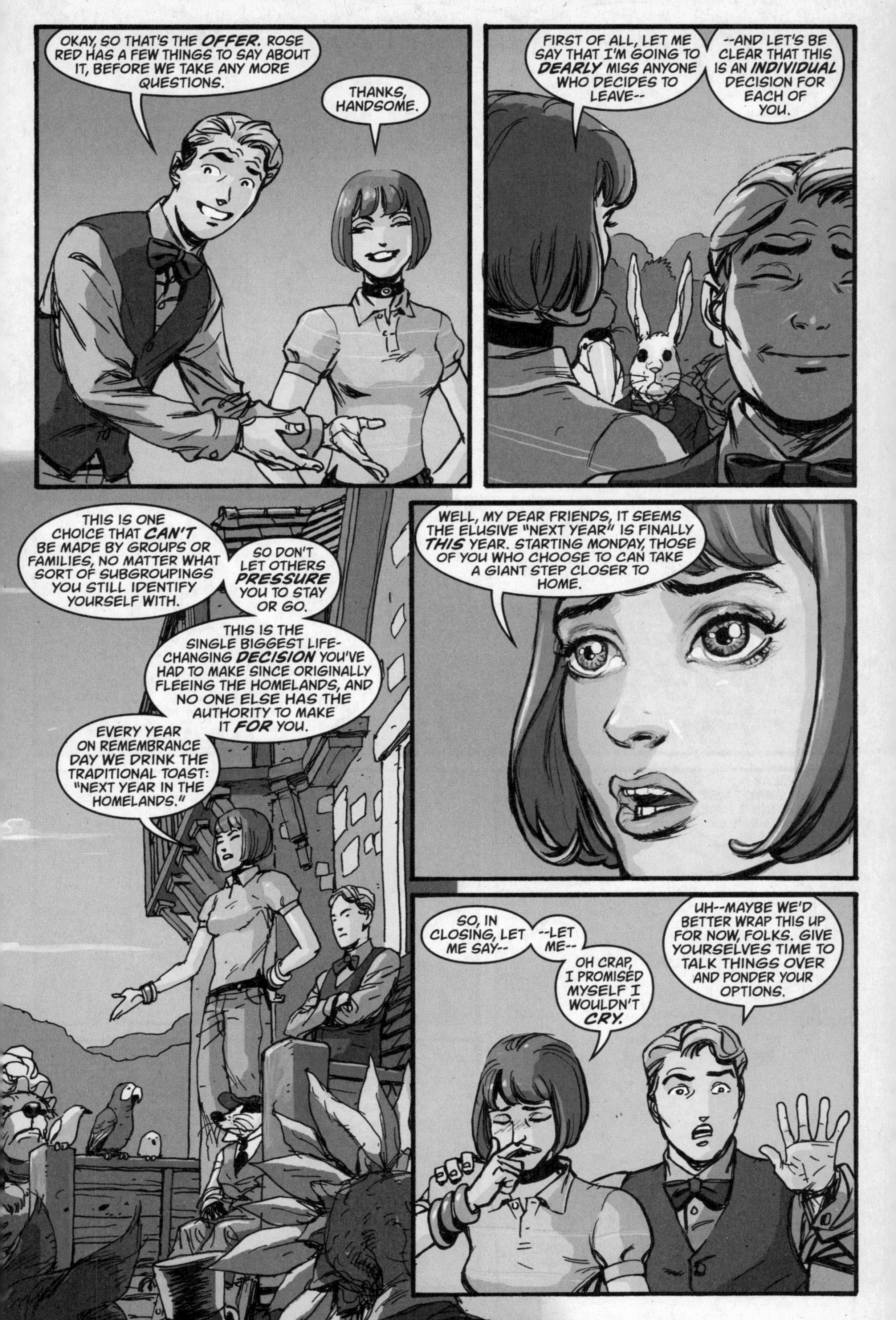
OKAY, SO THAT'S THE OFFER. ROSE RED HAS A FEW THINGS TO SAY ABOUT IT, BEFORE WE TAKE ANY MORE QUESTIONS.
THANKS, HANDSOME.
FIRST OF ALL, LET ME SAY THAT I'M GOING TO DEARLY MISS ANYONE WHO DECIDES TO LEAVE--
--AND LET'S BE CLEAR THAT THIS IS AN INDIVIDUAL DECISION FOR EACH OF YOU.
THIS IS ONE CHOICE THAT CAN'T BE MADE BY GROUPS OR FAMILIES, NO MATTER WHAT SORT OF SUBGROUPINGS YOU STILL IDENTIFY YOURSELF WITH.
SO DON'T LET OTHERS PRESSURE YOU TO STAY OR GO.
THIS IS THE SINGLE BIGGEST LIFE-CHANGING DECISION YOU'VE HAD TO MAKE SINCE ORIGINALLY FLEEING THE HOMELANDS, AND NO ONE ELSE HAS THE AUTHORITY TO MAKE IT FOR YOU.
EVERY YEAR ON REMEMBRANCE DAY WE DRINK THE TRADITIONAL TOAST: "NEXT YEAR IN THE HOMELANDS."
WELL, MY DEAR FRIENDS, IT SEEMS THE ELUSIVE "NEXT YEAR" IS FINALLY THIS YEAR. STARTING MONDAY, THOSE OF YOU WHO CHOOSE TO CAN TAKE A GIANT STEP CLOSER TO HOME.
SO, IN CLOSING, LET ME SAY--
--LET ME--
OH CRAP, I PROMISED MYSELF I WOULDN'T CRY.
UH--MAYBE WE'D BETTER WRAP THIS UP FOR NOW, FOLKS. GIVE YOURSELVES TIME TO TALK THINGS OVER AND PONDER YOUR OPTIONS.

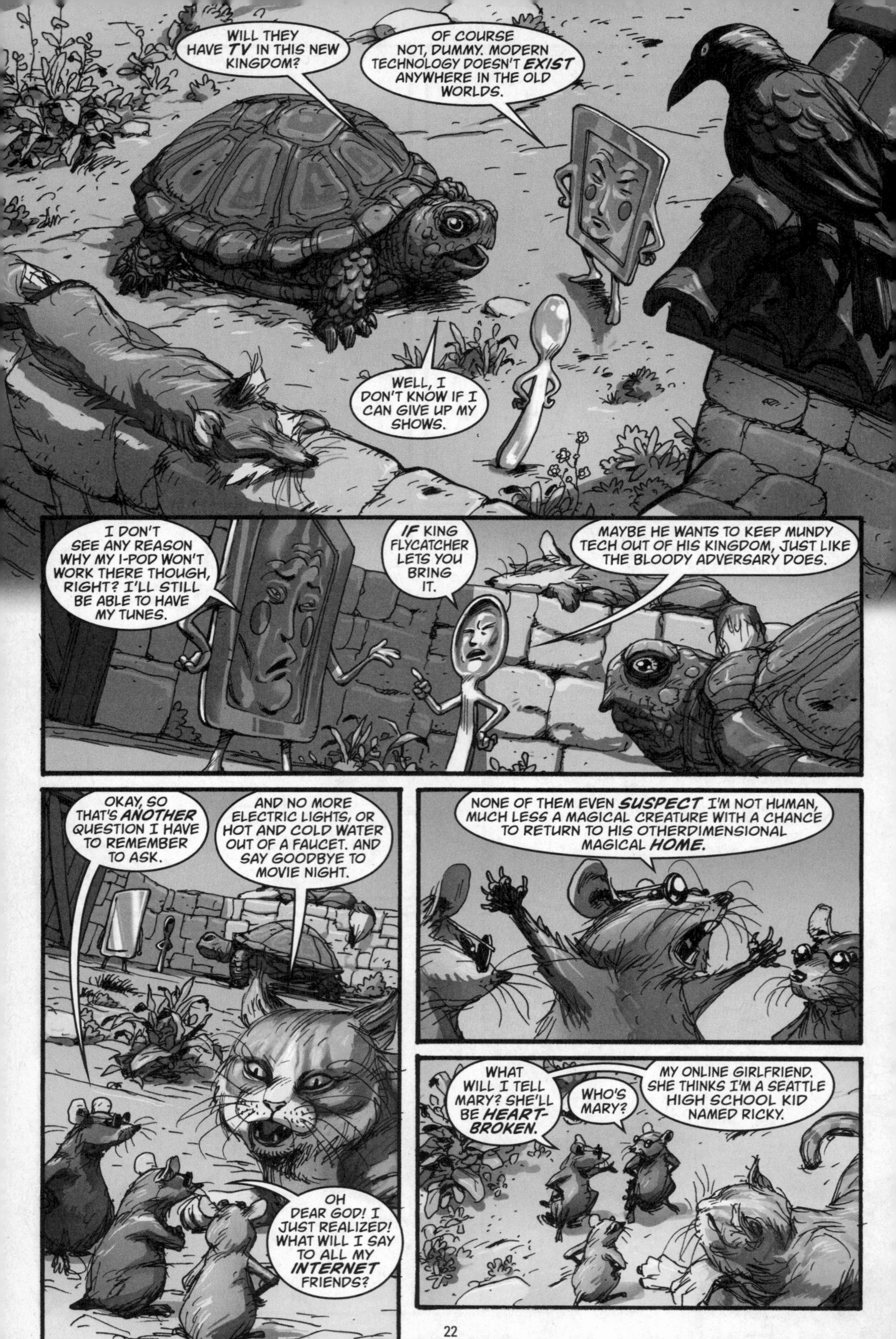
WILL THEY HAVE TV IN THIS NEW KINGDOM?
OF COURSE NOT, DUMMY. MODERN TECHNOLOGY DOESN'T EXIST ANYWHERE IN THE OLD WORLDS.
WELL, I DON'T KNOW IF I CAN GIVE UP MY SHOWS.
I DON'T SEE ANY REASON WHY MY I-POD WON'T WORK THERE THOUGH, RIGHT? I'LL STILL BE ABLE TO HAVE MY TUNES.
IF KING FLYCATCHER LETS YOU BRING IT.
MAYBE HE WANTS TO KEEP MUNDY TECH OUT OF HIS KINGDOM, JUST LIKE THE BLOODY ADVERSARY DOES.
OKAY, SO THAT'S ANOTHER QUESTION I HAVE TO REMEMBER TO ASK.
AND NO MORE ELECTRIC LIGHTS, OR HOT AND COLD WATER OUT OF A FAUCET. AND SAY GOODBYE TO MOVIE NIGHT.
OH DEAR GOD! I JUST REALIZED! WHAT WILL I SAY TO ALL MY INTERNET FRIENDS?
NONE OF THEM EVEN SUSPECT I'M NOT HUMAN, MUCH LESS A MAGICAL CREATURE WITH A CHANCE TO RETURN TO HIS OTHERDIMENSIONAL MAGICAL HOME.
WHAT WILL I TELL MARY? SHE'LL BE HEART-BROKEN.
WHO'S MARY?
MY ONLINE GIRLFRIEND. SHE THINKS I'M A SEATTLE HIGH SCHOOL KID NAMED RICKY.

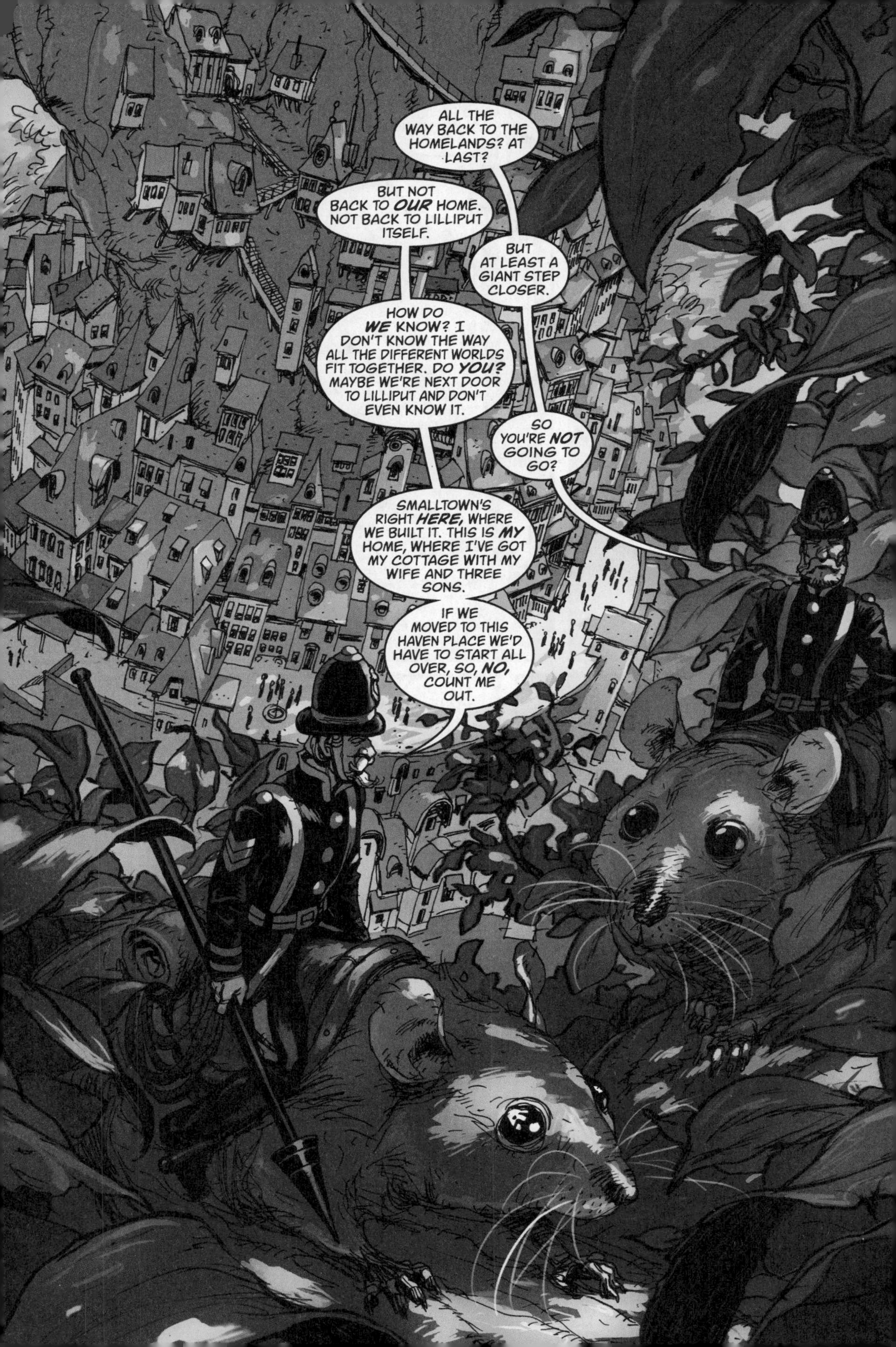
ALL THE WAY BACK TO THE HOMELANDS? AT LAST?
BUT NOT BACK TO OUR HOME. NOT BACK TO LILLIPUT ITSELF.
BUT AT LEAST A GIANT STEP CLOSER.
HOW DO WE KNOW? I DON'T KNOW THE WAY ALL THE DIFFERENT WORLDS FIT TOGETHER. DO YOU? MAYBE WE'RE NEXT DOOR TO LILLIPUT AND DON'T EVEN KNOW IT.
SO YOU'RE NOT GOING TO GO?
SMALLTOWN'S RIGHT HERE, WHERE WE BUILT IT. THIS IS MY HOME, WHERE I'VE GOT MY COTTAGE WITH MY WIFE AND THREE SONS.
IF WE MOVED TO THIS HAVEN PLACE WE'D HAVE TO START ALL OVER, SO, NO, COUNT ME OUT.

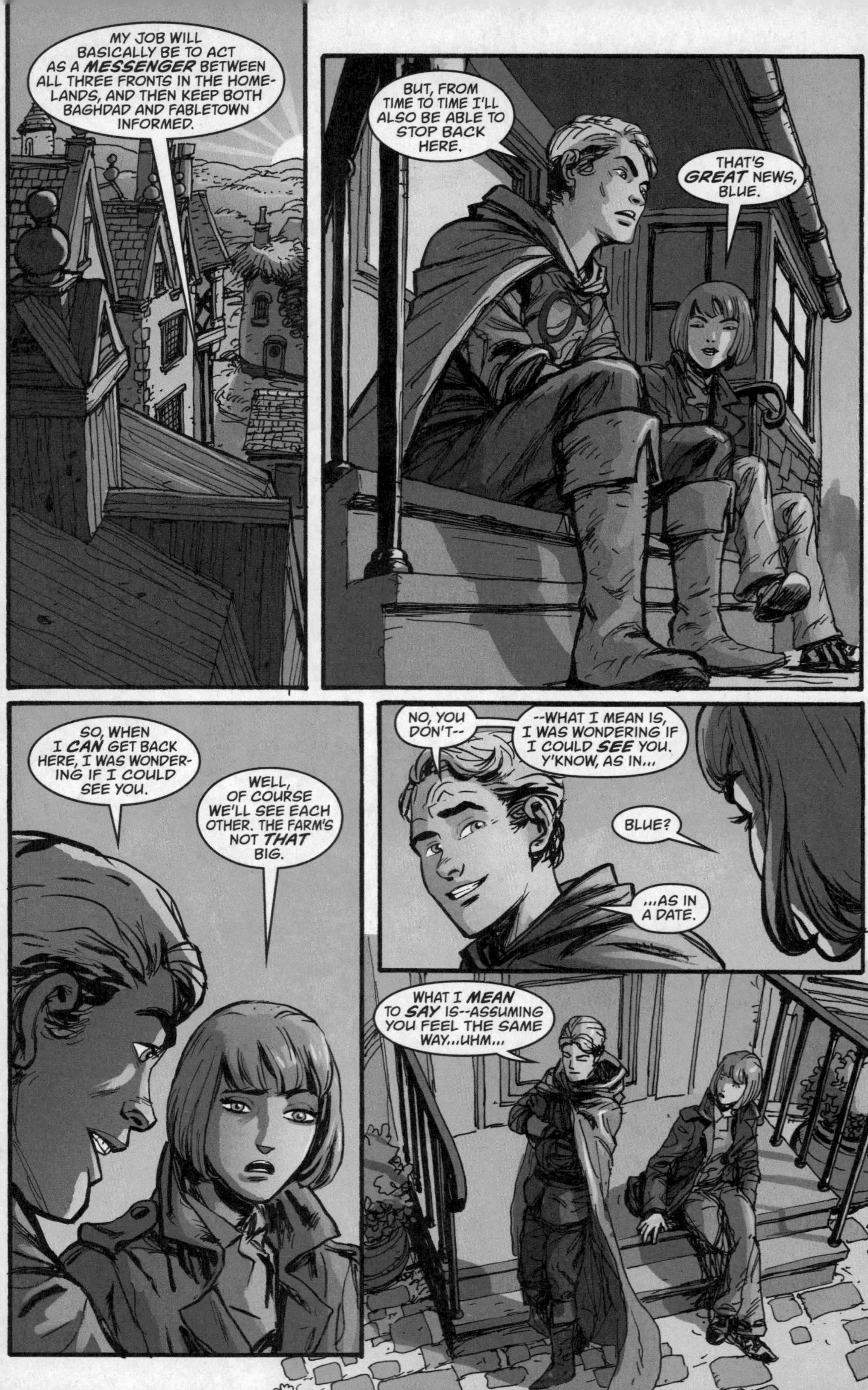
MY JOB WILL BASICALLY BE TO ACT AS A **MESSENGER** BETWEEN ALL THREE FRONTS IN THE HOME-LANDS, AND THEN KEEP BOTH BAGHDAD AND FABLETOWN INFORMED.
BUT, FROM TIME TO TIME I'LL ALSO BE ABLE TO STOP BACK HERE.
THAT'S **GREAT** NEWS, BLUE.
SO, WHEN I **CAN** GET BACK HERE, I WAS WONDER-ING IF I COULD SEE YOU.
WELL, OF COURSE WE'LL SEE EACH OTHER. THE FARM'S NOT **THAT** BIG.
NO, YOU DON'T--
--WHAT I MEAN IS, I WAS WONDERING IF I COULD **SEE** YOU. Y'KNOW, AS IN...
BLUE?
...AS IN A DATE.
WHAT I **MEAN** TO **SAY** IS--ASSUMING YOU FEEL THE SAME WAY...UHM...

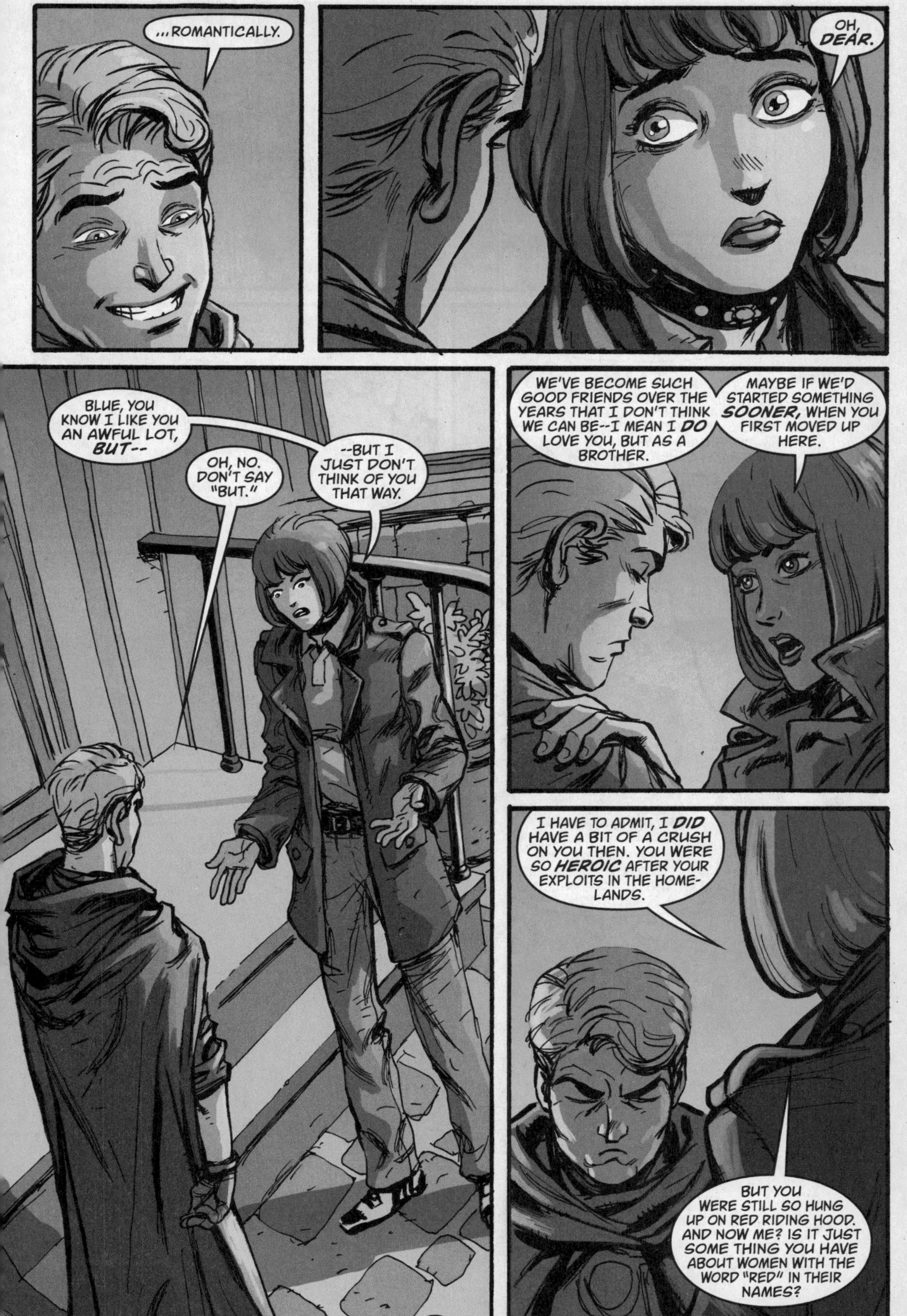
...ROMANTICALLY.
OH, DEAR.
BLUE, YOU KNOW I LIKE YOU AN AWFUL LOT, BUT--
OH, NO. DON'T SAY "BUT."
--BUT I JUST DON'T THINK OF YOU THAT WAY.
WE'VE BECOME SUCH GOOD FRIENDS OVER THE YEARS THAT I DON'T THINK WE CAN BE--I MEAN I DO LOVE YOU, BUT AS A BROTHER.
MAYBE IF WE'D STARTED SOMETHING SOONER, WHEN YOU FIRST MOVED UP HERE.
I HAVE TO ADMIT, I DID HAVE A BIT OF A CRUSH ON YOU THEN. YOU WERE SO HEROIC AFTER YOUR EXPLOITS IN THE HOME-LANDS.
BUT YOU WERE STILL SO HUNG UP ON RED RIDING HOOD. AND NOW ME? IS IT JUST SOME THING YOU HAVE ABOUT WOMEN WITH THE WORD "RED" IN THEIR NAMES?

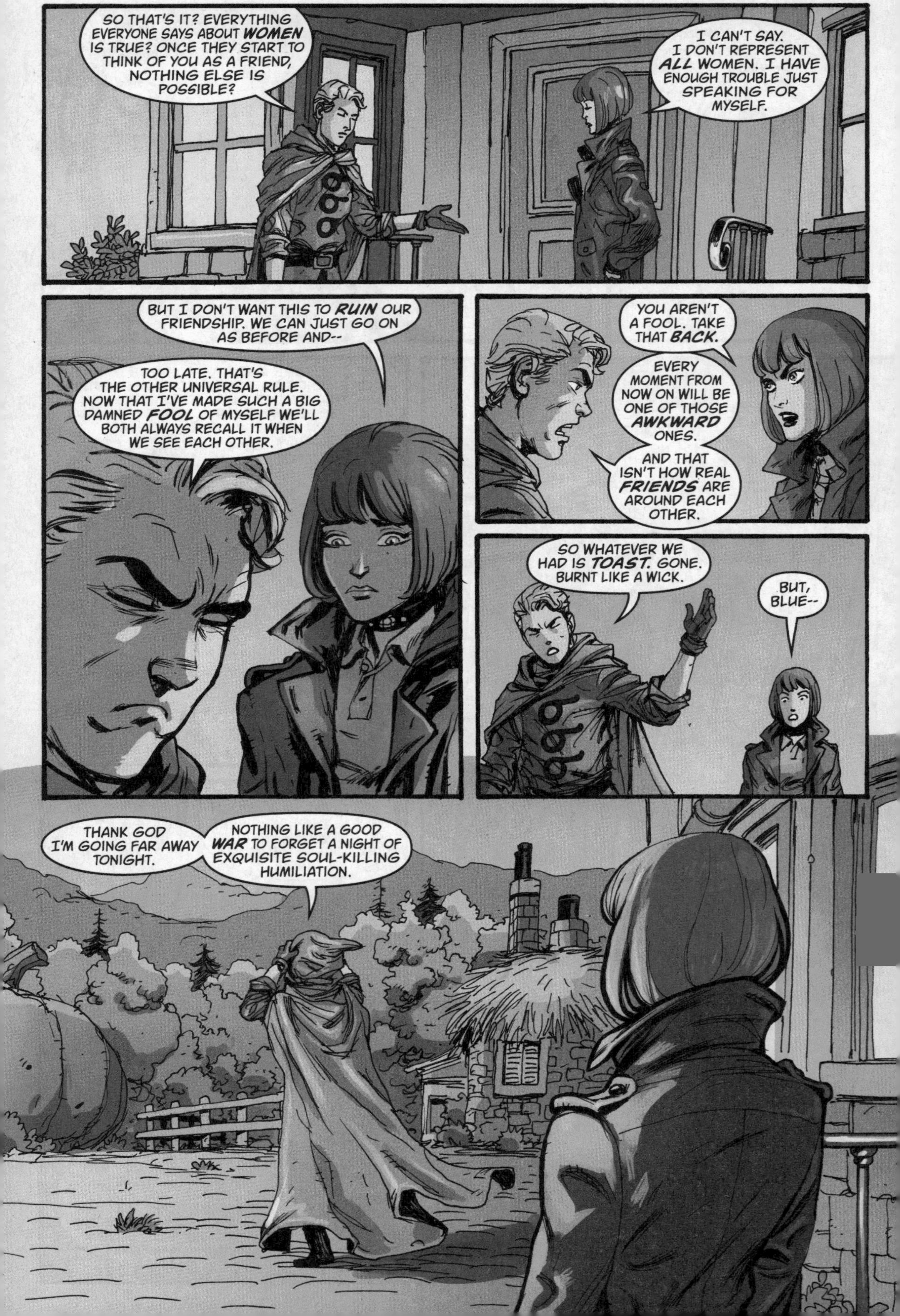
SO THAT'S IT? EVERYTHING EVERYONE SAYS ABOUT WOMEN IS TRUE? ONCE THEY START TO THINK OF YOU AS A FRIEND, NOTHING ELSE IS POSSIBLE?
I CAN'T SAY. I DON'T REPRESENT ALL WOMEN. I HAVE ENOUGH TROUBLE JUST SPEAKING FOR MYSELF.
BUT I DON'T WANT THIS TO RUIN OUR FRIENDSHIP. WE CAN JUST GO ON AS BEFORE AND--
TOO LATE. THAT'S THE OTHER UNIVERSAL RULE. NOW THAT I'VE MADE SUCH A BIG DAMNED FOOL OF MYSELF WE'LL BOTH ALWAYS RECALL IT WHEN WE SEE EACH OTHER.
YOU AREN'T A FOOL. TAKE THAT BACK.
EVERY MOMENT FROM NOW ON WILL BE ONE OF THOSE AWKWARD ONES.
AND THAT ISN'T HOW REAL FRIENDS ARE AROUND EACH OTHER.
SO WHATEVER WE HAD IS TOAST. GONE. BURNT LIKE A WICK.
BUT, BLUE--
THANK GOD I'M GOING FAR AWAY TONIGHT.
NOTHING LIKE A GOOD WAR TO FORGET A NIGHT OF EXQUISITE SOUL-KILLING HUMILIATION.

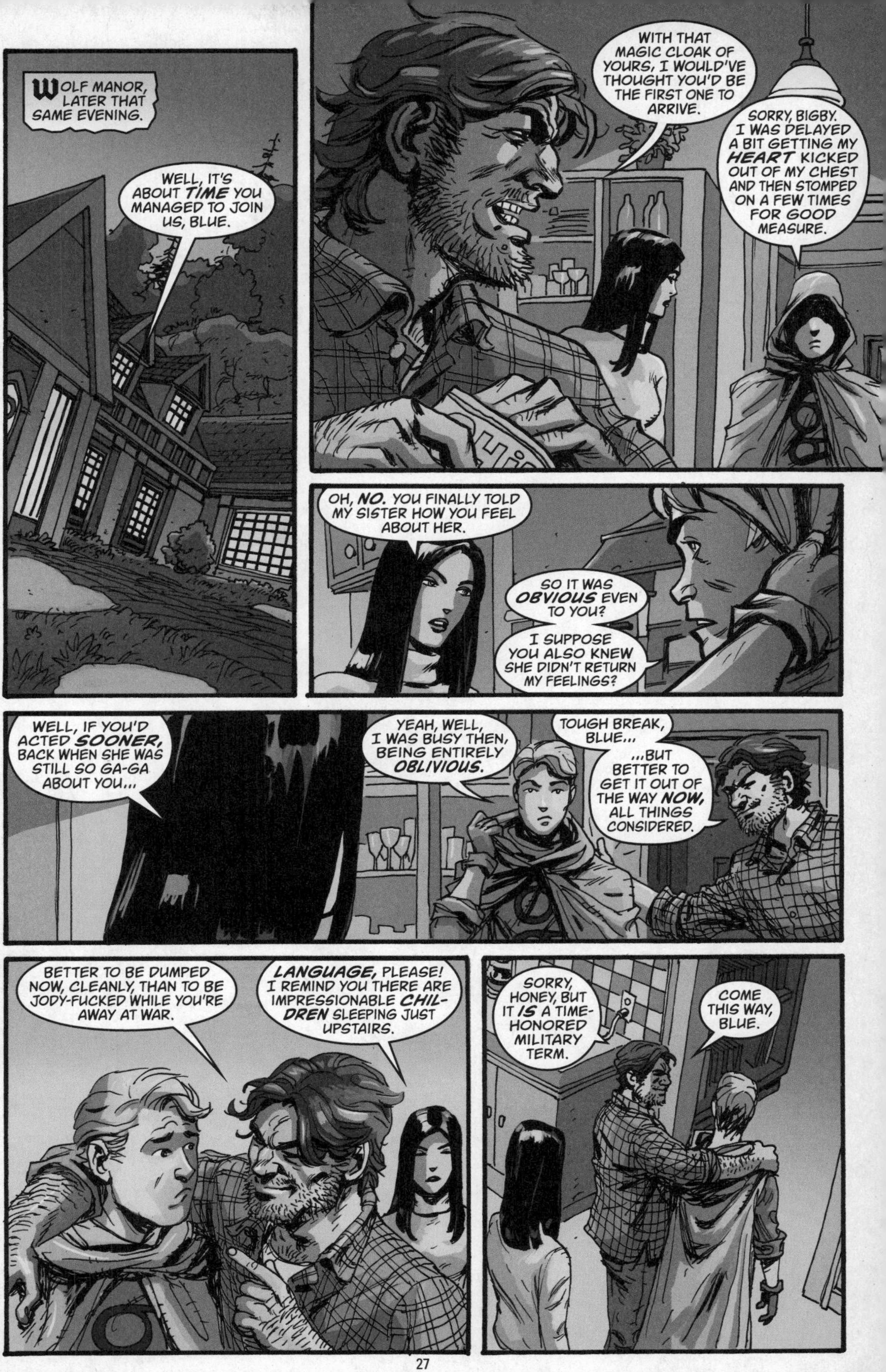
WOLF MANOR, LATER THAT SAME EVENING.
WELL, IT'S ABOUT TIME YOU MANAGED TO JOIN US, BLUE.
WITH THAT MAGIC CLOAK OF YOURS, I WOULD'VE THOUGHT YOU'D BE THE FIRST ONE TO ARRIVE.
SORRY, BIGBY. I WAS DELAYED A BIT GETTING MY HEART KICKED OUT OF MY CHEST AND THEN STOMPED ON A FEW TIMES FOR GOOD MEASURE.
OH, NO. YOU FINALLY TOLD MY SISTER HOW YOU FEEL ABOUT HER.
SO IT WAS OBVIOUS EVEN TO YOU?
I SUPPOSE YOU ALSO KNEW SHE DIDN'T RETURN MY FEELINGS?
WELL, IF YOU'D ACTED SOONER, BACK WHEN SHE WAS STILL SO GA-GA ABOUT YOU...
YEAH, WELL, I WAS BUSY THEN, BEING ENTIRELY OBLIVIOUS.
TOUGH BREAK, BLUE...
...BUT BETTER TO GET IT OUT OF THE WAY NOW, ALL THINGS CONSIDERED.
BETTER TO BE DUMPED NOW, CLEANLY, THAN TO BE JODY-FUCKED WHILE YOU'RE AWAY AT WAR.
LANGUAGE, PLEASE! I REMIND YOU THERE ARE IMPRESSIONABLE CHIL-DREN SLEEPING JUST UPSTAIRS.
SORRY, HONEY, BUT IT IS A TIME-HONORED MILITARY TERM.
COME THIS WAY, BLUE.

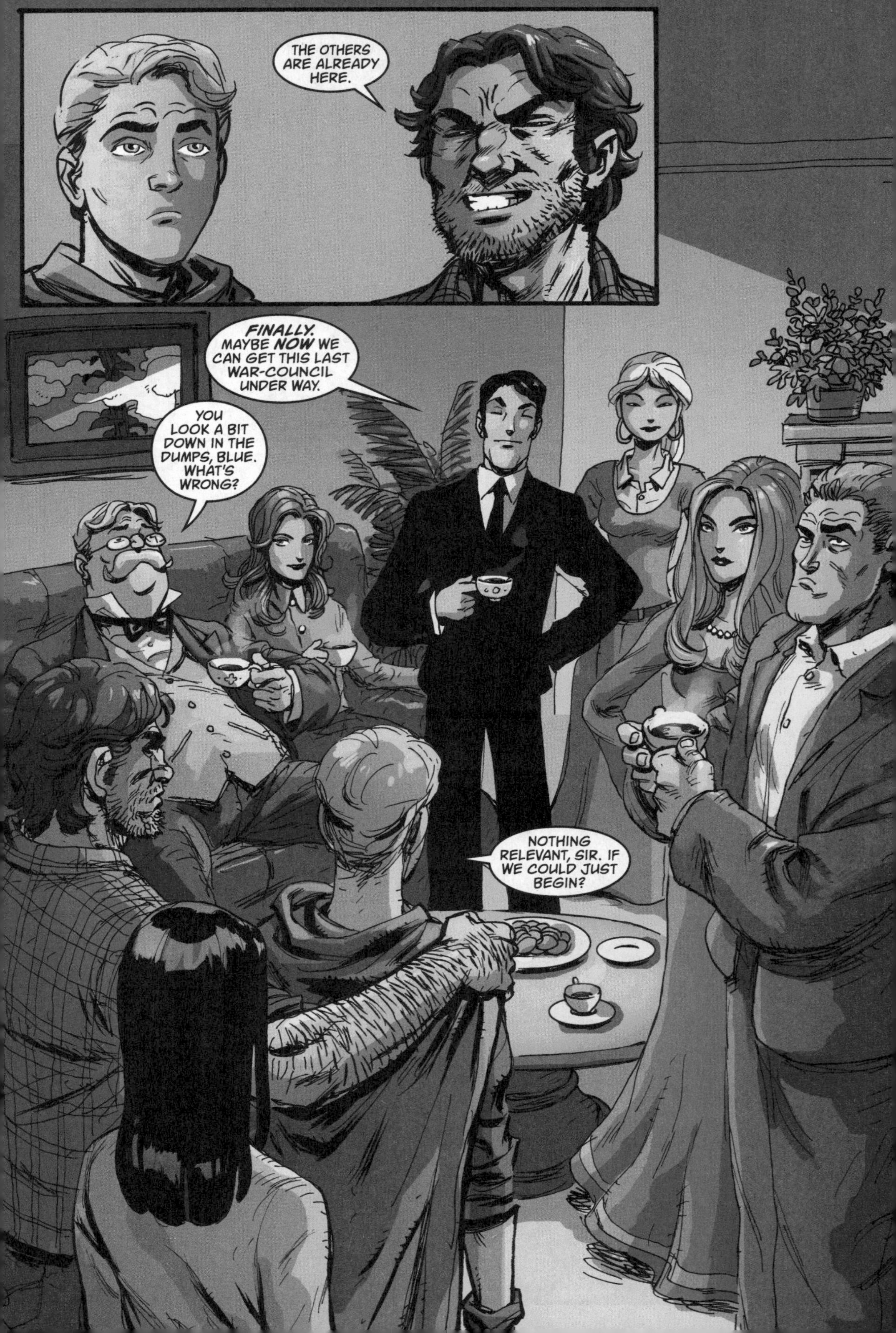
THE OTHERS ARE ALREADY HERE.
FINALLY. MAYBE *NOW* WE CAN GET THIS LAST WAR-COUNCIL UNDER WAY.
YOU LOOK A BIT DOWN IN THE DUMPS, BLUE. WHAT'S WRONG?
NOTHING RELEVANT, SIR. IF WE COULD JUST BEGIN?

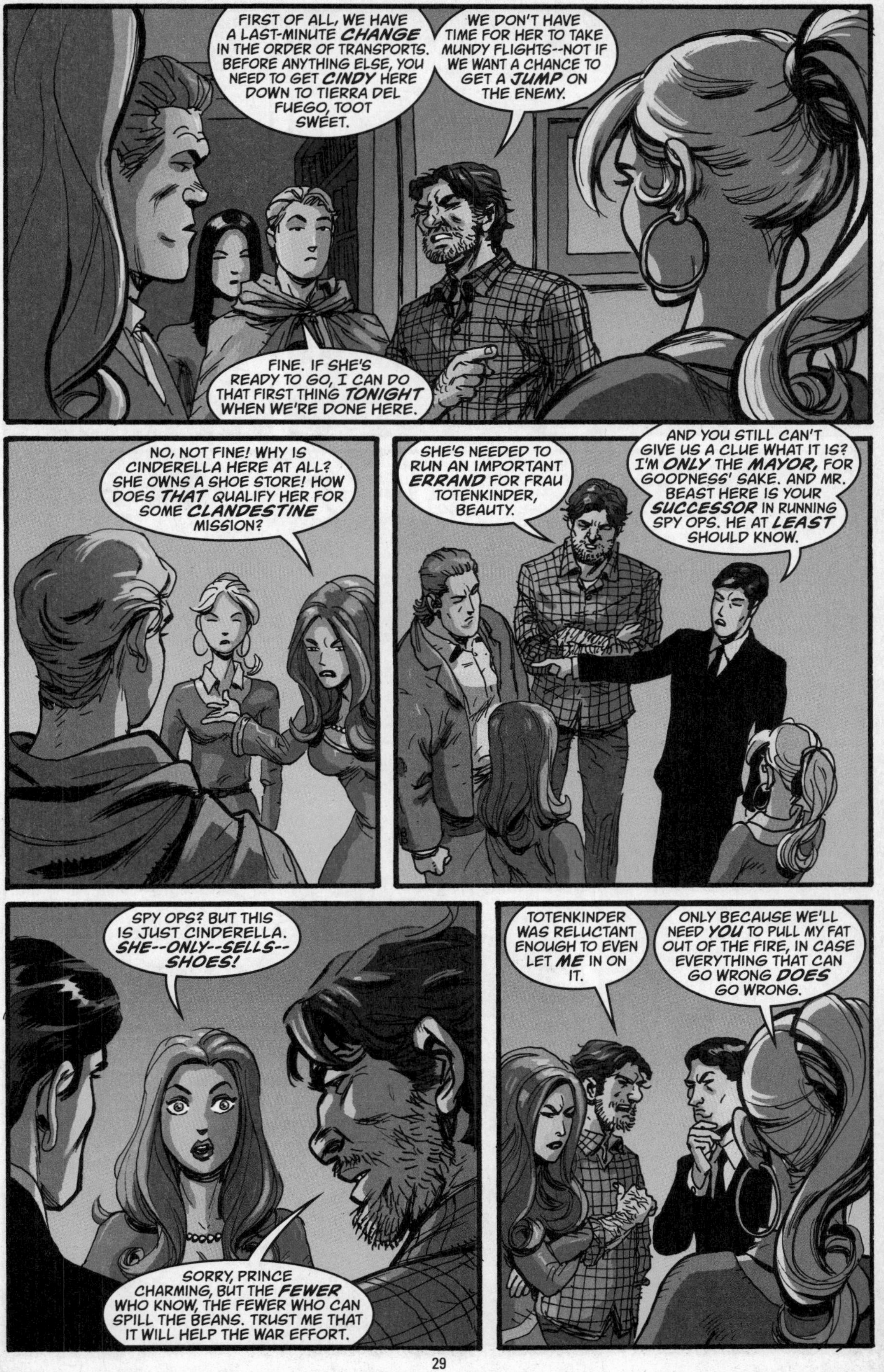
FIRST OF ALL, WE HAVE A LAST-MINUTE CHANGE IN THE ORDER OF TRANSPORTS. BEFORE ANYTHING ELSE, YOU NEED TO GET CINDY HERE DOWN TO TIERRA DEL FUEGO, TOOT SWEET.
WE DON'T HAVE TIME FOR HER TO TAKE MUNDY FLIGHTS--NOT IF WE WANT A CHANCE TO GET A JUMP ON THE ENEMY.
FINE. IF SHE'S READY TO GO, I CAN DO THAT FIRST THING TONIGHT WHEN WE'RE DONE HERE.
NO, NOT FINE! WHY IS CINDERELLA HERE AT ALL? SHE OWNS A SHOE STORE! HOW DOES THAT QUALIFY HER FOR SOME CLANDESTINE MISSION?
SHE'S NEEDED TO RUN AN IMPORTANT ERRAND FOR FRAU TOTENKINDER, BEAUTY.
AND YOU STILL CAN'T GIVE US A CLUE WHAT IT IS? I'M ONLY THE MAYOR, FOR GOODNESS' SAKE. AND MR. BEAST HERE IS YOUR SUCCESSOR IN RUNNING SPY OPS. HE AT LEAST SHOULD KNOW.
SPY OPS? BUT THIS IS JUST CINDERELLA. SHE--ONLY--SELLS--SHOES!
SORRY, PRINCE CHARMING, BUT THE FEWER WHO KNOW, THE FEWER WHO CAN SPILL THE BEANS. TRUST ME THAT IT WILL HELP THE WAR EFFORT.
TOTENKINDER WAS RELUCTANT ENOUGH TO EVEN LET ME IN ON IT.
ONLY BECAUSE WE'LL NEED YOU TO PULL MY FAT OUT OF THE FIRE, IN CASE EVERYTHING THAT CAN GO WRONG DOES GO WRONG.

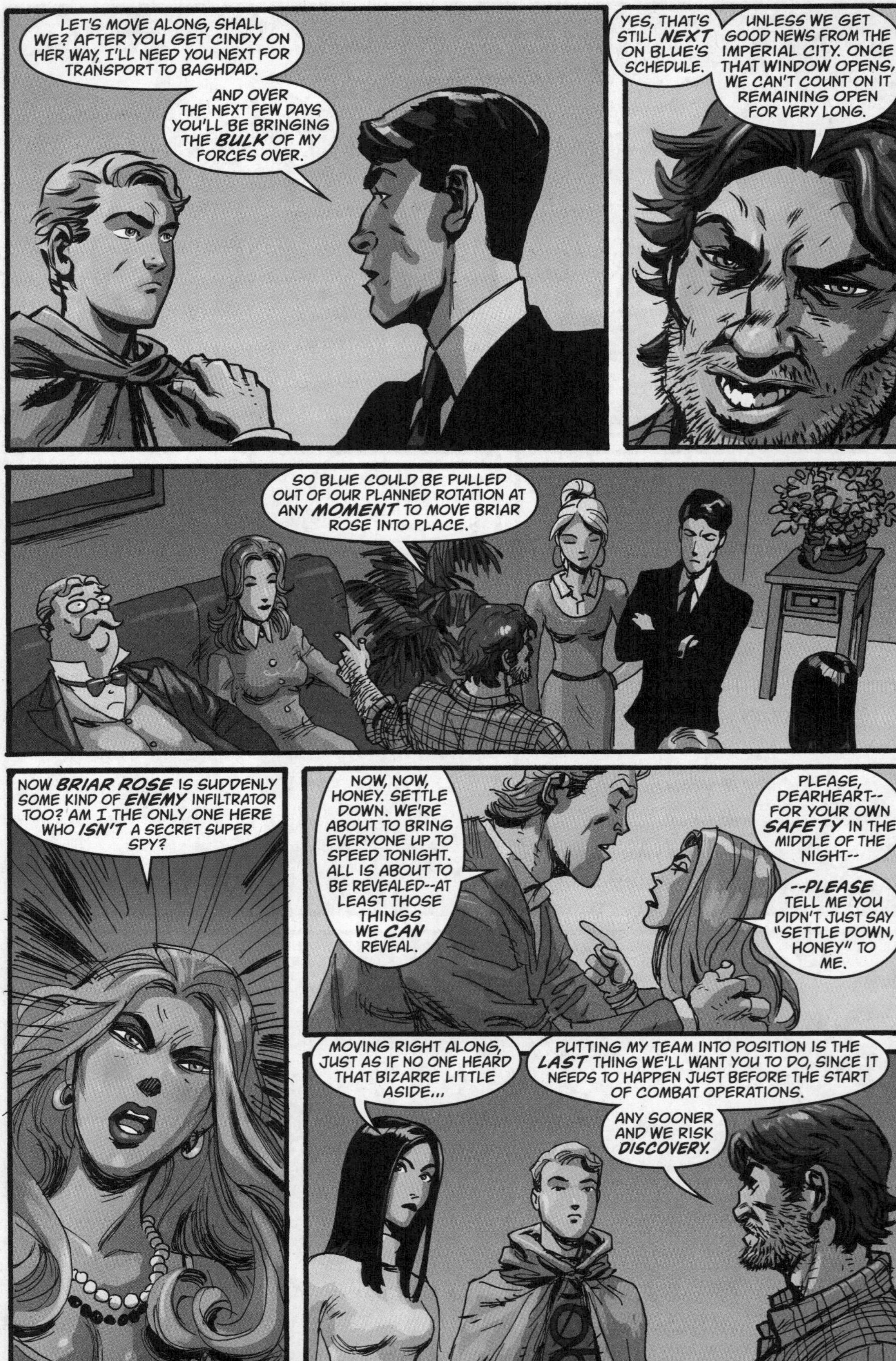
LET'S MOVE ALONG, SHALL WE? AFTER YOU GET CINDY ON HER WAY, I'LL NEED YOU NEXT FOR TRANSPORT TO BAGHDAD.
AND OVER THE NEXT FEW DAYS YOU'LL BE BRINGING THE *BULK* OF MY FORCES OVER.
YES, THAT'S STILL *NEXT* ON BLUE'S SCHEDULE.
UNLESS WE GET GOOD NEWS FROM THE IMPERIAL CITY. ONCE THAT WINDOW OPENS, WE CAN'T COUNT ON IT REMAINING OPEN FOR VERY LONG.
SO BLUE COULD BE PULLED OUT OF OUR PLANNED ROTATION AT ANY *MOMENT* TO MOVE BRIAR ROSE INTO PLACE.
NOW *BRIAR ROSE* IS SUDDENLY SOME KIND OF *ENEMY* INFILTRATOR TOO? AM I THE ONLY ONE HERE WHO *ISN'T* A SECRET SUPER SPY?
NOW, NOW, HONEY. SETTLE DOWN. WE'RE ABOUT TO BRING EVERYONE UP TO SPEED TONIGHT. ALL IS ABOUT TO BE REVEALED--AT LEAST THOSE THINGS WE *CAN* REVEAL.
PLEASE, DEARHEART--FOR YOUR OWN *SAFETY* IN THE MIDDLE OF THE NIGHT--
--*PLEASE* TELL ME YOU DIDN'T JUST SAY "SETTLE DOWN, HONEY" TO ME.
MOVING RIGHT ALONG, JUST AS IF NO ONE HEARD THAT BIZARRE LITTLE ASIDE...
PUTTING MY TEAM INTO POSITION IS THE *LAST* THING WE'LL WANT YOU TO DO, SINCE IT NEEDS TO HAPPEN JUST BEFORE THE START OF COMBAT OPERATIONS.
ANY SOONER AND WE RISK *DISCOVERY*.

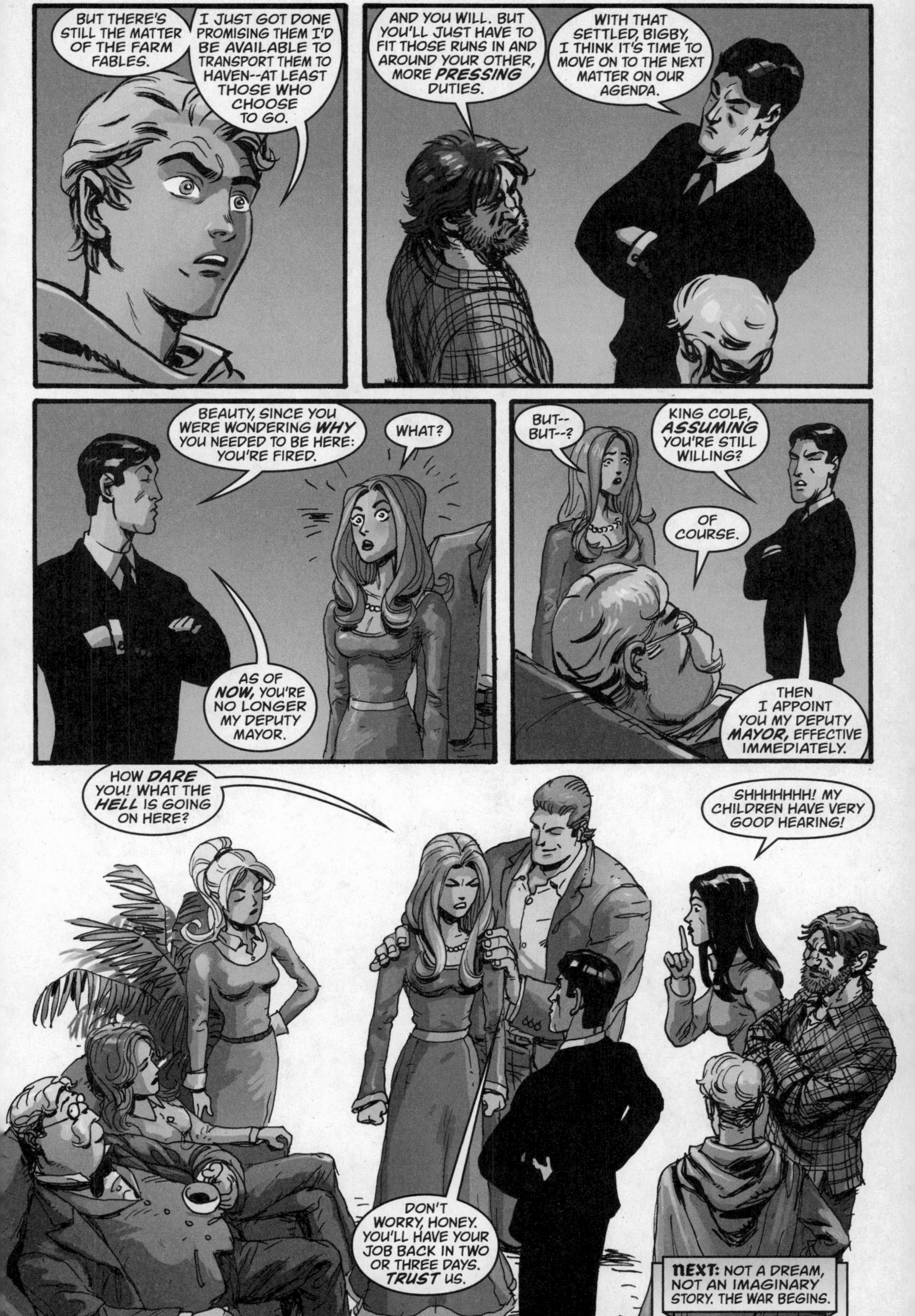

BUT THERE'S STILL THE MATTER OF THE FARM FABLES.
I JUST GOT DONE PROMISING THEM I'D BE AVAILABLE TO TRANSPORT THEM TO HAVEN--AT LEAST THOSE WHO CHOOSE TO GO.
AND YOU WILL. BUT YOU'LL JUST HAVE TO FIT THOSE RUNS IN AND AROUND YOUR OTHER, MORE PRESSING DUTIES.
WITH THAT SETTLED, BIGBY, I THINK IT'S TIME TO MOVE ON TO THE NEXT MATTER ON OUR AGENDA.
BEAUTY, SINCE YOU WERE WONDERING WHY YOU NEEDED TO BE HERE: YOU'RE FIRED.
WHAT?
AS OF NOW, YOU'RE NO LONGER MY DEPUTY MAYOR.
BUT-- BUT--?
KING COLE, ASSUMING YOU'RE STILL WILLING?
OF COURSE.
THEN I APPOINT YOU MY DEPUTY MAYOR, EFFECTIVE IMMEDIATELY.
HOW DARE YOU! WHAT THE HELL IS GOING ON HERE?
SHHHHHHH! MY CHILDREN HAVE VERY GOOD HEARING!
DON'T WORRY, HONEY. YOU'LL HAVE YOUR JOB BACK IN TWO OR THREE DAYS. TRUST US.
NEXT: NOT A DREAM, NOT AN IMAGINARY STORY. THE WAR BEGINS.

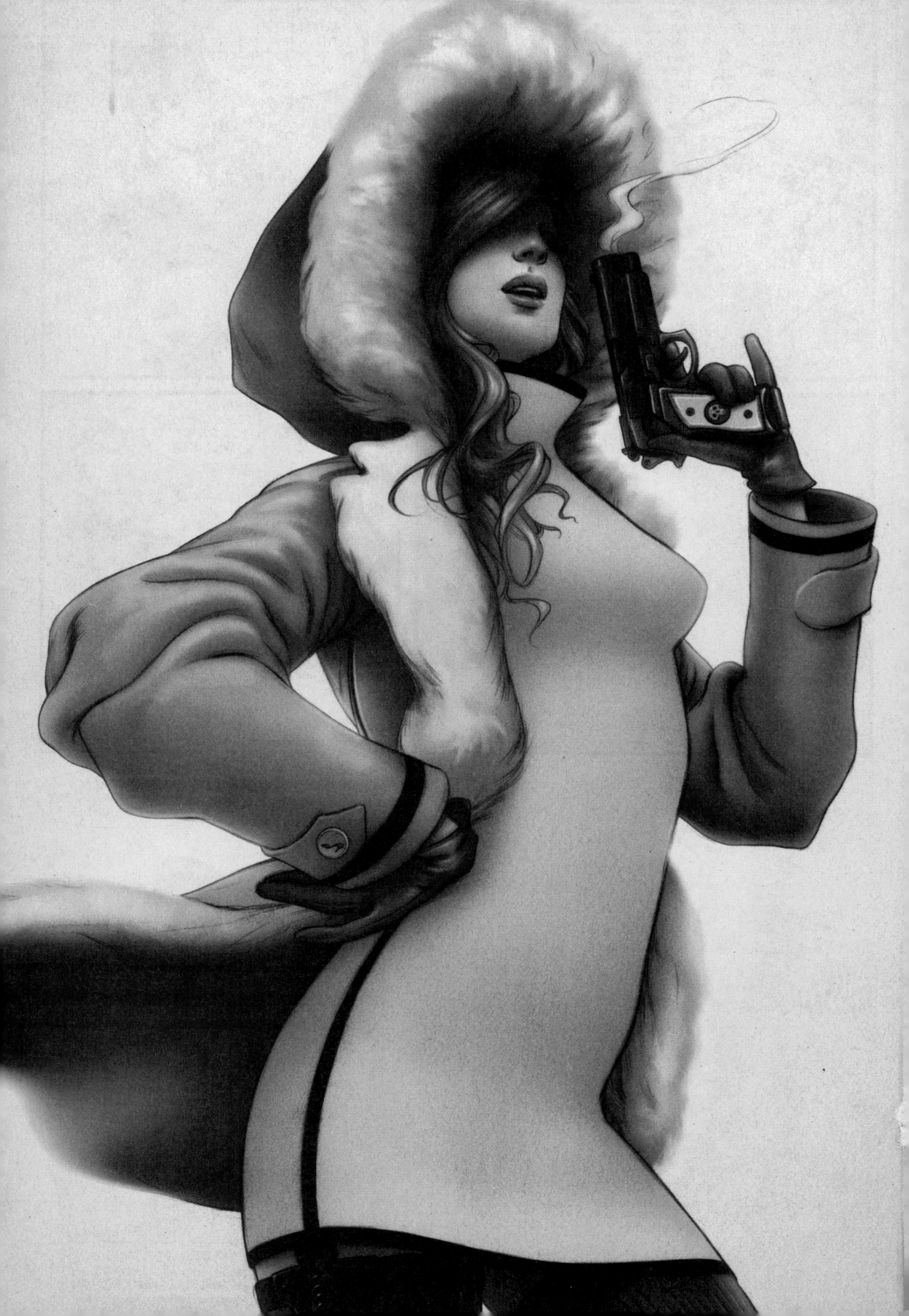

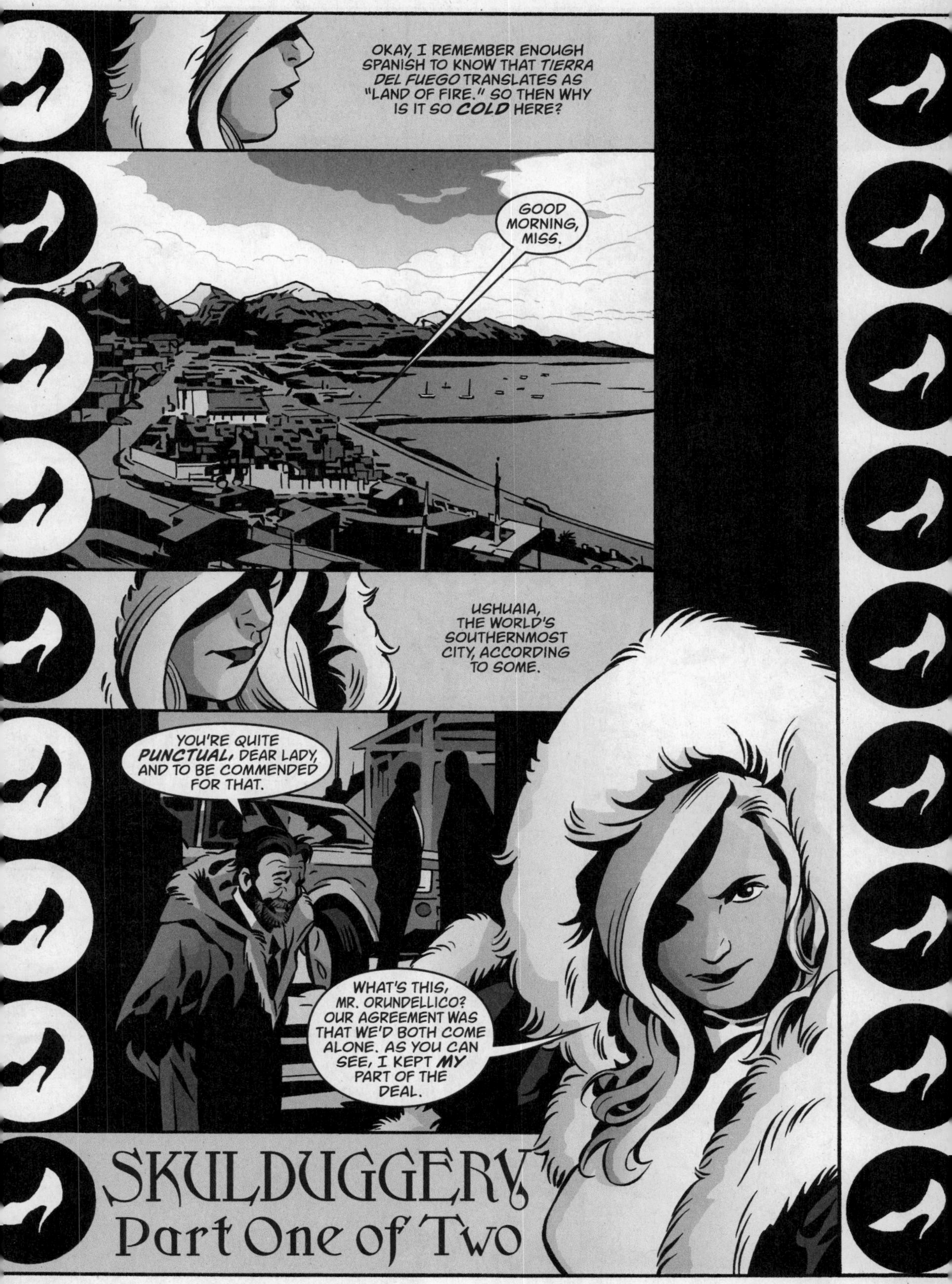

OKAY, I REMEMBER ENOUGH SPANISH TO KNOW THAT *TIERRA DEL FUEGO* TRANSLATES AS "LAND OF FIRE." SO THEN WHY IS IT SO **COLD** HERE?
GOOD MORNING, MISS.
USHUAIA, THE WORLD'S SOUTHERNMOST CITY, ACCORDING TO SOME.
YOU'RE QUITE **PUNCTUAL,** DEAR LADY, AND TO BE COMMENDED FOR THAT.
WHAT'S THIS, MR. ORUNDELLICO? OUR AGREEMENT WAS THAT WE'D BOTH COME ALONE. AS YOU CAN SEE, I KEPT **MY** PART OF THE DEAL.
SKULDUGGERY
Part One of Two

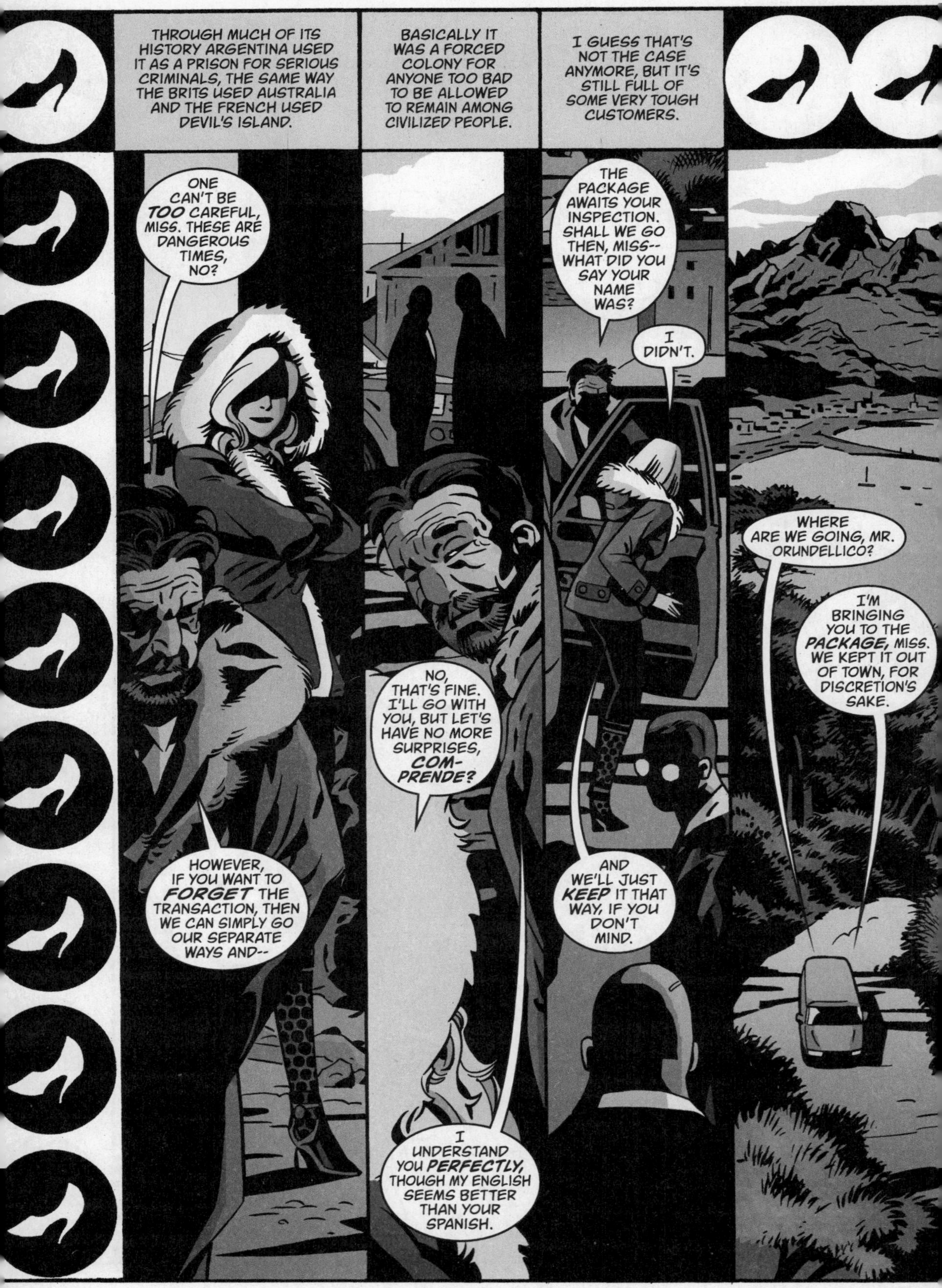
THROUGH MUCH OF ITS HISTORY ARGENTINA USED IT AS A PRISON FOR SERIOUS CRIMINALS, THE SAME WAY THE BRITS USED AUSTRALIA AND THE FRENCH USED DEVIL'S ISLAND.
BASICALLY IT WAS A FORCED COLONY FOR ANYONE TOO BAD TO BE ALLOWED TO REMAIN AMONG CIVILIZED PEOPLE.
I GUESS THAT'S NOT THE CASE ANYMORE, BUT IT'S STILL FULL OF SOME VERY TOUGH CUSTOMERS.
ONE CAN'T BE TOO CAREFUL, MISS. THESE ARE DANGEROUS TIMES, NO?
HOWEVER, IF YOU WANT TO FORGET THE TRANSACTION, THEN WE CAN SIMPLY GO OUR SEPARATE WAYS AND--
NO, THAT'S FINE. I'LL GO WITH YOU, BUT LET'S HAVE NO MORE SURPRISES, COMPRENDE?
I UNDERSTAND YOU PERFECTLY, THOUGH MY ENGLISH SEEMS BETTER THAN YOUR SPANISH.
THE PACKAGE AWAITS YOUR INSPECTION. SHALL WE GO THEN, MISS-- WHAT DID YOU SAY YOUR NAME WAS?
I DIDN'T.
AND WE'LL JUST KEEP IT THAT WAY, IF YOU DON'T MIND.
WHERE ARE WE GOING, MR. ORUNDELLICO?
I'M BRINGING YOU TO THE PACKAGE, MISS. WE KEPT IT OUT OF TOWN, FOR DISCRETION'S SAKE.

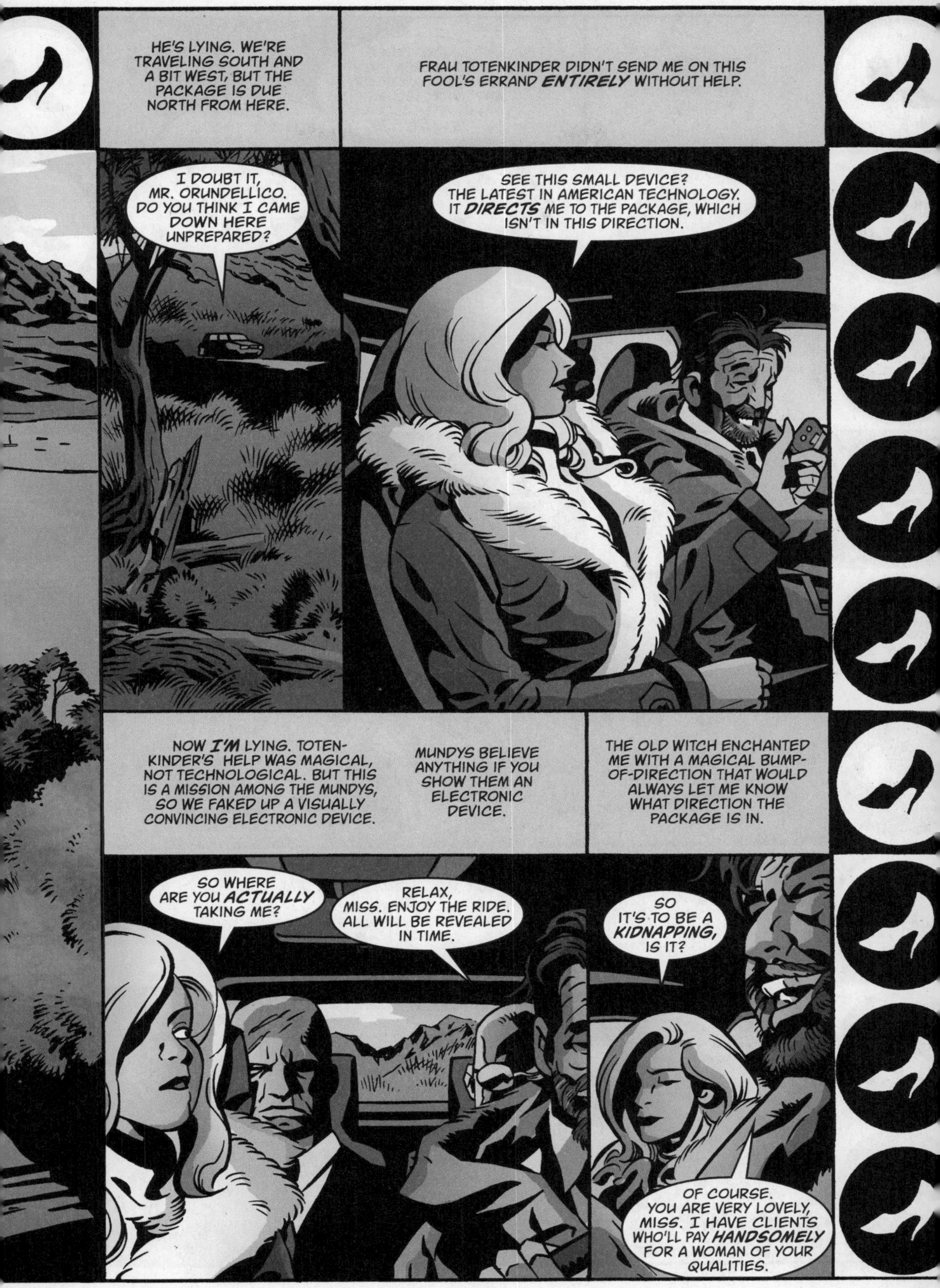
HE'S LYING. WE'RE TRAVELING SOUTH AND A BIT WEST, BUT THE PACKAGE IS DUE NORTH FROM HERE.
FRAU TOTENKINDER DIDN'T SEND ME ON THIS FOOL'S ERRAND *ENTIRELY* WITHOUT HELP.
I DOUBT IT, MR. ORUNDELLICO. DO YOU THINK I CAME DOWN HERE UNPREPARED?
SEE THIS SMALL DEVICE? THE LATEST IN AMERICAN TECHNOLOGY. IT *DIRECTS* ME TO THE PACKAGE, WHICH ISN'T IN THIS DIRECTION.
NOW *I'M* LYING. TOTEN-KINDER'S HELP WAS MAGICAL, NOT TECHNOLOGICAL. BUT THIS IS A MISSION AMONG THE MUNDYS, SO WE FAKED UP A VISUALLY CONVINCING ELECTRONIC DEVICE.
MUNDYS BELIEVE ANYTHING IF YOU SHOW THEM AN ELECTRONIC DEVICE.
THE OLD WITCH ENCHANTED ME WITH A MAGICAL BUMP-OF-DIRECTION THAT WOULD ALWAYS LET ME KNOW WHAT DIRECTION THE PACKAGE IS IN.
SO WHERE ARE YOU *ACTUALLY* TAKING ME?
RELAX, MISS. ENJOY THE RIDE. ALL WILL BE REVEALED IN TIME.
SO IT'S TO BE A *KIDNAPPING,* IS IT?
OF COURSE. YOU ARE VERY LOVELY, MISS. I HAVE CLIENTS WHO'LL PAY *HANDSOMELY* FOR A WOMAN OF YOUR QUALITIES.

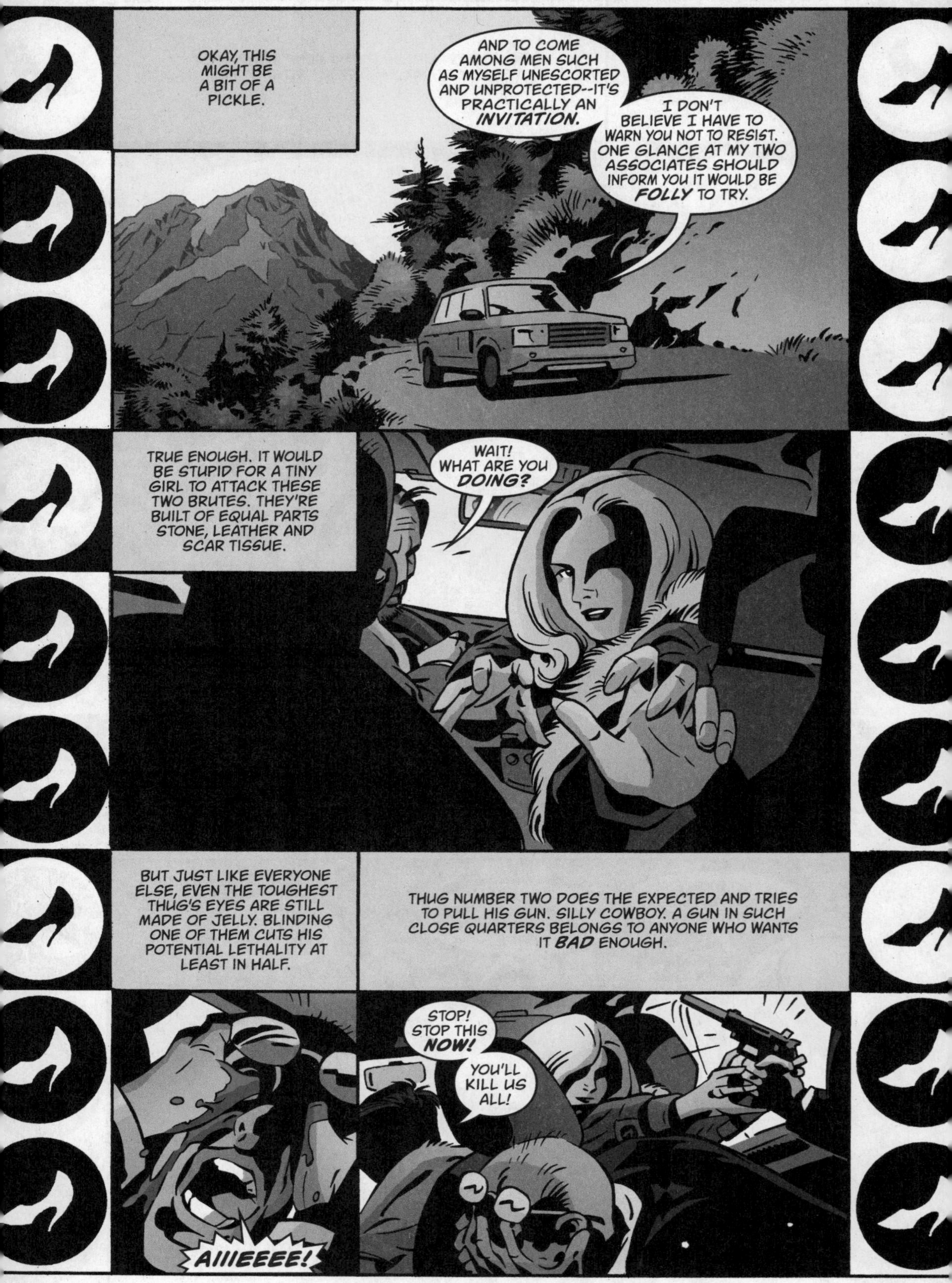
OKAY, THIS MIGHT BE A BIT OF A PICKLE.
AND TO COME AMONG MEN SUCH AS MYSELF UNESCORTED AND UNPROTECTED--IT'S PRACTICALLY AN INVITATION.
I DON'T BELIEVE I HAVE TO WARN YOU NOT TO RESIST. ONE GLANCE AT MY TWO ASSOCIATES SHOULD INFORM YOU IT WOULD BE FOLLY TO TRY.
TRUE ENOUGH. IT WOULD BE STUPID FOR A TINY GIRL TO ATTACK THESE TWO BRUTES. THEY'RE BUILT OF EQUAL PARTS STONE, LEATHER AND SCAR TISSUE.
WAIT! WHAT ARE YOU DOING?
BUT JUST LIKE EVERYONE ELSE, EVEN THE TOUGHEST THUG'S EYES ARE STILL MADE OF JELLY. BLINDING ONE OF THEM CUTS HIS POTENTIAL LETHALITY AT LEAST IN HALF.
AIIIEEEE!
THUG NUMBER TWO DOES THE EXPECTED AND TRIES TO PULL HIS GUN. SILLY COWBOY. A GUN IN SUCH CLOSE QUARTERS BELONGS TO ANYONE WHO WANTS IT BAD ENOUGH.
STOP! STOP THIS NOW!
YOU'LL KILL US ALL!

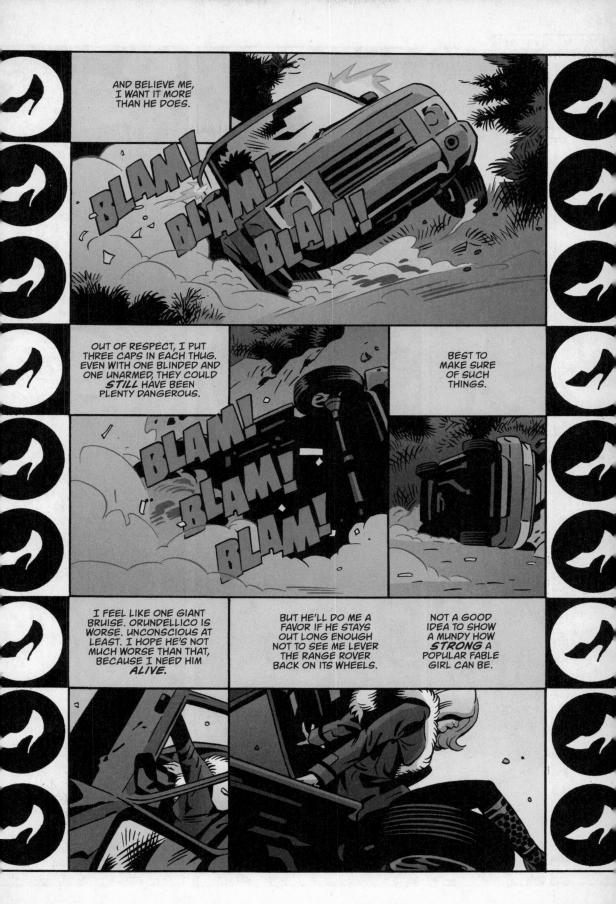

AND BELIEVE ME, I WANT IT MORE THAN HE DOES.

BLAM! BLAM! BLAM!

OUT OF RESPECT, I PUT THREE CAPS IN EACH THUG. EVEN WITH ONE BLINDED AND ONE UNARMED, THEY COULD *STILL* HAVE BEEN PLENTY DANGEROUS.

BEST TO MAKE SURE OF SUCH THINGS.

BLAM! BLAM! BLAM!

I FEEL LIKE ONE GIANT BRUISE. ORUNDELLICO IS WORSE. UNCONSCIOUS AT LEAST. I HOPE HE'S NOT MUCH WORSE THAN THAT, BECAUSE I NEED HIM *ALIVE.*

BUT HE'LL DO ME A FAVOR IF HE STAYS OUT LONG ENOUGH NOT TO SEE ME LEVER THE RANGE ROVER BACK ON ITS WHEELS.

NOT A GOOD IDEA TO SHOW A MUNDY HOW *STRONG* A POPULAR FABLE GIRL CAN BE.

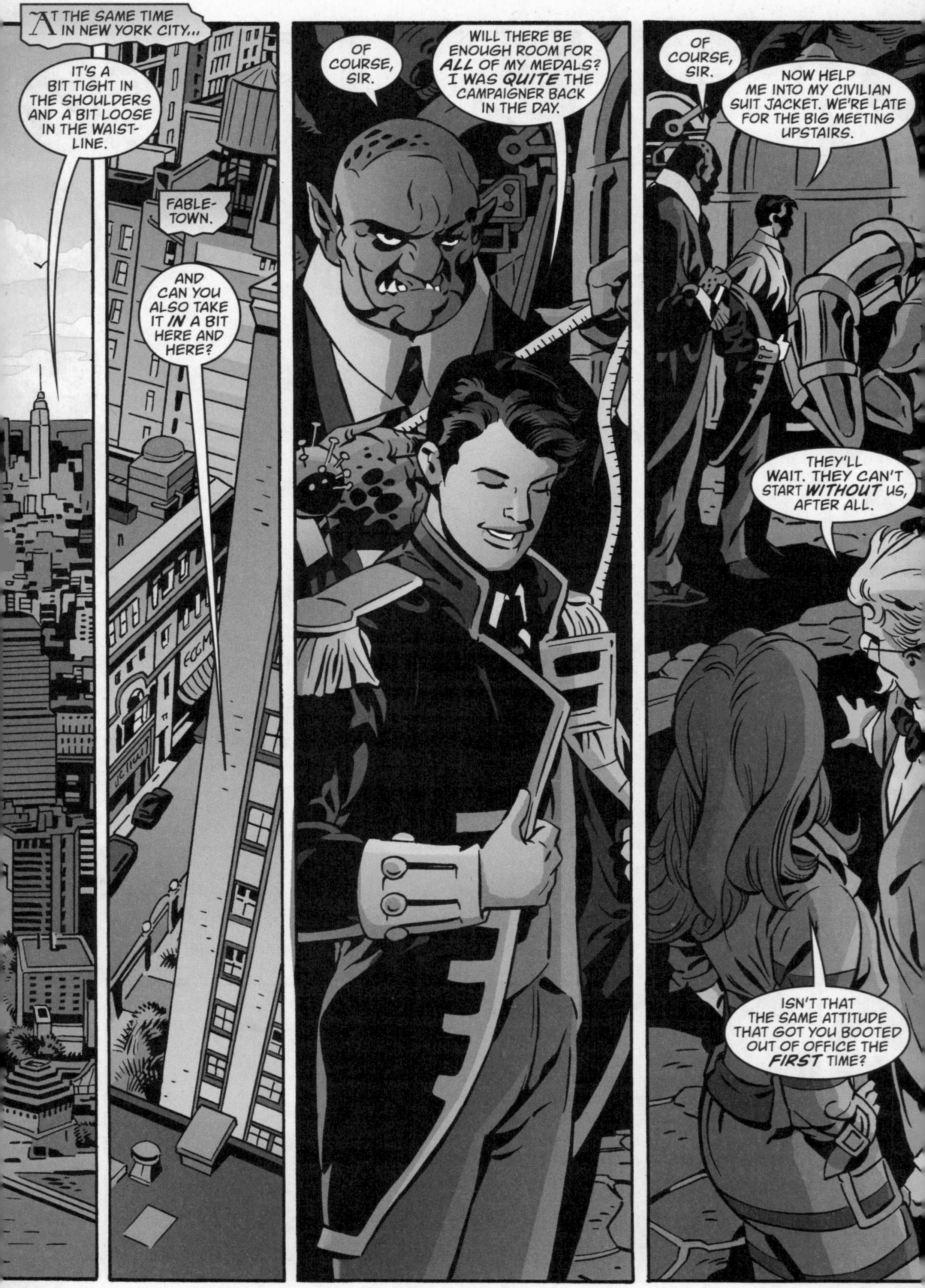
AT THE SAME TIME IN NEW YORK CITY...
IT'S A BIT TIGHT IN THE SHOULDERS AND A BIT LOOSE IN THE WAIST-LINE.
FABLE-TOWN.
AND CAN YOU ALSO TAKE IT IN A BIT HERE AND HERE?
OF COURSE, SIR.
WILL THERE BE ENOUGH ROOM FOR ALL OF MY MEDALS? I WAS QUITE THE CAMPAIGNER BACK IN THE DAY.
OF COURSE, SIR.
NOW HELP ME INTO MY CIVILIAN SUIT JACKET. WE'RE LATE FOR THE BIG MEETING UPSTAIRS.
THEY'LL WAIT. THEY CAN'T START WITHOUT US, AFTER ALL.
ISN'T THAT THE SAME ATTITUDE THAT GOT YOU BOOTED OUT OF OFFICE THE FIRST TIME?

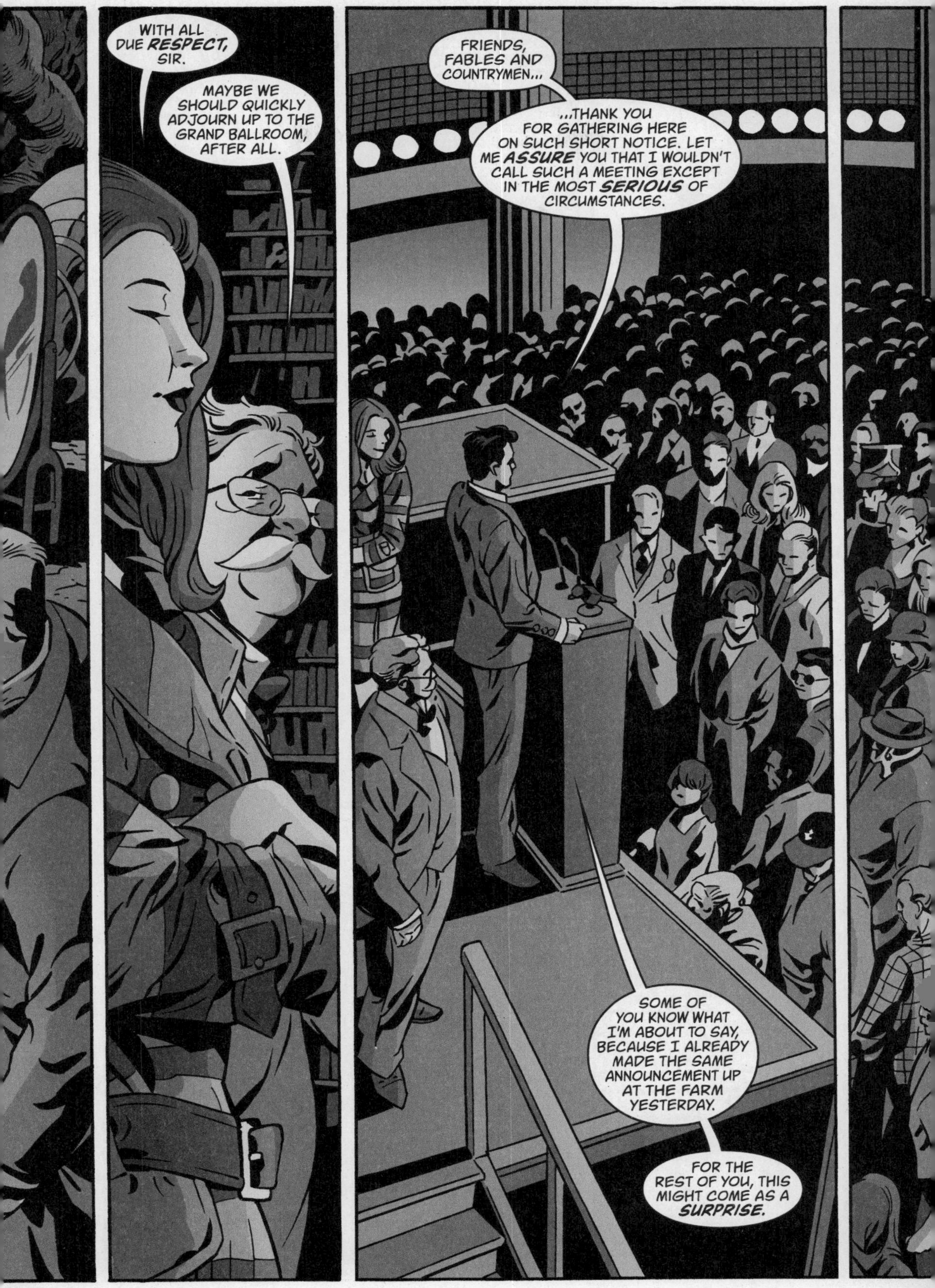
WITH ALL DUE *RESPECT*, SIR.
MAYBE WE SHOULD QUICKLY ADJOURN UP TO THE GRAND BALLROOM, AFTER ALL.
FRIENDS, FABLES AND COUNTRYMEN...
...THANK YOU FOR GATHERING HERE ON SUCH SHORT NOTICE. LET ME *ASSURE* YOU THAT I WOULDN'T CALL SUCH A MEETING EXCEPT IN THE MOST *SERIOUS* OF CIRCUMSTANCES.
SOME OF YOU KNOW WHAT I'M ABOUT TO SAY, BECAUSE I ALREADY MADE THE SAME ANNOUNCEMENT UP AT THE FARM YESTERDAY.
FOR THE REST OF YOU, THIS MIGHT COME AS A *SURPRISE*.

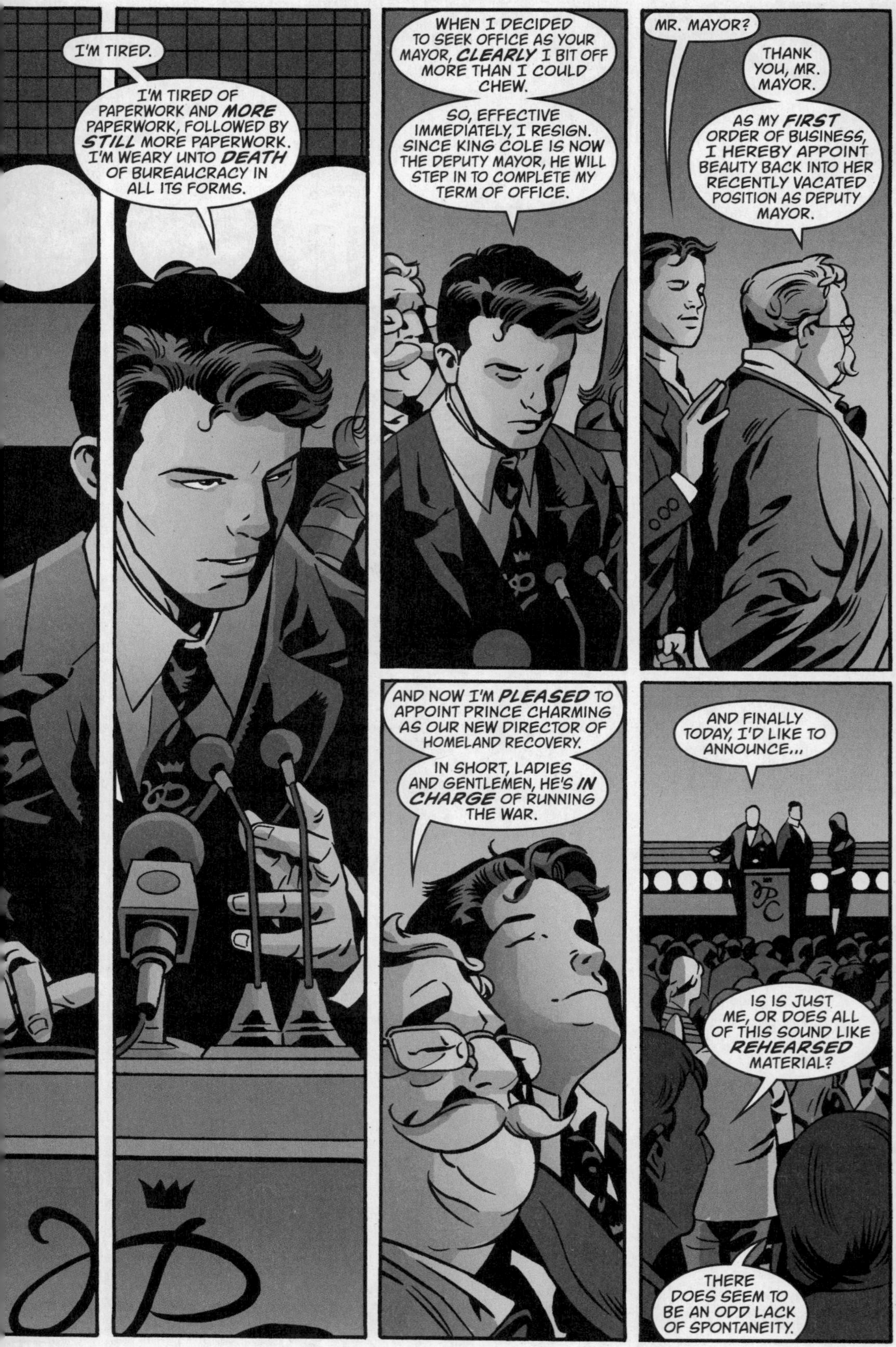

I'M TIRED.
I'M TIRED OF PAPERWORK AND MORE PAPERWORK, FOLLOWED BY STILL MORE PAPERWORK. I'M WEARY UNTO DEATH OF BUREAUCRACY IN ALL ITS FORMS.
WHEN I DECIDED TO SEEK OFFICE AS YOUR MAYOR, CLEARLY I BIT OFF MORE THAN I COULD CHEW.
SO, EFFECTIVE IMMEDIATELY, I RESIGN. SINCE KING COLE IS NOW THE DEPUTY MAYOR, HE WILL STEP IN TO COMPLETE MY TERM OF OFFICE.
MR. MAYOR?
THANK YOU, MR. MAYOR.
AS MY FIRST ORDER OF BUSINESS, I HEREBY APPOINT BEAUTY BACK INTO HER RECENTLY VACATED POSITION AS DEPUTY MAYOR.
AND NOW I'M PLEASED TO APPOINT PRINCE CHARMING AS OUR NEW DIRECTOR OF HOMELAND RECOVERY.
IN SHORT, LADIES AND GENTLEMEN, HE'S IN CHARGE OF RUNNING THE WAR.
AND FINALLY TODAY, I'D LIKE TO ANNOUNCE...
IS IS JUST ME, OR DOES ALL OF THIS SOUND LIKE REHEARSED MATERIAL?
THERE DOES SEEM TO BE AN ODD LACK OF SPONTANEITY.

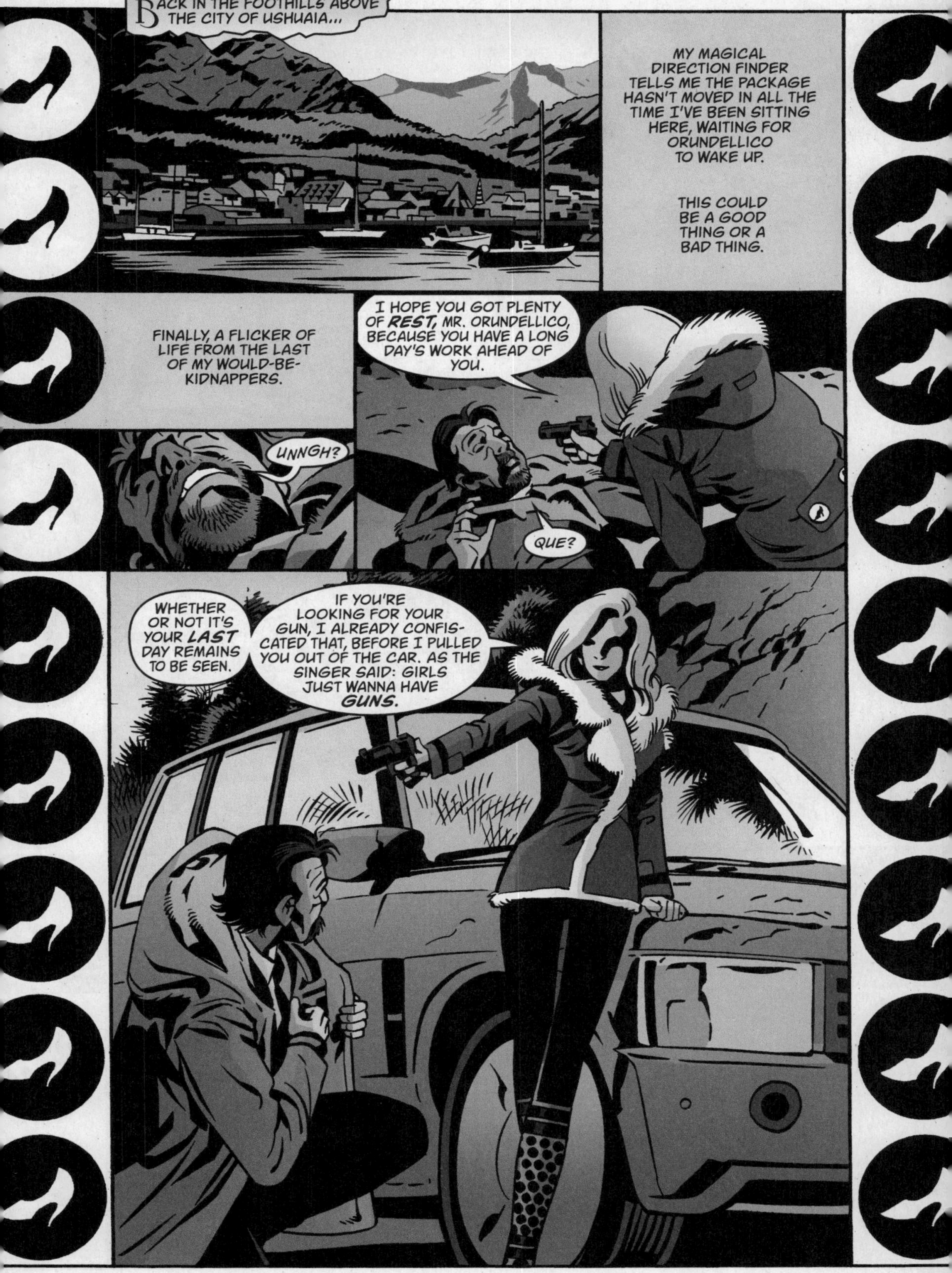
BACK IN THE FOOTHILLS ABOVE THE CITY OF USHUAIA...
MY MAGICAL DIRECTION FINDER TELLS ME THE PACKAGE HASN'T MOVED IN ALL THE TIME I'VE BEEN SITTING HERE, WAITING FOR ORUNDELLICO TO WAKE UP.
THIS COULD BE A GOOD THING OR A BAD THING.
FINALLY, A FLICKER OF LIFE FROM THE LAST OF MY WOULD-BE-KIDNAPPERS.
UNNGH?
I HOPE YOU GOT PLENTY OF REST, MR. ORUNDELLICO, BECAUSE YOU HAVE A LONG DAY'S WORK AHEAD OF YOU.
QUE?
WHETHER OR NOT IT'S YOUR LAST DAY REMAINS TO BE SEEN.
IF YOU'RE LOOKING FOR YOUR GUN, I ALREADY CONFISCATED THAT, BEFORE I PULLED YOU OUT OF THE CAR. AS THE SINGER SAID: GIRLS JUST WANNA HAVE GUNS.

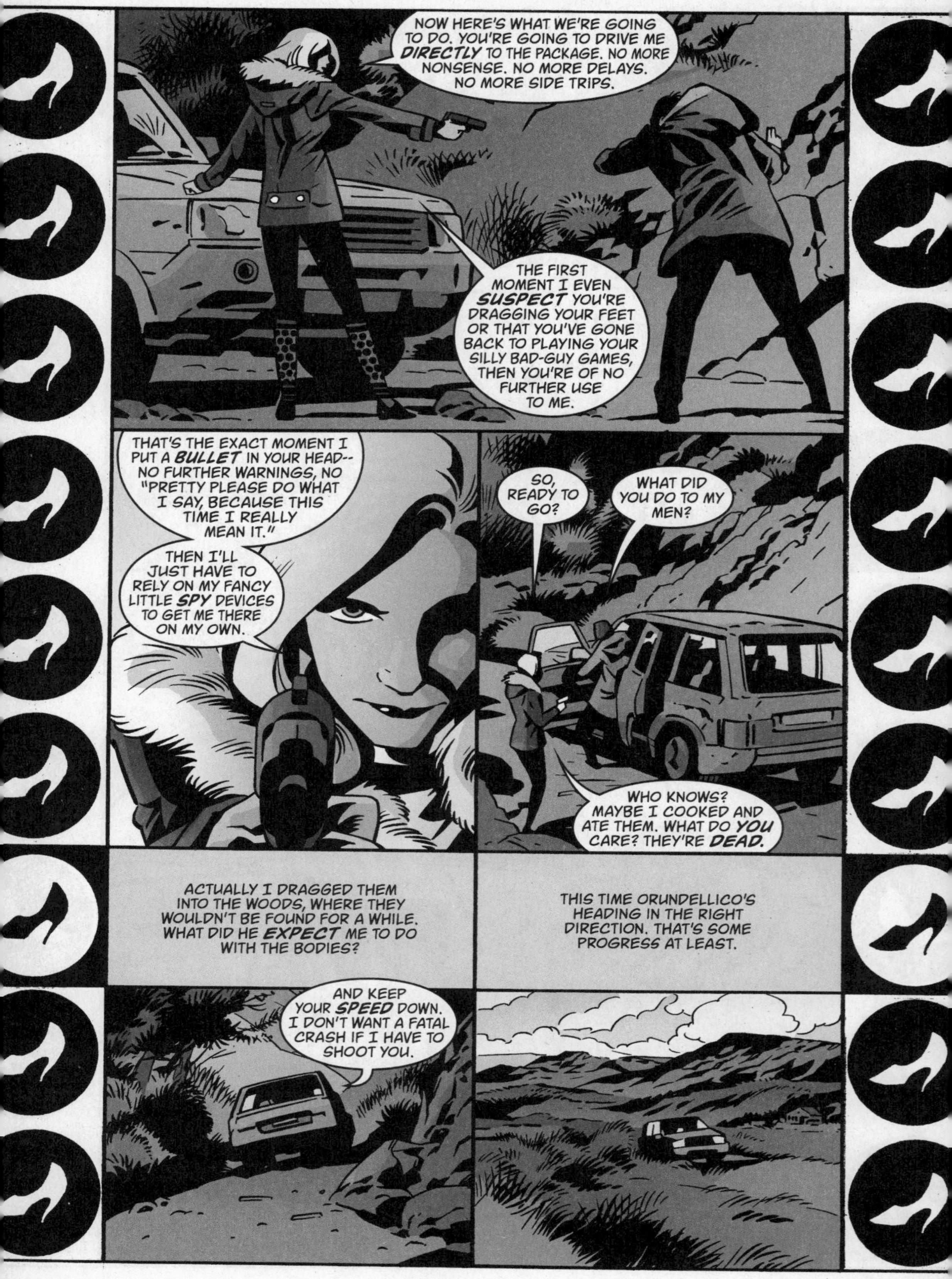
NOW HERE'S WHAT WE'RE GOING TO DO. YOU'RE GOING TO DRIVE ME DIRECTLY TO THE PACKAGE. NO MORE NONSENSE. NO MORE DELAYS. NO MORE SIDE TRIPS.
THE FIRST MOMENT I EVEN SUSPECT YOU'RE DRAGGING YOUR FEET OR THAT YOU'VE GONE BACK TO PLAYING YOUR SILLY BAD-GUY GAMES, THEN YOU'RE OF NO FURTHER USE TO ME.
THAT'S THE EXACT MOMENT I PUT A BULLET IN YOUR HEAD--NO FURTHER WARNINGS, NO "PRETTY PLEASE DO WHAT I SAY, BECAUSE THIS TIME I REALLY MEAN IT."
THEN I'LL JUST HAVE TO RELY ON MY FANCY LITTLE SPY DEVICES TO GET ME THERE ON MY OWN.
SO, READY TO GO?
WHAT DID YOU DO TO MY MEN?
WHO KNOWS? MAYBE I COOKED AND ATE THEM. WHAT DO YOU CARE? THEY'RE DEAD.
ACTUALLY I DRAGGED THEM INTO THE WOODS, WHERE THEY WOULDN'T BE FOUND FOR A WHILE. WHAT DID HE EXPECT ME TO DO WITH THE BODIES?
THIS TIME ORUNDELLICO'S HEADING IN THE RIGHT DIRECTION. THAT'S SOME PROGRESS AT LEAST.
AND KEEP YOUR SPEED DOWN. I DON'T WANT A FATAL CRASH IF I HAVE TO SHOOT YOU.

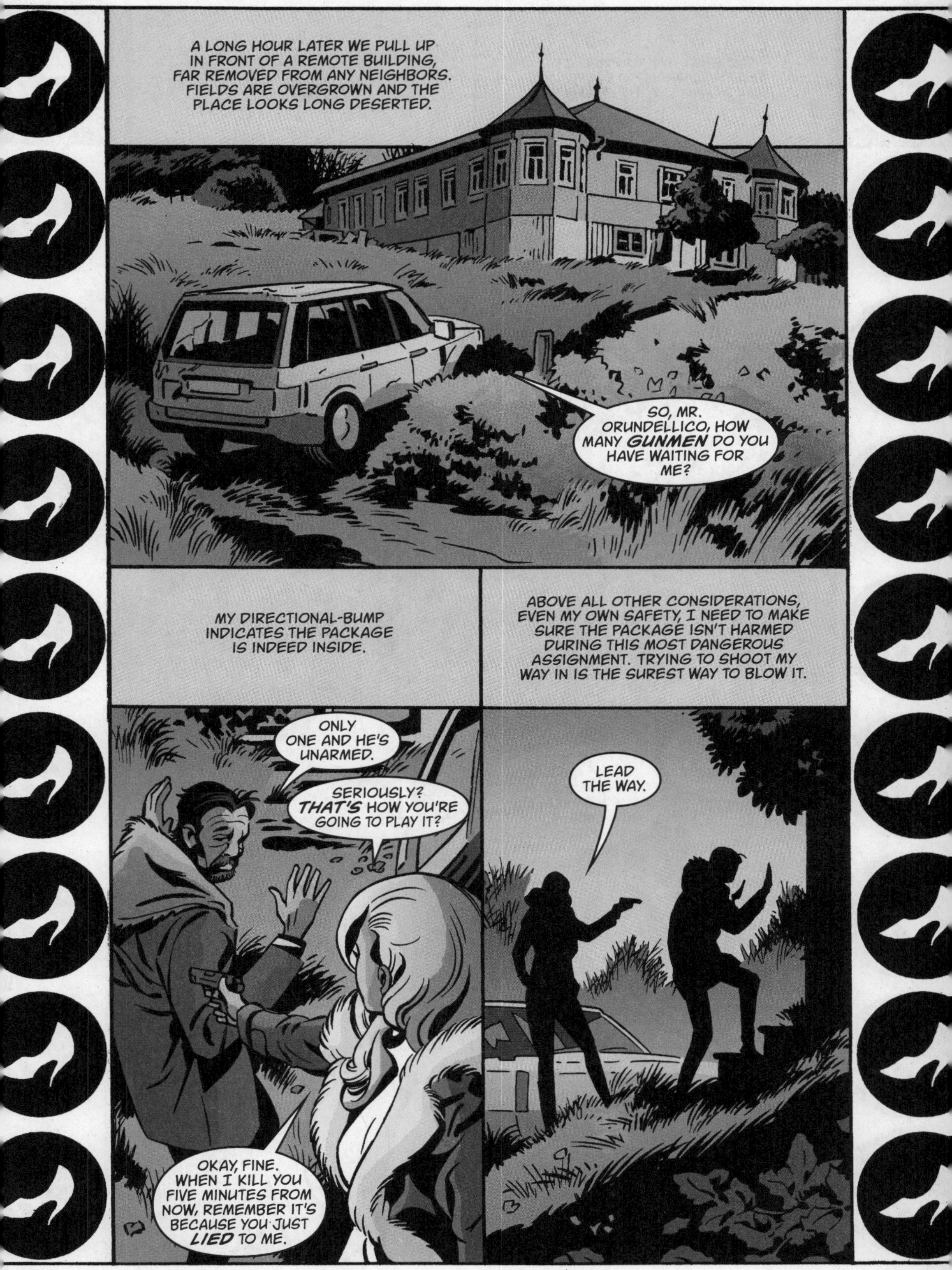
A LONG HOUR LATER WE PULL UP IN FRONT OF A REMOTE BUILDING, FAR REMOVED FROM ANY NEIGHBORS. FIELDS ARE OVERGROWN AND THE PLACE LOOKS LONG DESERTED.
SO, MR. ORUNDELLICO, HOW MANY GUNMEN DO YOU HAVE WAITING FOR ME?
MY DIRECTIONAL-BUMP INDICATES THE PACKAGE IS INDEED INSIDE.
ABOVE ALL OTHER CONSIDERATIONS, EVEN MY OWN SAFETY, I NEED TO MAKE SURE THE PACKAGE ISN'T HARMED DURING THIS MOST DANGEROUS ASSIGNMENT. TRYING TO SHOOT MY WAY IN IS THE SUREST WAY TO BLOW IT.
ONLY ONE AND HE'S UNARMED.
SERIOUSLY? THAT'S HOW YOU'RE GOING TO PLAY IT?
OKAY, FINE. WHEN I KILL YOU FIVE MINUTES FROM NOW, REMEMBER IT'S BECAUSE YOU JUST LIED TO ME.
LEAD THE WAY.

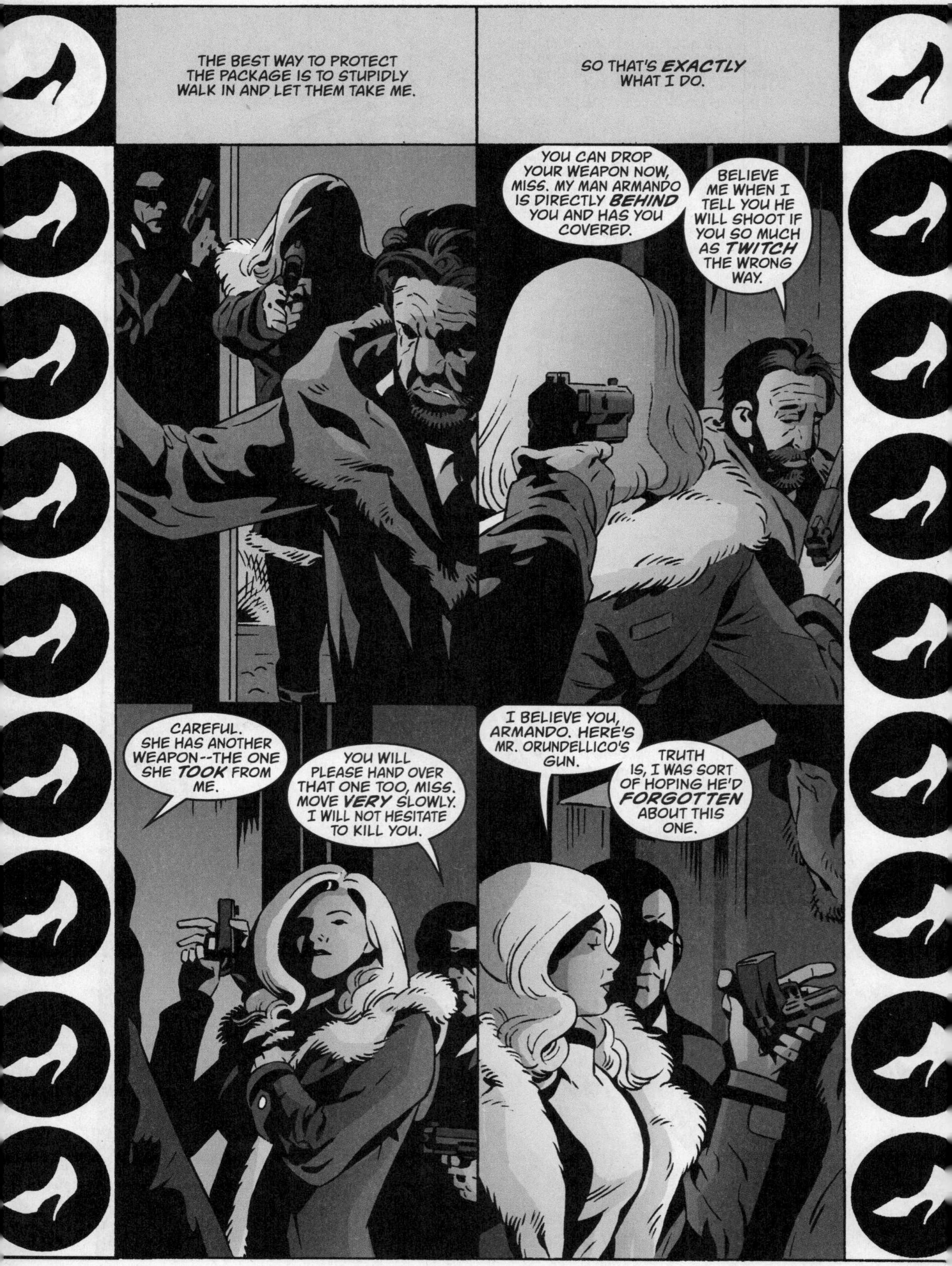
THE BEST WAY TO PROTECT THE PACKAGE IS TO STUPIDLY WALK IN AND LET THEM TAKE ME.
SO THAT'S EXACTLY WHAT I DO.
YOU CAN DROP YOUR WEAPON NOW, MISS. MY MAN ARMANDO IS DIRECTLY BEHIND YOU AND HAS YOU COVERED.
BELIEVE ME WHEN I TELL YOU HE WILL SHOOT IF YOU SO MUCH AS TWITCH THE WRONG WAY.
CAREFUL. SHE HAS ANOTHER WEAPON--THE ONE SHE TOOK FROM ME.
YOU WILL PLEASE HAND OVER THAT ONE TOO, MISS. MOVE VERY SLOWLY. I WILL NOT HESITATE TO KILL YOU.
I BELIEVE YOU, ARMANDO. HERE'S MR. ORUNDELLICO'S GUN.
TRUTH IS, I WAS SORT OF HOPING HE'D FORGOTTEN ABOUT THIS ONE.

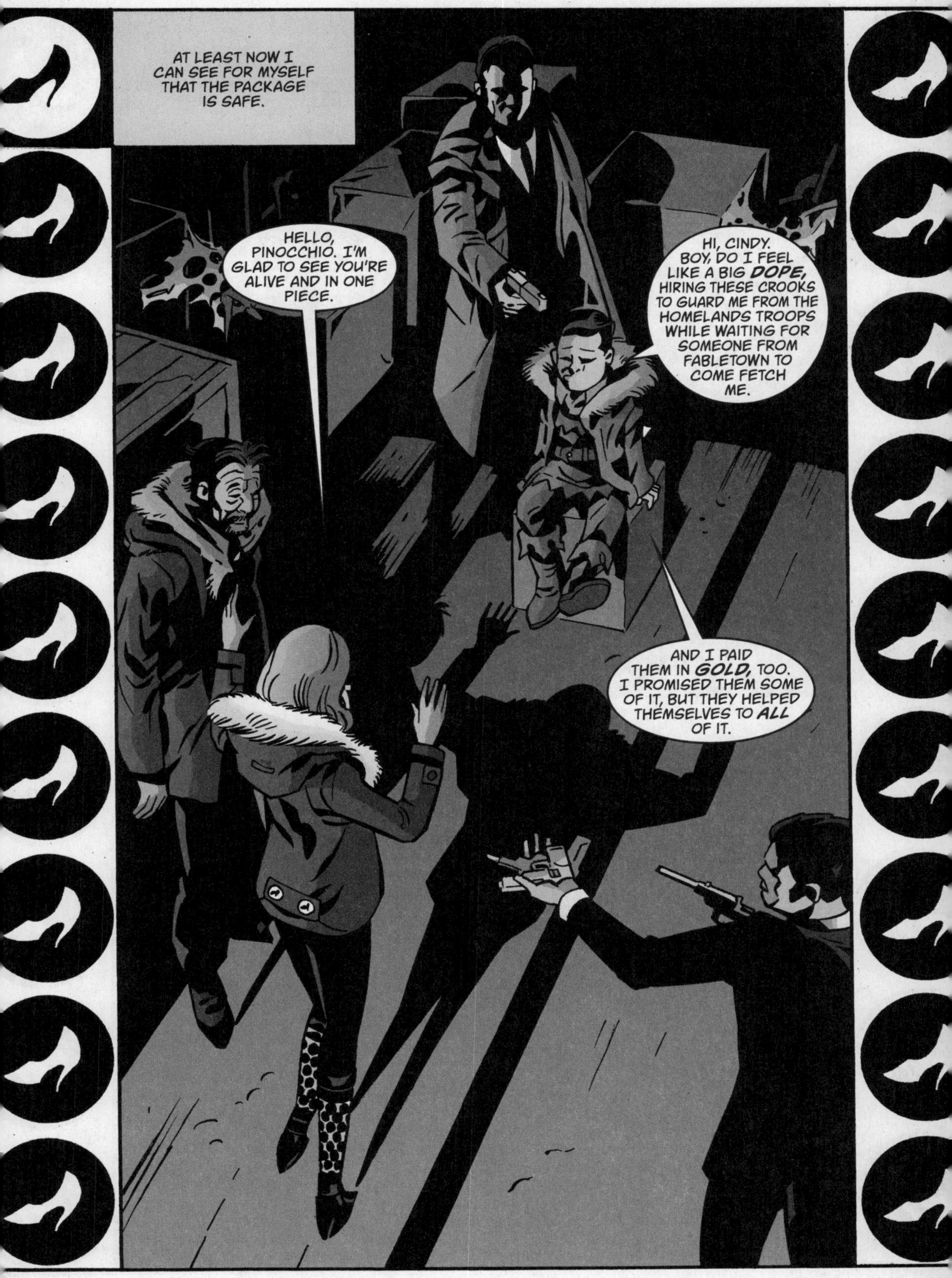
AT LEAST NOW I CAN SEE FOR MYSELF THAT THE PACKAGE IS SAFE.
HELLO, PINOCCHIO. I'M GLAD TO SEE YOU'RE ALIVE AND IN ONE PIECE.
HI, CINDY. BOY, DO I FEEL LIKE A BIG DOPE, HIRING THESE CROOKS TO GUARD ME FROM THE HOMELANDS TROOPS WHILE WAITING FOR SOMEONE FROM FABLETOWN TO COME FETCH ME.
AND I PAID THEM IN GOLD, TOO. I PROMISED THEM SOME OF IT, BUT THEY HELPED THEMSELVES TO ALL OF IT.

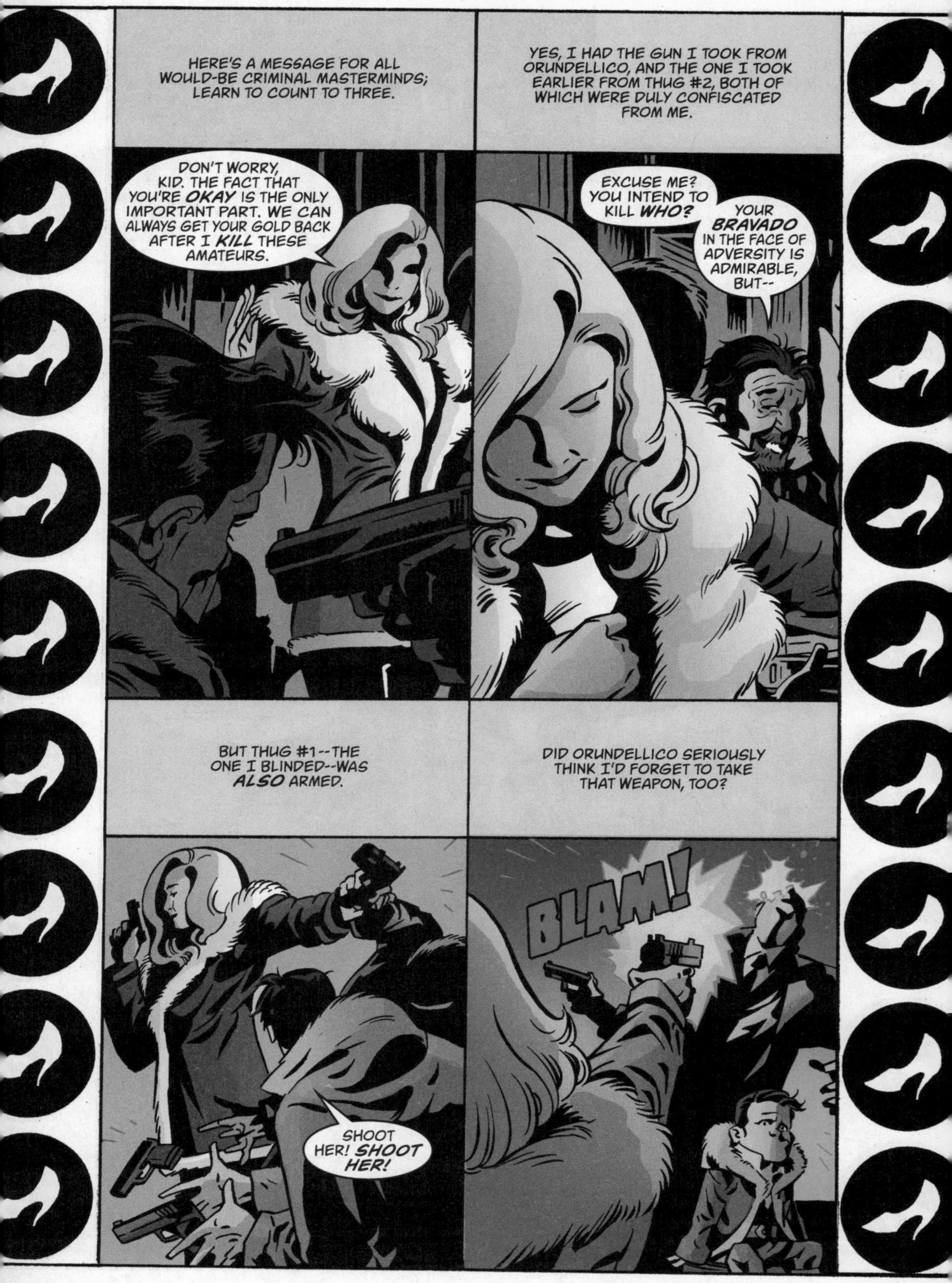
HERE'S A MESSAGE FOR ALL WOULD-BE CRIMINAL MASTERMINDS; LEARN TO COUNT TO THREE.
YES, I HAD THE GUN I TOOK FROM ORUNDELLICO, AND THE ONE I TOOK EARLIER FROM THUG #2, BOTH OF WHICH WERE DULY CONFISCATED FROM ME.
DON'T WORRY, KID. THE FACT THAT YOU'RE OKAY IS THE ONLY IMPORTANT PART. WE CAN ALWAYS GET YOUR GOLD BACK AFTER I KILL THESE AMATEURS.
EXCUSE ME? YOU INTEND TO KILL WHO?
YOUR BRAVADO IN THE FACE OF ADVERSITY IS ADMIRABLE, BUT--
BUT THUG #1--THE ONE I BLINDED--WAS ALSO ARMED.
DID ORUNDELLICO SERIOUSLY THINK I'D FORGET TO TAKE THAT WEAPON, TOO?
SHOOT HER! SHOOT HER!
BLAM!

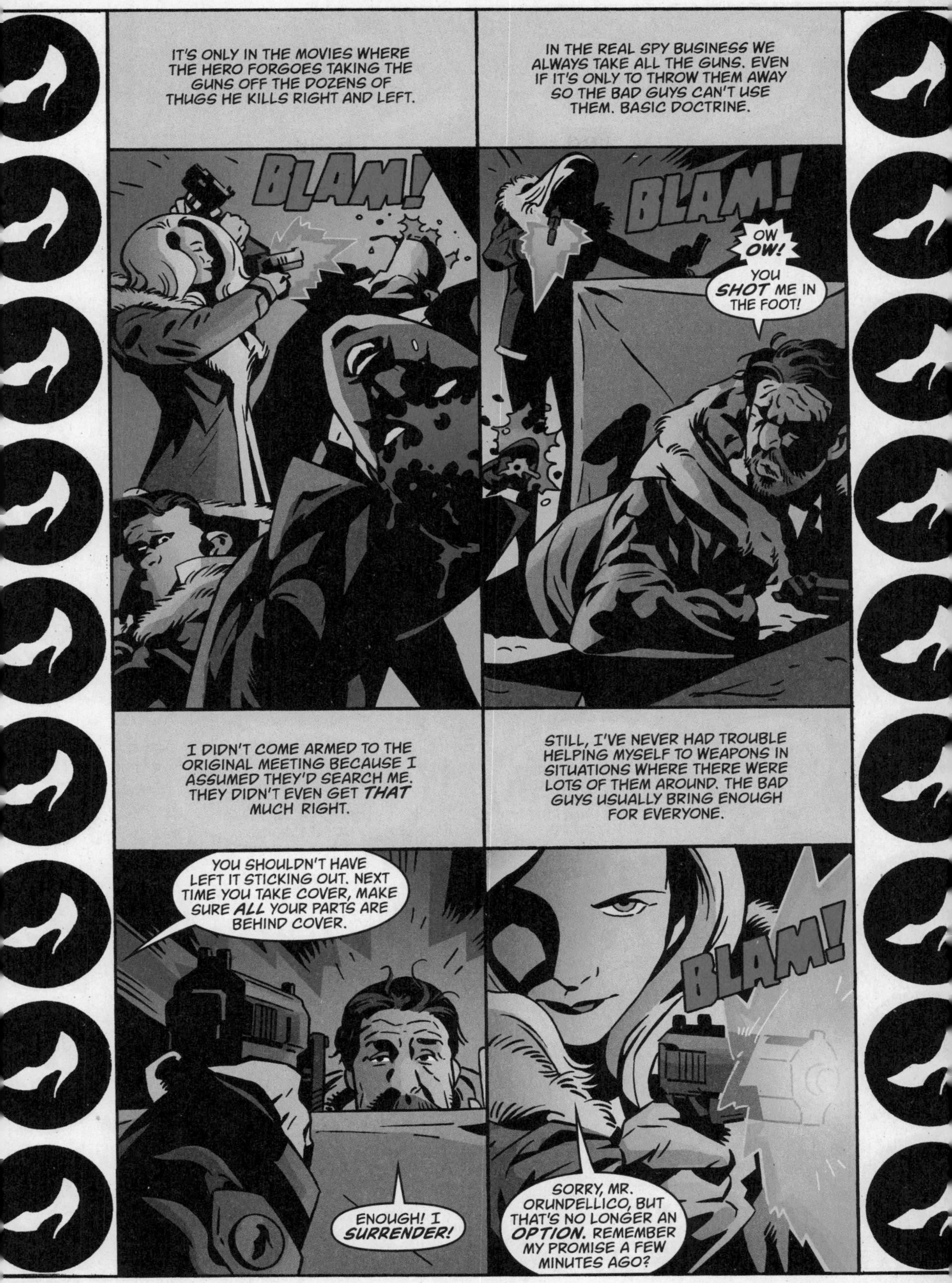

IT'S ONLY IN THE MOVIES WHERE THE HERO FORGOES TAKING THE GUNS OFF THE DOZENS OF THUGS HE KILLS RIGHT AND LEFT.
IN THE REAL SPY BUSINESS WE ALWAYS TAKE ALL THE GUNS. EVEN IF IT'S ONLY TO THROW THEM AWAY SO THE BAD GUYS CAN'T USE THEM. BASIC DOCTRINE.
BLAM!
BLAM!
OW OW!
YOU SHOT ME IN THE FOOT!
I DIDN'T COME ARMED TO THE ORIGINAL MEETING BECAUSE I ASSUMED THEY'D SEARCH ME. THEY DIDN'T EVEN GET THAT MUCH RIGHT.
STILL, I'VE NEVER HAD TROUBLE HELPING MYSELF TO WEAPONS IN SITUATIONS WHERE THERE WERE LOTS OF THEM AROUND. THE BAD GUYS USUALLY BRING ENOUGH FOR EVERYONE.
YOU SHOULDN'T HAVE LEFT IT STICKING OUT. NEXT TIME YOU TAKE COVER, MAKE SURE ALL YOUR PARTS ARE BEHIND COVER.
ENOUGH! I SURRENDER!
BLAM!
SORRY, MR. ORUNDELLICO, BUT THAT'S NO LONGER AN OPTION. REMEMBER MY PROMISE A FEW MINUTES AGO?

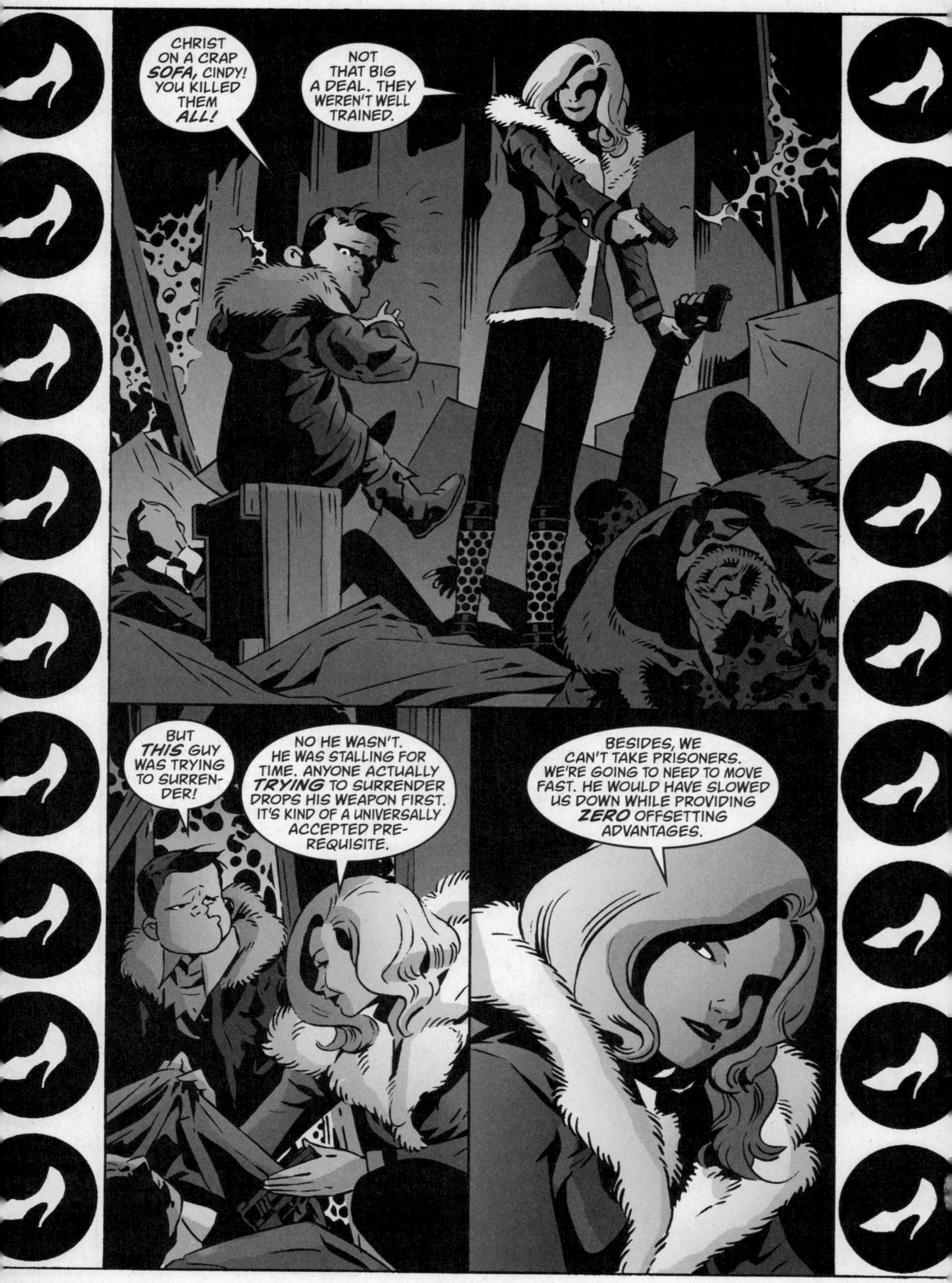
CHRIST ON A CRAP SOFA, CINDY! YOU KILLED THEM ALL!
NOT THAT BIG A DEAL. THEY WEREN'T WELL TRAINED.
BUT THIS GUY WAS TRYING TO SURREN-DER!
NO HE WASN'T. HE WAS STALLING FOR TIME. ANYONE ACTUALLY TRYING TO SURRENDER DROPS HIS WEAPON FIRST. IT'S KIND OF A UNIVERSALLY ACCEPTED PRE-REQUISITE.
BESIDES, WE CAN'T TAKE PRISONERS. WE'RE GOING TO NEED TO MOVE FAST. HE WOULD HAVE SLOWED US DOWN WHILE PROVIDING ZERO OFFSETTING ADVANTAGES.

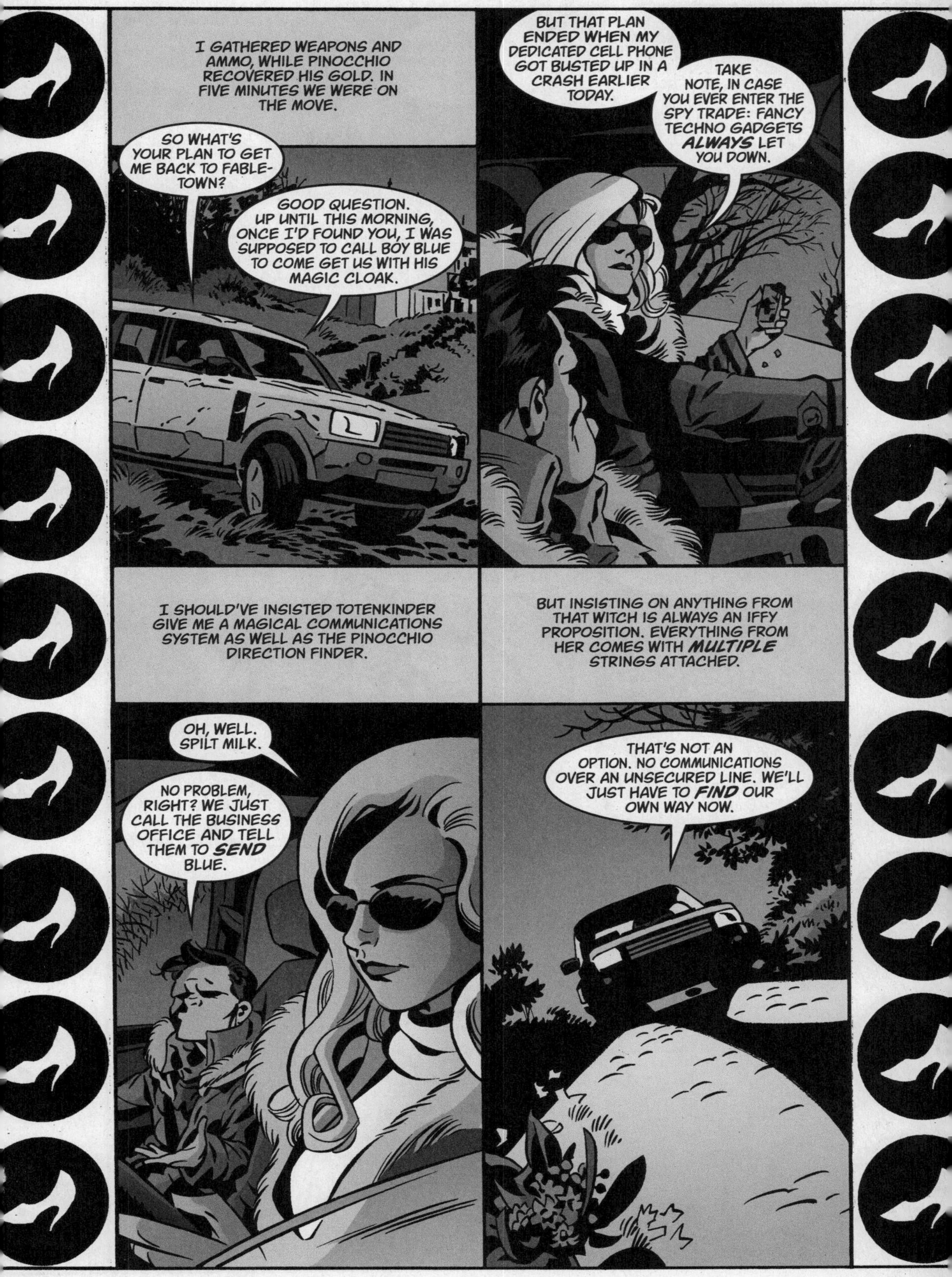
I GATHERED WEAPONS AND AMMO, WHILE PINOCCHIO RECOVERED HIS GOLD. IN FIVE MINUTES WE WERE ON THE MOVE.
SO WHAT'S YOUR PLAN TO GET ME BACK TO FABLE-TOWN?
GOOD QUESTION. UP UNTIL THIS MORNING, ONCE I'D FOUND YOU, I WAS SUPPOSED TO CALL BOY BLUE TO COME GET US WITH HIS MAGIC CLOAK.
BUT THAT PLAN ENDED WHEN MY DEDICATED CELL PHONE GOT BUSTED UP IN A CRASH EARLIER TODAY.
TAKE NOTE, IN CASE YOU EVER ENTER THE SPY TRADE: FANCY TECHNO GADGETS ALWAYS LET YOU DOWN.
I SHOULD'VE INSISTED TOTENKINDER GIVE ME A MAGICAL COMMUNICATIONS SYSTEM AS WELL AS THE PINOCCHIO DIRECTION FINDER.
BUT INSISTING ON ANYTHING FROM THAT WITCH IS ALWAYS AN IFFY PROPOSITION. EVERYTHING FROM HER COMES WITH MULTIPLE STRINGS ATTACHED.
OH, WELL. SPILT MILK.
NO PROBLEM, RIGHT? WE JUST CALL THE BUSINESS OFFICE AND TELL THEM TO SEND BLUE.
THAT'S NOT AN OPTION. NO COMMUNICATIONS OVER AN UNSECURED LINE. WE'LL JUST HAVE TO FIND OUR OWN WAY NOW.

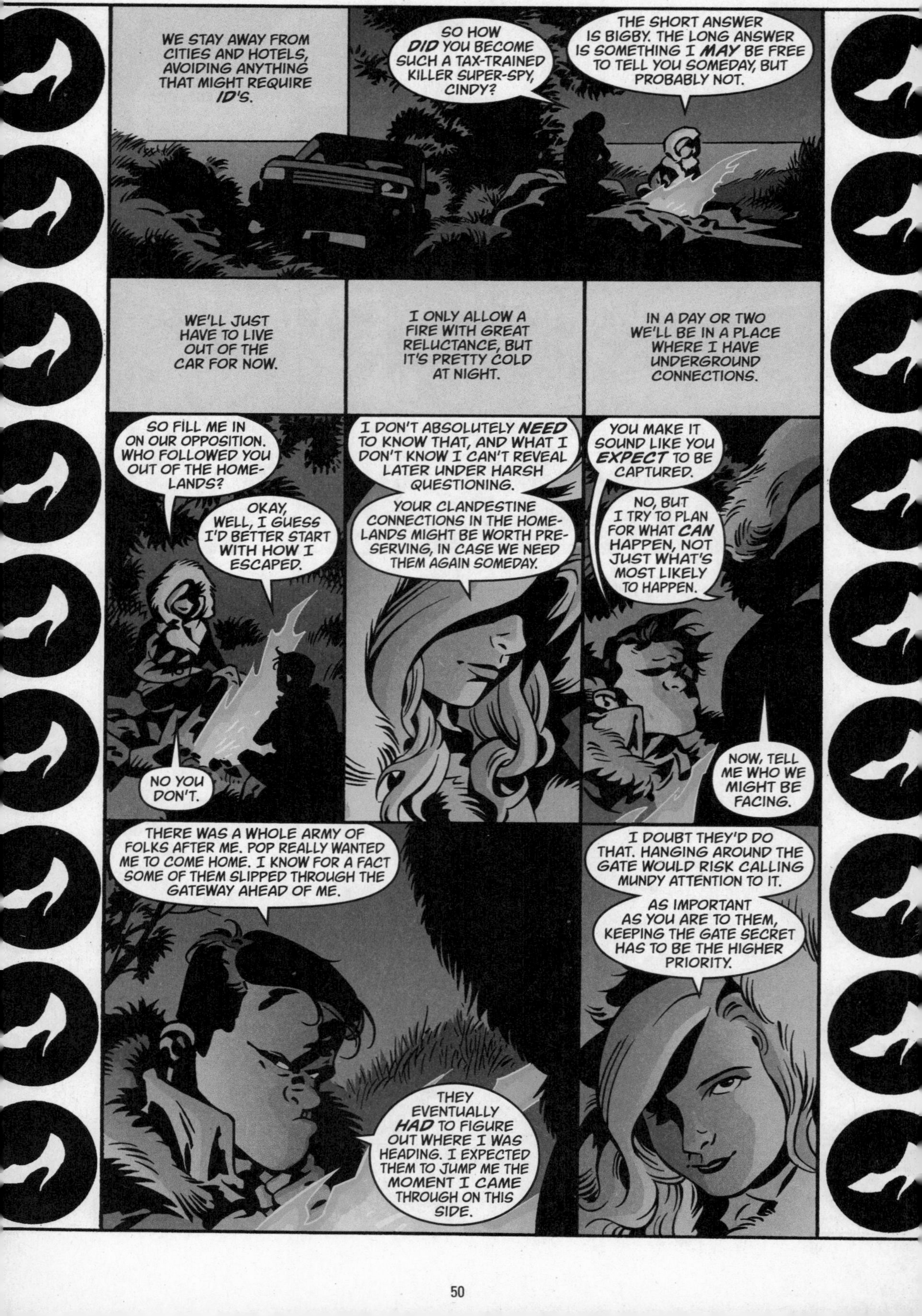
WE STAY AWAY FROM CITIES AND HOTELS, AVOIDING ANYTHING THAT MIGHT REQUIRE ID'S.
SO HOW DID YOU BECOME SUCH A TAX-TRAINED KILLER SUPER-SPY, CINDY?
THE SHORT ANSWER IS BIGBY. THE LONG ANSWER IS SOMETHING I MAY BE FREE TO TELL YOU SOMEDAY, BUT PROBABLY NOT.
WE'LL JUST HAVE TO LIVE OUT OF THE CAR FOR NOW.
I ONLY ALLOW A FIRE WITH GREAT RELUCTANCE, BUT IT'S PRETTY COLD AT NIGHT.
IN A DAY OR TWO WE'LL BE IN A PLACE WHERE I HAVE UNDERGROUND CONNECTIONS.
SO FILL ME IN ON OUR OPPOSITION. WHO FOLLOWED YOU OUT OF THE HOME-LANDS?
OKAY, WELL, I GUESS I'D BETTER START WITH HOW I ESCAPED.
NO YOU DON'T.
I DON'T ABSOLUTELY NEED TO KNOW THAT, AND WHAT I DON'T KNOW I CAN'T REVEAL LATER UNDER HARSH QUESTIONING.
YOUR CLANDESTINE CONNECTIONS IN THE HOME-LANDS MIGHT BE WORTH PRE-SERVING, IN CASE WE NEED THEM AGAIN SOMEDAY.
YOU MAKE IT SOUND LIKE YOU EXPECT TO BE CAPTURED.
NO, BUT I TRY TO PLAN FOR WHAT CAN HAPPEN, NOT JUST WHAT'S MOST LIKELY TO HAPPEN.
NOW, TELL ME WHO WE MIGHT BE FACING.
THERE WAS A WHOLE ARMY OF FOLKS AFTER ME. POP REALLY WANTED ME TO COME HOME. I KNOW FOR A FACT SOME OF THEM SLIPPED THROUGH THE GATEWAY AHEAD OF ME.
THEY EVENTUALLY HAD TO FIGURE OUT WHERE I WAS HEADING. I EXPECTED THEM TO JUMP ME THE MOMENT I CAME THROUGH ON THIS SIDE.
I DOUBT THEY'D DO THAT. HANGING AROUND THE GATE WOULD RISK CALLING MUNDY ATTENTION TO IT.
AS IMPORTANT AS YOU ARE TO THEM, KEEPING THE GATE SECRET HAS TO BE THE HIGHER PRIORITY.

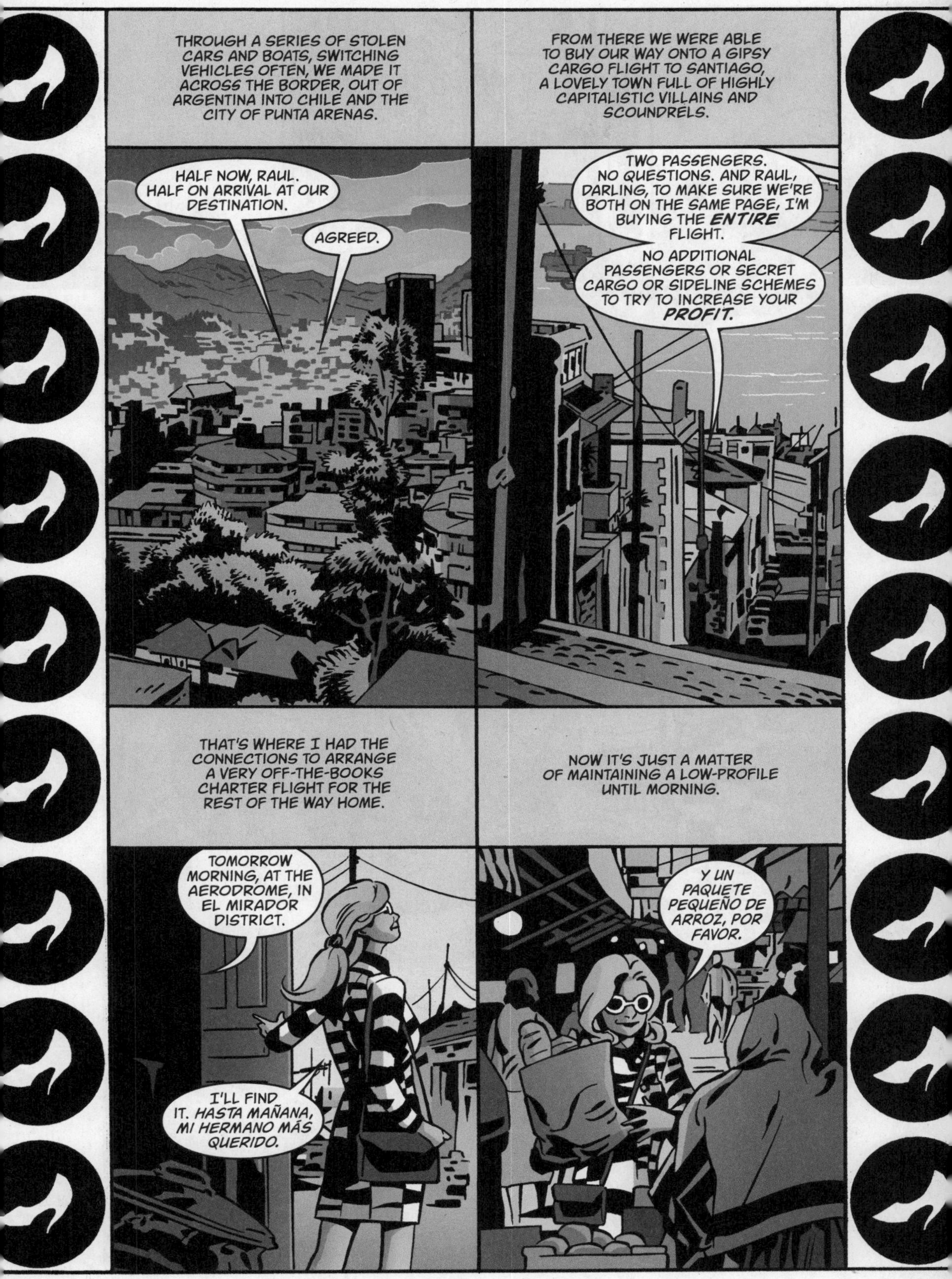
THROUGH A SERIES OF STOLEN CARS AND BOATS, SWITCHING VEHICLES OFTEN, WE MADE IT ACROSS THE BORDER, OUT OF ARGENTINA INTO CHILE AND THE CITY OF PUNTA ARENAS.
FROM THERE WE WERE ABLE TO BUY OUR WAY ONTO A GIPSY CARGO FLIGHT TO SANTIAGO, A LOVELY TOWN FULL OF HIGHLY CAPITALISTIC VILLAINS AND SCOUNDRELS.
HALF NOW, RAUL. HALF ON ARRIVAL AT OUR DESTINATION.
AGREED.
TWO PASSENGERS. NO QUESTIONS. AND RAUL, DARLING, TO MAKE SURE WE'RE BOTH ON THE SAME PAGE, I'M BUYING THE *ENTIRE* FLIGHT.
NO ADDITIONAL PASSENGERS OR SECRET CARGO OR SIDELINE SCHEMES TO TRY TO INCREASE YOUR *PROFIT.*
THAT'S WHERE I HAD THE CONNECTIONS TO ARRANGE A VERY OFF-THE-BOOKS CHARTER FLIGHT FOR THE REST OF THE WAY HOME.
NOW IT'S JUST A MATTER OF MAINTAINING A LOW-PROFILE UNTIL MORNING.
TOMORROW MORNING, AT THE AERODROME, IN EL MIRADOR DISTRICT.
I'LL FIND IT. *HASTA MAÑANA, MI HERMANO MÁS QUERIDO.*
Y UN PAQUETE PEQUEÑO DE ARROZ, POR FAVOR.

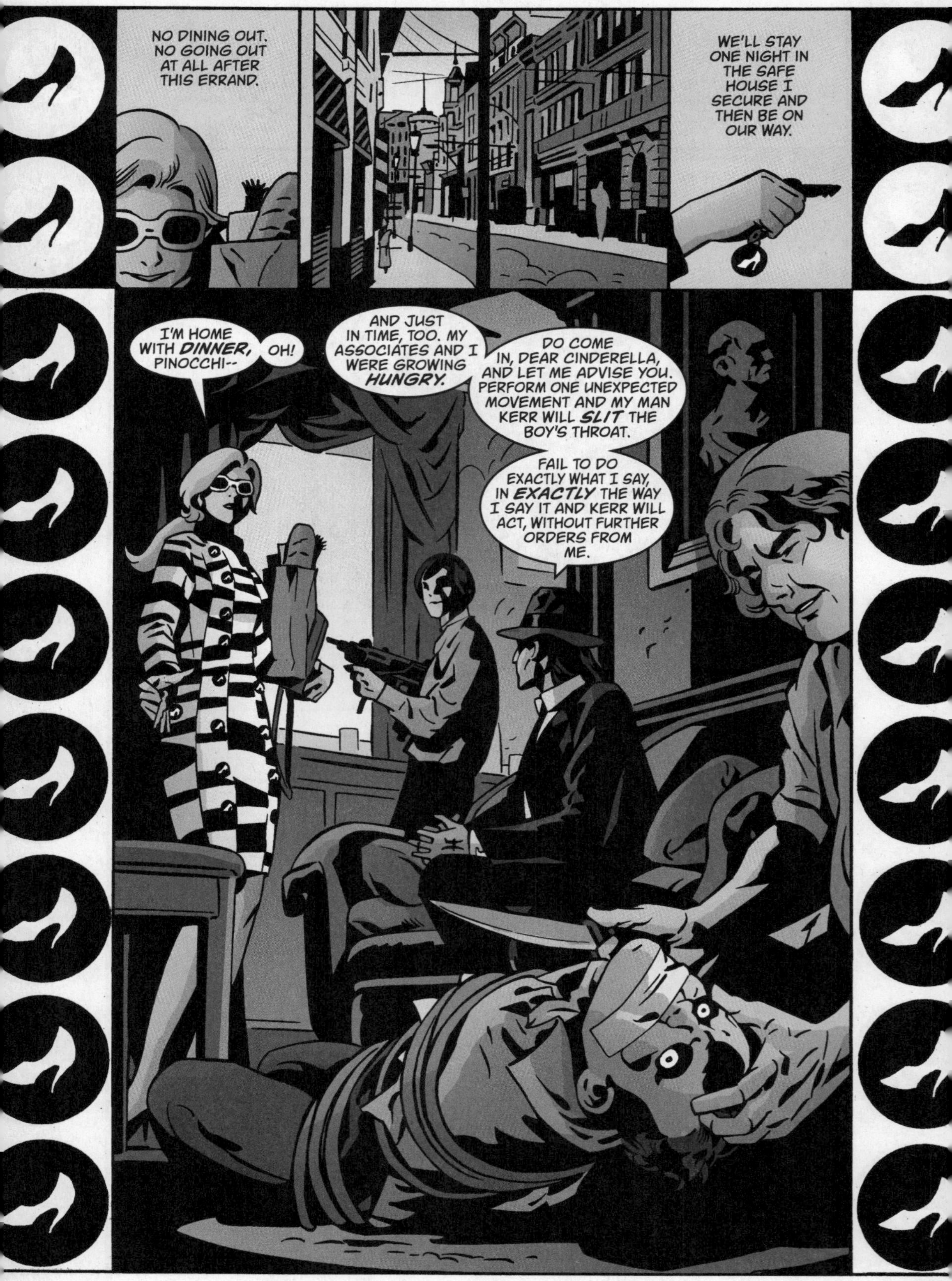
NO DINING OUT. NO GOING OUT AT ALL AFTER THIS ERRAND.
WE'LL STAY ONE NIGHT IN THE SAFE HOUSE I SECURE AND THEN BE ON OUR WAY.
I'M HOME WITH **DINNER,** PINOCCHI--
OH!
AND JUST IN TIME, TOO. MY ASSOCIATES AND I WERE GROWING **HUNGRY.**
DO COME IN, DEAR CINDERELLA, AND LET ME ADVISE YOU. PERFORM ONE UNEXPECTED MOVEMENT AND MY MAN KERR WILL **SLIT** THE BOY'S THROAT.
FAIL TO DO EXACTLY WHAT I SAY, IN **EXACTLY** THE WAY I SAY IT AND KERR WILL ACT, WITHOUT FURTHER ORDERS FROM ME.

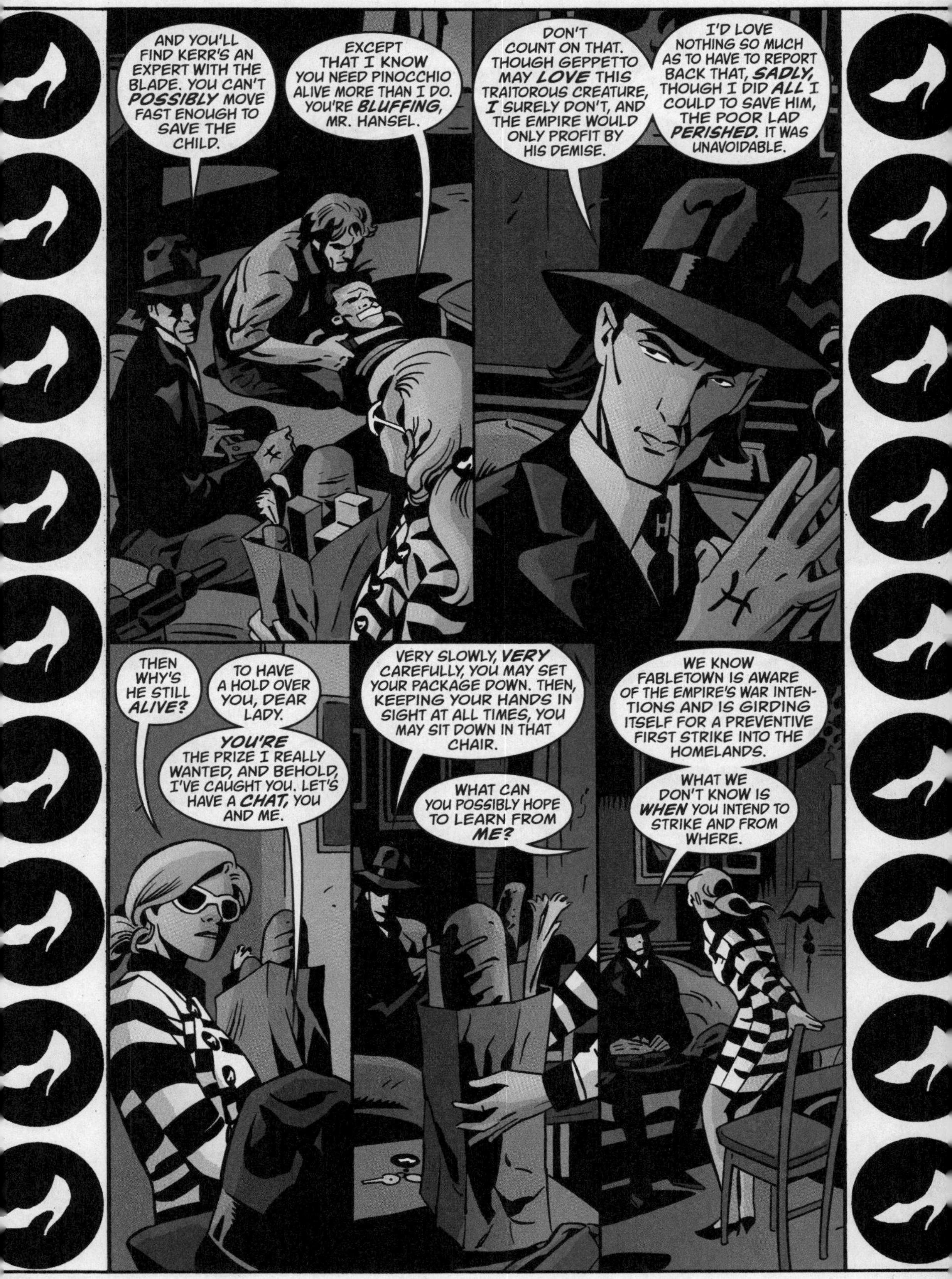
AND YOU'LL FIND KERR'S AN EXPERT WITH THE BLADE. YOU CAN'T POSSIBLY MOVE FAST ENOUGH TO SAVE THE CHILD.
EXCEPT THAT I KNOW YOU NEED PINOCCHIO ALIVE MORE THAN I DO. YOU'RE BLUFFING, MR. HANSEL.
DON'T COUNT ON THAT. THOUGH GEPPETTO MAY LOVE THIS TRAITOROUS CREATURE, I SURELY DON'T, AND THE EMPIRE WOULD ONLY PROFIT BY HIS DEMISE.
I'D LOVE NOTHING SO MUCH AS TO HAVE TO REPORT BACK THAT, SADLY, THOUGH I DID ALL I COULD TO SAVE HIM, THE POOR LAD PERISHED. IT WAS UNAVOIDABLE.
THEN WHY'S HE STILL ALIVE?
TO HAVE A HOLD OVER YOU, DEAR LADY.
YOU'RE THE PRIZE I REALLY WANTED, AND BEHOLD, I'VE CAUGHT YOU. LET'S HAVE A CHAT, YOU AND ME.
VERY SLOWLY, VERY CAREFULLY, YOU MAY SET YOUR PACKAGE DOWN. THEN, KEEPING YOUR HANDS IN SIGHT AT ALL TIMES, YOU MAY SIT DOWN IN THAT CHAIR.
WHAT CAN YOU POSSIBLY HOPE TO LEARN FROM ME?
WE KNOW FABLETOWN IS AWARE OF THE EMPIRE'S WAR INTENTIONS AND IS GIRDING ITSELF FOR A PREVENTIVE FIRST STRIKE INTO THE HOMELANDS.
WHAT WE DON'T KNOW IS WHEN YOU INTEND TO STRIKE AND FROM WHERE.

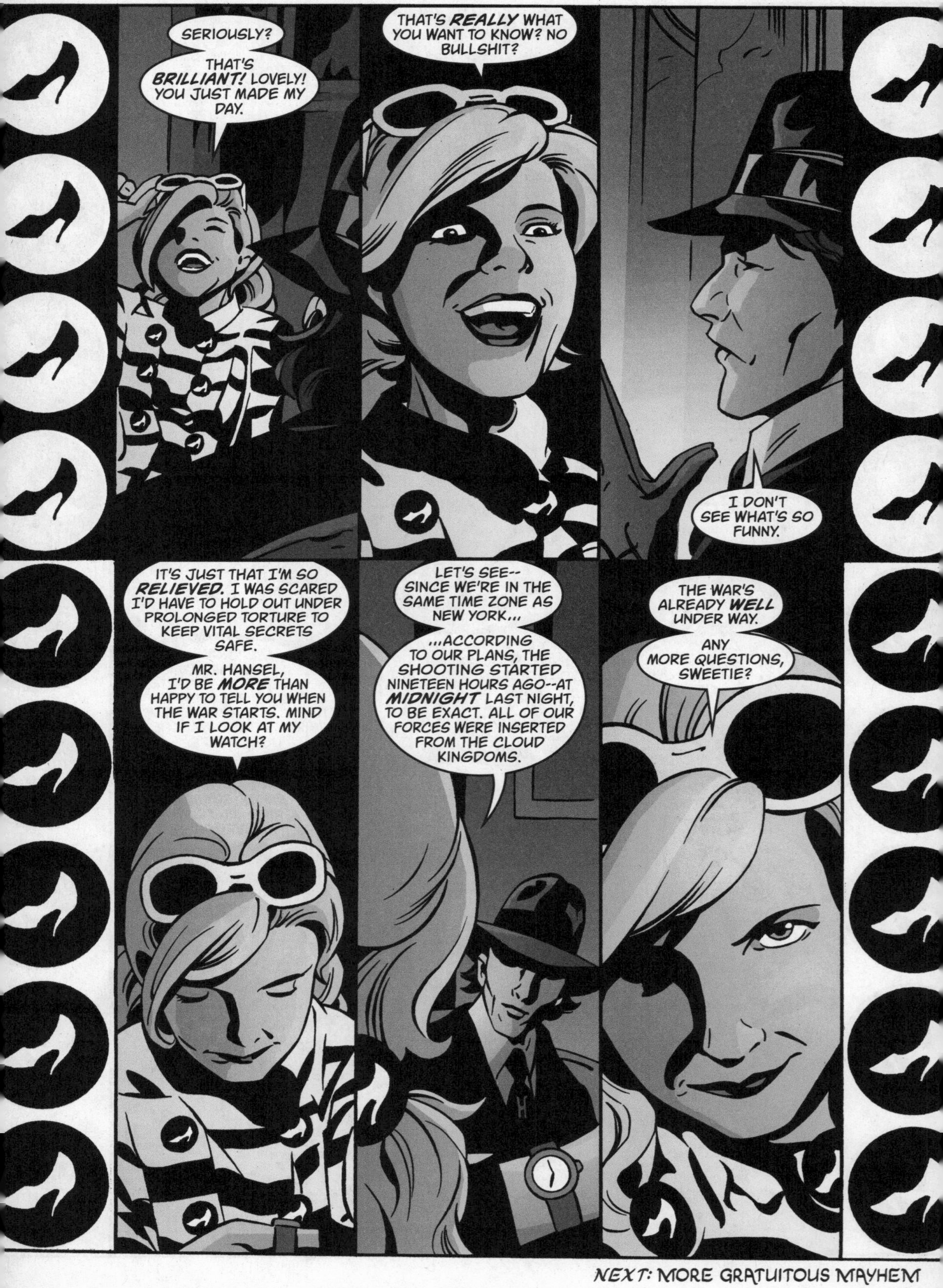
SERIOUSLY?
THAT'S BRILLIANT! LOVELY! YOU JUST MADE MY DAY.
THAT'S REALLY WHAT YOU WANT TO KNOW? NO BULLSHIT?
I DON'T SEE WHAT'S SO FUNNY.
IT'S JUST THAT I'M SO RELIEVED. I WAS SCARED I'D HAVE TO HOLD OUT UNDER PROLONGED TORTURE TO KEEP VITAL SECRETS SAFE.
MR. HANSEL, I'D BE MORE THAN HAPPY TO TELL YOU WHEN THE WAR STARTS. MIND IF I LOOK AT MY WATCH?
LET'S SEE-- SINCE WE'RE IN THE SAME TIME ZONE AS NEW YORK...
...ACCORDING TO OUR PLANS, THE SHOOTING STARTED NINETEEN HOURS AGO--AT MIDNIGHT LAST NIGHT, TO BE EXACT. ALL OF OUR FORCES WERE INSERTED FROM THE CLOUD KINGDOMS.
THE WAR'S ALREADY WELL UNDER WAY.
ANY MORE QUESTIONS, SWEETIE?

NEXT: MORE GRATUITOUS MAYHEM

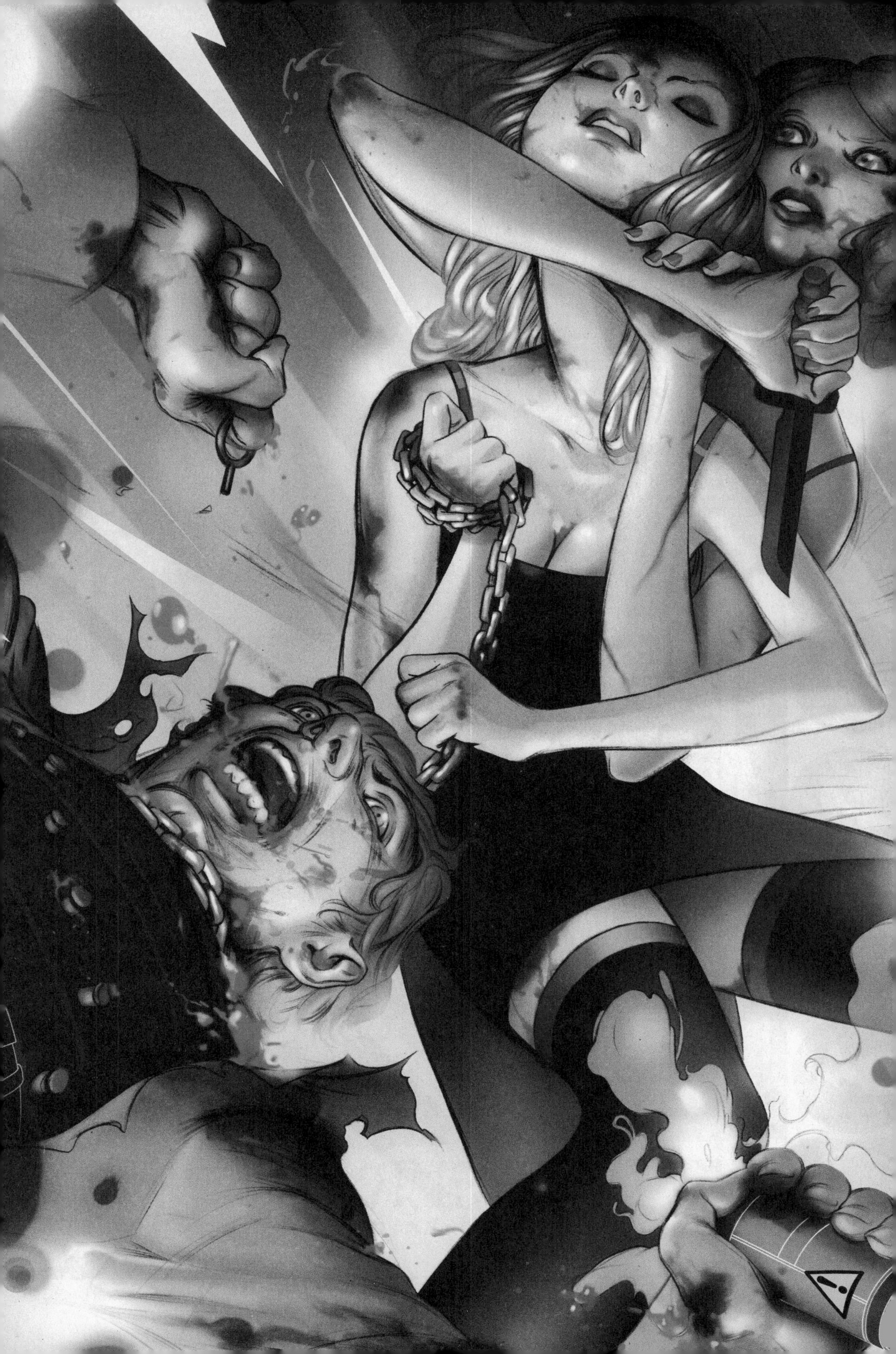

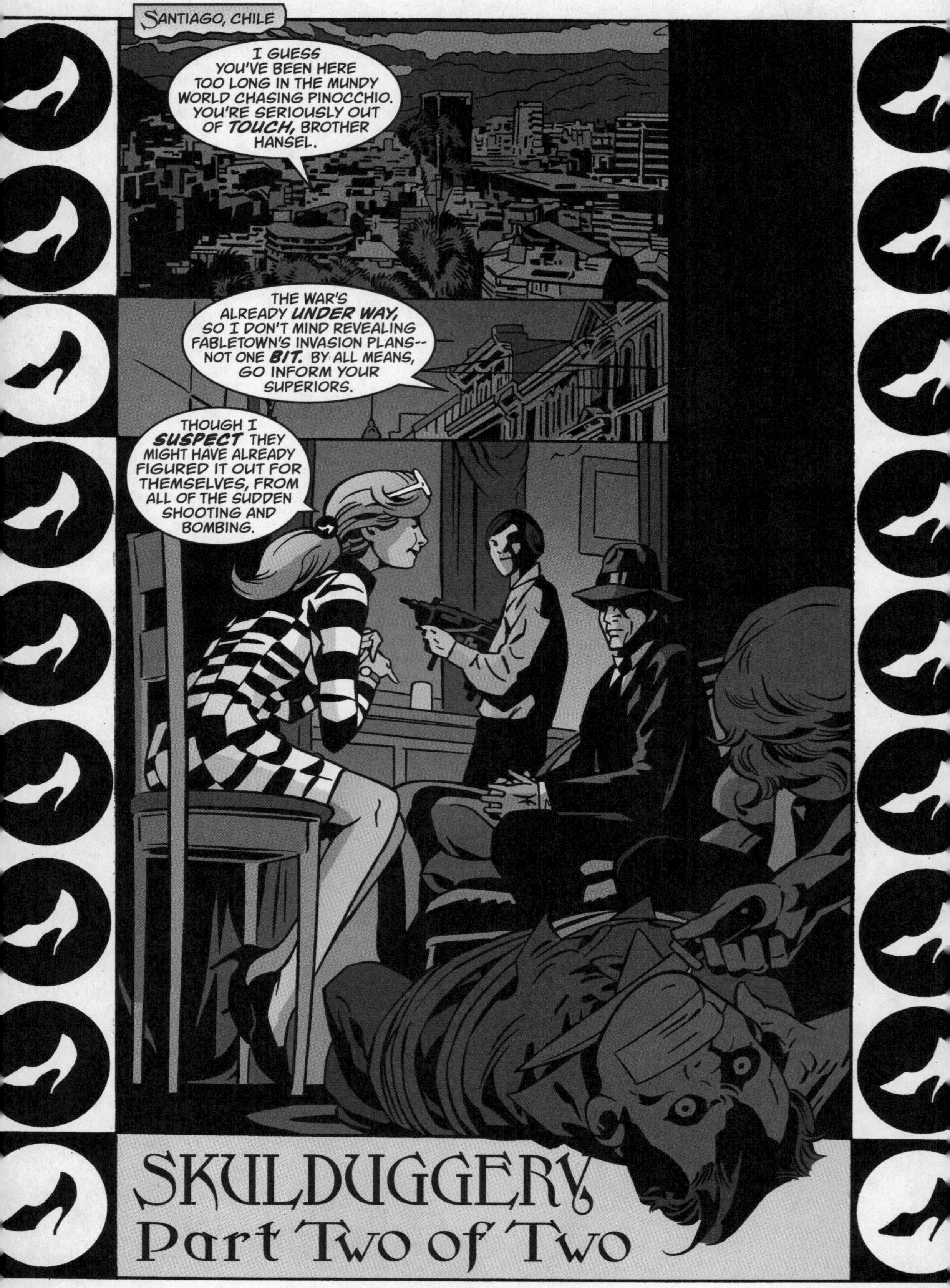
SANTIAGO, CHILE
I GUESS YOU'VE BEEN HERE TOO LONG IN THE MUNDY WORLD CHASING PINOCCHIO. YOU'RE SERIOUSLY OUT OF *TOUCH,* BROTHER HANSEL.
THE WAR'S ALREADY *UNDER WAY,* SO I DON'T MIND REVEALING FABLETOWN'S INVASION PLANS--NOT ONE *BIT.* BY ALL MEANS, GO INFORM YOUR SUPERIORS.
THOUGH I *SUSPECT* THEY MIGHT HAVE ALREADY FIGURED IT OUT FOR THEMSELVES, FROM ALL OF THE SUDDEN SHOOTING AND BOMBING.
SKULDUGGERY
Part Two of Two

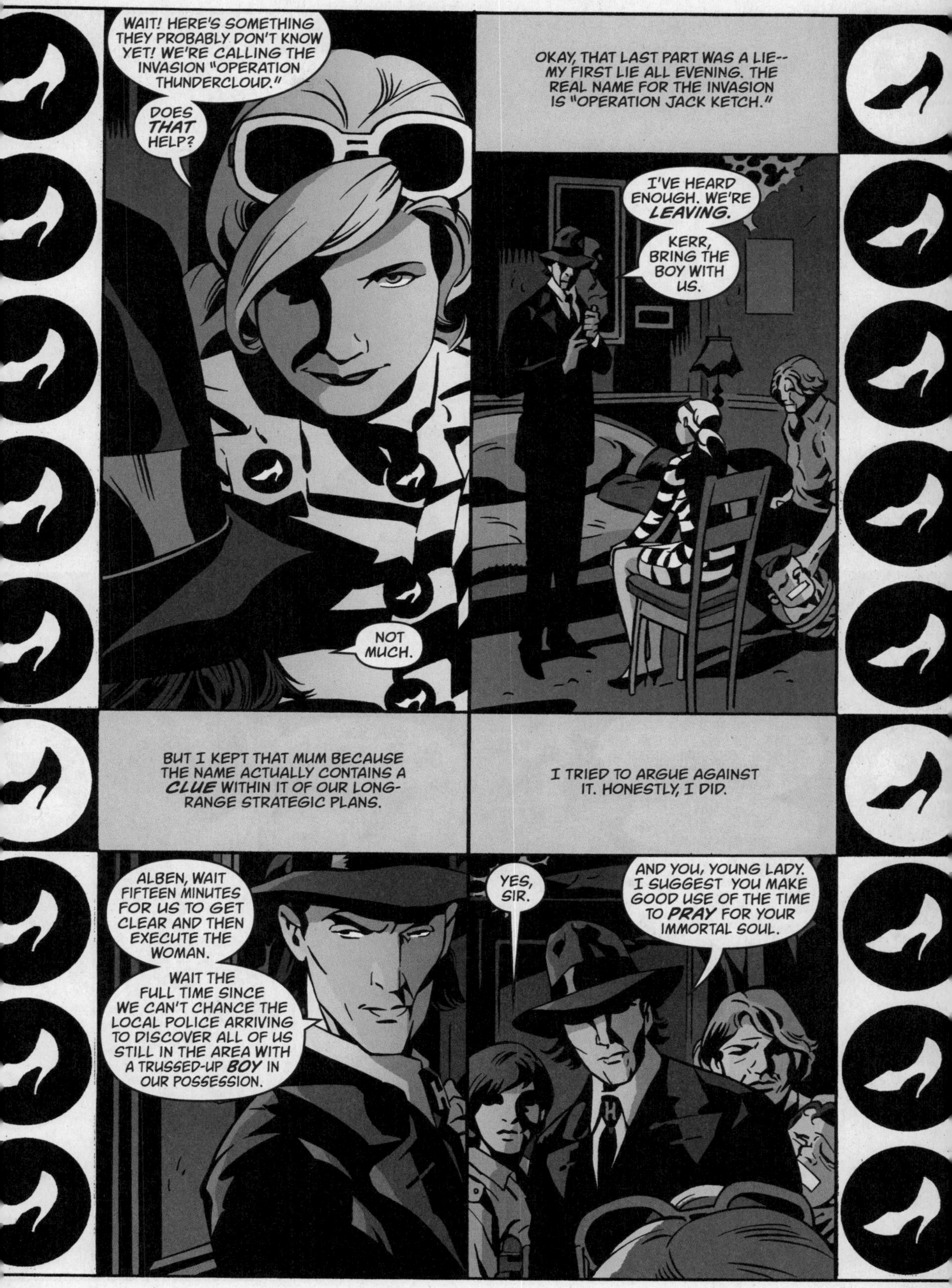
WAIT! HERE'S SOMETHING THEY PROBABLY DON'T KNOW YET! WE'RE CALLING THE INVASION "OPERATION THUNDERCLOUD."
DOES THAT HELP?
NOT MUCH.
OKAY, THAT LAST PART WAS A LIE-- MY FIRST LIE ALL EVENING. THE REAL NAME FOR THE INVASION IS "OPERATION JACK KETCH."
I'VE HEARD ENOUGH. WE'RE LEAVING.
KERR, BRING THE BOY WITH US.
BUT I KEPT THAT MUM BECAUSE THE NAME ACTUALLY CONTAINS A CLUE WITHIN IT OF OUR LONG-RANGE STRATEGIC PLANS.
I TRIED TO ARGUE AGAINST IT. HONESTLY, I DID.
ALBEN, WAIT FIFTEEN MINUTES FOR US TO GET CLEAR AND THEN EXECUTE THE WOMAN.
WAIT THE FULL TIME SINCE WE CAN'T CHANCE THE LOCAL POLICE ARRIVING TO DISCOVER ALL OF US STILL IN THE AREA WITH A TRUSSED-UP BOY IN OUR POSSESSION.
YES, SIR.
AND YOU, YOUNG LADY. I SUGGEST YOU MAKE GOOD USE OF THE TIME TO PRAY FOR YOUR IMMORTAL SOUL.

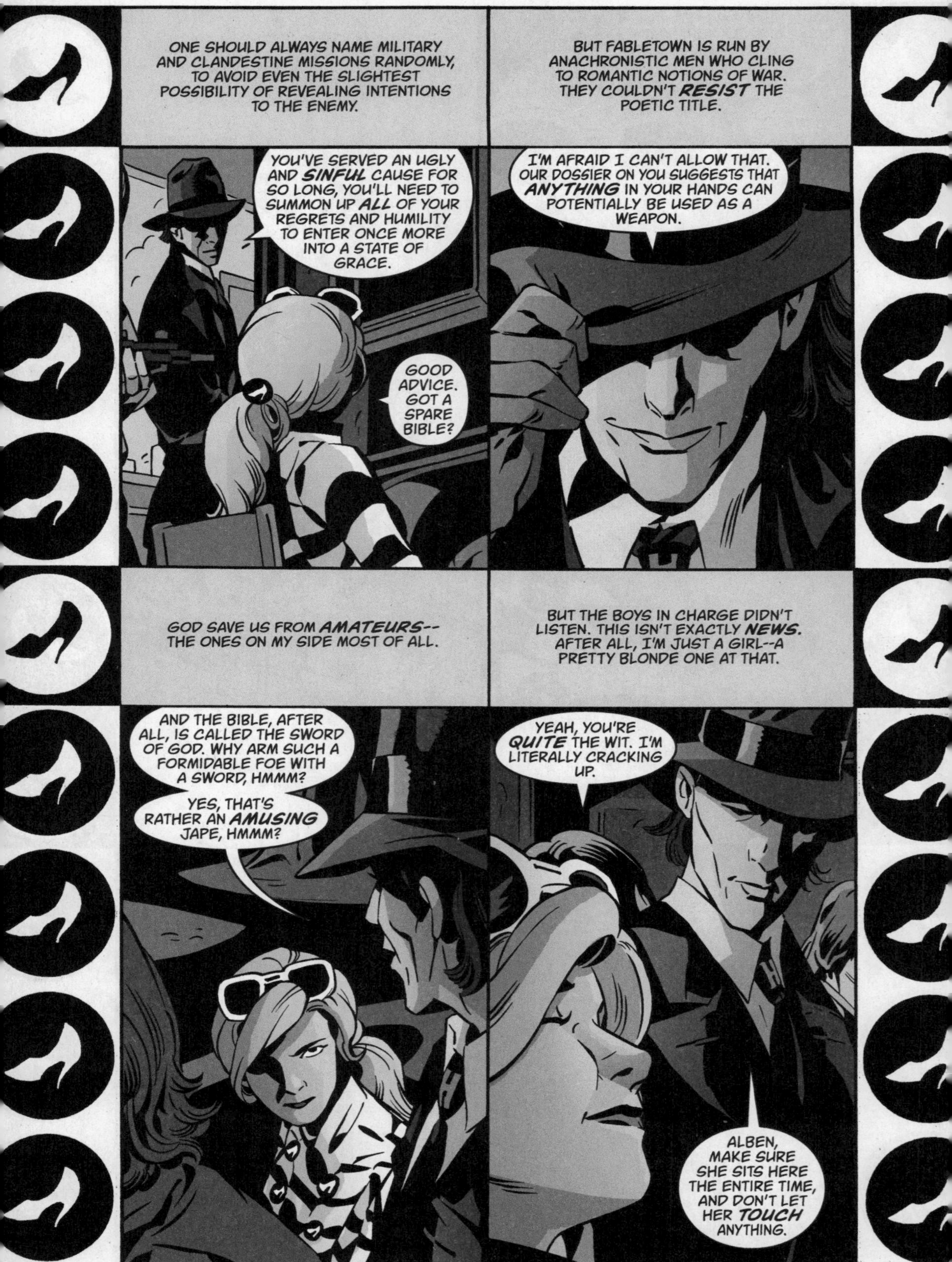
ONE SHOULD ALWAYS NAME MILITARY AND CLANDESTINE MISSIONS RANDOMLY, TO AVOID EVEN THE SLIGHTEST POSSIBILITY OF REVEALING INTENTIONS TO THE ENEMY.
BUT FABLETOWN IS RUN BY ANACHRONISTIC MEN WHO CLING TO ROMANTIC NOTIONS OF WAR. THEY COULDN'T RESIST THE POETIC TITLE.
YOU'VE SERVED AN UGLY AND SINFUL CAUSE FOR SO LONG, YOU'LL NEED TO SUMMON UP ALL OF YOUR REGRETS AND HUMILITY TO ENTER ONCE MORE INTO A STATE OF GRACE.
GOOD ADVICE. GOT A SPARE BIBLE?
I'M AFRAID I CAN'T ALLOW THAT. OUR DOSSIER ON YOU SUGGESTS THAT ANYTHING IN YOUR HANDS CAN POTENTIALLY BE USED AS A WEAPON.
GOD SAVE US FROM AMATEURS-- THE ONES ON MY SIDE MOST OF ALL.
BUT THE BOYS IN CHARGE DIDN'T LISTEN. THIS ISN'T EXACTLY NEWS. AFTER ALL, I'M JUST A GIRL--A PRETTY BLONDE ONE AT THAT.
AND THE BIBLE, AFTER ALL, IS CALLED THE SWORD OF GOD. WHY ARM SUCH A FORMIDABLE FOE WITH A SWORD, HMMM?
YES, THAT'S RATHER AN AMUSING JAPE, HMMM?
YEAH, YOU'RE QUITE THE WIT. I'M LITERALLY CRACKING UP.
ALBEN, MAKE SURE SHE SITS HERE THE ENTIRE TIME, AND DON'T LET HER TOUCH ANYTHING.

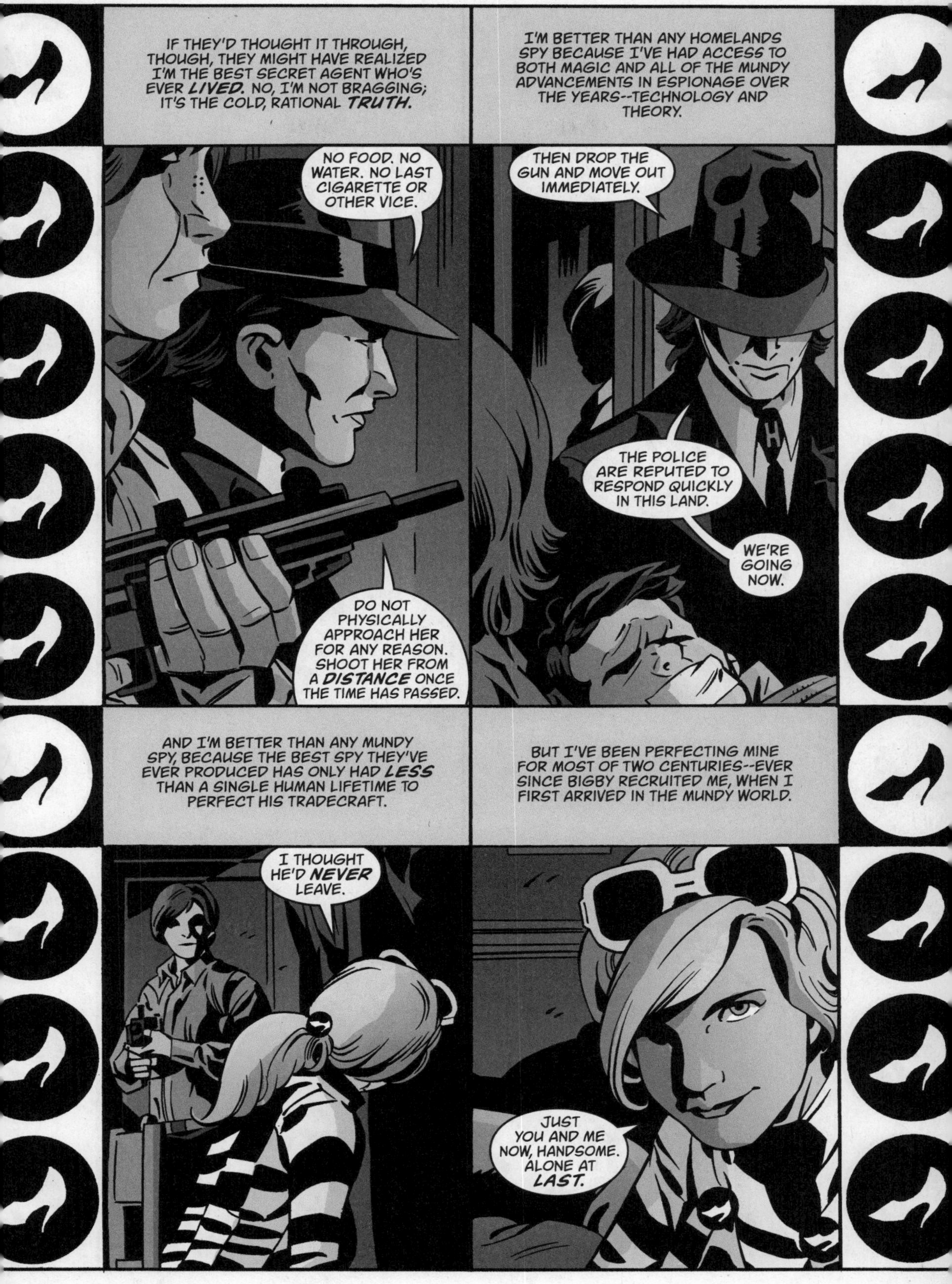
IF THEY'D THOUGHT IT THROUGH, THOUGH, THEY MIGHT HAVE REALIZED I'M THE BEST SECRET AGENT WHO'S EVER LIVED. NO, I'M NOT BRAGGING; IT'S THE COLD, RATIONAL TRUTH.
I'M BETTER THAN ANY HOMELANDS SPY BECAUSE I'VE HAD ACCESS TO BOTH MAGIC AND ALL OF THE MUNDY ADVANCEMENTS IN ESPIONAGE OVER THE YEARS--TECHNOLOGY AND THEORY.
NO FOOD. NO WATER. NO LAST CIGARETTE OR OTHER VICE.
DO NOT PHYSICALLY APPROACH HER FOR ANY REASON. SHOOT HER FROM A DISTANCE ONCE THE TIME HAS PASSED.
THEN DROP THE GUN AND MOVE OUT IMMEDIATELY.
THE POLICE ARE REPUTED TO RESPOND QUICKLY IN THIS LAND.
WE'RE GOING NOW.
AND I'M BETTER THAN ANY MUNDY SPY, BECAUSE THE BEST SPY THEY'VE EVER PRODUCED HAS ONLY HAD LESS THAN A SINGLE HUMAN LIFETIME TO PERFECT HIS TRADECRAFT.
BUT I'VE BEEN PERFECTING MINE FOR MOST OF TWO CENTURIES--EVER SINCE BIGBY RECRUITED ME, WHEN I FIRST ARRIVED IN THE MUNDY WORLD.
I THOUGHT HE'D NEVER LEAVE.
JUST YOU AND ME NOW, HANDSOME. ALONE AT LAST.

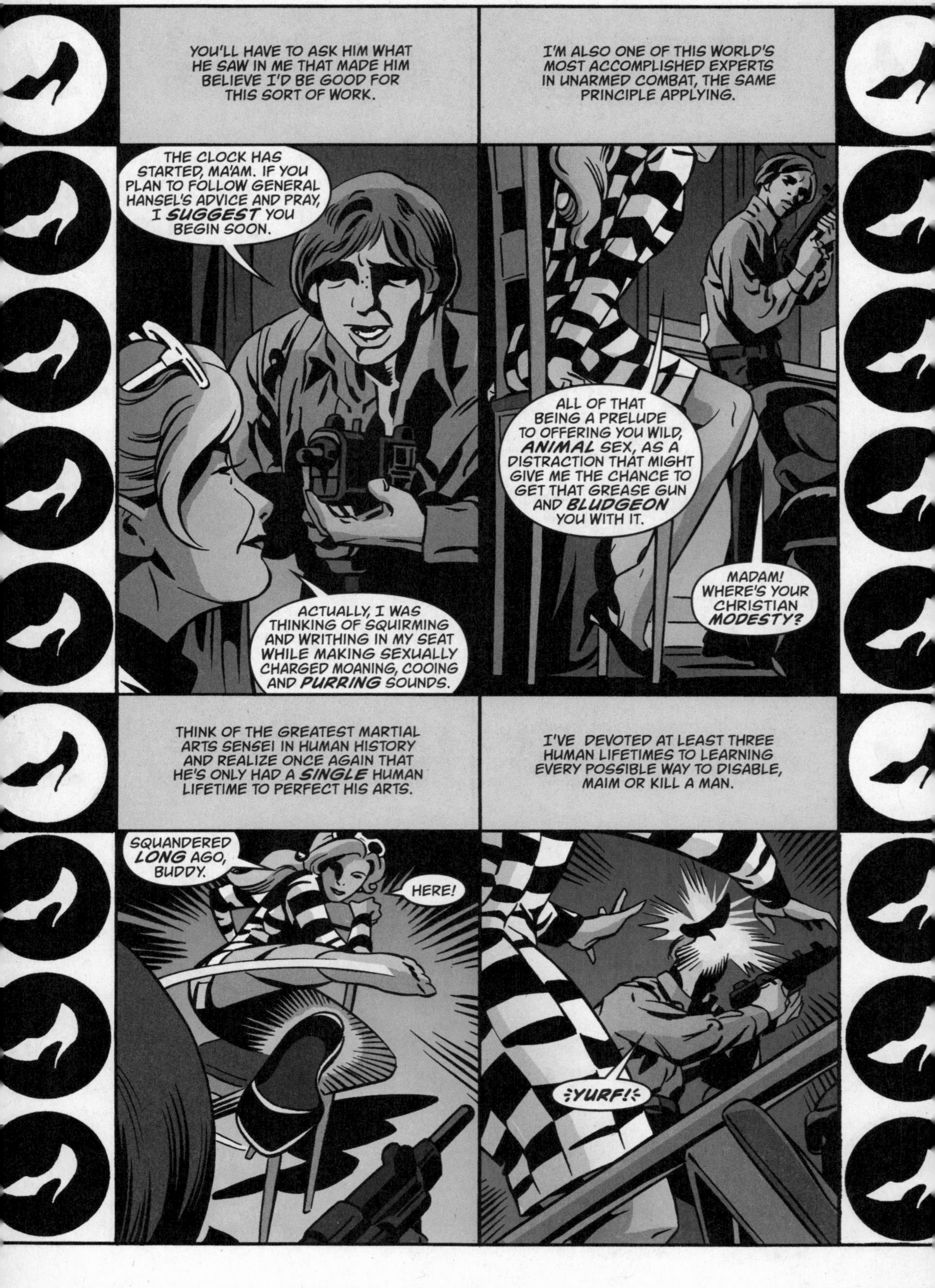

YOU'LL HAVE TO ASK HIM WHAT HE SAW IN ME THAT MADE HIM BELIEVE I'D BE GOOD FOR THIS SORT OF WORK.
I'M ALSO ONE OF THIS WORLD'S MOST ACCOMPLISHED EXPERTS IN UNARMED COMBAT, THE SAME PRINCIPLE APPLYING.
THE CLOCK HAS STARTED, MA'AM. IF YOU PLAN TO FOLLOW GENERAL HANSEL'S ADVICE AND PRAY, I SUGGEST YOU BEGIN SOON.
ACTUALLY, I WAS THINKING OF SQUIRMING AND WRITHING IN MY SEAT WHILE MAKING SEXUALLY CHARGED MOANING, COOING AND PURRING SOUNDS.
ALL OF THAT BEING A PRELUDE TO OFFERING YOU WILD, ANIMAL SEX, AS A DISTRACTION THAT MIGHT GIVE ME THE CHANCE TO GET THAT GREASE GUN AND BLUDGEON YOU WITH IT.
MADAM! WHERE'S YOUR CHRISTIAN MODESTY?
THINK OF THE GREATEST MARTIAL ARTS SENSEI IN HUMAN HISTORY AND REALIZE ONCE AGAIN THAT HE'S ONLY HAD A SINGLE HUMAN LIFETIME TO PERFECT HIS ARTS.
I'VE DEVOTED AT LEAST THREE HUMAN LIFETIMES TO LEARNING EVERY POSSIBLE WAY TO DISABLE, MAIM OR KILL A MAN.
SQUANDERED LONG AGO, BUDDY.
HERE!
YURF!

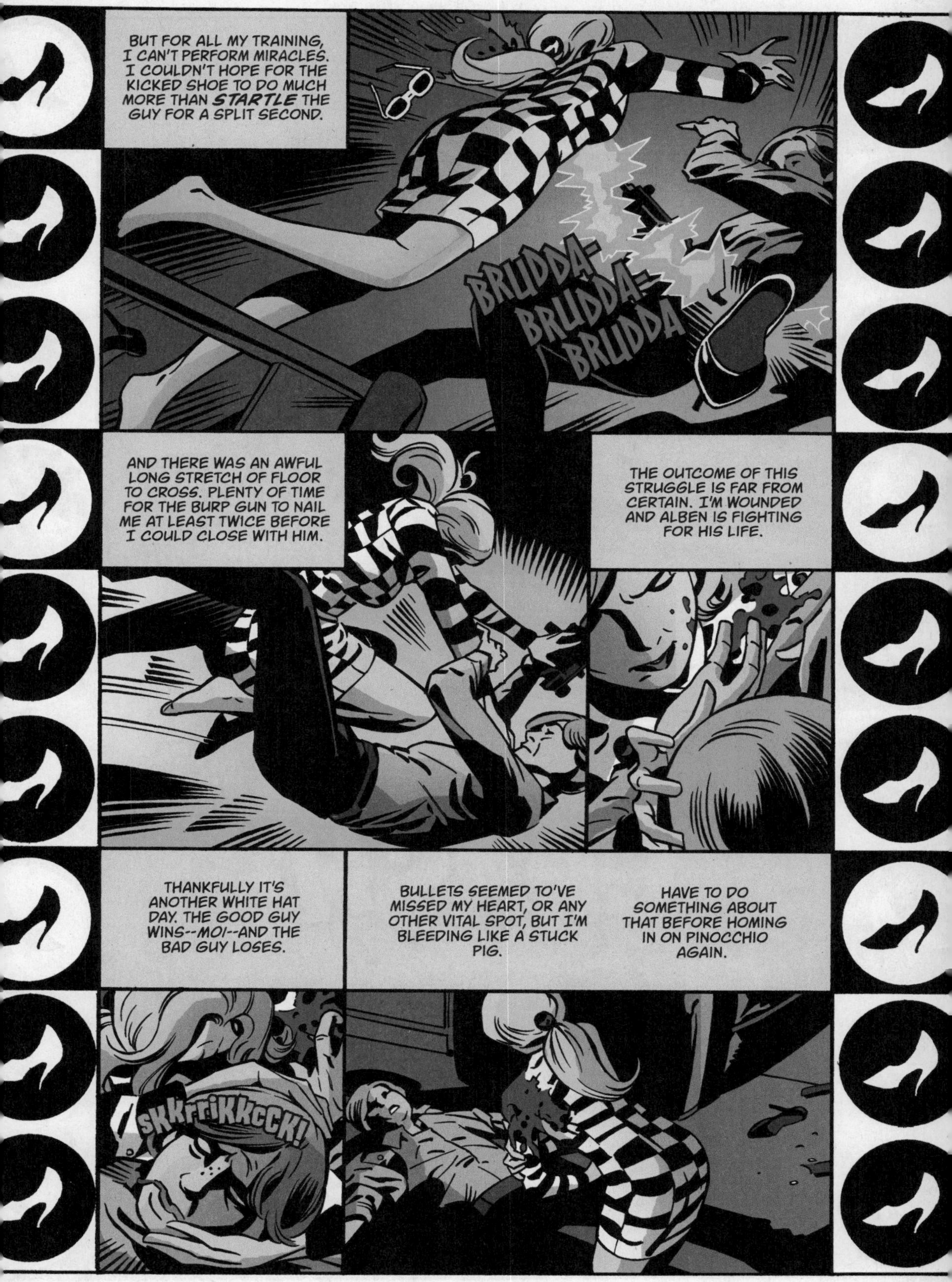
BUT FOR ALL MY TRAINING, I CAN'T PERFORM MIRACLES. I COULDN'T HOPE FOR THE KICKED SHOE TO DO MUCH MORE THAN *STARTLE* THE GUY FOR A SPLIT SECOND.
BRUDDA-BRUDDA-BRUDDA
AND THERE WAS AN AWFUL LONG STRETCH OF FLOOR TO CROSS. PLENTY OF TIME FOR THE BURP GUN TO NAIL ME AT LEAST TWICE BEFORE I COULD CLOSE WITH HIM.
THE OUTCOME OF THIS STRUGGLE IS FAR FROM CERTAIN. I'M WOUNDED AND ALBEN IS FIGHTING FOR HIS LIFE.
THANKFULLY IT'S ANOTHER WHITE HAT DAY. THE GOOD GUY WINS--*MOI*--AND THE BAD GUY LOSES.
SKKRRIKKCCK!
BULLETS SEEMED TO'VE MISSED MY HEART, OR ANY OTHER VITAL SPOT, BUT I'M BLEEDING LIKE A STUCK PIG.
HAVE TO DO SOMETHING ABOUT THAT BEFORE HOMING IN ON PINOCCHIO AGAIN.

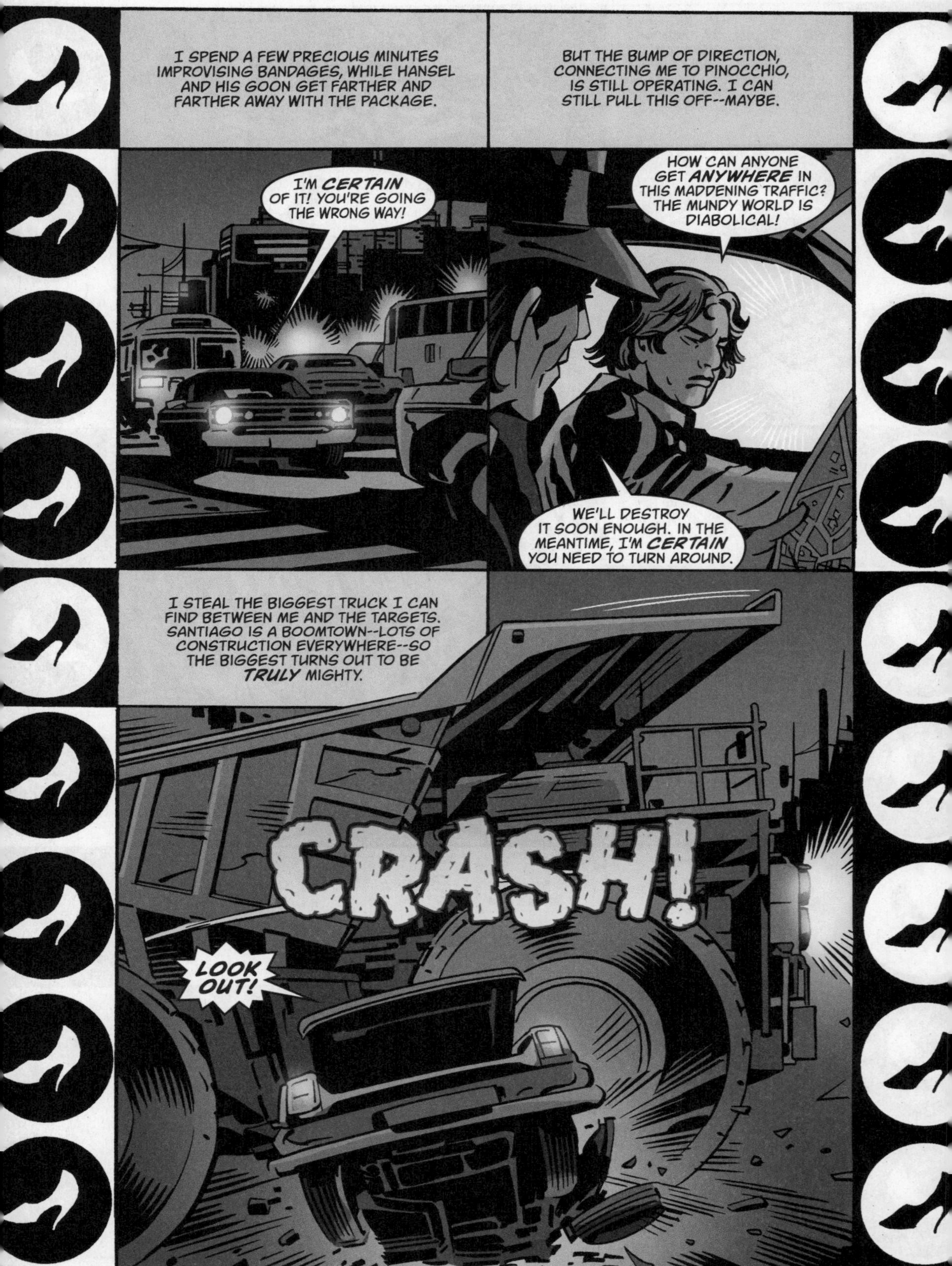
I SPEND A FEW PRECIOUS MINUTES IMPROVISING BANDAGES, WHILE HANSEL AND HIS GOON GET FARTHER AND FARTHER AWAY WITH THE PACKAGE.
BUT THE BUMP OF DIRECTION, CONNECTING ME TO PINOCCHIO, IS STILL OPERATING. I CAN STILL PULL THIS OFF--MAYBE.
I'M CERTAIN OF IT! YOU'RE GOING THE WRONG WAY!
HOW CAN ANYONE GET ANYWHERE IN THIS MADDENING TRAFFIC? THE MUNDY WORLD IS DIABOLICAL!
WE'LL DESTROY IT SOON ENOUGH. IN THE MEANTIME, I'M CERTAIN YOU NEED TO TURN AROUND.
I STEAL THE BIGGEST TRUCK I CAN FIND BETWEEN ME AND THE TARGETS. SANTIAGO IS A BOOMTOWN--LOTS OF CONSTRUCTION EVERYWHERE--SO THE BIGGEST TURNS OUT TO BE TRULY MIGHTY.
CRASH!
LOOK OUT!

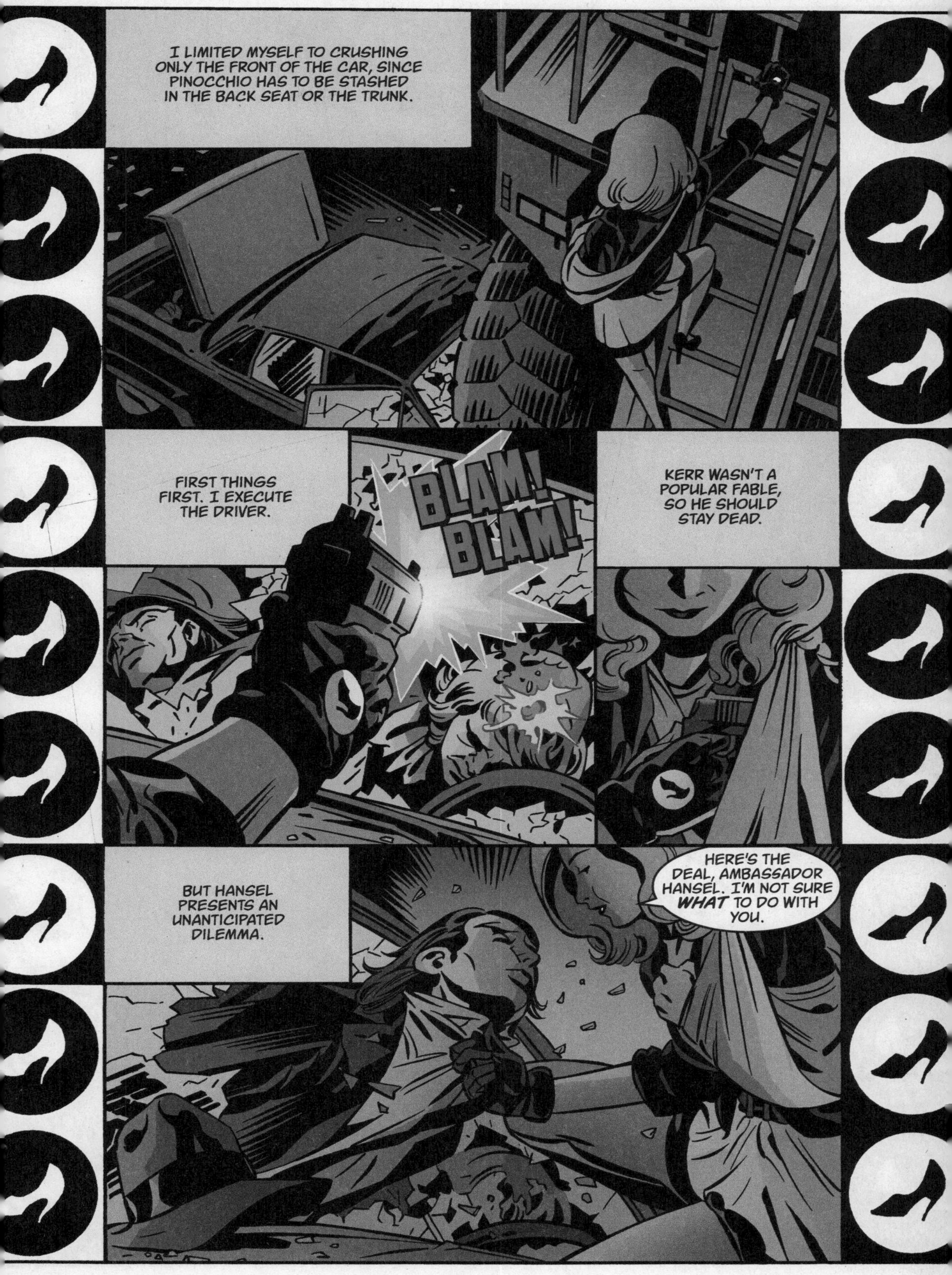

I LIMITED MYSELF TO CRUSHING ONLY THE FRONT OF THE CAR, SINCE PINOCCHIO HAS TO BE STASHED IN THE BACK SEAT OR THE TRUNK.
FIRST THINGS FIRST. I EXECUTE THE DRIVER.
BLAM! BLAM!
KERR WASN'T A POPULAR FABLE, SO HE SHOULD STAY DEAD.
BUT HANSEL PRESENTS AN UNANTICIPATED DILEMMA.
HERE'S THE DEAL, AMBASSADOR HANSEL. I'M NOT SURE *WHAT* TO DO WITH YOU.

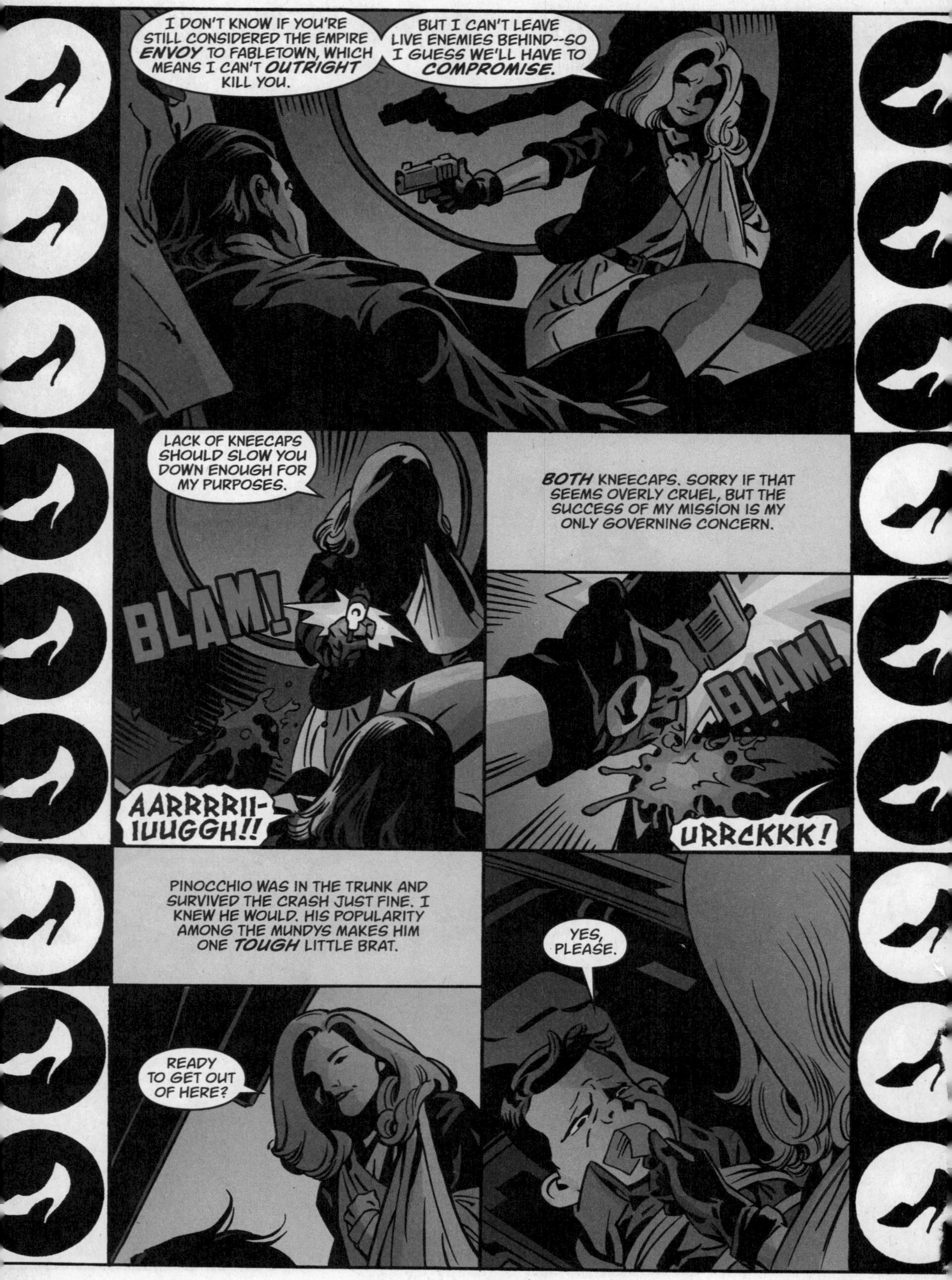
I DON'T KNOW IF YOU'RE STILL CONSIDERED THE EMPIRE *ENVOY* TO FABLETOWN, WHICH MEANS I CAN'T *OUTRIGHT* KILL YOU.
BUT I CAN'T LEAVE LIVE ENEMIES BEHIND--SO I GUESS WE'LL HAVE TO *COMPROMISE.*
LACK OF KNEECAPS SHOULD SLOW YOU DOWN ENOUGH FOR MY PURPOSES.
BLAM!
AARRRRII-IUUGGH!!
BOTH KNEECAPS. SORRY IF THAT SEEMS OVERLY CRUEL, BUT THE SUCCESS OF MY MISSION IS MY ONLY GOVERNING CONCERN.
BLAM!
URRCKKK!
PINOCCHIO WAS IN THE TRUNK AND SURVIVED THE CRASH JUST FINE. I KNEW HE WOULD. HIS POPULARITY AMONG THE MUNDYS MAKES HIM ONE *TOUGH* LITTLE BRAT.
READY TO GET OUT OF HERE?
YES, PLEASE.

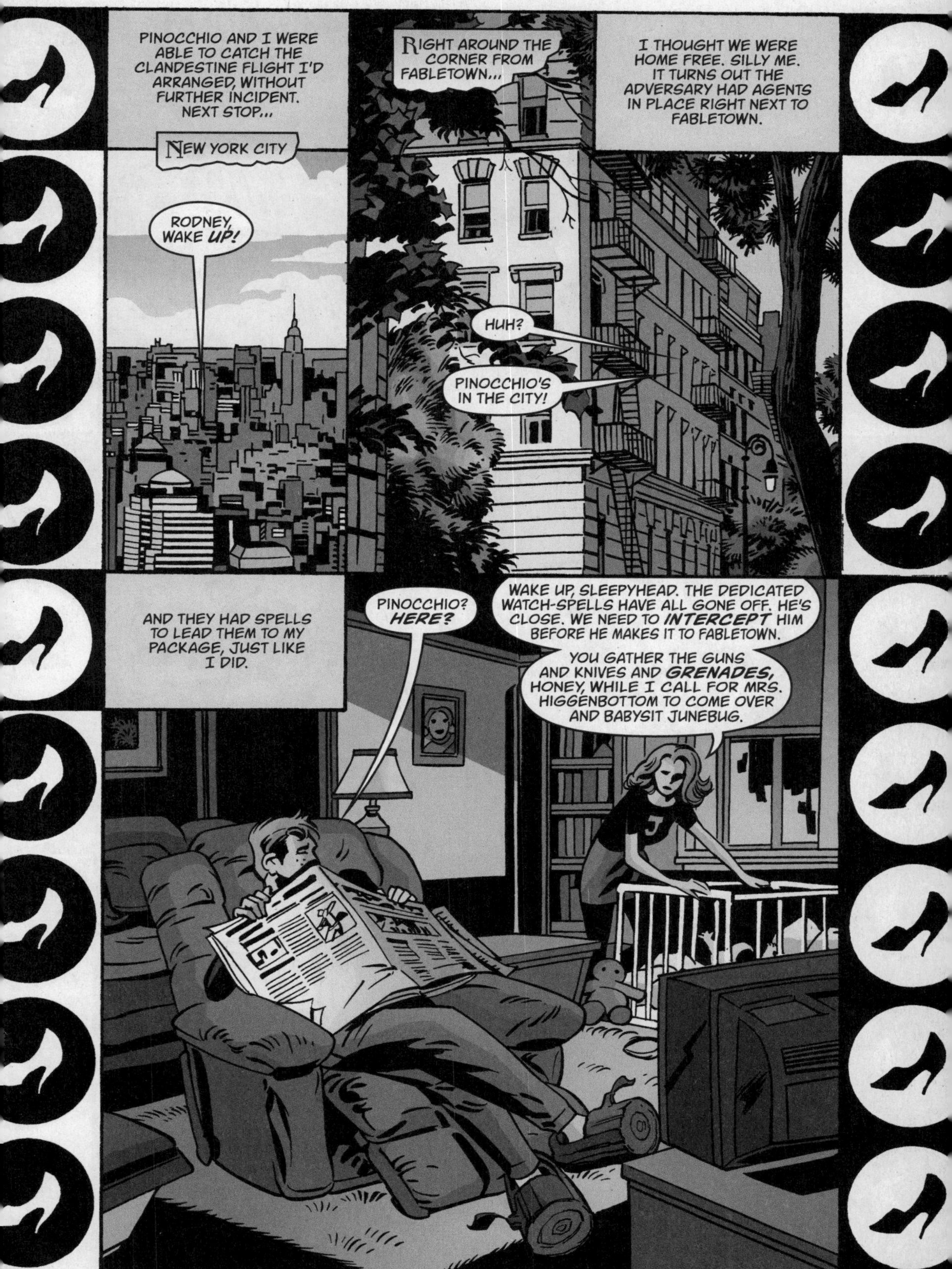
PINOCCHIO AND I WERE ABLE TO CATCH THE CLANDESTINE FLIGHT I'D ARRANGED, WITHOUT FURTHER INCIDENT. NEXT STOP...
NEW YORK CITY
RODNEY, WAKE UP!
RIGHT AROUND THE CORNER FROM FABLETOWN...
I THOUGHT WE WERE HOME FREE. SILLY ME. IT TURNS OUT THE ADVERSARY HAD AGENTS IN PLACE RIGHT NEXT TO FABLETOWN.
HUH?
PINOCCHIO'S IN THE CITY!
AND THEY HAD SPELLS TO LEAD THEM TO MY PACKAGE, JUST LIKE I DID.
PINOCCHIO? HERE?
WAKE UP, SLEEPYHEAD. THE DEDICATED WATCH-SPELLS HAVE ALL GONE OFF. HE'S CLOSE. WE NEED TO INTERCEPT HIM BEFORE HE MAKES IT TO FABLETOWN.
YOU GATHER THE GUNS AND KNIVES AND GRENADES, HONEY, WHILE I CALL FOR MRS. HIGGENBOTTOM TO COME OVER AND BABYSIT JUNEBUG.

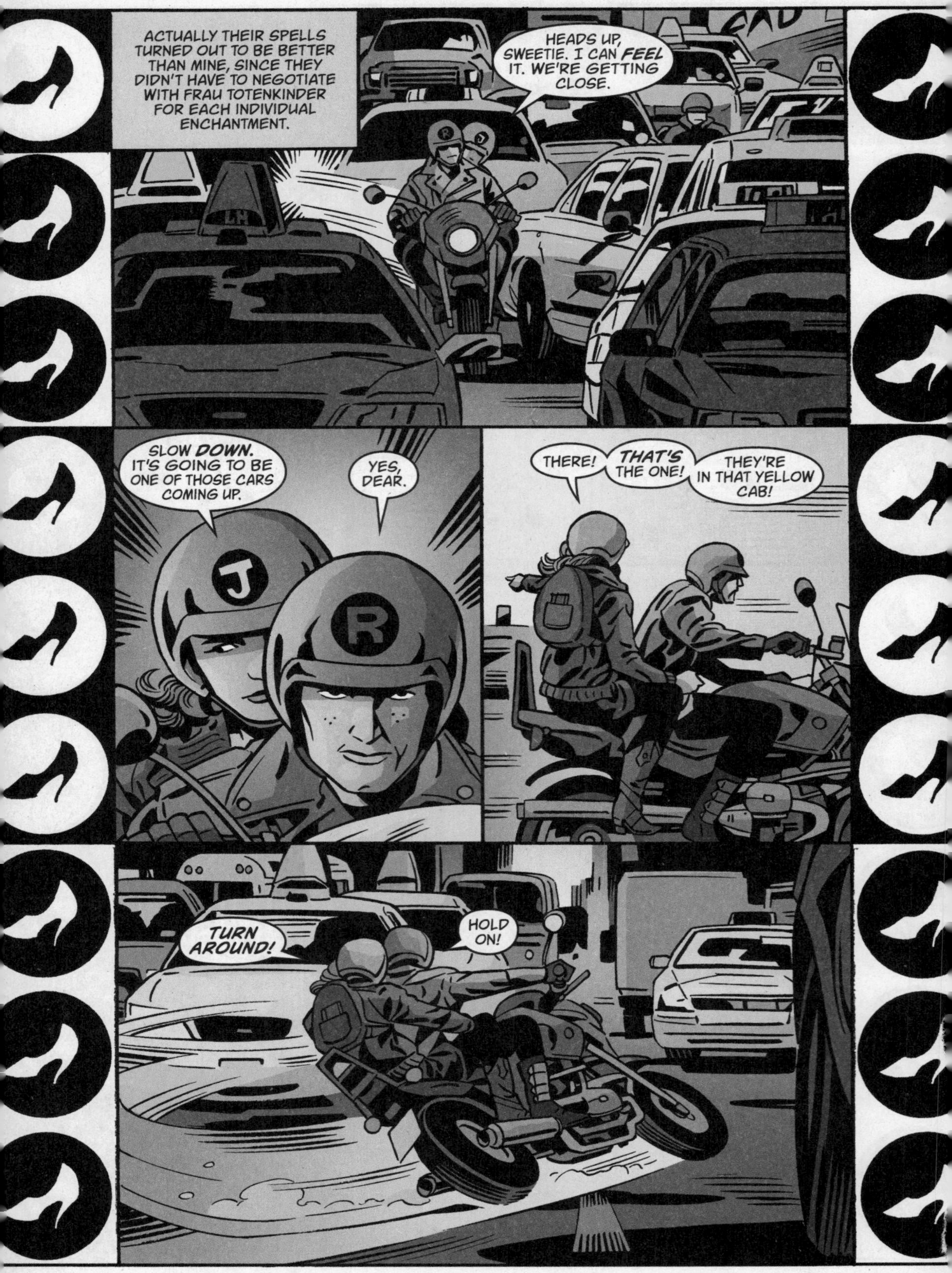
ACTUALLY THEIR SPELLS TURNED OUT TO BE BETTER THAN MINE, SINCE THEY DIDN'T HAVE TO NEGOTIATE WITH FRAU TOTENKINDER FOR EACH INDIVIDUAL ENCHANTMENT.
HEADS UP, SWEETIE. I CAN *FEEL* IT. WE'RE GETTING CLOSE.
SLOW **DOWN.** IT'S GOING TO BE ONE OF THOSE CARS COMING UP.
YES, DEAR.
THERE!
THAT'S THE ONE!
THEY'RE IN THAT YELLOW CAB!
TURN AROUND!
HOLD ON!

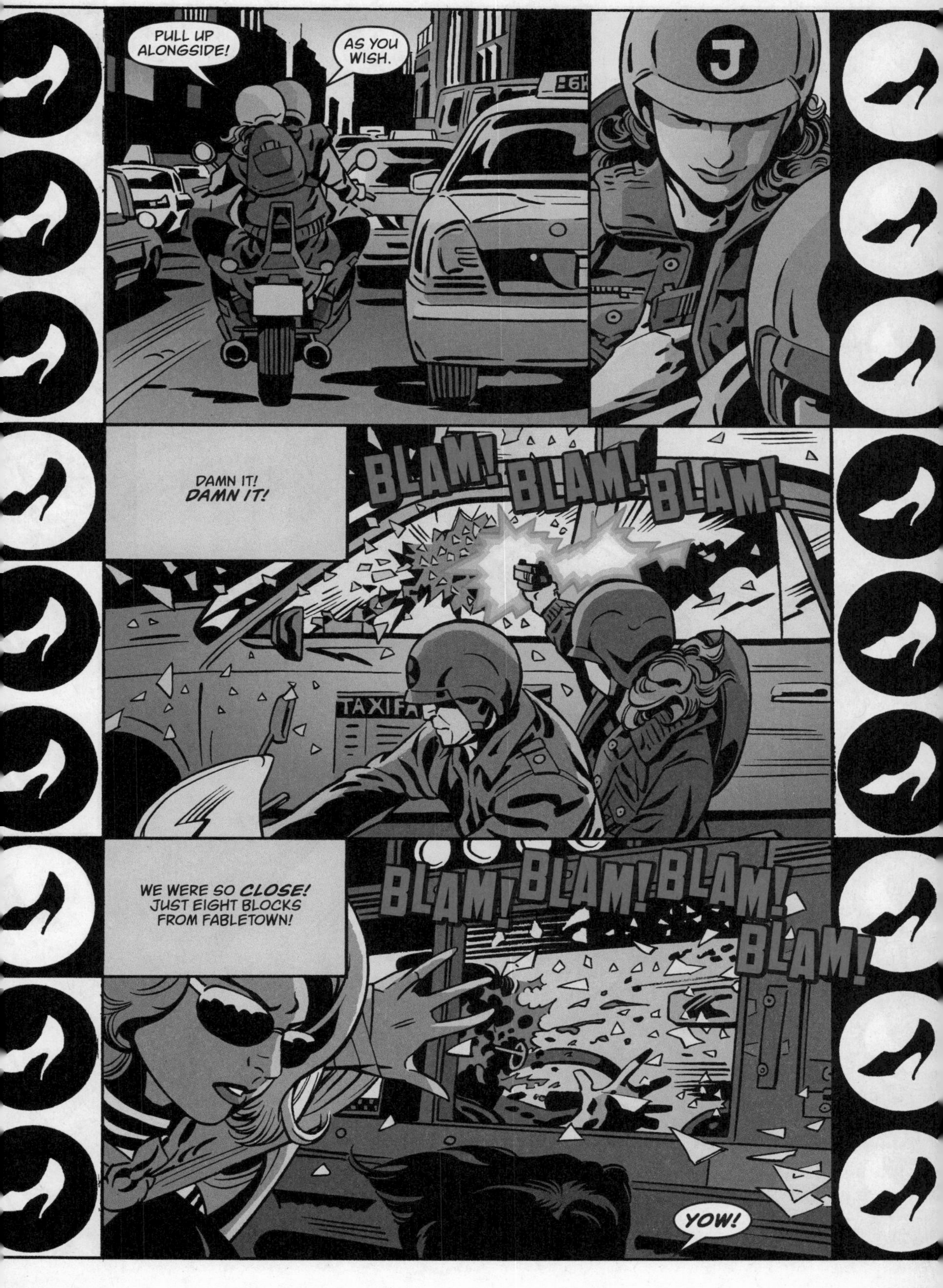
PULL UP ALONGSIDE!
AS YOU WISH.
6H
J
DAMN IT! *DAMN IT!*
BLAM! BLAM! BLAM!
TAXIFA
WE WERE SO *CLOSE!* JUST EIGHT BLOCKS FROM FABLETOWN!
BLAM! BLAM! BLAM! BLAM!
YOW!

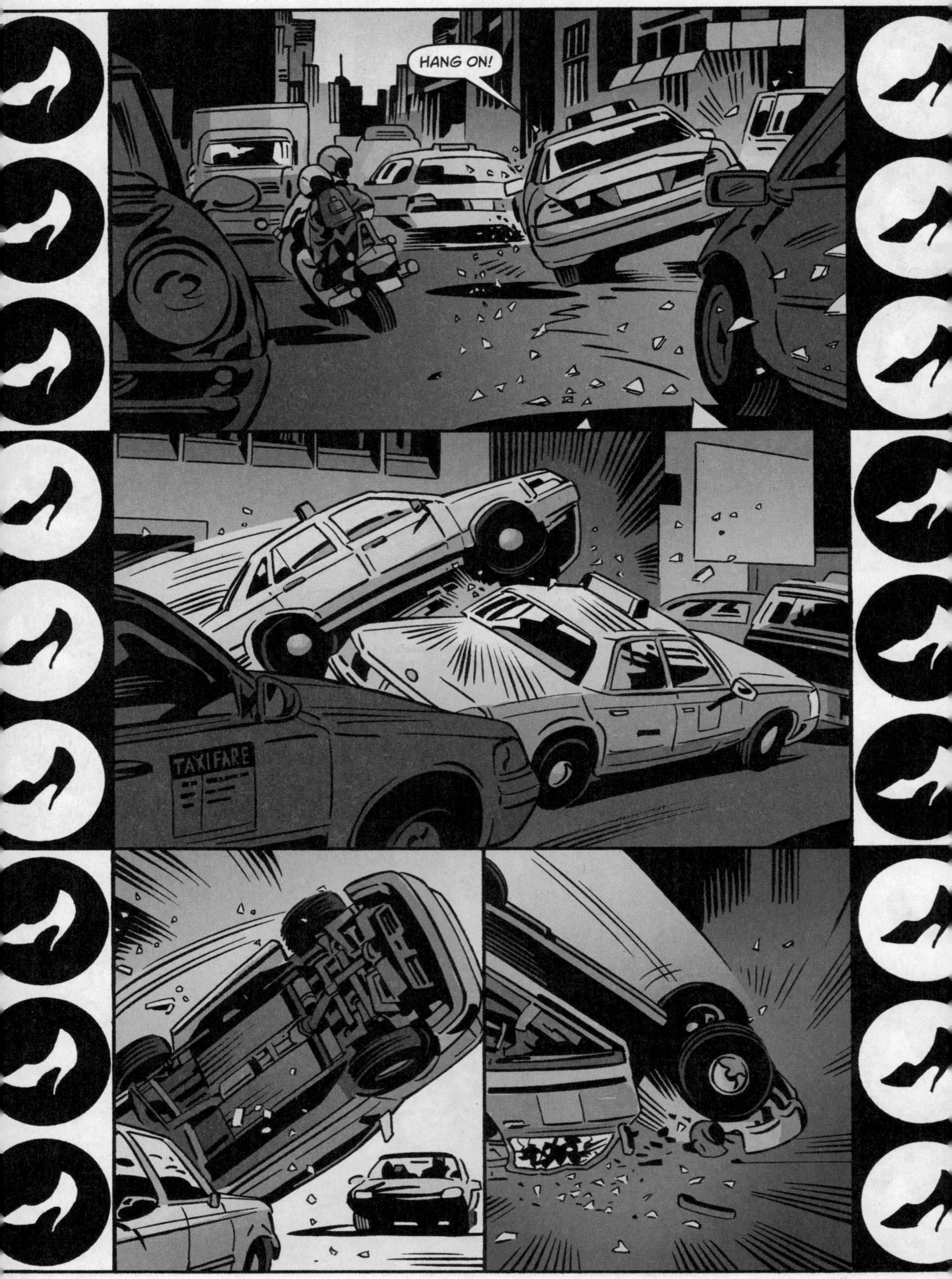
HANG ON!
TAXIFARE

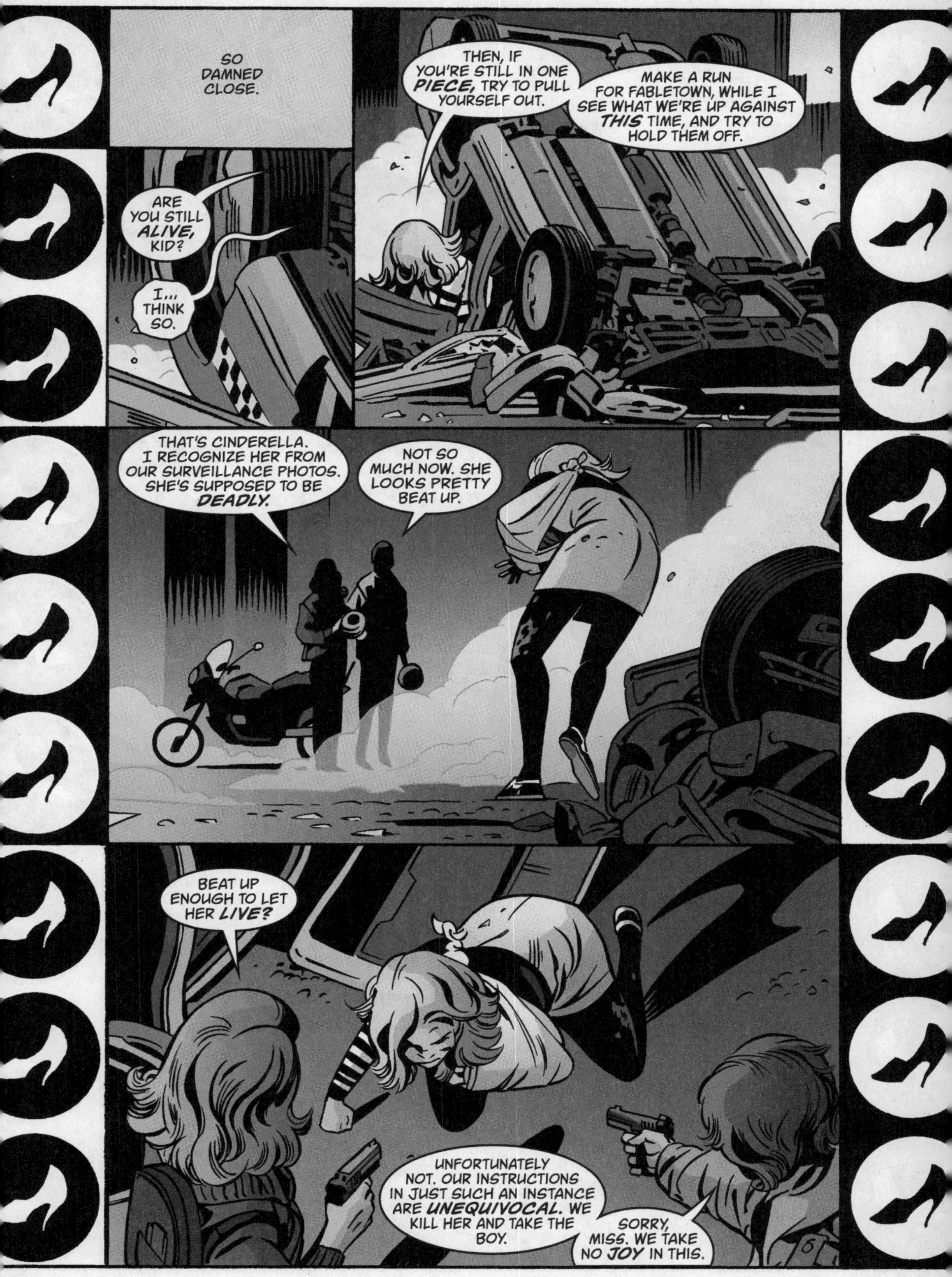
SO DAMNED CLOSE.
ARE YOU STILL ALIVE, KID?
I... THINK SO.
THEN, IF YOU'RE STILL IN ONE PIECE, TRY TO PULL YOURSELF OUT.
MAKE A RUN FOR FABLETOWN, WHILE I SEE WHAT WE'RE UP AGAINST THIS TIME, AND TRY TO HOLD THEM OFF.
THAT'S CINDERELLA. I RECOGNIZE HER FROM OUR SURVEILLANCE PHOTOS. SHE'S SUPPOSED TO BE DEADLY.
NOT SO MUCH NOW. SHE LOOKS PRETTY BEAT UP.
BEAT UP ENOUGH TO LET HER LIVE?
UNFORTUNATELY NOT. OUR INSTRUCTIONS IN JUST SUCH AN INSTANCE ARE UNEQUIVOCAL. WE KILL HER AND TAKE THE BOY.
SORRY, MISS. WE TAKE NO JOY IN THIS.

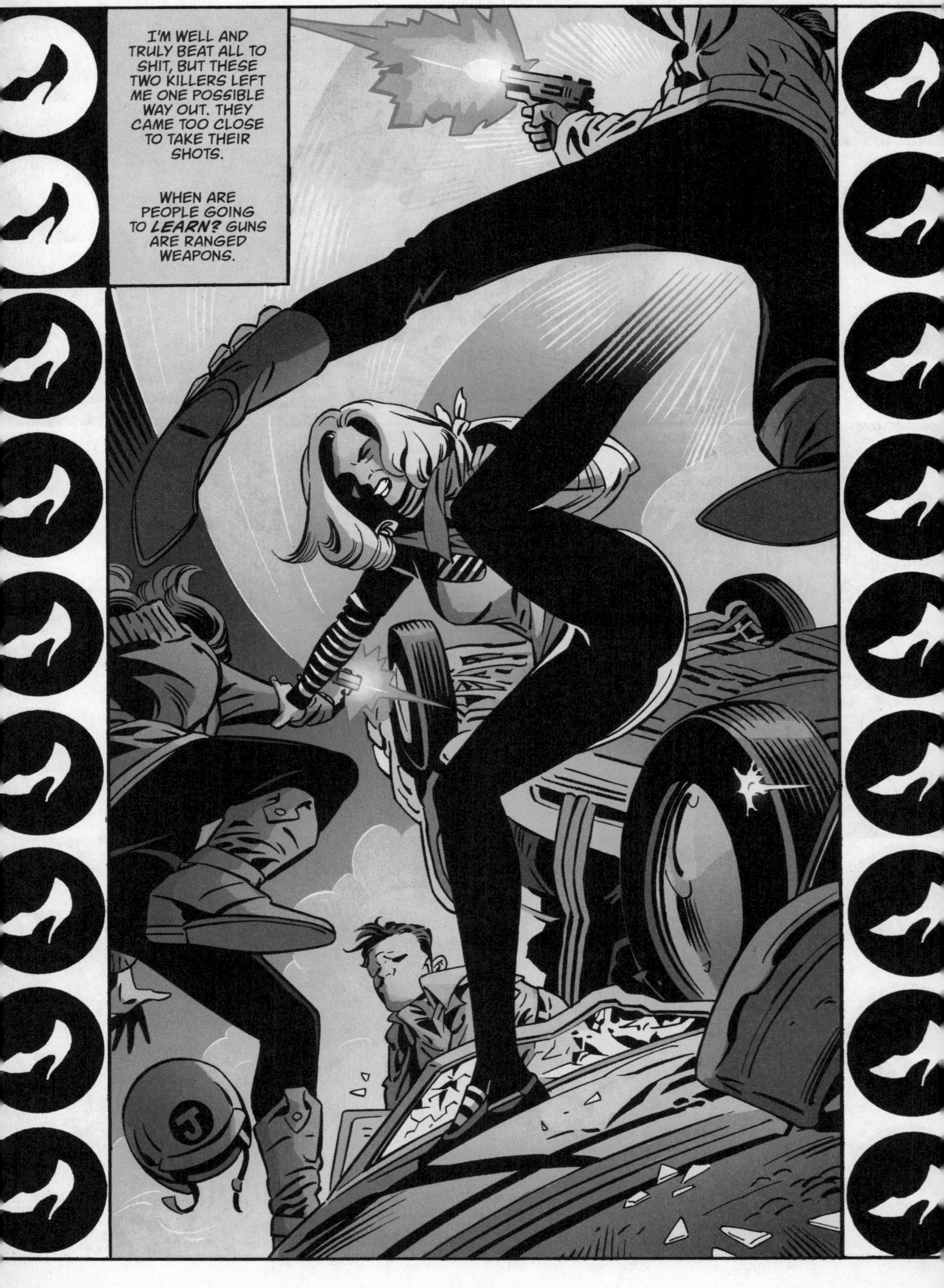
I'M WELL AND TRULY BEAT ALL TO SHIT, BUT THESE TWO KILLERS LEFT ME ONE POSSIBLE WAY OUT. THEY CAME TOO CLOSE TO TAKE THEIR SHOTS.
WHEN ARE PEOPLE GOING TO LEARN? GUNS ARE RANGED WEAPONS.

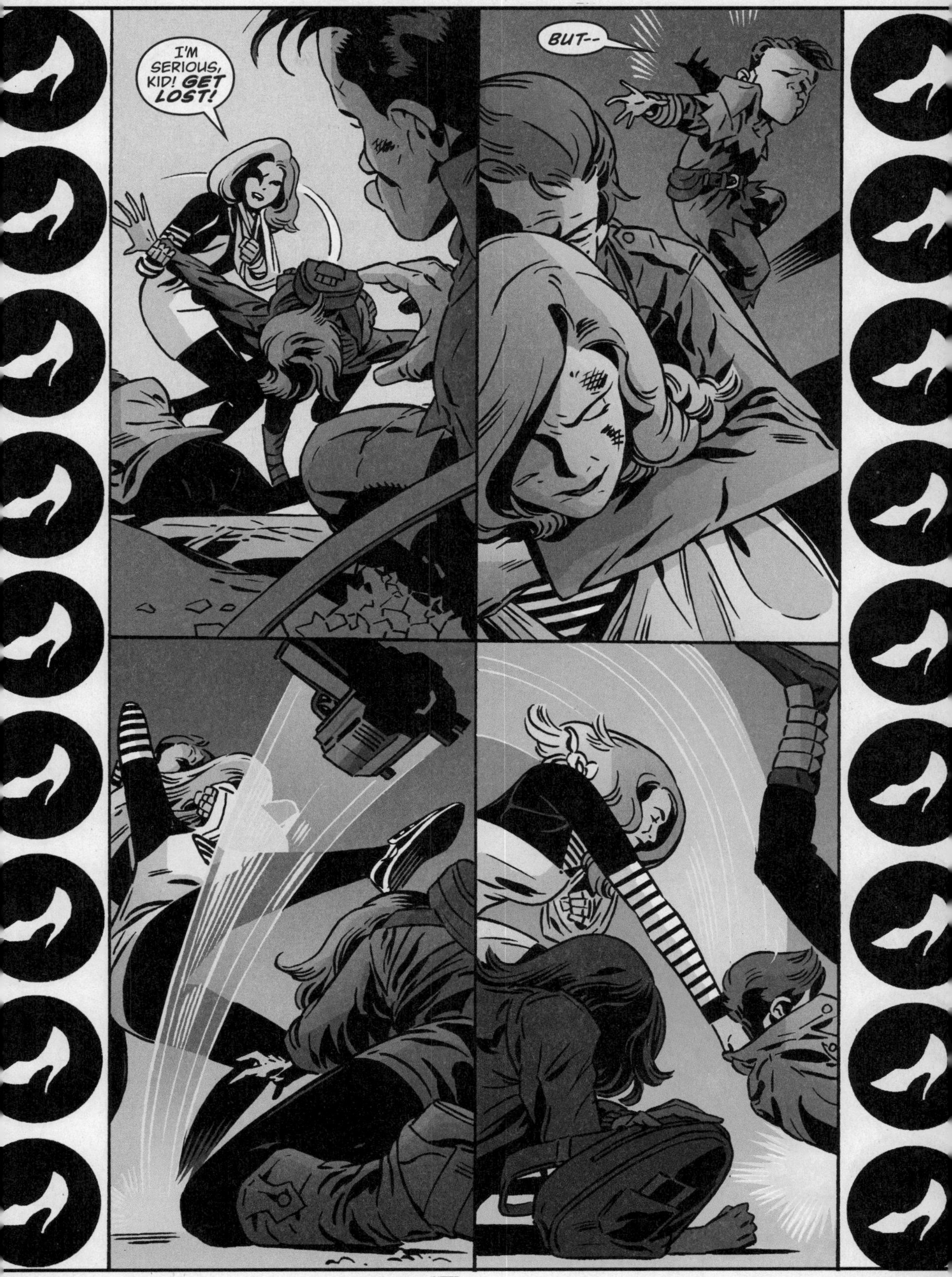
I'M SERIOUS, KID! GET LOST!
BUT--

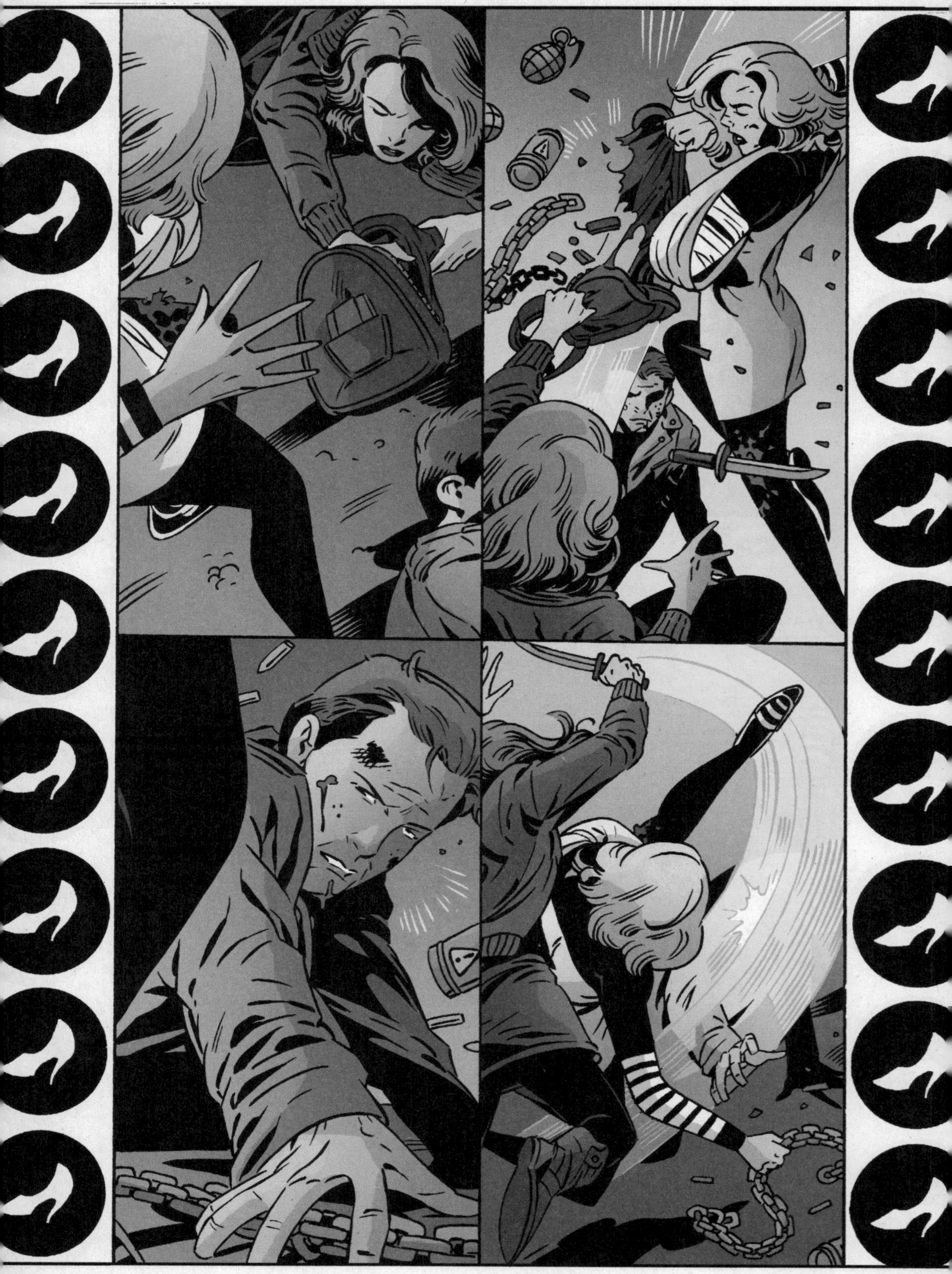

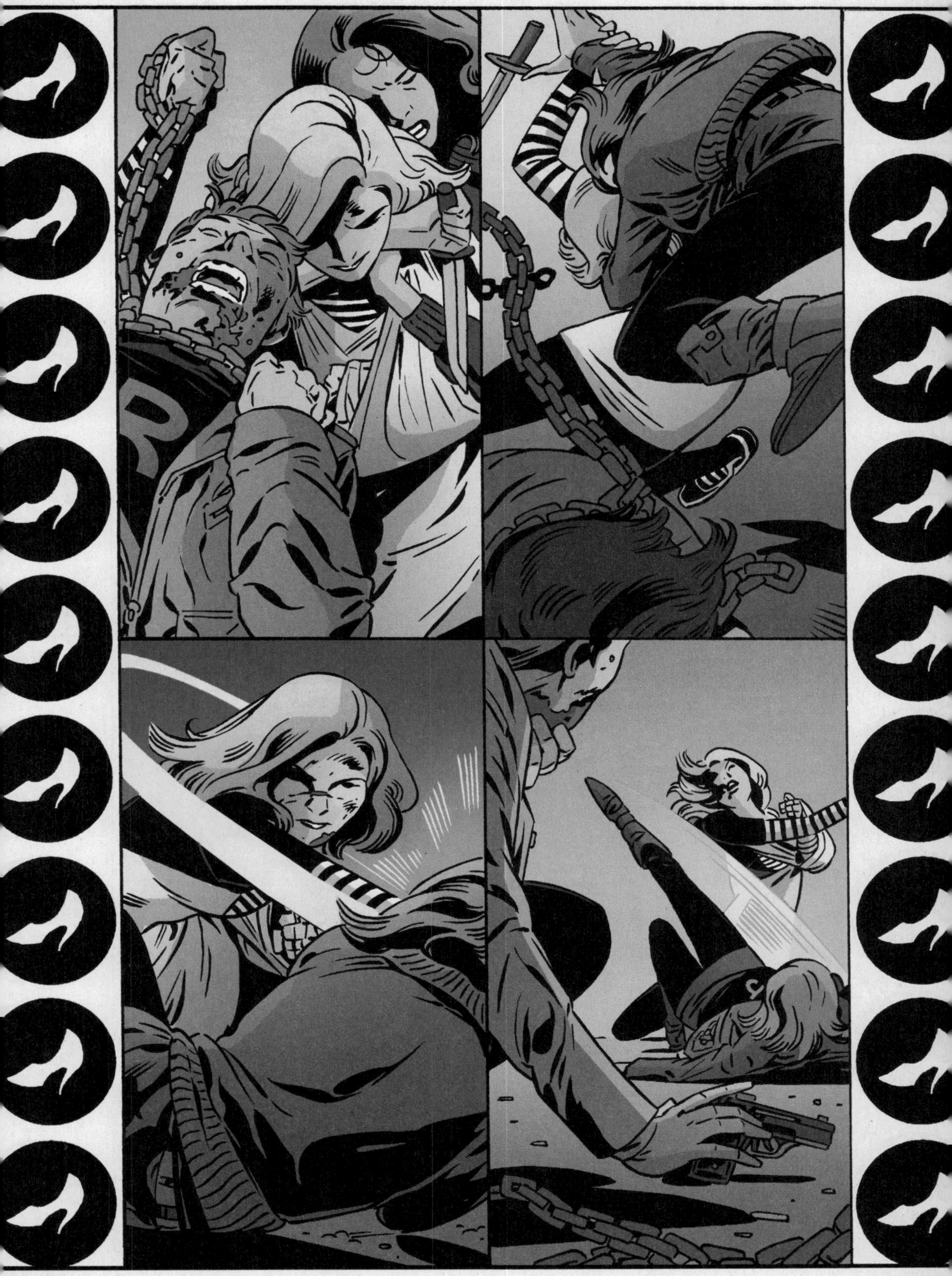

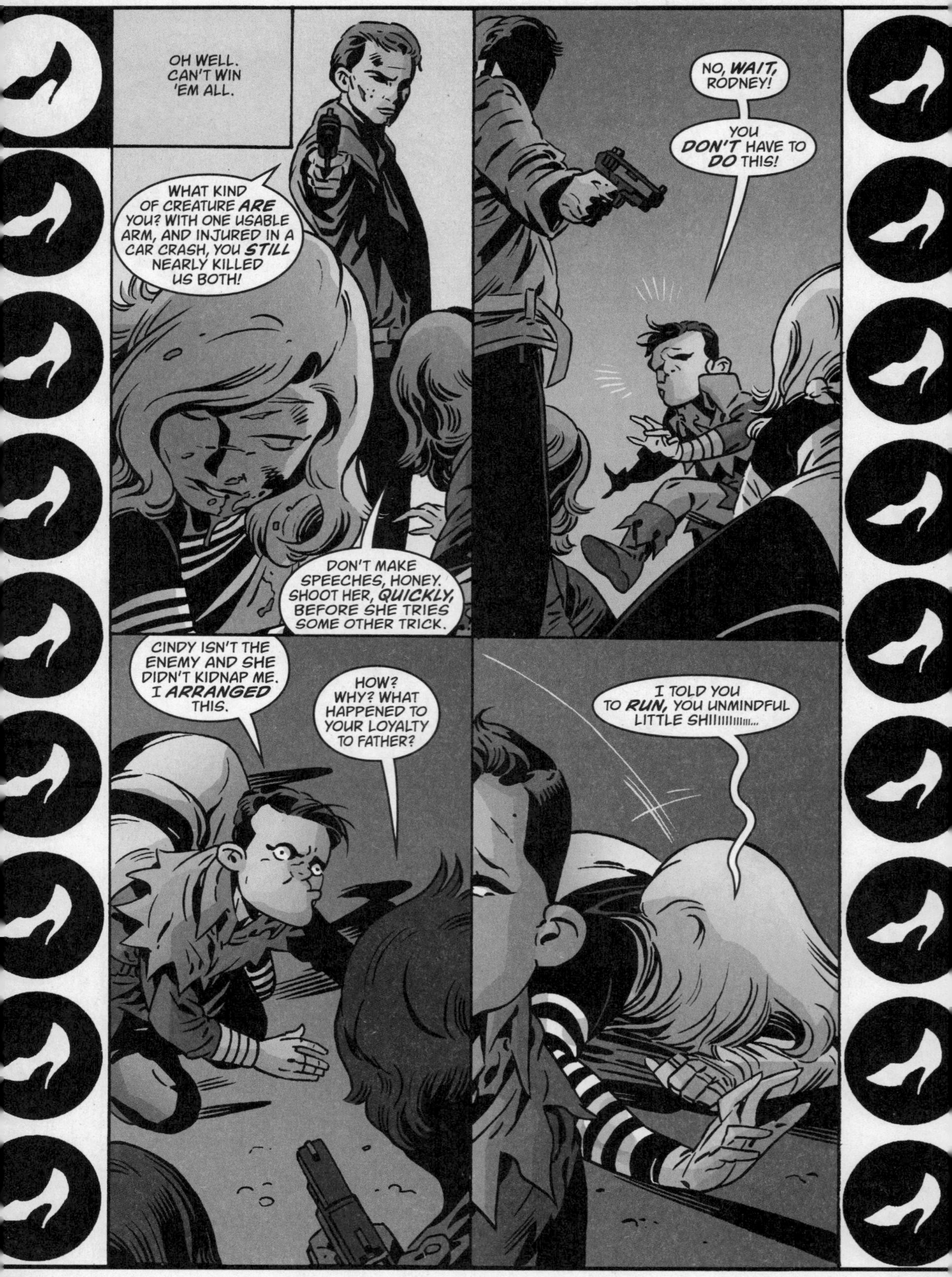

OH WELL. CAN'T WIN 'EM ALL.
WHAT KIND OF CREATURE ARE YOU? WITH ONE USABLE ARM, AND INJURED IN A CAR CRASH, YOU STILL NEARLY KILLED US BOTH!
DON'T MAKE SPEECHES, HONEY. SHOOT HER, QUICKLY, BEFORE SHE TRIES SOME OTHER TRICK.
NO, WAIT, RODNEY!
YOU DON'T HAVE TO DO THIS!
CINDY ISN'T THE ENEMY AND SHE DIDN'T KIDNAP ME. I ARRANGED THIS.
HOW? WHY? WHAT HAPPENED TO YOUR LOYALTY TO FATHER?
I TOLD YOU TO RUN, YOU UNMINDFUL LITTLE SHIIIIIIIIIIIII...

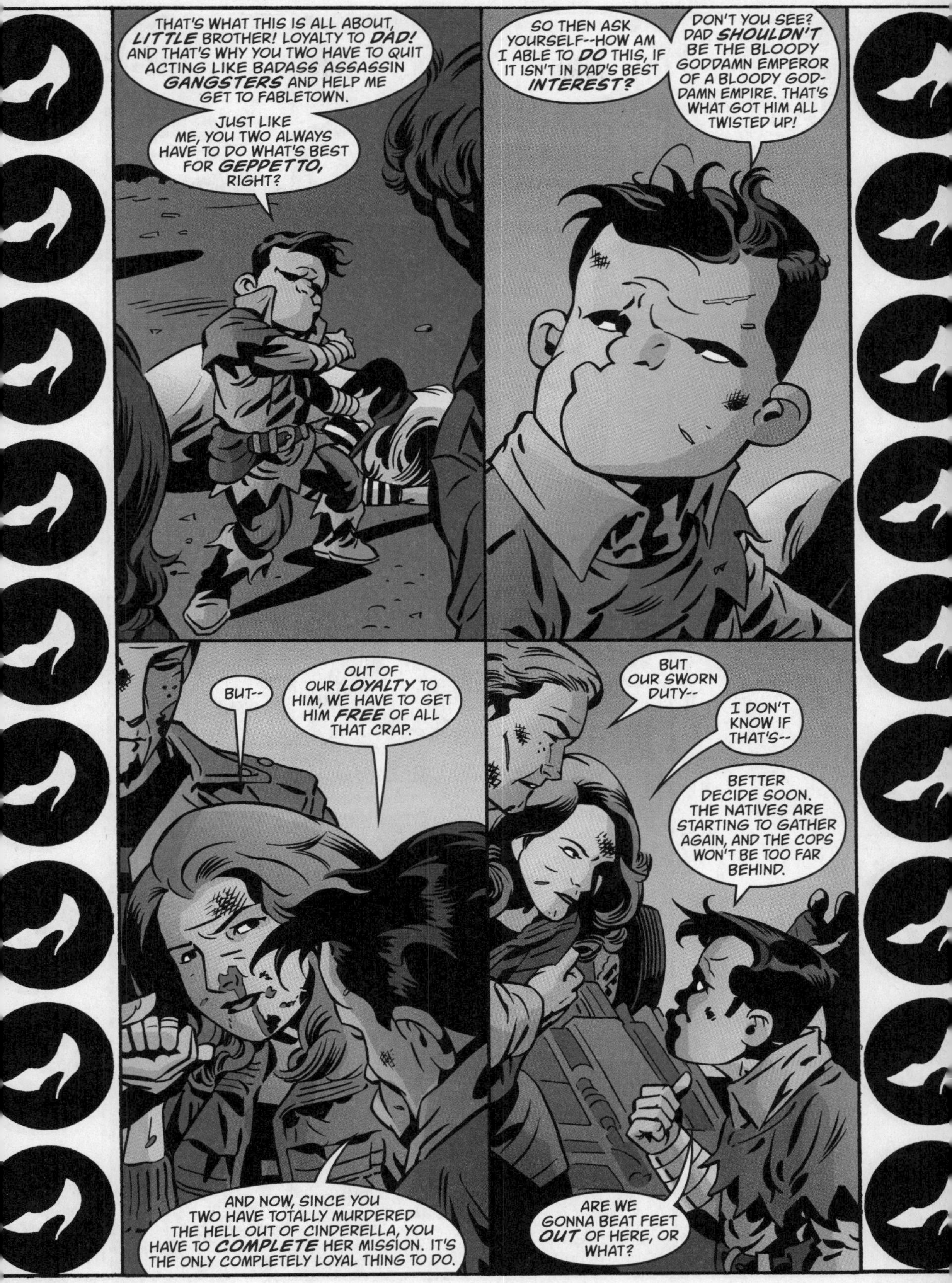
THAT'S WHAT THIS IS ALL ABOUT, LITTLE BROTHER! LOYALTY TO DAD! AND THAT'S WHY YOU TWO HAVE TO QUIT ACTING LIKE BADASS ASSASSIN GANGSTERS AND HELP ME GET TO FABLETOWN.
JUST LIKE ME, YOU TWO ALWAYS HAVE TO DO WHAT'S BEST FOR GEPPETTO, RIGHT?
SO THEN ASK YOURSELF--HOW AM I ABLE TO DO THIS, IF IT ISN'T IN DAD'S BEST INTEREST?
DON'T YOU SEE? DAD SHOULDN'T BE THE BLOODY GODDAMN EMPEROR OF A BLOODY GOD-DAMN EMPIRE. THAT'S WHAT GOT HIM ALL TWISTED UP!
BUT--
OUT OF OUR LOYALTY TO HIM, WE HAVE TO GET HIM FREE OF ALL THAT CRAP.
AND NOW, SINCE YOU TWO HAVE TOTALLY MURDERED THE HELL OUT OF CINDERELLA, YOU HAVE TO COMPLETE HER MISSION. IT'S THE ONLY COMPLETELY LOYAL THING TO DO.
BUT OUR SWORN DUTY--
I DON'T KNOW IF THAT'S--
BETTER DECIDE SOON. THE NATIVES ARE STARTING TO GATHER AGAIN, AND THE COPS WON'T BE TOO FAR BEHIND.
ARE WE GONNA BEAT FEET OUT OF HERE, OR WHAT?

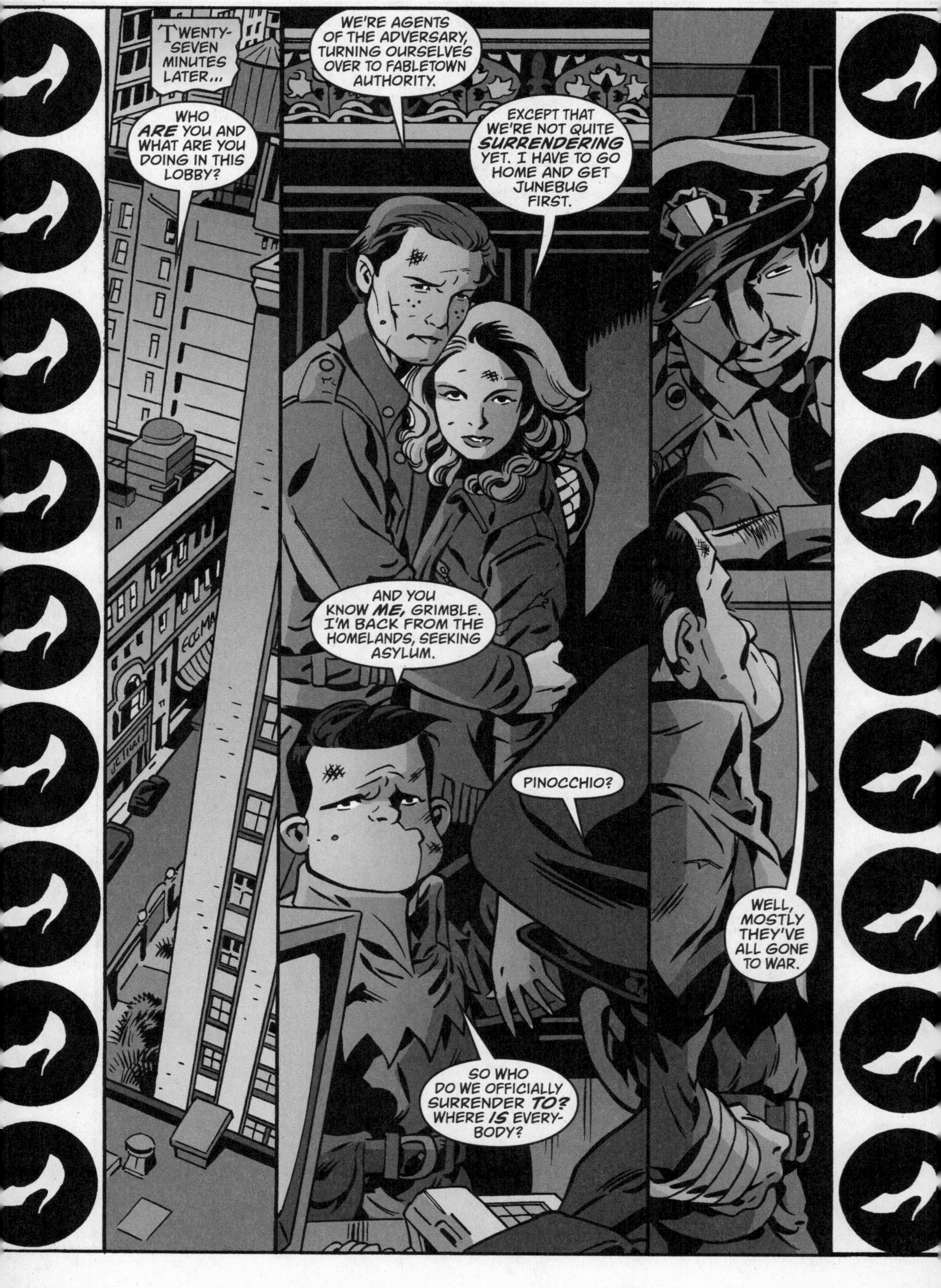

TWENTY-SEVEN MINUTES LATER...
WHO *ARE* YOU AND WHAT ARE YOU DOING IN THIS LOBBY?
WE'RE AGENTS OF THE ADVERSARY, TURNING OURSELVES OVER TO FABLETOWN AUTHORITY.
EXCEPT THAT WE'RE NOT QUITE *SURRENDERING* YET. I HAVE TO GO HOME AND GET JUNEBUG FIRST.
AND YOU KNOW *ME,* GRIMBLE. I'M BACK FROM THE HOMELANDS, SEEKING ASYLUM.
PINOCCHIO?
SO WHO DO WE OFFICIALLY SURRENDER *TO?* WHERE *IS* EVERYBODY?
WELL, MOSTLY THEY'VE ALL GONE TO WAR.

A FEW DAYS LATER IN A NEW YORK MUNDY HOSPITAL...

NO, I'M NOT DEAD YET.

IT'LL TAKE MORE THAN *THIS* TO CASH IN MY CHIPS.

WE'RE JUST SO GLAD YOU'RE OKAY.

BUT DID YOU HAVE TO GET YOURSELF SENT TO A *MUNDY* HOSPITAL?

DON'T WORRY. I'M JUST A NORMAL JANE DOE WITH TRAUMATIC *MEMORY* LOSS AFTER BEING AN UNFORTUNATE BYSTANDER IN SOME DRIVE-BY *GANG* SHOOTING.

BUT THE DOCTORS ARE BEGINNING TO GET A BIT CURIOUS AT HOW FAST I'M *MENDING*, SO THE SOONER YOU CAN BUST ME OUT OF HERE, THE BETTER.

WE'RE WORKING ON IT. JUST CONTINUE TO PLAY DUMB IN THE MEANTIME.

EASY ENOUGH FOR ME.

I MADE A LOT OF DUMB MISTAKES ON THIS ONE. HOW'S THE *BRAT* DOING?

WHO CAN SAY?

THEY WHISKED HIM UP TO WOLF MANOR FOR DEBRIEFING. THAT'S THE NEW *NERVE CENTER* OF OUR WAR PLANNING.

LEAVING BEAUTY AND ME DOWN HERE TO PRESIDE OVER AN EMPTY FABLETOWN. BUT *RELAX*, CINDY.

SLEEP THE SLEEP OF THE JUST, KNOWING THAT YOU COMPLETED YOUR MISSION.

I GUESS I CAN LIVE WITH THAT.

NEXT: THE BATTLESHIP

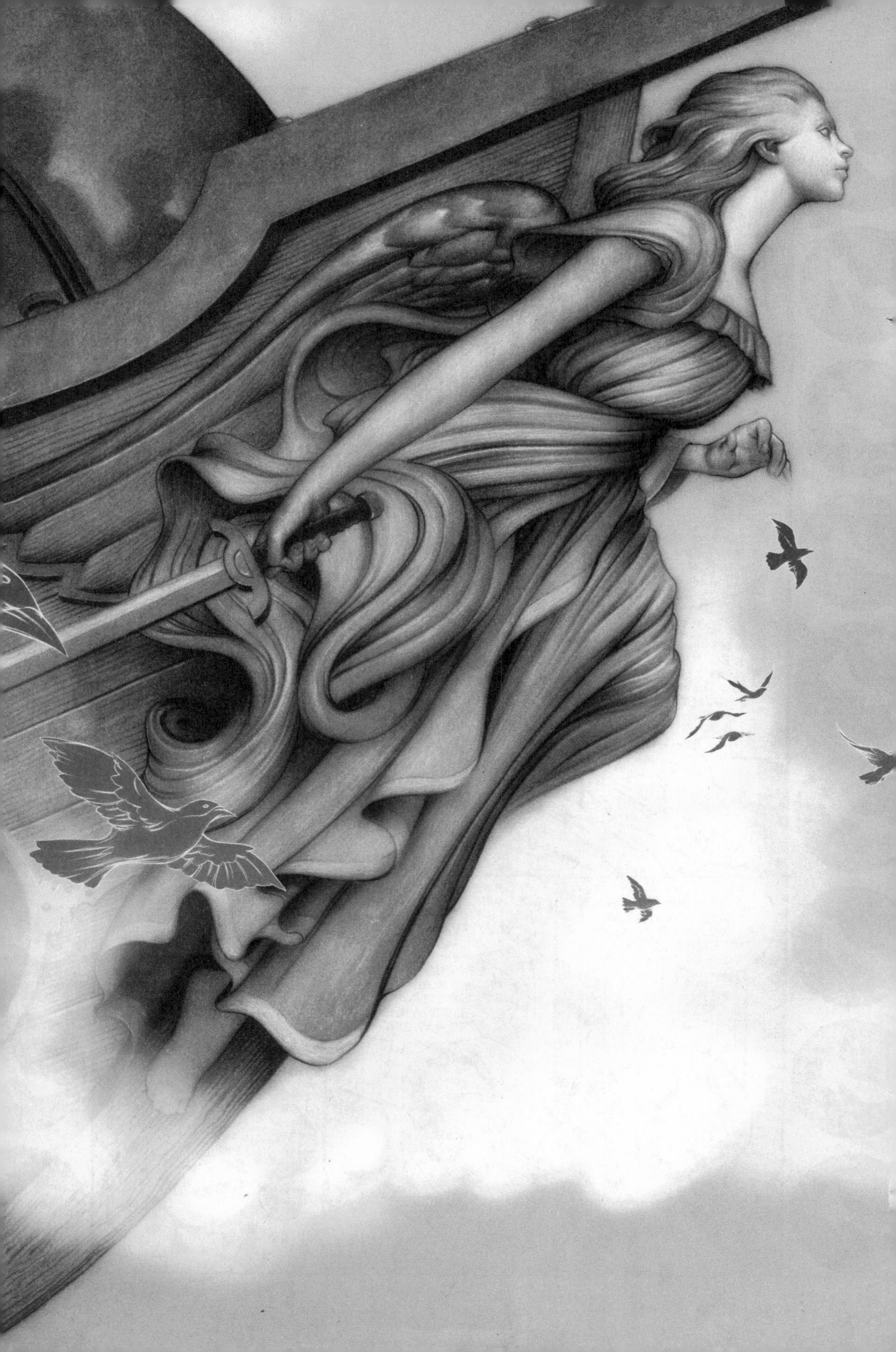

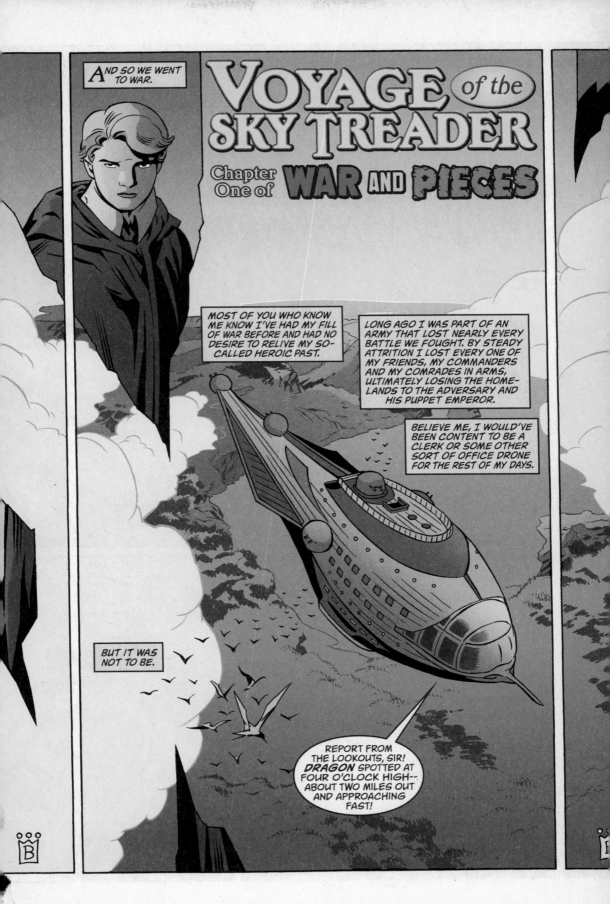

AND SO WE WENT TO WAR.

VOYAGE of the SKY TREADER
Chapter One of WAR AND PIECES

MOST OF YOU WHO KNOW ME KNOW I'VE HAD MY FILL OF WAR BEFORE AND HAD NO DESIRE TO RELIVE MY SO-CALLED HEROIC PAST.

LONG AGO I WAS PART OF AN ARMY THAT LOST NEARLY EVERY BATTLE WE FOUGHT. BY STEADY ATTRITION I LOST EVERY ONE OF MY FRIENDS, MY COMMANDERS AND MY COMRADES IN ARMS, ULTIMATELY LOSING THE HOMELANDS TO THE ADVERSARY AND HIS PUPPET EMPEROR.

BELIEVE ME, I WOULD'VE BEEN CONTENT TO BE A CLERK OR SOME OTHER SORT OF OFFICE DRONE FOR THE REST OF MY DAYS.

BUT IT WAS NOT TO BE.

REPORT FROM THE LOOKOUTS, SIR! *DRAGON* SPOTTED AT FOUR O'CLOCK HIGH-- ABOUT TWO MILES OUT AND APPROACHING FAST!

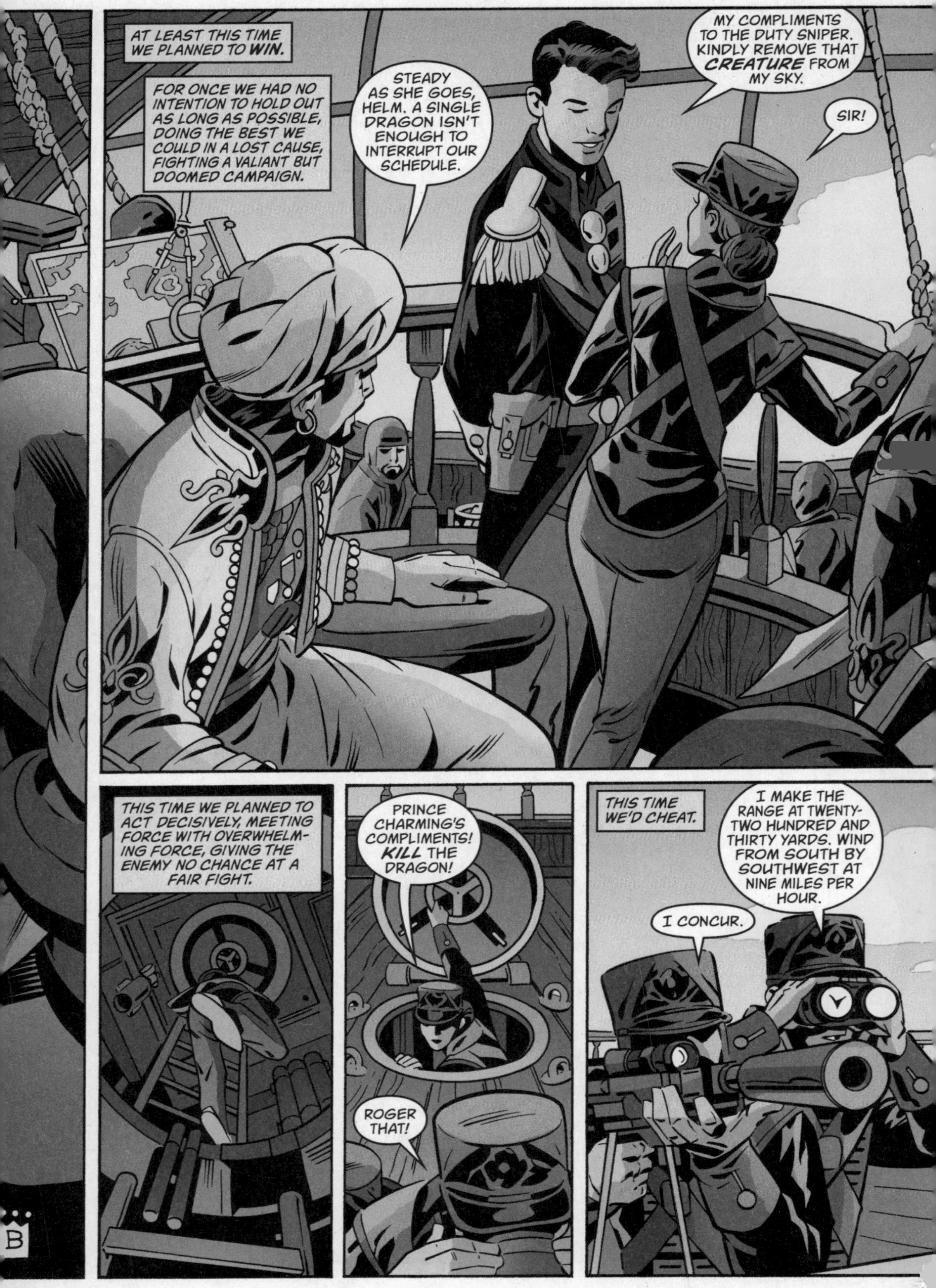
AT LEAST THIS TIME WE PLANNED TO **WIN**.
FOR ONCE WE HAD NO INTENTION TO HOLD OUT AS LONG AS POSSIBLE, DOING THE BEST WE COULD IN A LOST CAUSE, FIGHTING A VALIANT BUT DOOMED CAMPAIGN.
STEADY AS SHE GOES, HELM. A SINGLE DRAGON ISN'T ENOUGH TO INTERRUPT OUR SCHEDULE.
MY COMPLIMENTS TO THE DUTY SNIPER. KINDLY REMOVE THAT **CREATURE** FROM MY SKY.
SIR!
THIS TIME WE PLANNED TO ACT DECISIVELY, MEETING FORCE WITH OVERWHELMING FORCE, GIVING THE ENEMY NO CHANCE AT A FAIR FIGHT.
PRINCE CHARMING'S COMPLIMENTS! **KILL** THE DRAGON!
ROGER THAT!
THIS TIME WE'D CHEAT.
I MAKE THE RANGE AT TWENTY-TWO HUNDRED AND THIRTY YARDS. WIND FROM SOUTH BY SOUTHWEST AT NINE MILES PER HOUR.
I CONCUR.

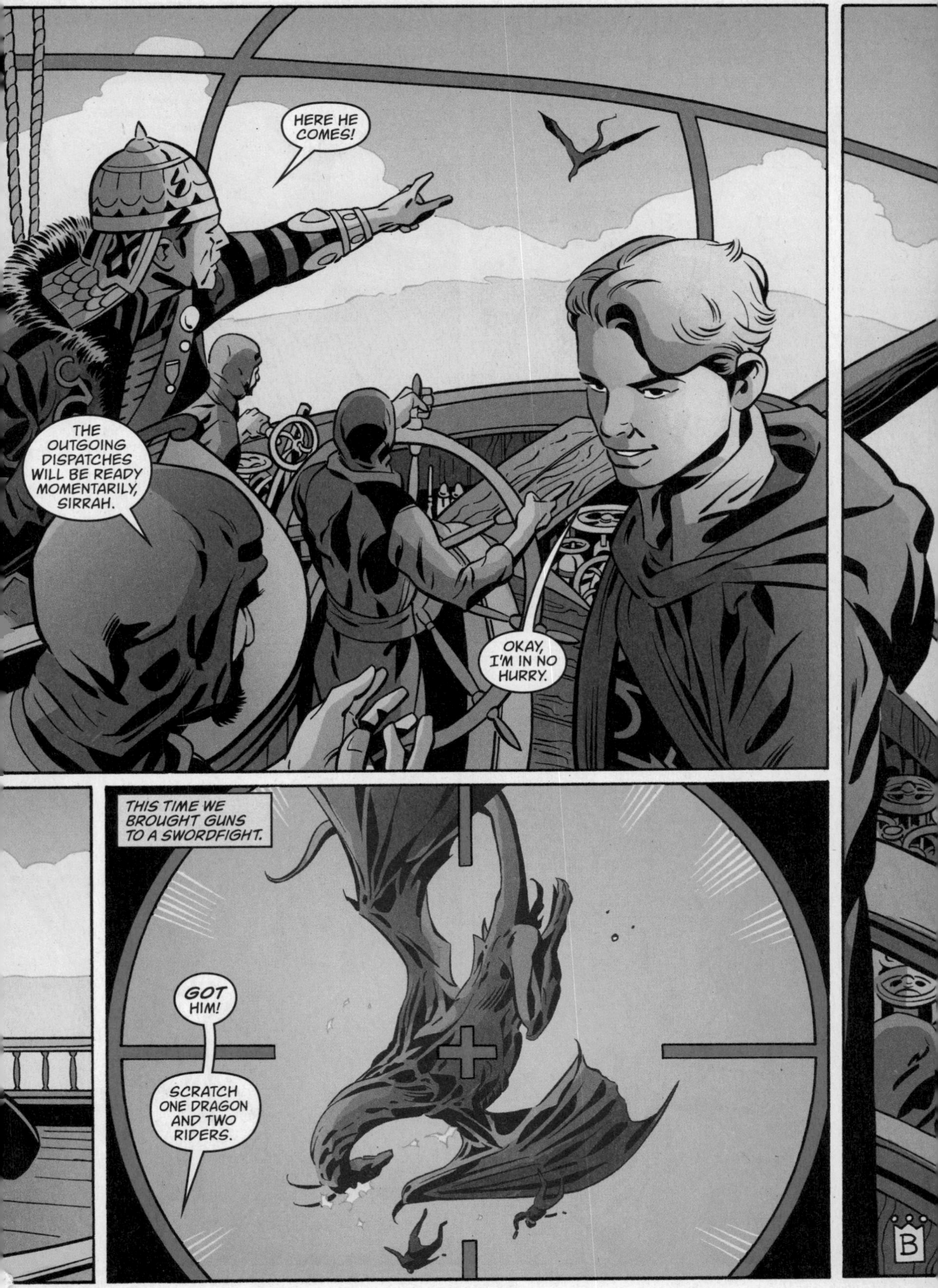
HERE HE COMES!
THE OUTGOING DISPATCHES WILL BE READY MOMENTARILY, SIRRAH.
OKAY, I'M IN NO HURRY.
THIS TIME WE BROUGHT GUNS TO A SWORDFIGHT.
GOT HIM!
SCRATCH ONE DRAGON AND TWO RIDERS.

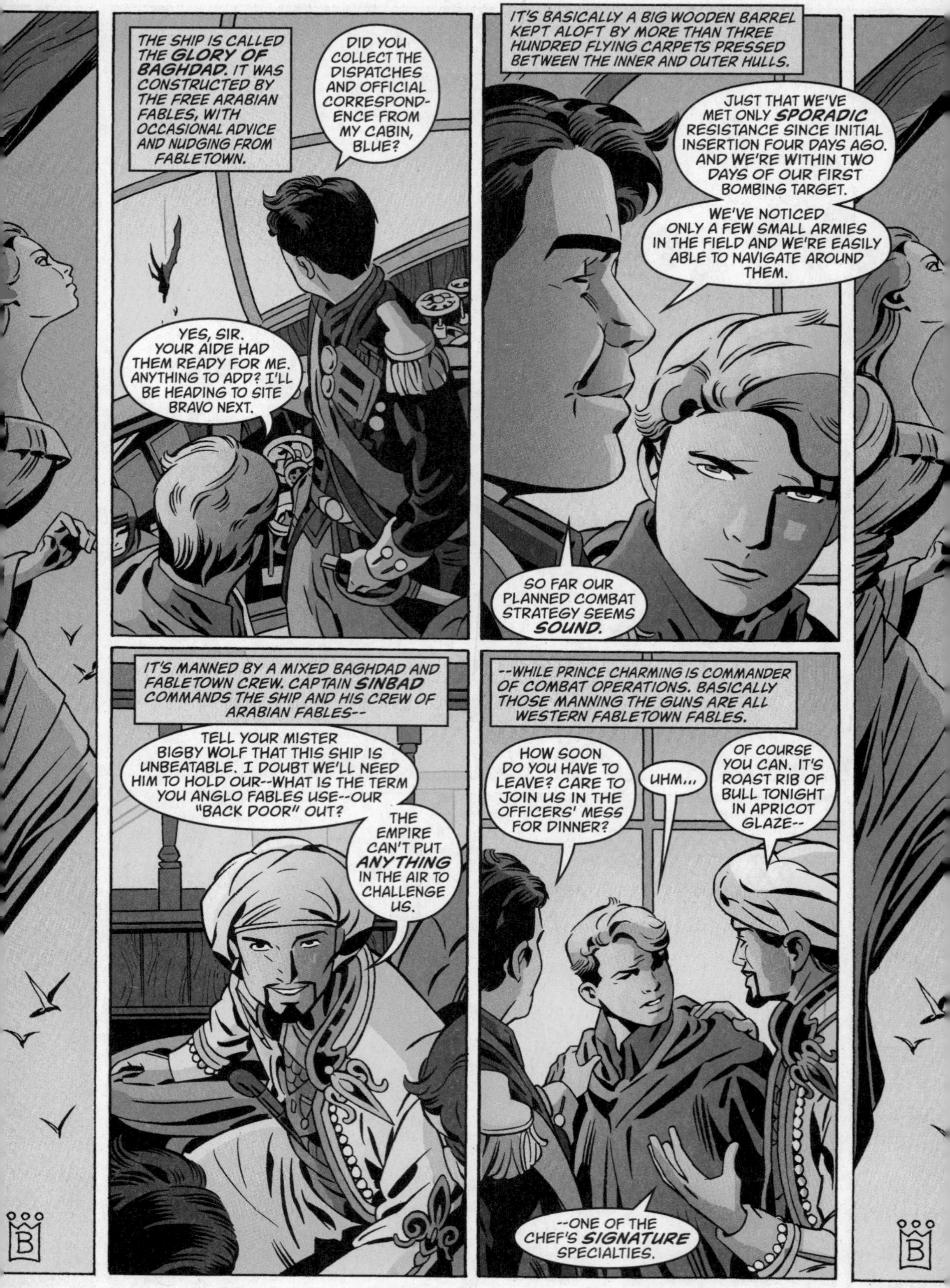
THE SHIP IS CALLED THE GLORY OF BAGHDAD. IT WAS CONSTRUCTED BY THE FREE ARABIAN FABLES, WITH OCCASIONAL ADVICE AND NUDGING FROM FABLETOWN.
DID YOU COLLECT THE DISPATCHES AND OFFICIAL CORRESPONDENCE FROM MY CABIN, BLUE?
YES, SIR. YOUR AIDE HAD THEM READY FOR ME. ANYTHING TO ADD? I'LL BE HEADING TO SITE BRAVO NEXT.
IT'S BASICALLY A BIG WOODEN BARREL KEPT ALOFT BY MORE THAN THREE HUNDRED FLYING CARPETS PRESSED BETWEEN THE INNER AND OUTER HULLS.
JUST THAT WE'VE MET ONLY SPORADIC RESISTANCE SINCE INITIAL INSERTION FOUR DAYS AGO. AND WE'RE WITHIN TWO DAYS OF OUR FIRST BOMBING TARGET.
WE'VE NOTICED ONLY A FEW SMALL ARMIES IN THE FIELD AND WE'RE EASILY ABLE TO NAVIGATE AROUND THEM.
SO FAR OUR PLANNED COMBAT STRATEGY SEEMS SOUND.
IT'S MANNED BY A MIXED BAGHDAD AND FABLETOWN CREW. CAPTAIN SINBAD COMMANDS THE SHIP AND HIS CREW OF ARABIAN FABLES--
TELL YOUR MISTER BIGBY WOLF THAT THIS SHIP IS UNBEATABLE. I DOUBT WE'LL NEED HIM TO HOLD OUR--WHAT IS THE TERM YOU ANGLO FABLES USE--OUR "BACK DOOR" OUT?
THE EMPIRE CAN'T PUT ANYTHING IN THE AIR TO CHALLENGE US.
--WHILE PRINCE CHARMING IS COMMANDER OF COMBAT OPERATIONS. BASICALLY THOSE MANNING THE GUNS ARE ALL WESTERN FABLETOWN FABLES.
HOW SOON DO YOU HAVE TO LEAVE? CARE TO JOIN US IN THE OFFICERS' MESS FOR DINNER?
UHM...
OF COURSE YOU CAN. IT'S ROAST RIB OF BULL TONIGHT IN APRICOT GLAZE--
--ONE OF THE CHEF'S SIGNATURE SPECIALTIES.

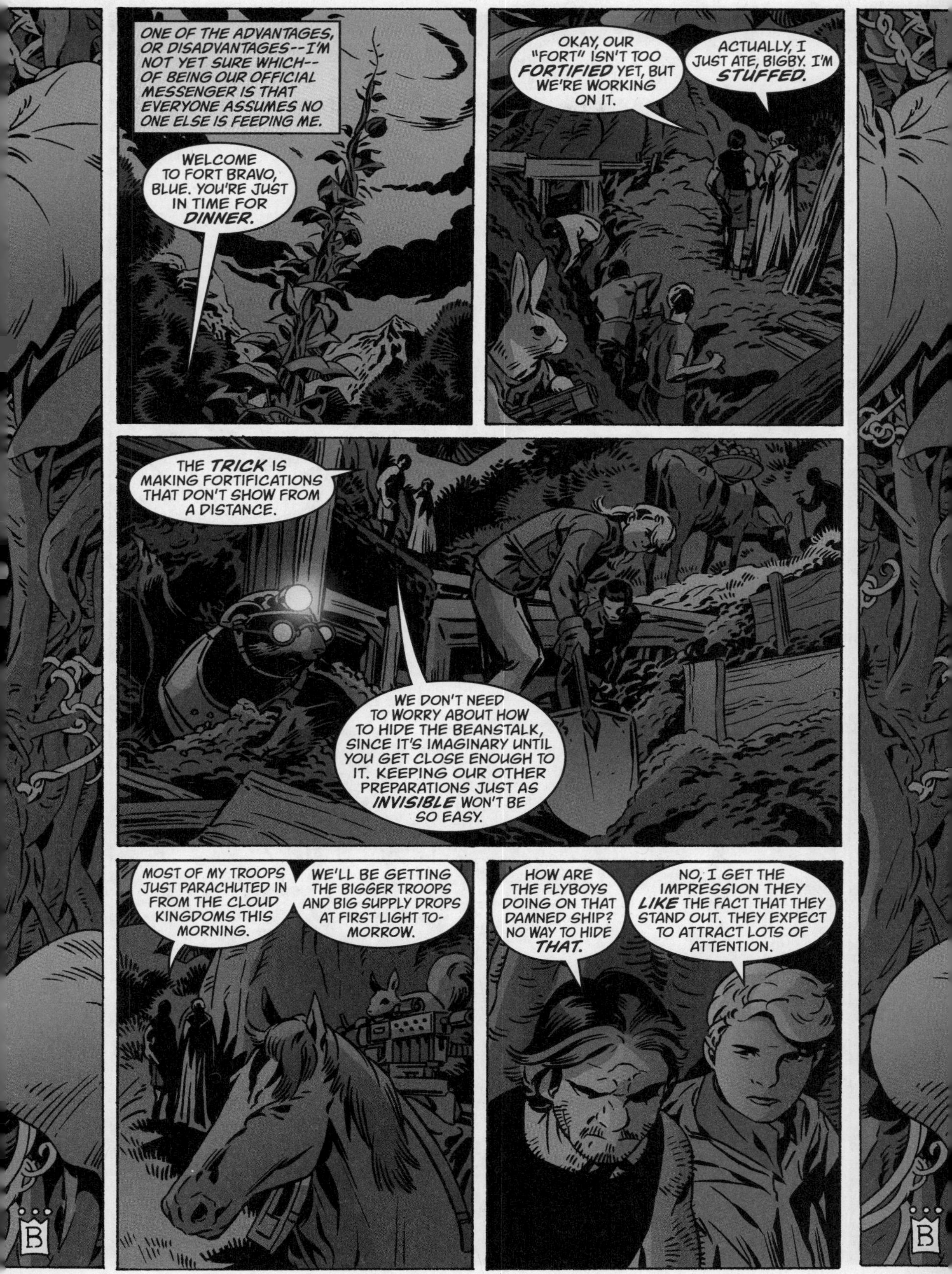
ONE OF THE ADVANTAGES, OR DISADVANTAGES--I'M NOT YET SURE WHICH--OF BEING OUR OFFICIAL MESSENGER IS THAT EVERYONE ASSUMES NO ONE ELSE IS FEEDING ME.
WELCOME TO FORT BRAVO, BLUE. YOU'RE JUST IN TIME FOR DINNER.
OKAY, OUR "FORT" ISN'T TOO FORTIFIED YET, BUT WE'RE WORKING ON IT.
ACTUALLY, I JUST ATE, BIGBY. I'M STUFFED.
THE TRICK IS MAKING FORTIFICATIONS THAT DON'T SHOW FROM A DISTANCE.
WE DON'T NEED TO WORRY ABOUT HOW TO HIDE THE BEANSTALK, SINCE IT'S IMAGINARY UNTIL YOU GET CLOSE ENOUGH TO IT. KEEPING OUR OTHER PREPARATIONS JUST AS INVISIBLE WON'T BE SO EASY.
MOST OF MY TROOPS JUST PARACHUTED IN FROM THE CLOUD KINGDOMS THIS MORNING.
WE'LL BE GETTING THE BIGGER TROOPS AND BIG SUPPLY DROPS AT FIRST LIGHT TO-MORROW.
HOW ARE THE FLYBOYS DOING ON THAT DAMNED SHIP? NO WAY TO HIDE THAT.
NO, I GET THE IMPRESSION THEY LIKE THE FACT THAT THEY STAND OUT. THEY EXPECT TO ATTRACT LOTS OF ATTENTION.

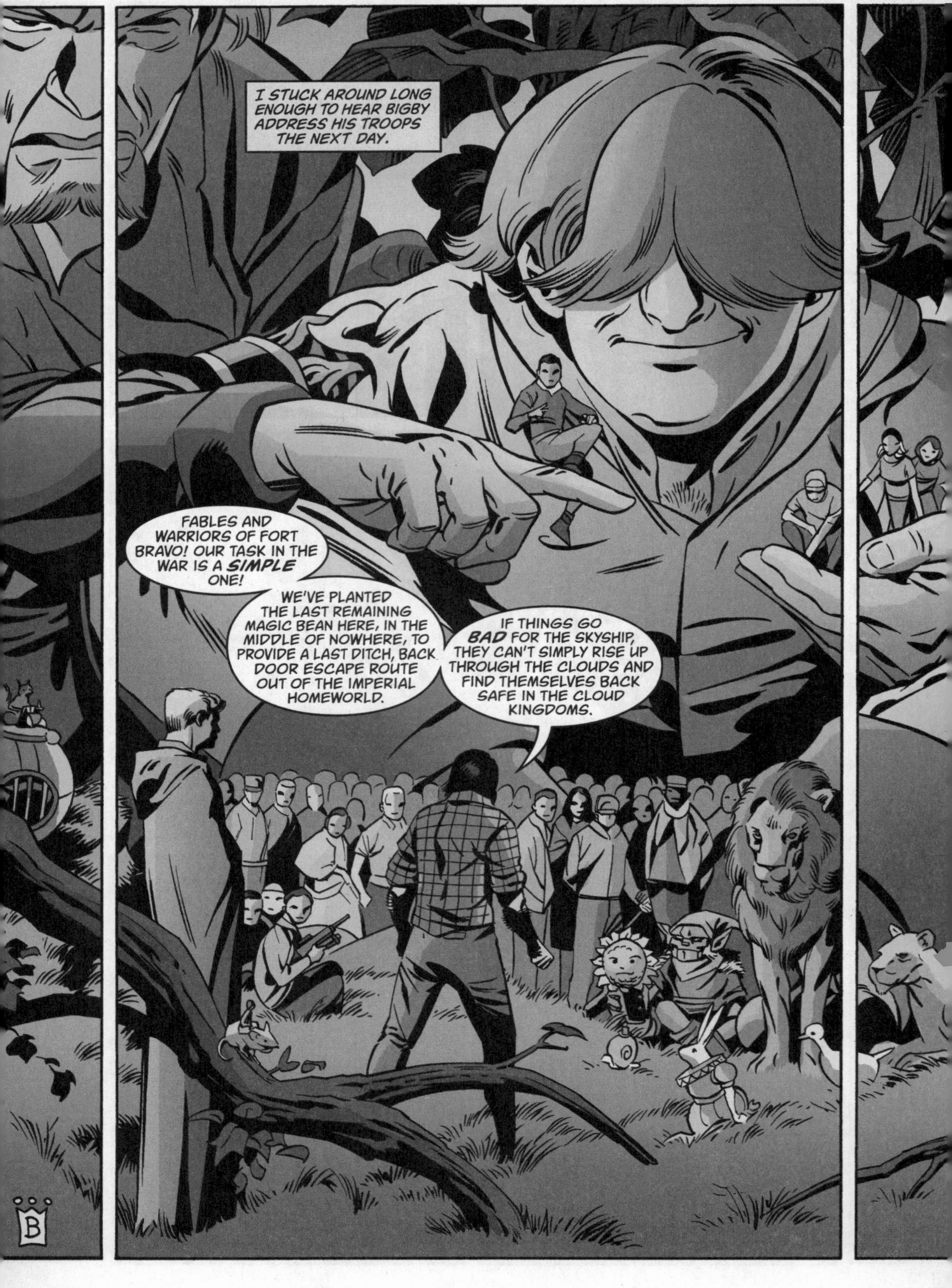
I STUCK AROUND LONG ENOUGH TO HEAR BIGBY ADDRESS HIS TROOPS THE NEXT DAY.
FABLES AND WARRIORS OF FORT BRAVO! OUR TASK IN THE WAR IS A *SIMPLE* ONE!
WE'VE PLANTED THE LAST REMAINING MAGIC BEAN HERE, IN THE MIDDLE OF NOWHERE, TO PROVIDE A LAST DITCH, BACK DOOR ESCAPE ROUTE OUT OF THE IMPERIAL HOMEWORLD.
IF THINGS GO *BAD* FOR THE SKYSHIP, THEY CAN'T SIMPLY RISE UP THROUGH THE CLOUDS AND FIND THEMSELVES BACK SAFE IN THE CLOUD KINGDOMS.

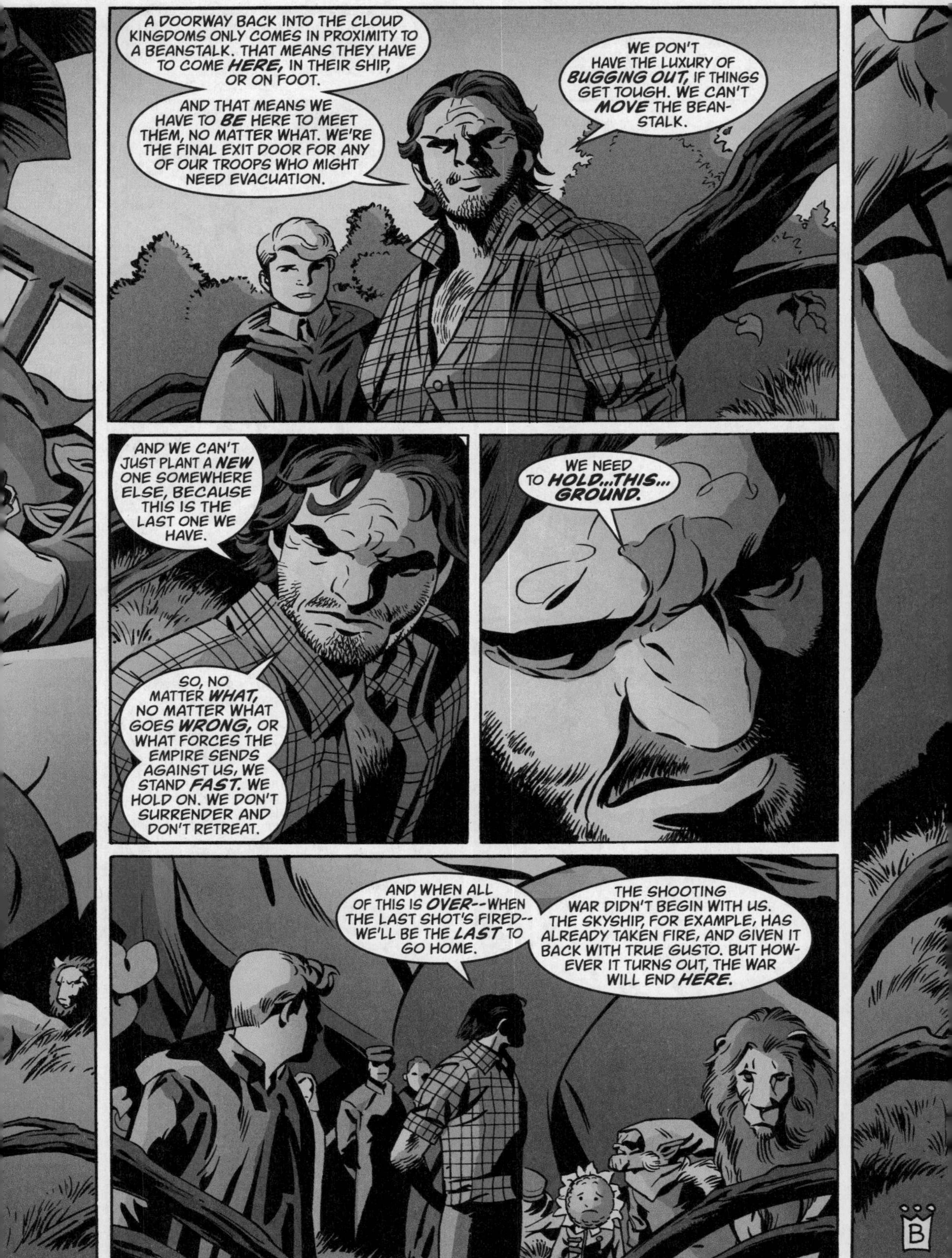
A DOORWAY BACK INTO THE CLOUD KINGDOMS ONLY COMES IN PROXIMITY TO A BEANSTALK. THAT MEANS THEY HAVE TO COME *HERE,* IN THEIR SHIP, OR ON FOOT.
AND THAT MEANS WE HAVE TO *BE* HERE TO MEET THEM, NO MATTER WHAT. WE'RE THE FINAL EXIT DOOR FOR ANY OF OUR TROOPS WHO MIGHT NEED EVACUATION.
WE DON'T HAVE THE LUXURY OF *BUGGING OUT,* IF THINGS GET TOUGH. WE CAN'T *MOVE* THE BEAN-STALK.
AND WE CAN'T JUST PLANT A *NEW* ONE SOMEWHERE ELSE, BECAUSE THIS IS THE LAST ONE WE HAVE.
SO, NO MATTER *WHAT,* NO MATTER WHAT GOES *WRONG,* OR WHAT FORCES THE EMPIRE SENDS AGAINST US, WE STAND *FAST.* WE HOLD ON. WE DON'T SURRENDER AND DON'T RETREAT.
WE NEED TO *HOLD...THIS... GROUND.*
AND WHEN ALL OF THIS IS *OVER*--WHEN THE LAST SHOT'S FIRED--WE'LL BE THE *LAST* TO GO HOME.
THE SHOOTING WAR DIDN'T BEGIN WITH US. THE SKYSHIP, FOR EXAMPLE, HAS ALREADY TAKEN FIRE, AND GIVEN IT BACK WITH TRUE GUSTO. BUT HOW-EVER IT TURNS OUT, THE WAR WILL END *HERE.*

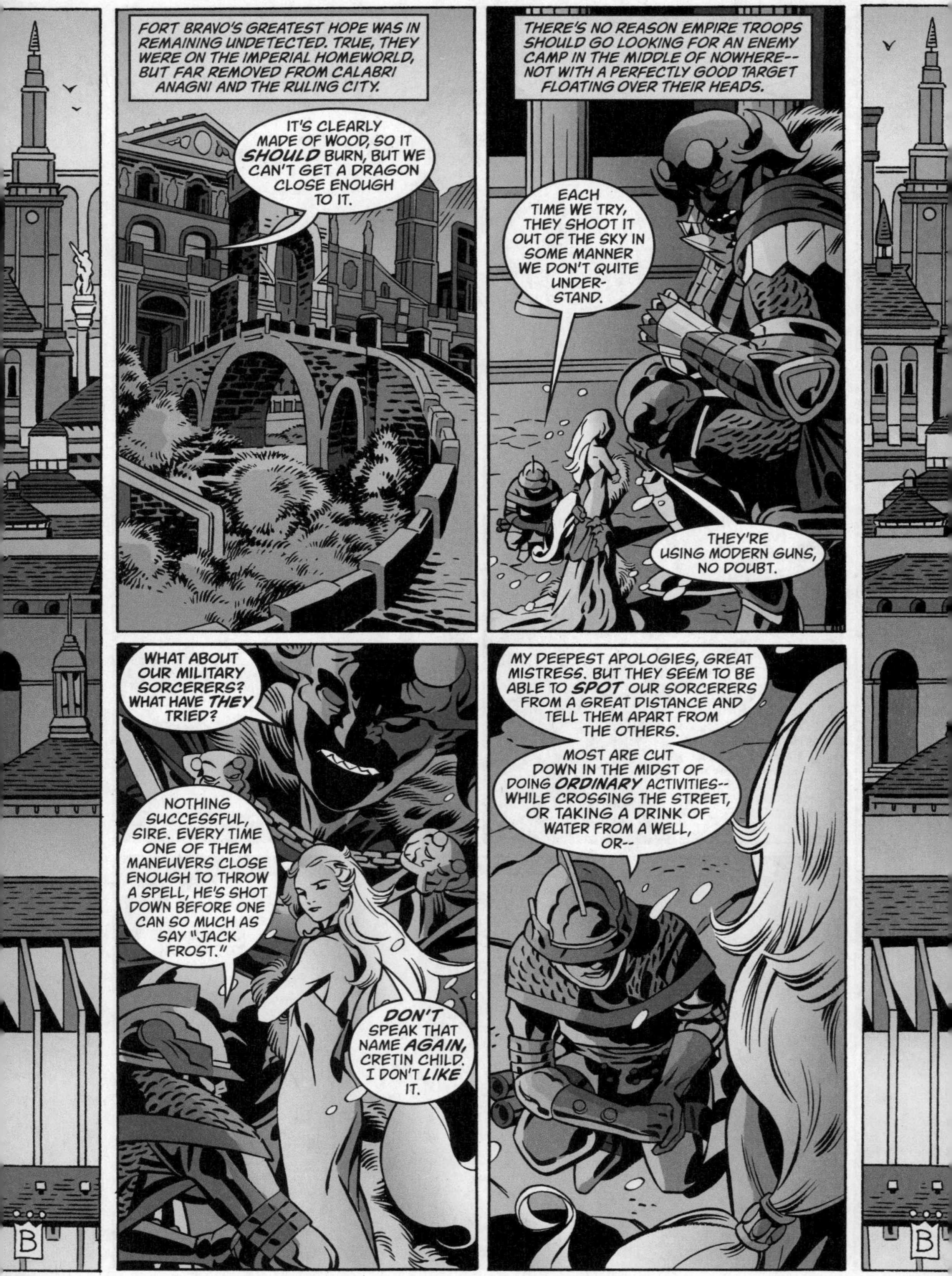
FORT BRAVO'S GREATEST HOPE WAS IN REMAINING UNDETECTED. TRUE, THEY WERE ON THE IMPERIAL HOMEWORLD, BUT FAR REMOVED FROM CALABRI ANAGNI AND THE RULING CITY.
IT'S CLEARLY MADE OF WOOD, SO IT SHOULD BURN, BUT WE CAN'T GET A DRAGON CLOSE ENOUGH TO IT.
THERE'S NO REASON EMPIRE TROOPS SHOULD GO LOOKING FOR AN ENEMY CAMP IN THE MIDDLE OF NOWHERE--NOT WITH A PERFECTLY GOOD TARGET FLOATING OVER THEIR HEADS.
EACH TIME WE TRY, THEY SHOOT IT OUT OF THE SKY IN SOME MANNER WE DON'T QUITE UNDER-STAND.
THEY'RE USING MODERN GUNS, NO DOUBT.
WHAT ABOUT OUR MILITARY SORCERERS? WHAT HAVE THEY TRIED?
NOTHING SUCCESSFUL, SIRE. EVERY TIME ONE OF THEM MANEUVERS CLOSE ENOUGH TO THROW A SPELL, HE'S SHOT DOWN BEFORE ONE CAN SO MUCH AS SAY "JACK FROST."
DON'T SPEAK THAT NAME AGAIN, CRETIN CHILD. I DON'T LIKE IT.
MY DEEPEST APOLOGIES, GREAT MISTRESS. BUT THEY SEEM TO BE ABLE TO SPOT OUR SORCERERS FROM A GREAT DISTANCE AND TELL THEM APART FROM THE OTHERS.
MOST ARE CUT DOWN IN THE MIDST OF DOING ORDINARY ACTIVITIES--WHILE CROSSING THE STREET, OR TAKING A DRINK OF WATER FROM A WELL, OR--

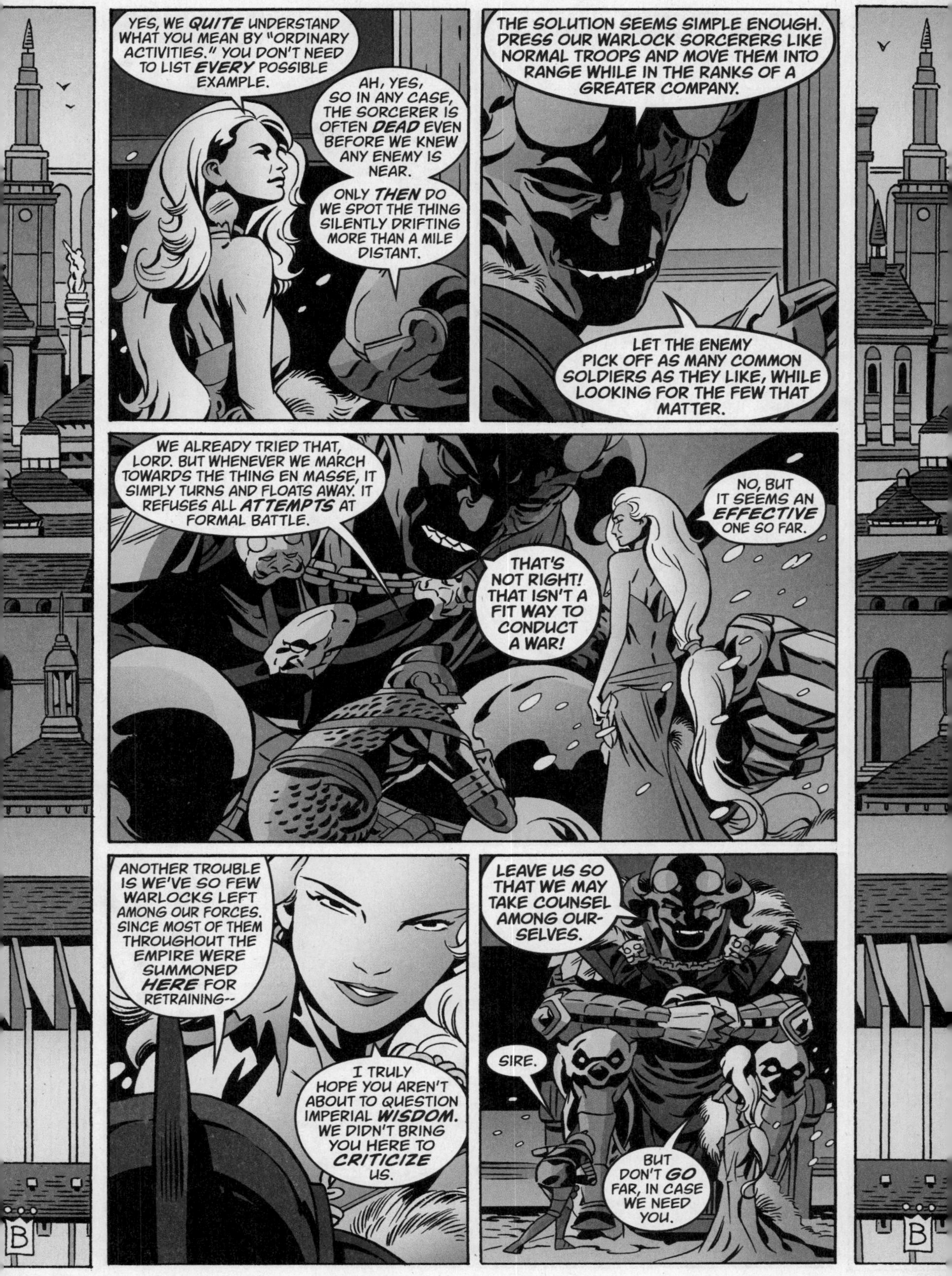
YES, WE QUITE UNDERSTAND WHAT YOU MEAN BY "ORDINARY ACTIVITIES." YOU DON'T NEED TO LIST EVERY POSSIBLE EXAMPLE.
AH, YES, SO IN ANY CASE, THE SORCERER IS OFTEN DEAD EVEN BEFORE WE KNEW ANY ENEMY IS NEAR.
ONLY THEN DO WE SPOT THE THING SILENTLY DRIFTING MORE THAN A MILE DISTANT.
THE SOLUTION SEEMS SIMPLE ENOUGH. DRESS OUR WARLOCK SORCERERS LIKE NORMAL TROOPS AND MOVE THEM INTO RANGE WHILE IN THE RANKS OF A GREATER COMPANY.
LET THE ENEMY PICK OFF AS MANY COMMON SOLDIERS AS THEY LIKE, WHILE LOOKING FOR THE FEW THAT MATTER.
WE ALREADY TRIED THAT, LORD. BUT WHENEVER WE MARCH TOWARDS THE THING EN MASSE, IT SIMPLY TURNS AND FLOATS AWAY. IT REFUSES ALL ATTEMPTS AT FORMAL BATTLE.
THAT'S NOT RIGHT! THAT ISN'T A FIT WAY TO CONDUCT A WAR!
NO, BUT IT SEEMS AN EFFECTIVE ONE SO FAR.
ANOTHER TROUBLE IS WE'VE SO FEW WARLOCKS LEFT AMONG OUR FORCES. SINCE MOST OF THEM THROUGHOUT THE EMPIRE WERE SUMMONED HERE FOR RETRAINING--
I TRULY HOPE YOU AREN'T ABOUT TO QUESTION IMPERIAL WISDOM. WE DIDN'T BRING YOU HERE TO CRITICIZE US.
LEAVE US SO THAT WE MAY TAKE COUNSEL AMONG OUR-SELVES.
SIRE.
BUT DON'T GO FAR, IN CASE WE NEED YOU.

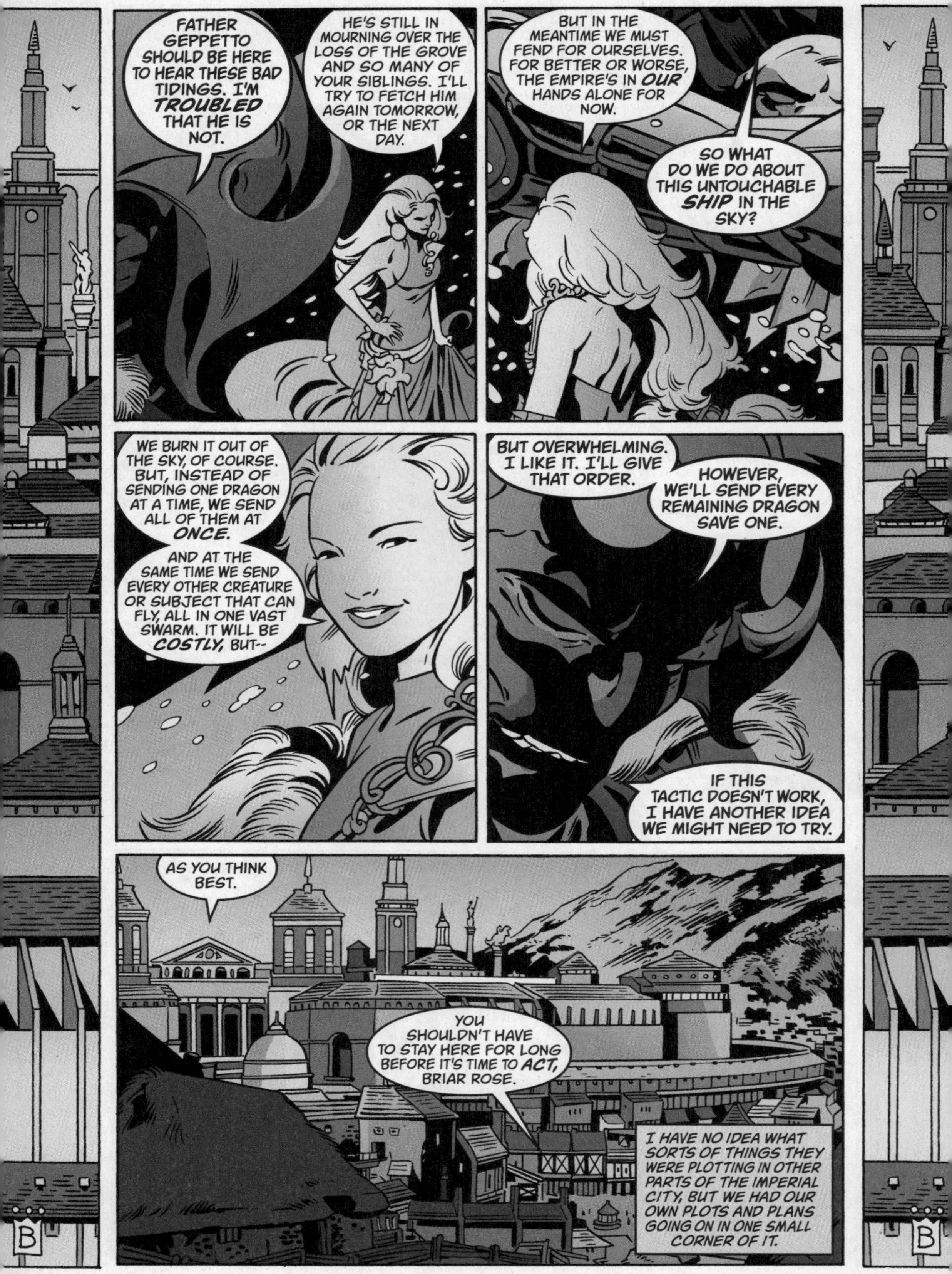
FATHER GEPPETTO SHOULD BE HERE TO HEAR THESE BAD TIDINGS. I'M TROUBLED THAT HE IS NOT.
HE'S STILL IN MOURNING OVER THE LOSS OF THE GROVE AND SO MANY OF YOUR SIBLINGS. I'LL TRY TO FETCH HIM AGAIN TOMORROW, OR THE NEXT DAY.
BUT IN THE MEANTIME WE MUST FEND FOR OURSELVES. FOR BETTER OR WORSE, THE EMPIRE'S IN OUR HANDS ALONE FOR NOW.
SO WHAT DO WE DO ABOUT THIS UNTOUCHABLE SHIP IN THE SKY?
WE BURN IT OUT OF THE SKY, OF COURSE. BUT, INSTEAD OF SENDING ONE DRAGON AT A TIME, WE SEND ALL OF THEM AT ONCE.
AND AT THE SAME TIME WE SEND EVERY OTHER CREATURE OR SUBJECT THAT CAN FLY, ALL IN ONE VAST SWARM. IT WILL BE COSTLY, BUT--
BUT OVERWHELMING. I LIKE IT. I'LL GIVE THAT ORDER.
HOWEVER, WE'LL SEND EVERY REMAINING DRAGON SAVE ONE.
IF THIS TACTIC DOESN'T WORK, I HAVE ANOTHER IDEA WE MIGHT NEED TO TRY.
AS YOU THINK BEST.
YOU SHOULDN'T HAVE TO STAY HERE FOR LONG BEFORE IT'S TIME TO ACT, BRIAR ROSE.
I HAVE NO IDEA WHAT SORTS OF THINGS THEY WERE PLOTTING IN OTHER PARTS OF THE IMPERIAL CITY, BUT WE HAD OUR OWN PLOTS AND PLANS GOING ON IN ONE SMALL CORNER OF IT.

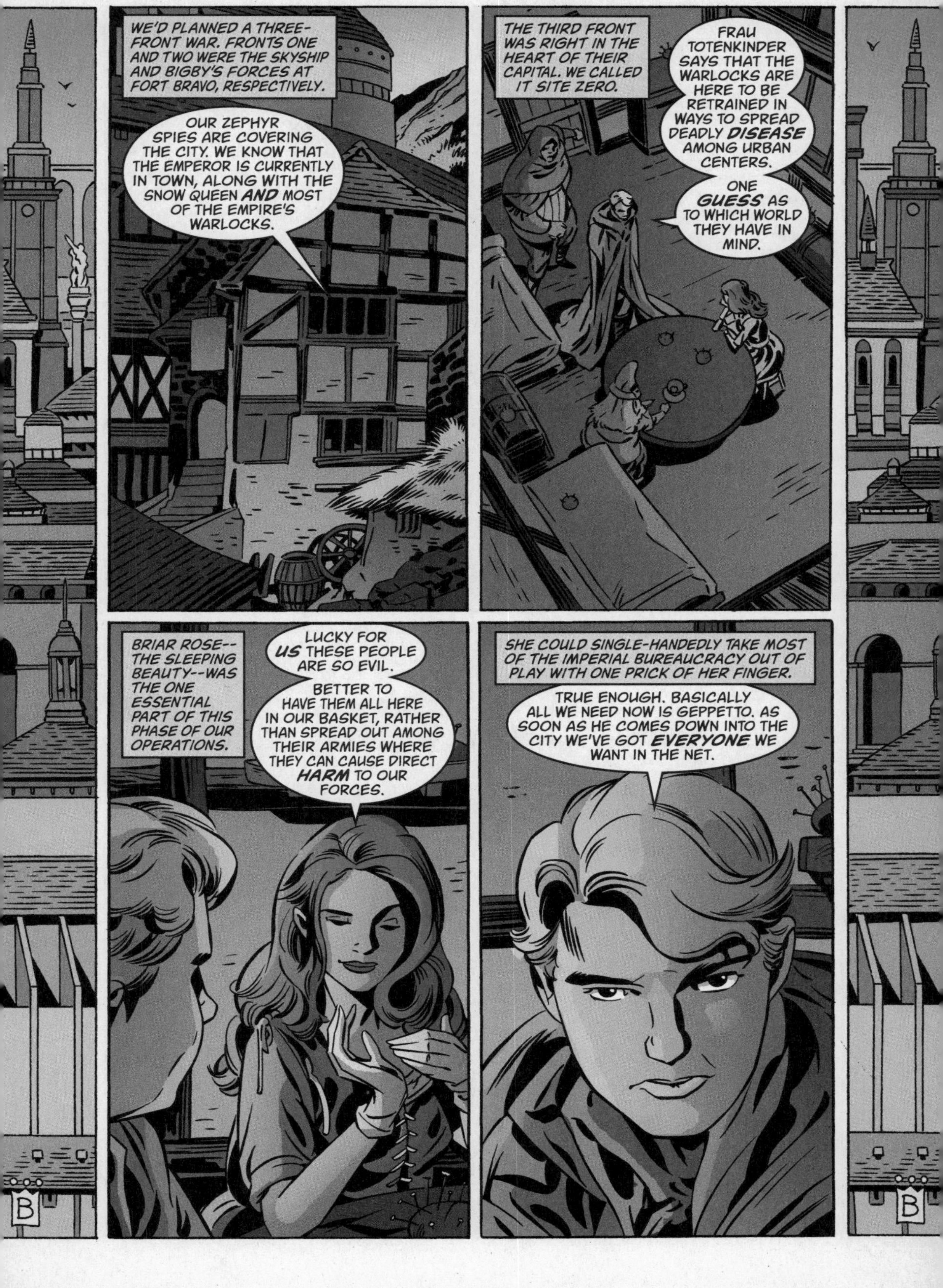

WE'D PLANNED A THREE-FRONT WAR. FRONTS ONE AND TWO WERE THE SKYSHIP AND BIGBY'S FORCES AT FORT BRAVO, RESPECTIVELY.
OUR ZEPHYR SPIES ARE COVERING THE CITY. WE KNOW THAT THE EMPEROR IS CURRENTLY IN TOWN, ALONG WITH THE SNOW QUEEN AND MOST OF THE EMPIRE'S WARLOCKS.
THE THIRD FRONT WAS RIGHT IN THE HEART OF THEIR CAPITAL. WE CALLED IT SITE ZERO.
FRAU TOTENKINDER SAYS THAT THE WARLOCKS ARE HERE TO BE RETRAINED IN WAYS TO SPREAD DEADLY DISEASE AMONG URBAN CENTERS.
ONE GUESS AS TO WHICH WORLD THEY HAVE IN MIND.
BRIAR ROSE--THE SLEEPING BEAUTY--WAS THE ONE ESSENTIAL PART OF THIS PHASE OF OUR OPERATIONS.
LUCKY FOR US THESE PEOPLE ARE SO EVIL.
BETTER TO HAVE THEM ALL HERE IN OUR BASKET, RATHER THAN SPREAD OUT AMONG THEIR ARMIES WHERE THEY CAN CAUSE DIRECT HARM TO OUR FORCES.
SHE COULD SINGLE-HANDEDLY TAKE MOST OF THE IMPERIAL BUREAUCRACY OUT OF PLAY WITH ONE PRICK OF HER FINGER.
TRUE ENOUGH. BASICALLY ALL WE NEED NOW IS GEPPETTO. AS SOON AS HE COMES DOWN INTO THE CITY WE'VE GOT EVERYONE WE WANT IN THE NET.

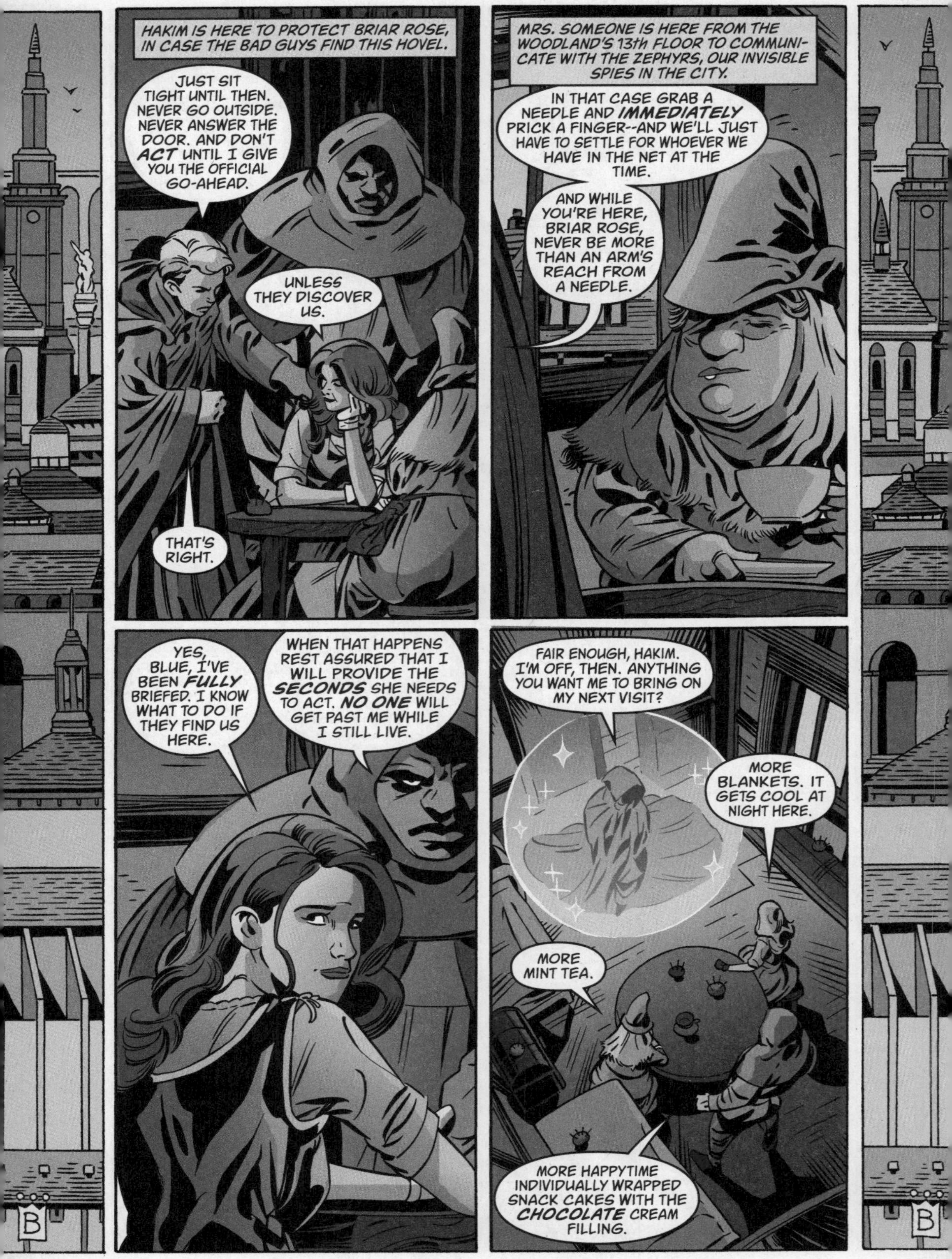
HAKIM IS HERE TO PROTECT BRIAR ROSE, IN CASE THE BAD GUYS FIND THIS HOVEL.
JUST SIT TIGHT UNTIL THEN. NEVER GO OUTSIDE. NEVER ANSWER THE DOOR. AND DON'T ACT UNTIL I GIVE YOU THE OFFICIAL GO-AHEAD.
UNLESS THEY DISCOVER US.
THAT'S RIGHT.
MRS. SOMEONE IS HERE FROM THE WOODLAND'S 13th FLOOR TO COMMUNICATE WITH THE ZEPHYRS, OUR INVISIBLE SPIES IN THE CITY.
IN THAT CASE GRAB A NEEDLE AND IMMEDIATELY PRICK A FINGER--AND WE'LL JUST HAVE TO SETTLE FOR WHOEVER WE HAVE IN THE NET AT THE TIME.
AND WHILE YOU'RE HERE, BRIAR ROSE, NEVER BE MORE THAN AN ARM'S REACH FROM A NEEDLE.
YES, BLUE, I'VE BEEN FULLY BRIEFED. I KNOW WHAT TO DO IF THEY FIND US HERE.
WHEN THAT HAPPENS REST ASSURED THAT I WILL PROVIDE THE SECONDS SHE NEEDS TO ACT. NO ONE WILL GET PAST ME WHILE I STILL LIVE.
FAIR ENOUGH, HAKIM. I'M OFF, THEN. ANYTHING YOU WANT ME TO BRING ON MY NEXT VISIT?
MORE BLANKETS. IT GETS COOL AT NIGHT HERE.
MORE MINT TEA.
MORE HAPPYTIME INDIVIDUALLY WRAPPED SNACK CAKES WITH THE CHOCOLATE CREAM FILLING.

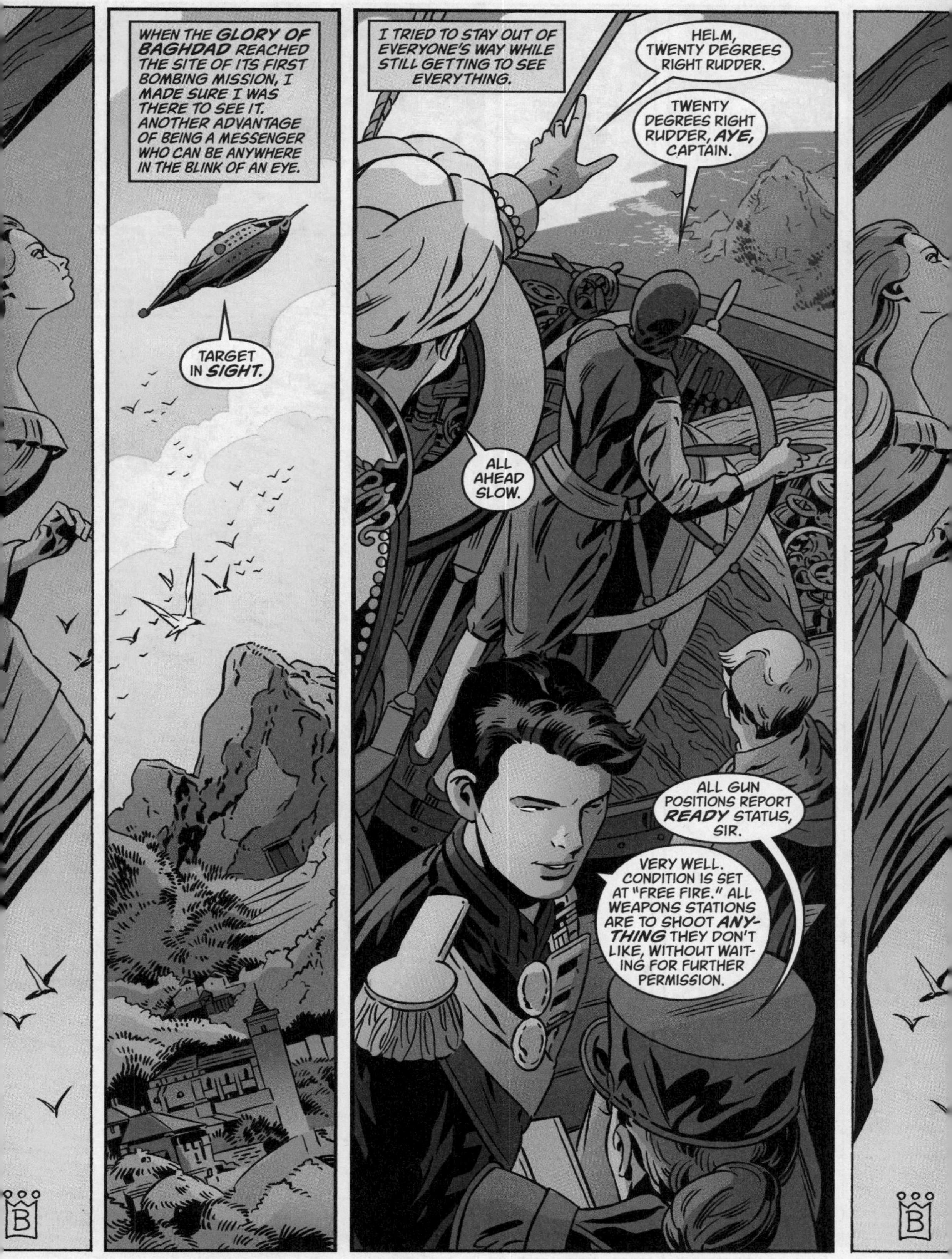
WHEN THE GLORY OF BAGHDAD REACHED THE SITE OF ITS FIRST BOMBING MISSION, I MADE SURE I WAS THERE TO SEE IT. ANOTHER ADVANTAGE OF BEING A MESSENGER WHO CAN BE ANYWHERE IN THE BLINK OF AN EYE.
TARGET IN SIGHT.
I TRIED TO STAY OUT OF EVERYONE'S WAY WHILE STILL GETTING TO SEE EVERYTHING.
HELM, TWENTY DEGREES RIGHT RUDDER.
TWENTY DEGREES RIGHT RUDDER, AYE, CAPTAIN.
ALL AHEAD SLOW.
ALL GUN POSITIONS REPORT READY STATUS, SIR.
VERY WELL. CONDITION IS SET AT "FREE FIRE." ALL WEAPONS STATIONS ARE TO SHOOT ANYTHING THEY DON'T LIKE, WITHOUT WAITING FOR FURTHER PERMISSION.

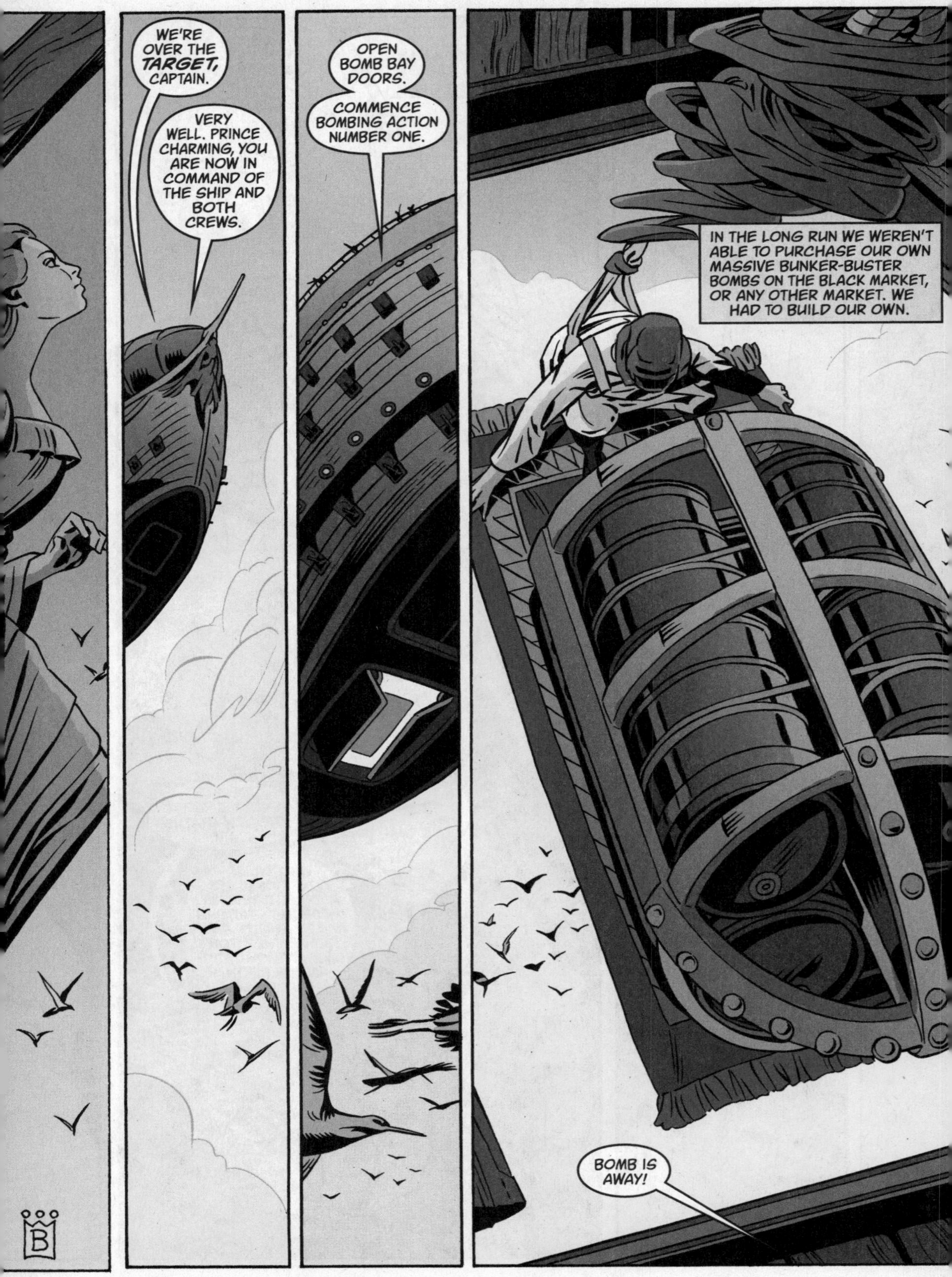
WE'RE OVER THE TARGET, CAPTAIN.
VERY WELL. PRINCE CHARMING, YOU ARE NOW IN COMMAND OF THE SHIP AND BOTH CREWS.
OPEN BOMB BAY DOORS.
COMMENCE BOMBING ACTION NUMBER ONE.
IN THE LONG RUN WE WEREN'T ABLE TO PURCHASE OUR OWN MASSIVE BUNKER-BUSTER BOMBS ON THE BLACK MARKET, OR ANY OTHER MARKET. WE HAD TO BUILD OUR OWN.
BOMB IS AWAY!

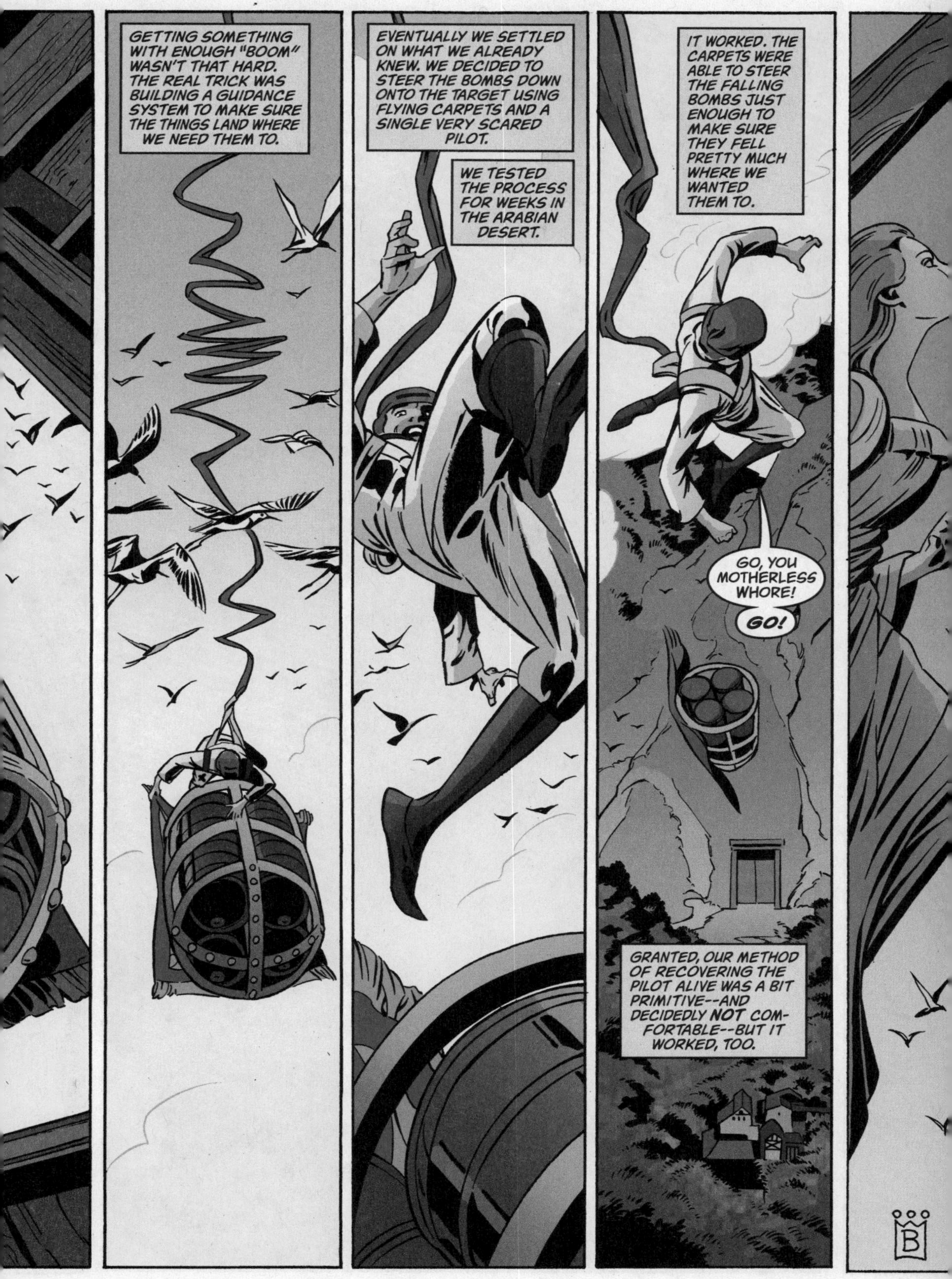
GETTING SOMETHING WITH ENOUGH "BOOM" WASN'T THAT HARD. THE REAL TRICK WAS BUILDING A GUIDANCE SYSTEM TO MAKE SURE THE THINGS LAND WHERE WE NEED THEM TO.
EVENTUALLY WE SETTLED ON WHAT WE ALREADY KNEW. WE DECIDED TO STEER THE BOMBS DOWN ONTO THE TARGET USING FLYING CARPETS AND A SINGLE VERY SCARED PILOT.
WE TESTED THE PROCESS FOR WEEKS IN THE ARABIAN DESERT.
IT WORKED. THE CARPETS WERE ABLE TO STEER THE FALLING BOMBS JUST ENOUGH TO MAKE SURE THEY FELL PRETTY MUCH WHERE WE WANTED THEM TO.
GO, YOU MOTHERLESS WHORE!
GO!
GRANTED, OUR METHOD OF RECOVERING THE PILOT ALIVE WAS A BIT PRIMITIVE--AND DECIDEDLY NOT COM-FORTABLE--BUT IT WORKED, TOO.

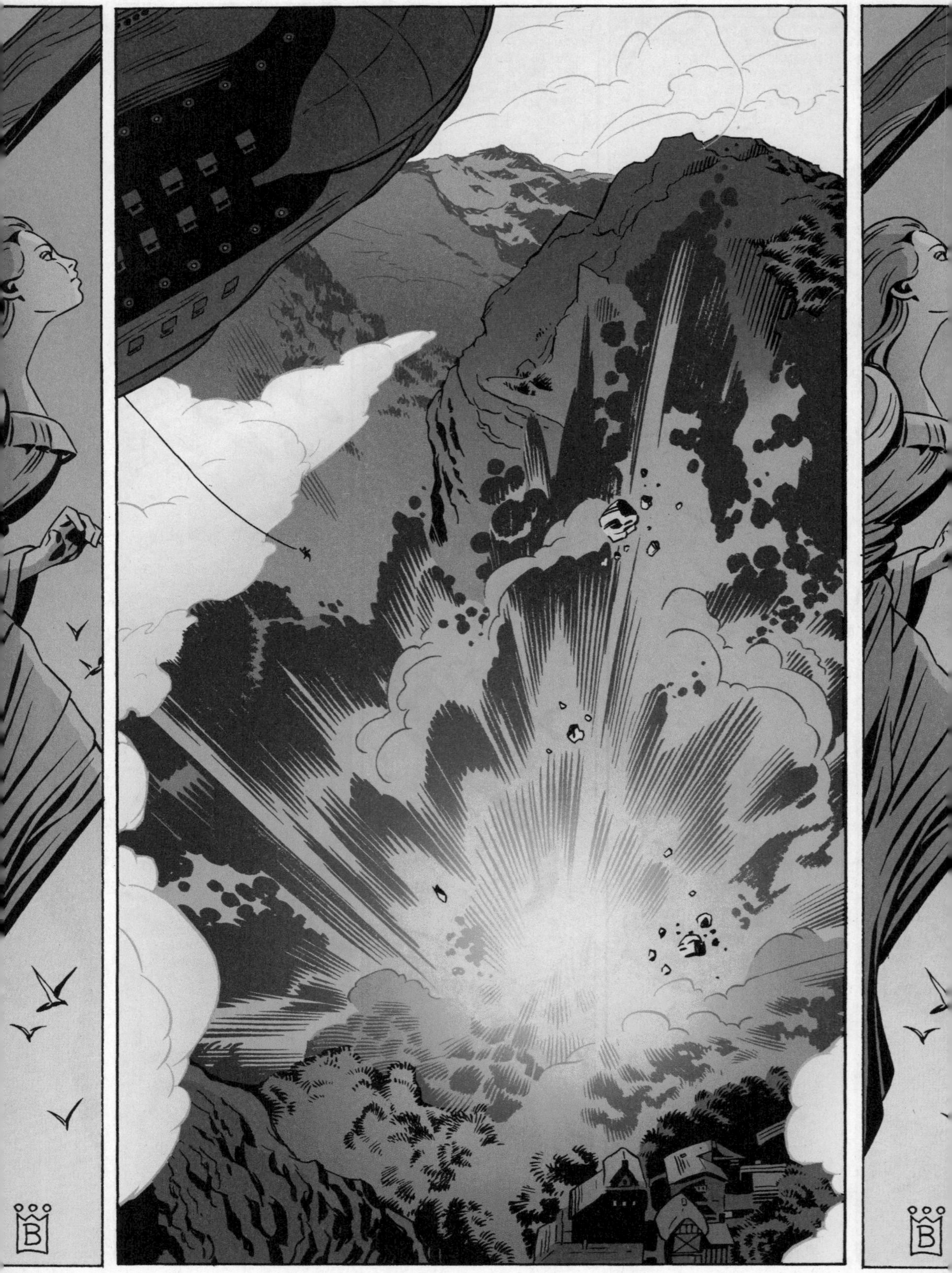

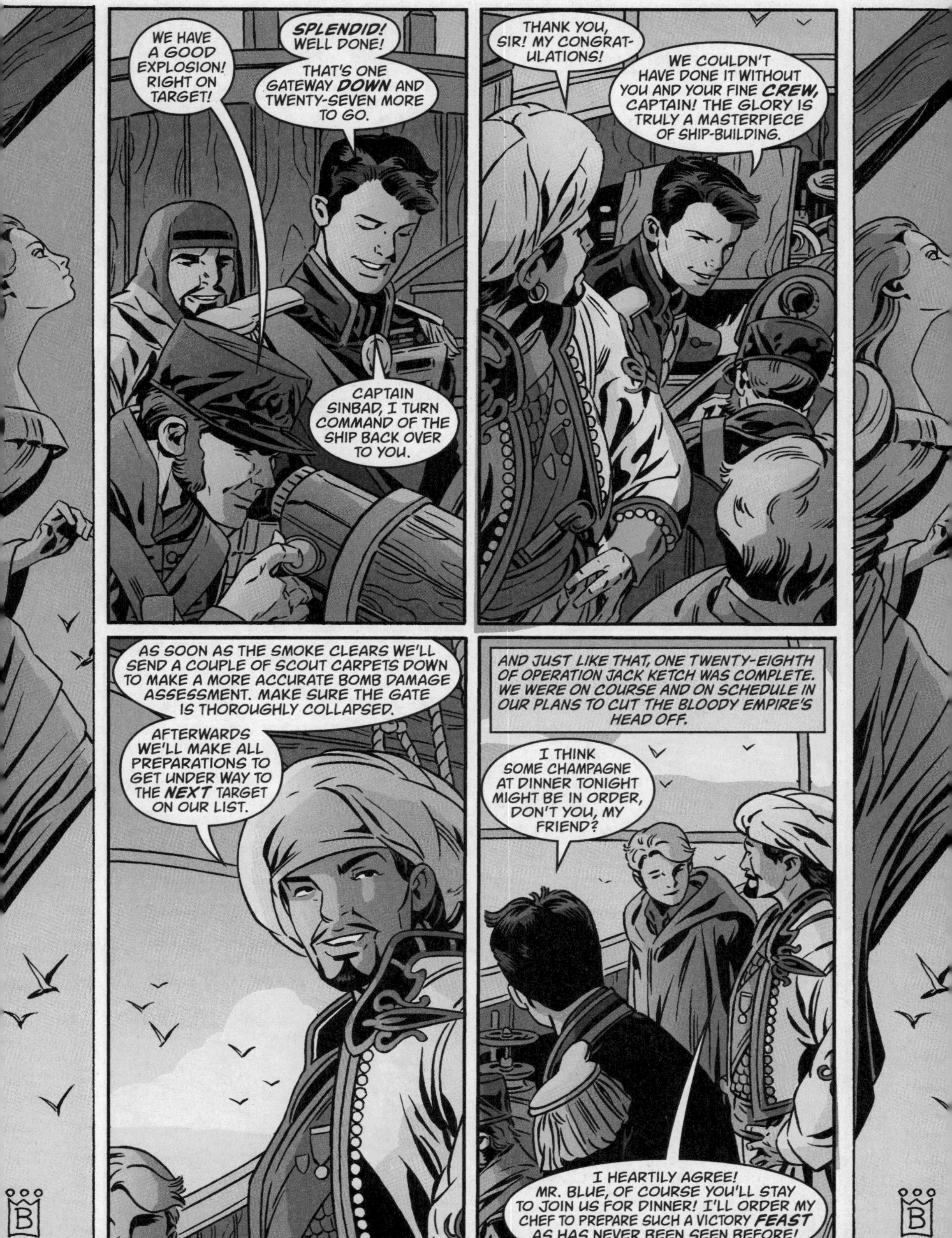
WE HAVE A GOOD EXPLOSION! RIGHT ON TARGET!
SPLENDID! WELL DONE!
THAT'S ONE GATEWAY DOWN AND TWENTY-SEVEN MORE TO GO.
CAPTAIN SINBAD, I TURN COMMAND OF THE SHIP BACK OVER TO YOU.
THANK YOU, SIR! MY CONGRAT-ULATIONS!
WE COULDN'T HAVE DONE IT WITHOUT YOU AND YOUR FINE CREW, CAPTAIN! THE GLORY IS TRULY A MASTERPIECE OF SHIP-BUILDING.
AS SOON AS THE SMOKE CLEARS WE'LL SEND A COUPLE OF SCOUT CARPETS DOWN TO MAKE A MORE ACCURATE BOMB DAMAGE ASSESSMENT. MAKE SURE THE GATE IS THOROUGHLY COLLAPSED.
AFTERWARDS WE'LL MAKE ALL PREPARATIONS TO GET UNDER WAY TO THE NEXT TARGET ON OUR LIST.
AND JUST LIKE THAT, ONE TWENTY-EIGHTH OF OPERATION JACK KETCH WAS COMPLETE. WE WERE ON COURSE AND ON SCHEDULE IN OUR PLANS TO CUT THE BLOODY EMPIRE'S HEAD OFF.
I THINK SOME CHAMPAGNE AT DINNER TONIGHT MIGHT BE IN ORDER, DON'T YOU, MY FRIEND?
I HEARTILY AGREE! MR. BLUE, OF COURSE YOU'LL STAY TO JOIN US FOR DINNER! I'LL ORDER MY CHEF TO PREPARE SUCH A VICTORY FEAST AS HAS NEVER BEEN SEEN BEFORE!

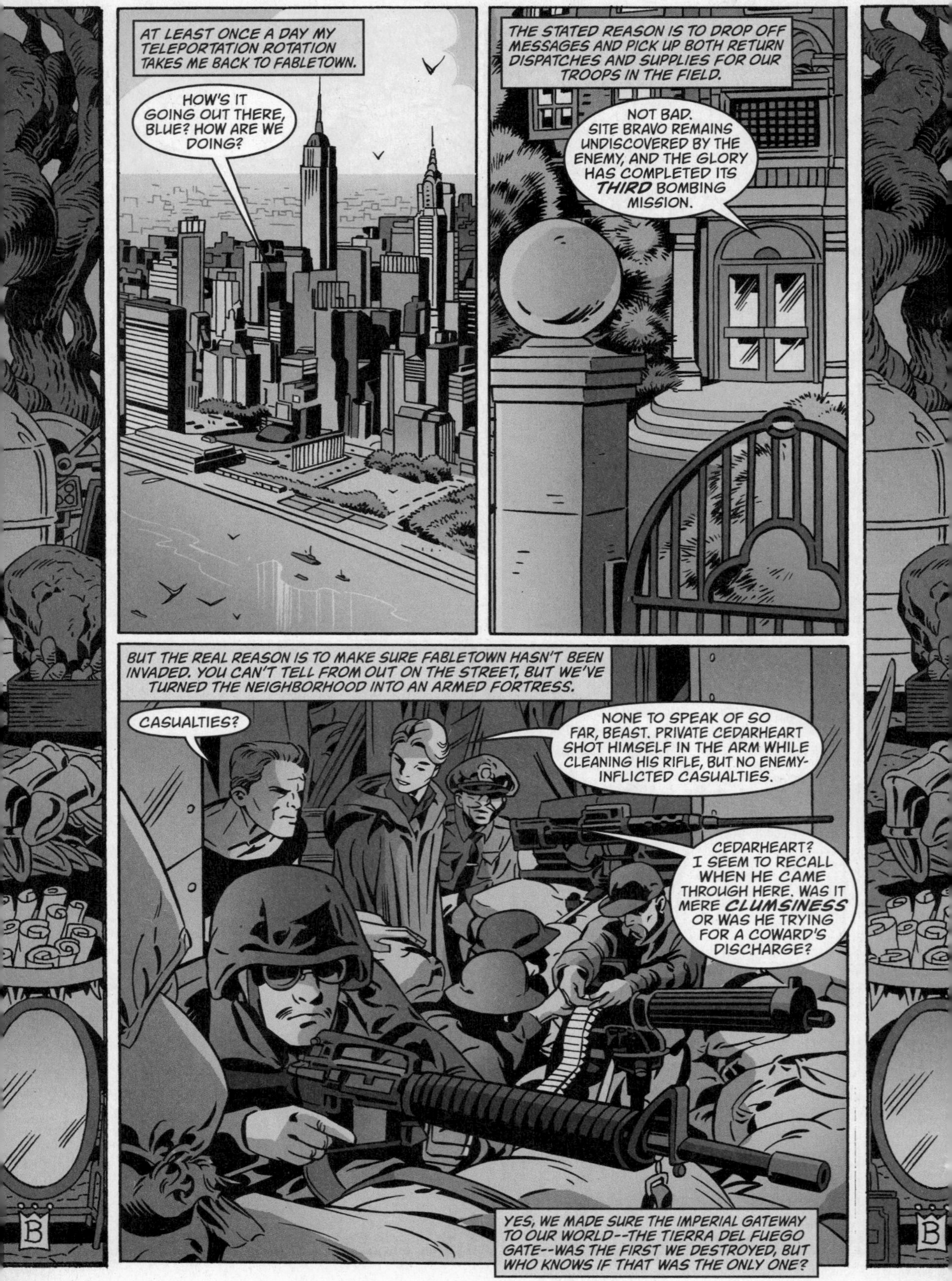

AT LEAST ONCE A DAY MY TELEPORTATION ROTATION TAKES ME BACK TO FABLETOWN.
HOW'S IT GOING OUT THERE, BLUE? HOW ARE WE DOING?
THE STATED REASON IS TO DROP OFF MESSAGES AND PICK UP BOTH RETURN DISPATCHES AND SUPPLIES FOR OUR TROOPS IN THE FIELD.
NOT BAD. SITE BRAVO REMAINS UNDISCOVERED BY THE ENEMY, AND THE GLORY HAS COMPLETED ITS THIRD BOMBING MISSION.
BUT THE REAL REASON IS TO MAKE SURE FABLETOWN HASN'T BEEN INVADED. YOU CAN'T TELL FROM OUT ON THE STREET, BUT WE'VE TURNED THE NEIGHBORHOOD INTO AN ARMED FORTRESS.
CASUALTIES?
NONE TO SPEAK OF SO FAR, BEAST. PRIVATE CEDARHEART SHOT HIMSELF IN THE ARM WHILE CLEANING HIS RIFLE, BUT NO ENEMY-INFLICTED CASUALTIES.
CEDARHEART? I SEEM TO RECALL WHEN HE CAME THROUGH HERE. WAS IT MERE CLUMSINESS OR WAS HE TRYING FOR A COWARD'S DISCHARGE?
YES, WE MADE SURE THE IMPERIAL GATEWAY TO OUR WORLD--THE TIERRA DEL FUEGO GATE--WAS THE FIRST WE DESTROYED, BUT WHO KNOWS IF THAT WAS THE ONLY ONE?

WHO CAN SAY? I DON'T KNOW THE FELLOW.

HERE'S THE DAILY PACKET FOR WOLF MANOR.

DID YOU GET A CHANCE TO SHOP FOR MORE OF *HAKIM'S* SNACK CAKES? HE GOES THROUGH THEM DAILY.

UNLIKE FABLETOWN, THE FARM DOESN'T NEED TO HIDE THE FACT THAT IT'S PREPARED FOR AN INVASION.

AFTER SEEING SNOW AT THE MANOR I'LL BE GOING TO BAGHDAD'S WEAPONS DEPOT TO LOAD ANOTHER BIG *BOMB* INTO THE CLOAK.

OH, *GOOD*. CAN YOU TAKE ME UP TO WOLF MANOR WITH YOU? I WAS SUPPOSED TO GET UP THERE THIS MORNING, BUT ADMINISTRATING THINGS CAME UP AND--

SURE. NO PROBLEM, ROSE.

WOLF MANOR HAS BECOME THE NERVE CENTER OF OUR WAR OPERATIONS.

REGARDLESS OF HOW SUCCESSFUL THEY'VE BEEN, WE NEED TO MAKE SURE THE GLORY HAS THREE BIG BOMBS IN THEIR HOLD AT *ALL* TIMES.

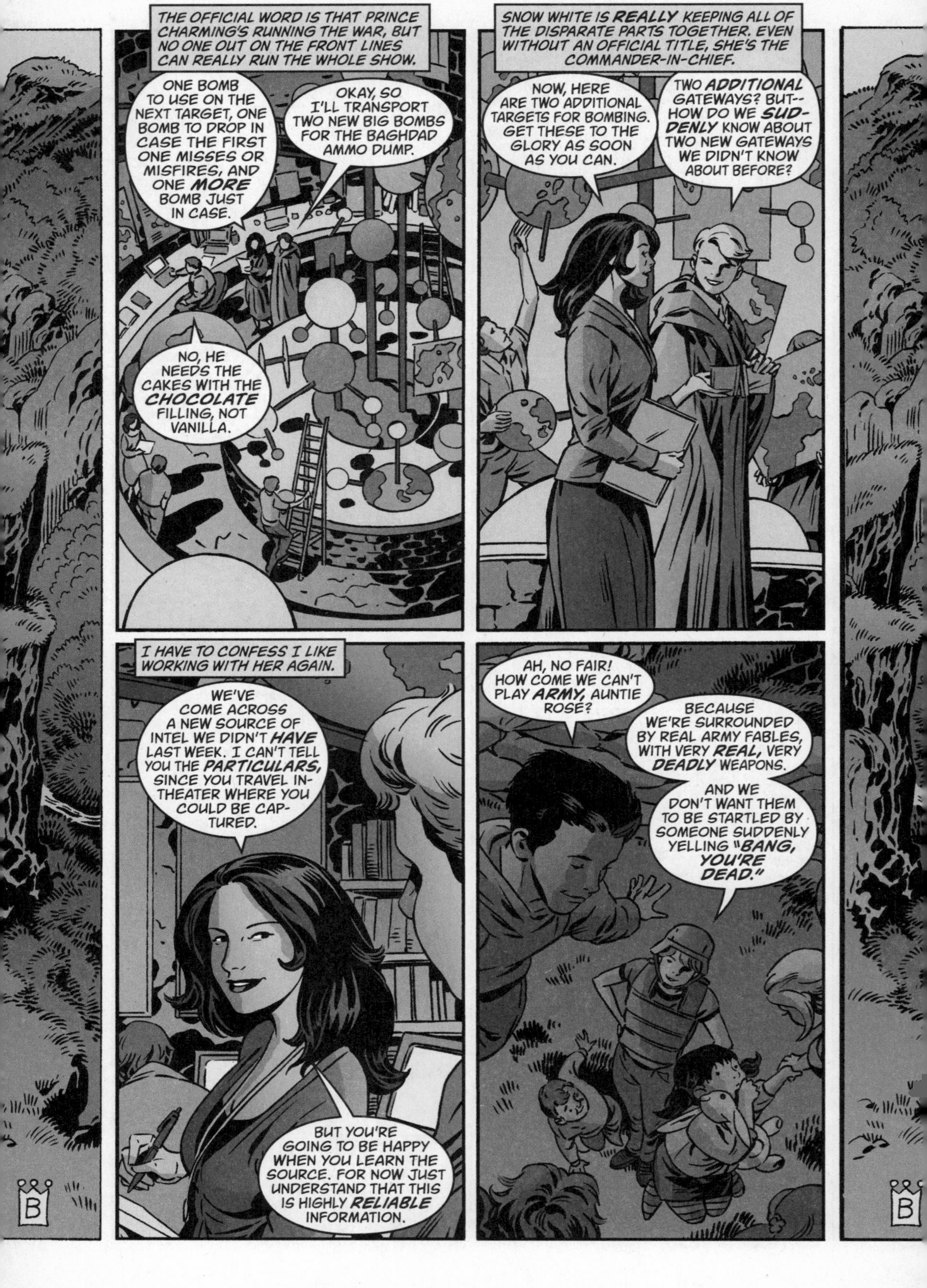

THE OFFICIAL WORD IS THAT PRINCE CHARMING'S RUNNING THE WAR, BUT NO ONE OUT ON THE FRONT LINES CAN REALLY RUN THE WHOLE SHOW.
ONE BOMB TO USE ON THE NEXT TARGET, ONE BOMB TO DROP IN CASE THE FIRST ONE MISSES OR MISFIRES, AND ONE MORE BOMB JUST IN CASE.
OKAY, SO I'LL TRANSPORT TWO NEW BIG BOMBS FOR THE BAGHDAD AMMO DUMP.
NO, HE NEEDS THE CAKES WITH THE CHOCOLATE FILLING, NOT VANILLA.
SNOW WHITE IS REALLY KEEPING ALL OF THE DISPARATE PARTS TOGETHER. EVEN WITHOUT AN OFFICIAL TITLE, SHE'S THE COMMANDER-IN-CHIEF.
NOW, HERE ARE TWO ADDITIONAL TARGETS FOR BOMBING. GET THESE TO THE GLORY AS SOON AS YOU CAN.
TWO ADDITIONAL GATEWAYS? BUT--HOW DO WE SUDDENLY KNOW ABOUT TWO NEW GATEWAYS WE DIDN'T KNOW ABOUT BEFORE?
I HAVE TO CONFESS I LIKE WORKING WITH HER AGAIN.
WE'VE COME ACROSS A NEW SOURCE OF INTEL WE DIDN'T HAVE LAST WEEK. I CAN'T TELL YOU THE PARTICULARS, SINCE YOU TRAVEL IN-THEATER WHERE YOU COULD BE CAPTURED.
BUT YOU'RE GOING TO BE HAPPY WHEN YOU LEARN THE SOURCE. FOR NOW JUST UNDERSTAND THAT THIS IS HIGHLY RELIABLE INFORMATION.
AH, NO FAIR! HOW COME WE CAN'T PLAY ARMY, AUNTIE ROSE?
BECAUSE WE'RE SURROUNDED BY REAL ARMY FABLES, WITH VERY REAL, VERY DEADLY WEAPONS.
AND WE DON'T WANT THEM TO BE STARTLED BY SOMEONE SUDDENLY YELLING "BANG, YOU'RE DEAD."

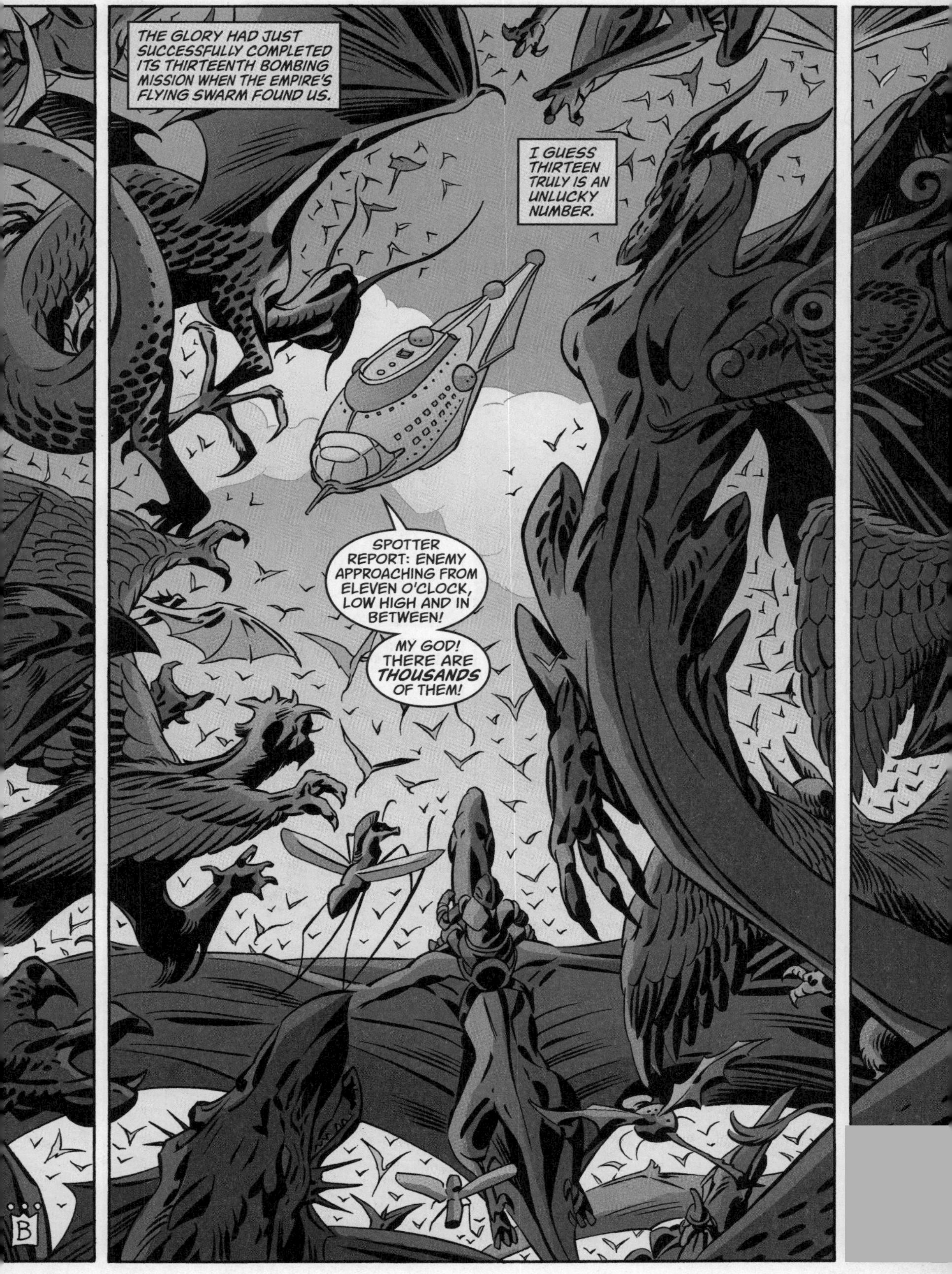
THE GLORY HAD JUST SUCCESSFULLY COMPLETED ITS THIRTEENTH BOMBING MISSION WHEN THE EMPIRE'S FLYING SWARM FOUND US.
I GUESS THIRTEEN TRULY IS AN UNLUCKY NUMBER.
SPOTTER REPORT: ENEMY APPROACHING FROM ELEVEN O'CLOCK, LOW HIGH AND IN BETWEEN!
MY GOD! THERE ARE THOUSANDS OF THEM!
B

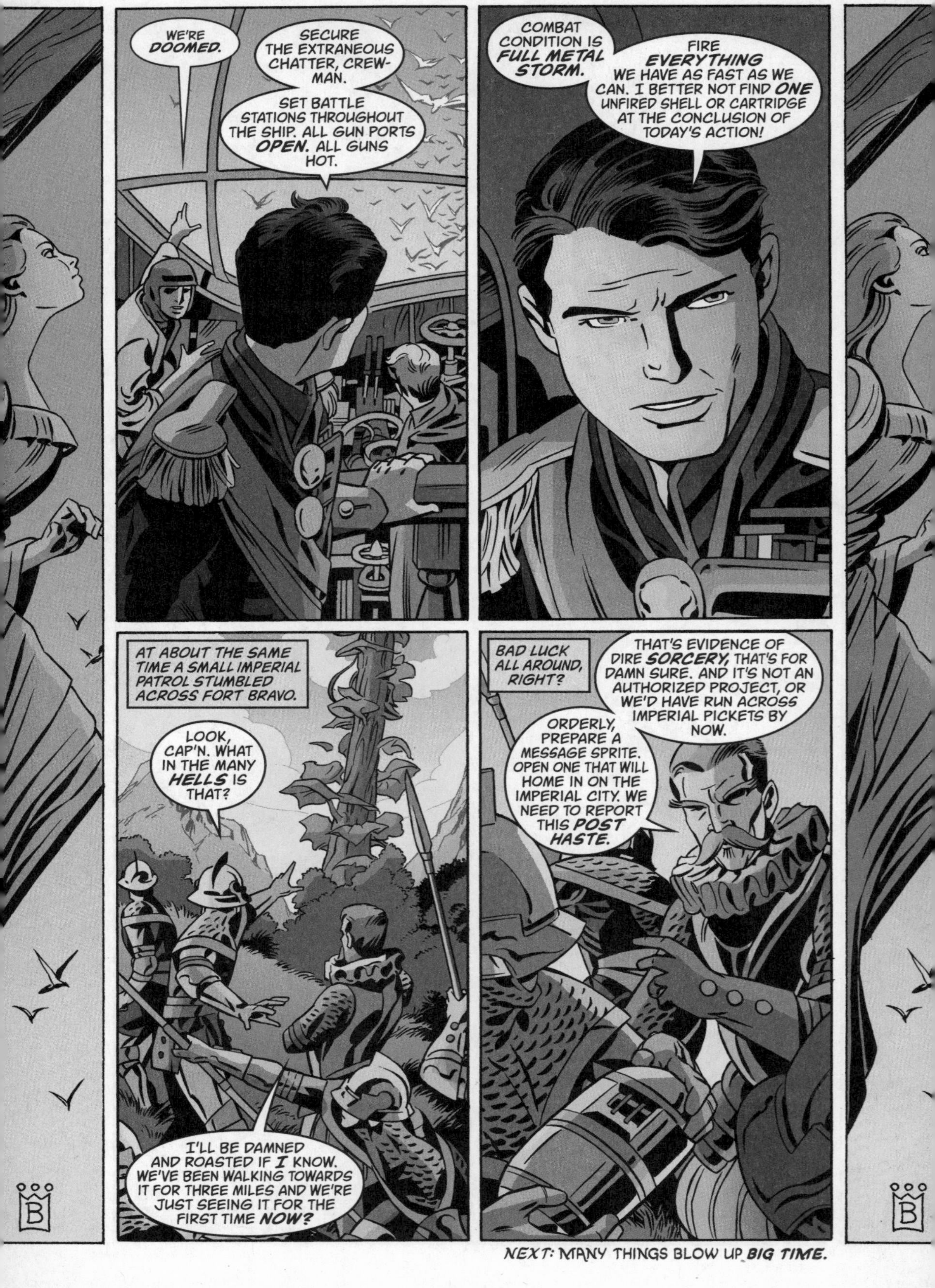
WE'RE DOOMED.
SECURE THE EXTRANEOUS CHATTER, CREW-MAN.
SET BATTLE STATIONS THROUGHOUT THE SHIP. ALL GUN PORTS OPEN. ALL GUNS HOT.
COMBAT CONDITION IS FULL METAL STORM.
FIRE EVERYTHING WE HAVE AS FAST AS WE CAN. I BETTER NOT FIND ONE UNFIRED SHELL OR CARTRIDGE AT THE CONCLUSION OF TODAY'S ACTION!
AT ABOUT THE SAME TIME A SMALL IMPERIAL PATROL STUMBLED ACROSS FORT BRAVO.
LOOK, CAP'N. WHAT IN THE MANY HELLS IS THAT?
I'LL BE DAMNED AND ROASTED IF I KNOW. WE'VE BEEN WALKING TOWARDS IT FOR THREE MILES AND WE'RE JUST SEEING IT FOR THE FIRST TIME NOW?
BAD LUCK ALL AROUND, RIGHT?
THAT'S EVIDENCE OF DIRE SORCERY, THAT'S FOR DAMN SURE. AND IT'S NOT AN AUTHORIZED PROJECT, OR WE'D HAVE RUN ACROSS IMPERIAL PICKETS BY NOW.
ORDERLY, PREPARE A MESSAGE SPRITE. OPEN ONE THAT WILL HOME IN ON THE IMPERIAL CITY. WE NEED TO REPORT THIS POST HASTE.
NEXT: MANY THINGS BLOW UP BIG TIME.

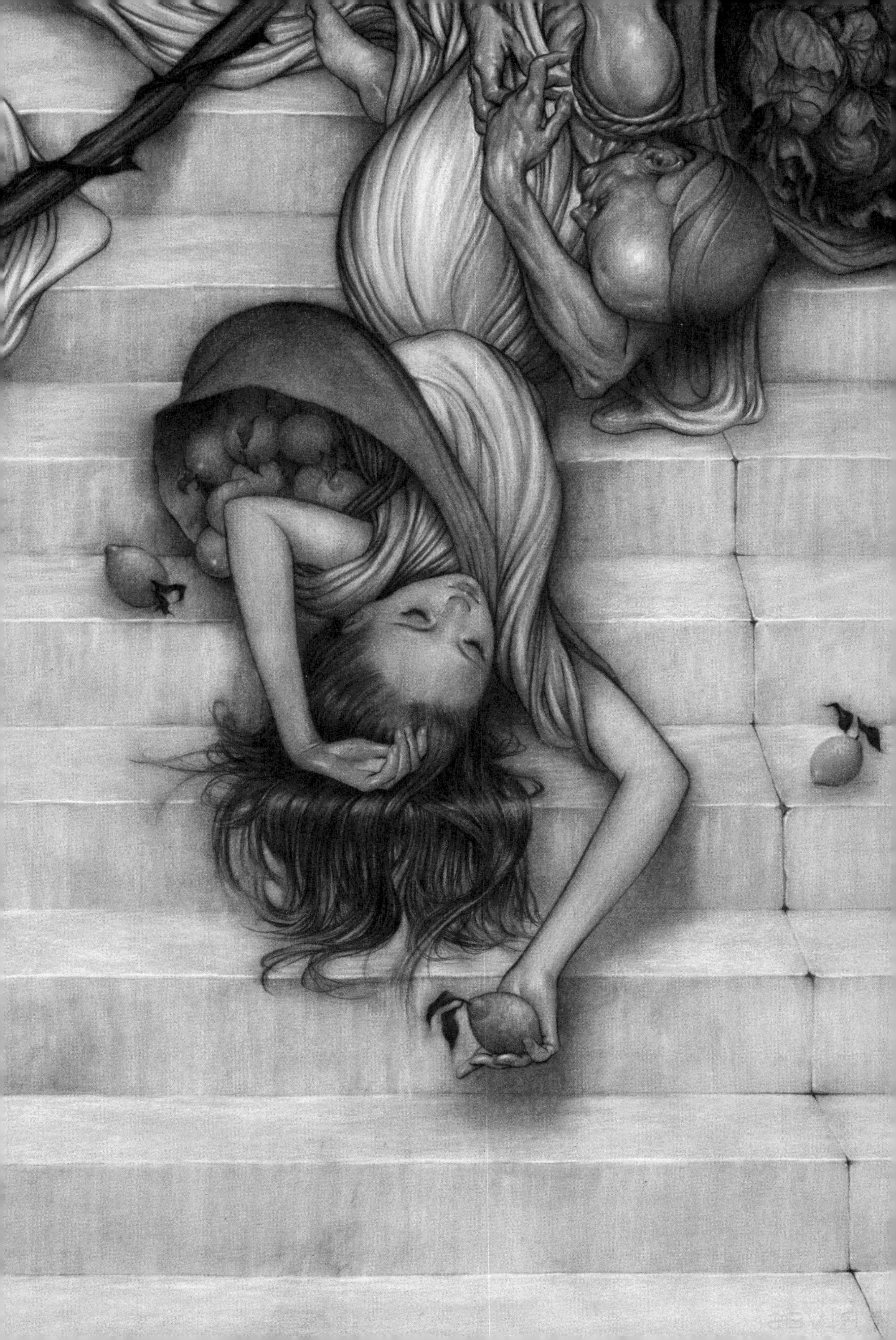

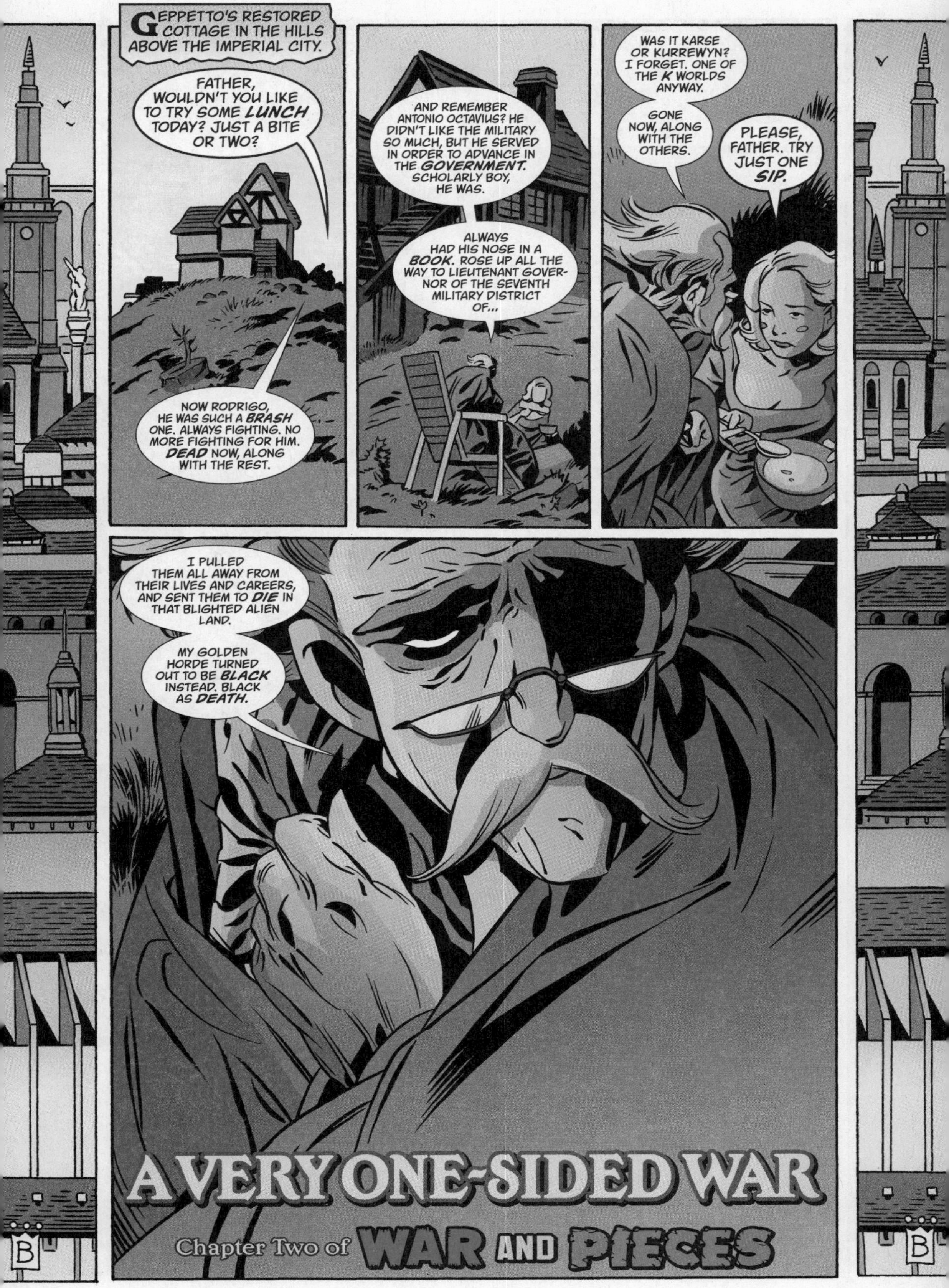
GEPPETTO'S RESTORED COTTAGE IN THE HILLS ABOVE THE IMPERIAL CITY.
FATHER, WOULDN'T YOU LIKE TO TRY SOME LUNCH TODAY? JUST A BITE OR TWO?
NOW RODRIGO, HE WAS SUCH A BRASH ONE. ALWAYS FIGHTING. NO MORE FIGHTING FOR HIM. DEAD NOW, ALONG WITH THE REST.
AND REMEMBER ANTONIO OCTAVIUS? HE DIDN'T LIKE THE MILITARY SO MUCH, BUT HE SERVED IN ORDER TO ADVANCE IN THE GOVERNMENT. SCHOLARLY BOY, HE WAS.
ALWAYS HAD HIS NOSE IN A BOOK. ROSE UP ALL THE WAY TO LIEUTENANT GOVERNOR OF THE SEVENTH MILITARY DISTRICT OF...
WAS IT KARSE OR KURREWYN? I FORGET. ONE OF THE K WORLDS ANYWAY.
GONE NOW, ALONG WITH THE OTHERS.
PLEASE, FATHER. TRY JUST ONE SIP.
I PULLED THEM ALL AWAY FROM THEIR LIVES AND CAREERS, AND SENT THEM TO DIE IN THAT BLIGHTED ALIEN LAND.
MY GOLDEN HORDE TURNED OUT TO BE BLACK INSTEAD. BLACK AS DEATH.
A VERY ONE-SIDED WAR
Chapter Two of WAR AND PIECES

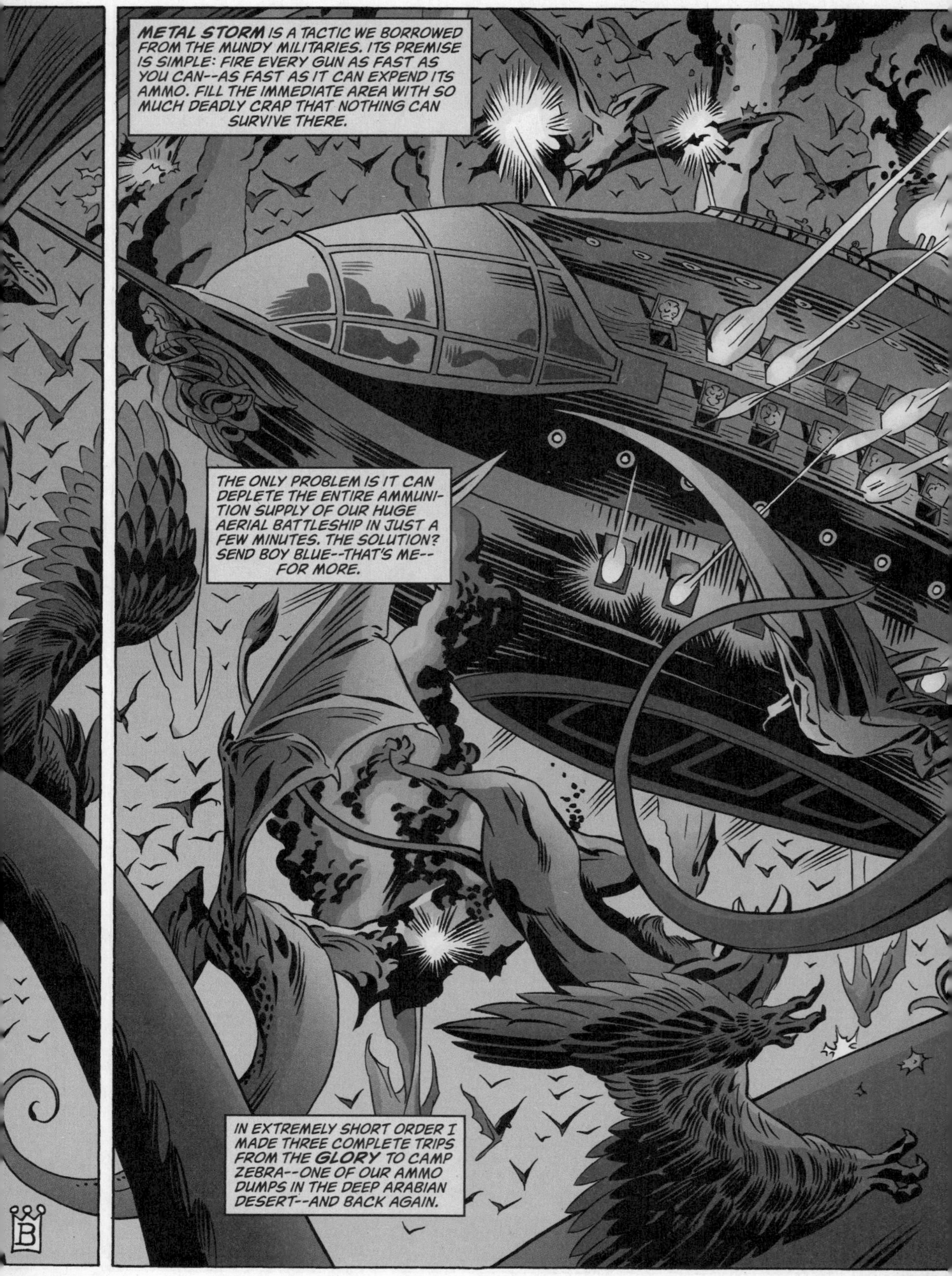
METAL STORM IS A TACTIC WE BORROWED FROM THE MUNDY MILITARIES. ITS PREMISE IS SIMPLE: FIRE EVERY GUN AS FAST AS YOU CAN--AS FAST AS IT CAN EXPEND ITS AMMO. FILL THE IMMEDIATE AREA WITH SO MUCH DEADLY CRAP THAT NOTHING CAN SURVIVE THERE.
THE ONLY PROBLEM IS IT CAN DEPLETE THE ENTIRE AMMUNITION SUPPLY OF OUR HUGE AERIAL BATTLESHIP IN JUST A FEW MINUTES. THE SOLUTION? SEND BOY BLUE--THAT'S ME--FOR MORE.
IN EXTREMELY SHORT ORDER I MADE THREE COMPLETE TRIPS FROM THE GLORY TO CAMP ZEBRA--ONE OF OUR AMMO DUMPS IN THE DEEP ARABIAN DESERT--AND BACK AGAIN.

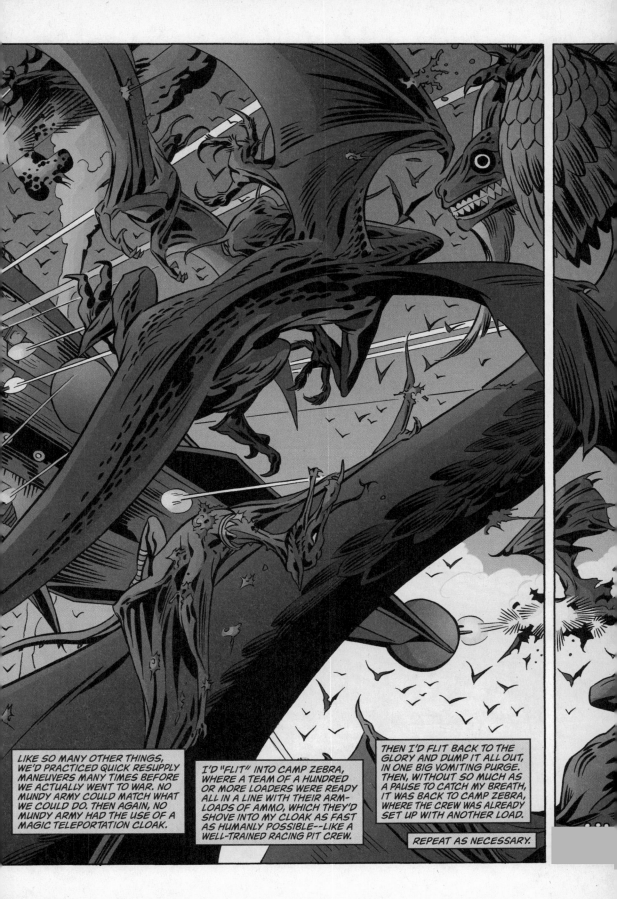

LIKE SO MANY OTHER THINGS, WE'D PRACTICED QUICK RESUPPLY MANEUVERS MANY TIMES BEFORE WE ACTUALLY WENT TO WAR. NO MUNDY ARMY COULD MATCH WHAT WE COULD DO. THEN AGAIN, NO MUNDY ARMY HAD THE USE OF A MAGIC TELEPORTATION CLOAK.

I'D "FLIT" INTO CAMP ZEBRA, WHERE A TEAM OF A HUNDRED OR MORE LOADERS WERE READY ALL IN A LINE WITH THEIR ARM-LOADS OF AMMO, WHICH THEY'D SHOVE INTO MY CLOAK AS FAST AS HUMANLY POSSIBLE--LIKE A WELL-TRAINED RACING PIT CREW.

THEN I'D FLIT BACK TO THE GLORY AND DUMP IT ALL OUT, IN ONE BIG VOMITING PURGE. THEN, WITHOUT SO MUCH AS A PAUSE TO CATCH MY BREATH, IT WAS BACK TO CAMP ZEBRA, WHERE THE CREW WAS ALREADY SET UP WITH ANOTHER LOAD.

REPEAT AS NECESSARY.

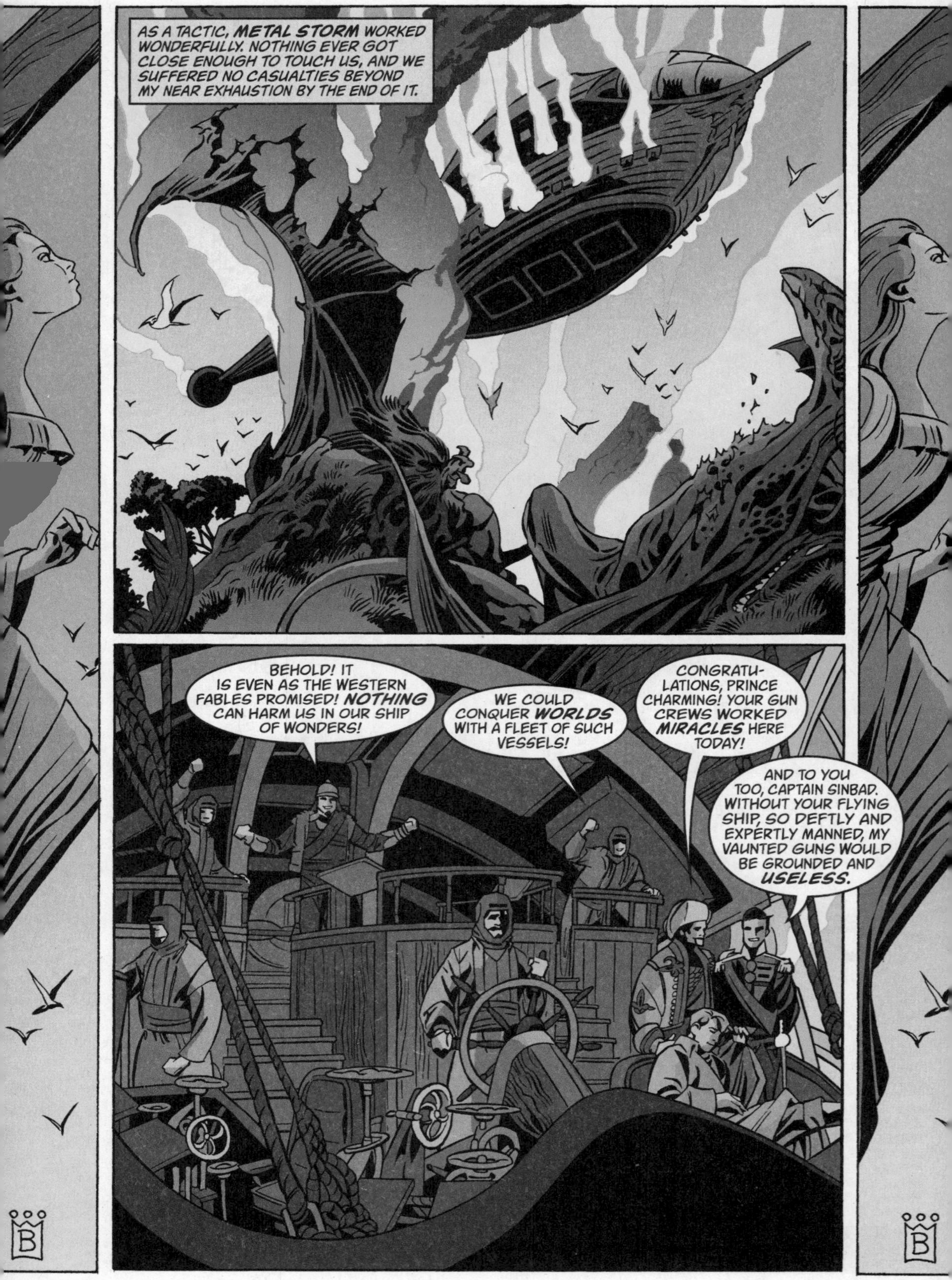
AS A TACTIC, METAL STORM WORKED WONDERFULLY. NOTHING EVER GOT CLOSE ENOUGH TO TOUCH US, AND WE SUFFERED NO CASUALTIES BEYOND MY NEAR EXHAUSTION BY THE END OF IT.
BEHOLD! IT IS EVEN AS THE WESTERN FABLES PROMISED! NOTHING CAN HARM US IN OUR SHIP OF WONDERS!
WE COULD CONQUER WORLDS WITH A FLEET OF SUCH VESSELS!
CONGRATU-LATIONS, PRINCE CHARMING! YOUR GUN CREWS WORKED MIRACLES HERE TODAY!
AND TO YOU TOO, CAPTAIN SINBAD. WITHOUT YOUR FLYING SHIP, SO DEFTLY AND EXPERTLY MANNED, MY VAUNTED GUNS WOULD BE GROUNDED AND USELESS.

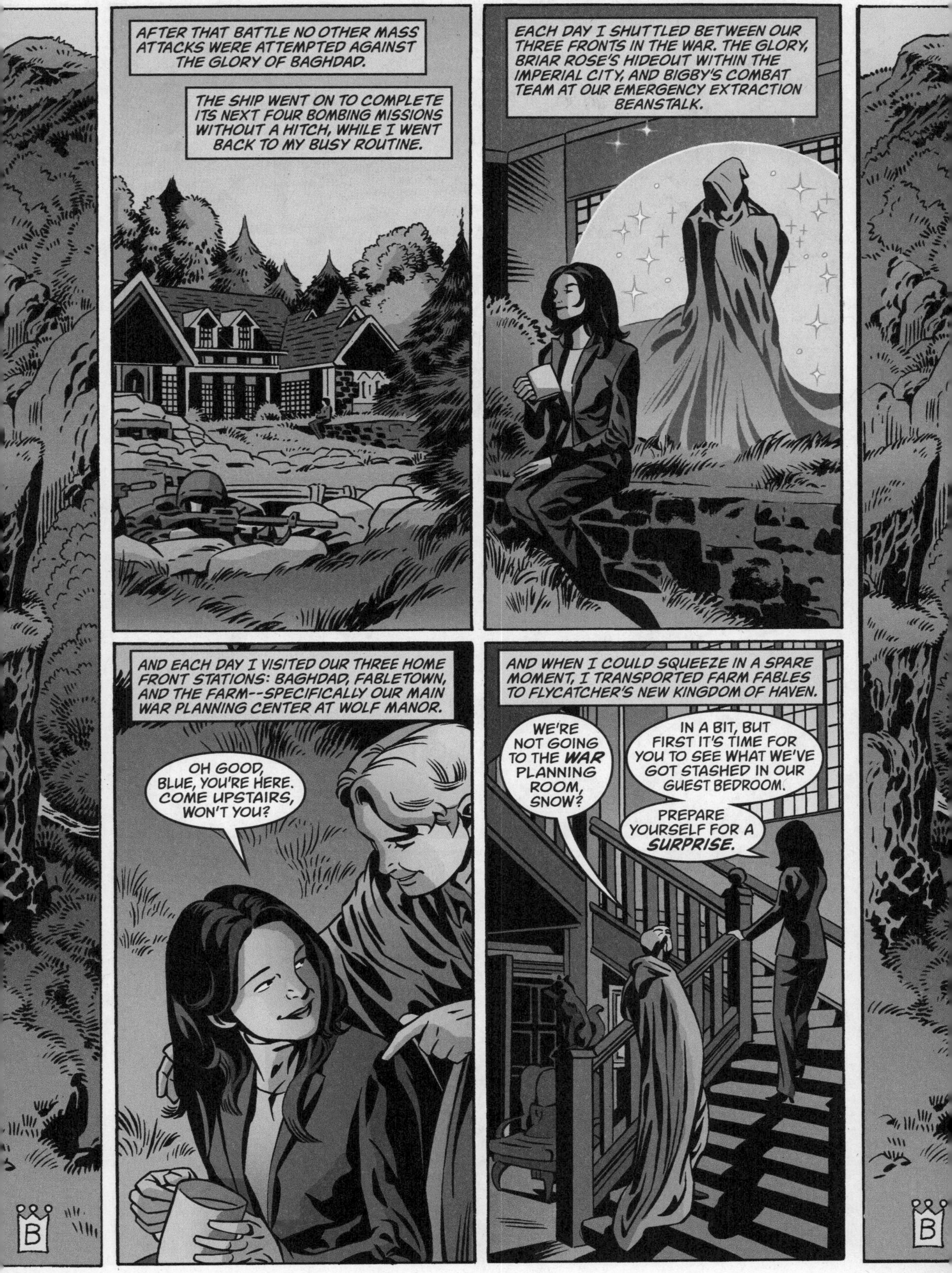
AFTER THAT BATTLE NO OTHER MASS ATTACKS WERE ATTEMPTED AGAINST THE GLORY OF BAGHDAD.
THE SHIP WENT ON TO COMPLETE ITS NEXT FOUR BOMBING MISSIONS WITHOUT A HITCH, WHILE I WENT BACK TO MY BUSY ROUTINE.
EACH DAY I SHUTTLED BETWEEN OUR THREE FRONTS IN THE WAR. THE GLORY, BRIAR ROSE'S HIDEOUT WITHIN THE IMPERIAL CITY, AND BIGBY'S COMBAT TEAM AT OUR EMERGENCY EXTRACTION BEANSTALK.
AND EACH DAY I VISITED OUR THREE HOME FRONT STATIONS: BAGHDAD, FABLETOWN, AND THE FARM--SPECIFICALLY OUR MAIN WAR PLANNING CENTER AT WOLF MANOR.
OH GOOD, BLUE, YOU'RE HERE. COME UPSTAIRS, WON'T YOU?
AND WHEN I COULD SQUEEZE IN A SPARE MOMENT, I TRANSPORTED FARM FABLES TO FLYCATCHER'S NEW KINGDOM OF HAVEN.
WE'RE NOT GOING TO THE WAR PLANNING ROOM, SNOW?
IN A BIT, BUT FIRST IT'S TIME FOR YOU TO SEE WHAT WE'VE GOT STASHED IN OUR GUEST BEDROOM.
PREPARE YOURSELF FOR A SURPRISE.

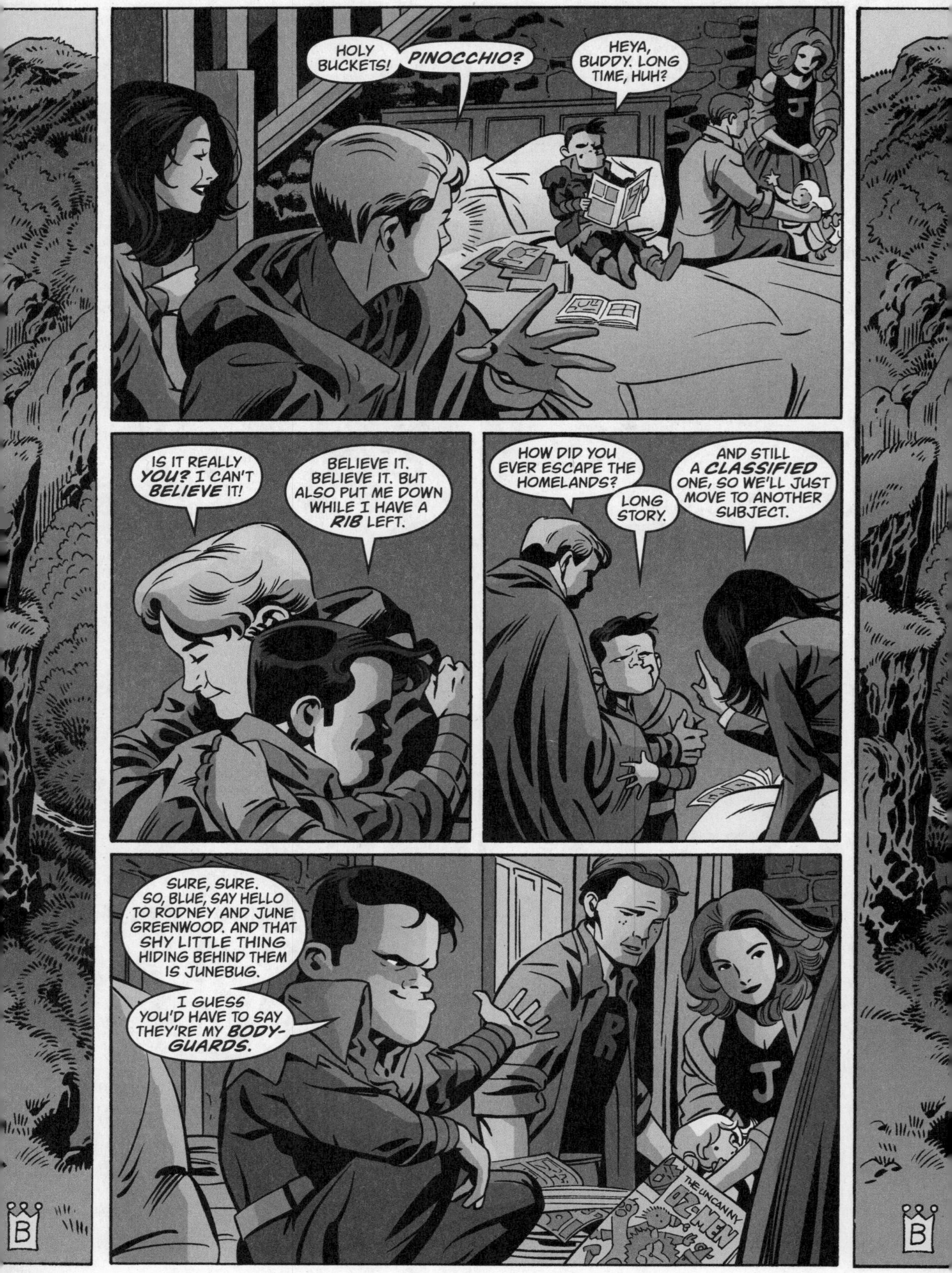

HOLY BUCKETS! PINOCCHIO?
HEYA, BUDDY. LONG TIME, HUH?
IS IT REALLY YOU? I CAN'T BELIEVE IT!
BELIEVE IT. BELIEVE IT. BUT ALSO PUT ME DOWN WHILE I HAVE A RIB LEFT.
HOW DID YOU EVER ESCAPE THE HOMELANDS?
LONG STORY.
AND STILL A CLASSIFIED ONE, SO WE'LL JUST MOVE TO ANOTHER SUBJECT.
SURE, SURE. SO, BLUE, SAY HELLO TO RODNEY AND JUNE GREENWOOD. AND THAT SHY LITTLE THING HIDING BEHIND THEM IS JUNEBUG.
I GUESS YOU'D HAVE TO SAY THEY'RE MY BODY-GUARDS.
THE UNCANNY OZ-MEN

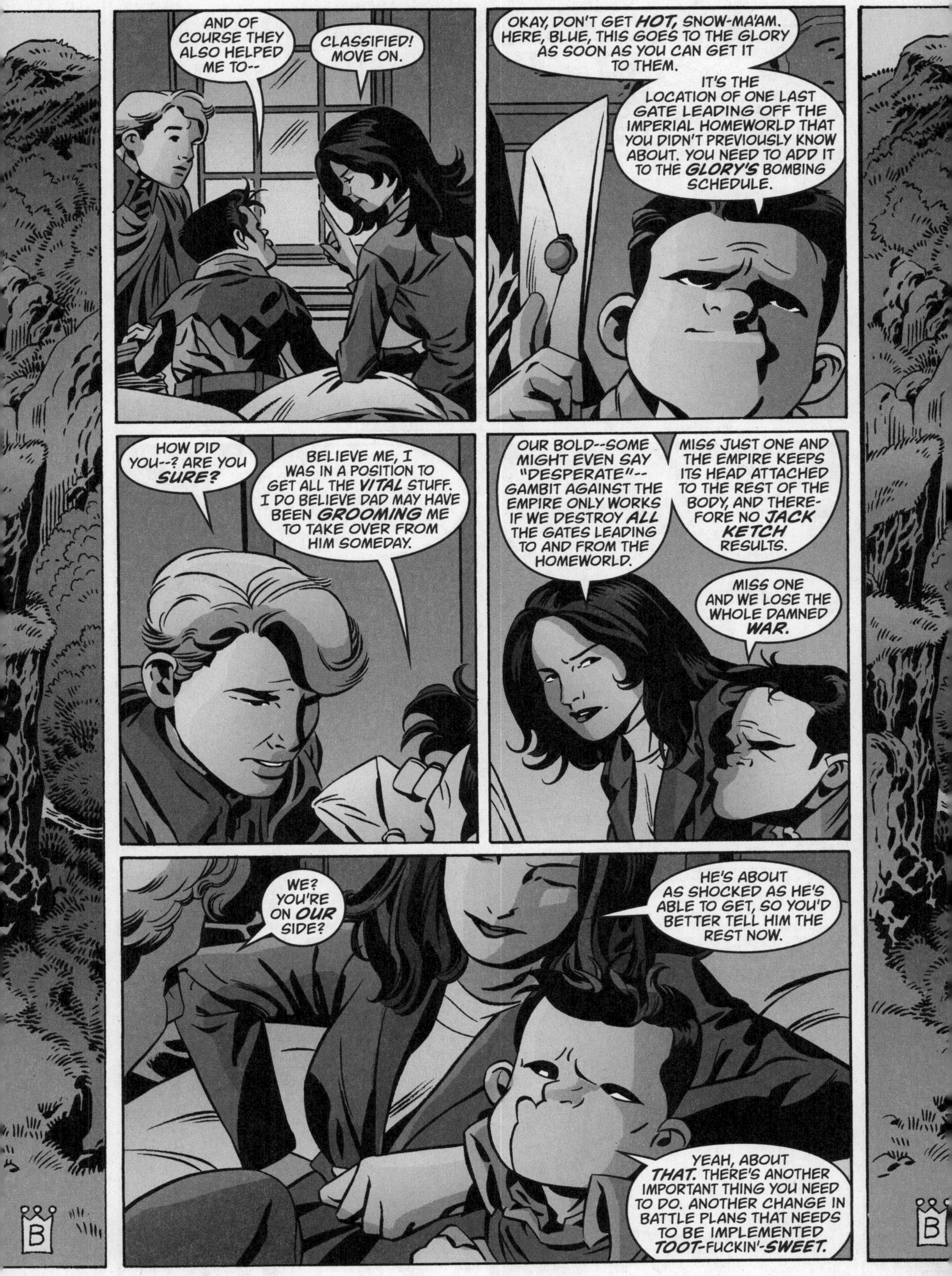
AND OF COURSE THEY ALSO HELPED ME TO--
CLASSIFIED! MOVE ON.
OKAY, DON'T GET HOT, SNOW-MA'AM. HERE, BLUE, THIS GOES TO THE GLORY AS SOON AS YOU CAN GET IT TO THEM.
IT'S THE LOCATION OF ONE LAST GATE LEADING OFF THE IMPERIAL HOMEWORLD THAT YOU DIDN'T PREVIOUSLY KNOW ABOUT. YOU NEED TO ADD IT TO THE GLORY'S BOMBING SCHEDULE.
HOW DID YOU--? ARE YOU SURE?
BELIEVE ME, I WAS IN A POSITION TO GET ALL THE VITAL STUFF. I DO BELIEVE DAD MAY HAVE BEEN GROOMING ME TO TAKE OVER FROM HIM SOMEDAY.
OUR BOLD--SOME MIGHT EVEN SAY "DESPERATE"--GAMBIT AGAINST THE EMPIRE ONLY WORKS IF WE DESTROY ALL THE GATES LEADING TO AND FROM THE HOMEWORLD.
MISS JUST ONE AND THE EMPIRE KEEPS ITS HEAD ATTACHED TO THE REST OF THE BODY, AND THEREFORE NO JACK KETCH RESULTS.
MISS ONE AND WE LOSE THE WHOLE DAMNED WAR.
WE? YOU'RE ON OUR SIDE?
HE'S ABOUT AS SHOCKED AS HE'S ABLE TO GET, SO YOU'D BETTER TELL HIM THE REST NOW.
YEAH, ABOUT THAT. THERE'S ANOTHER IMPORTANT THING YOU NEED TO DO. ANOTHER CHANGE IN BATTLE PLANS THAT NEEDS TO BE IMPLEMENTED TOOT-FUCKIN'-SWEET.

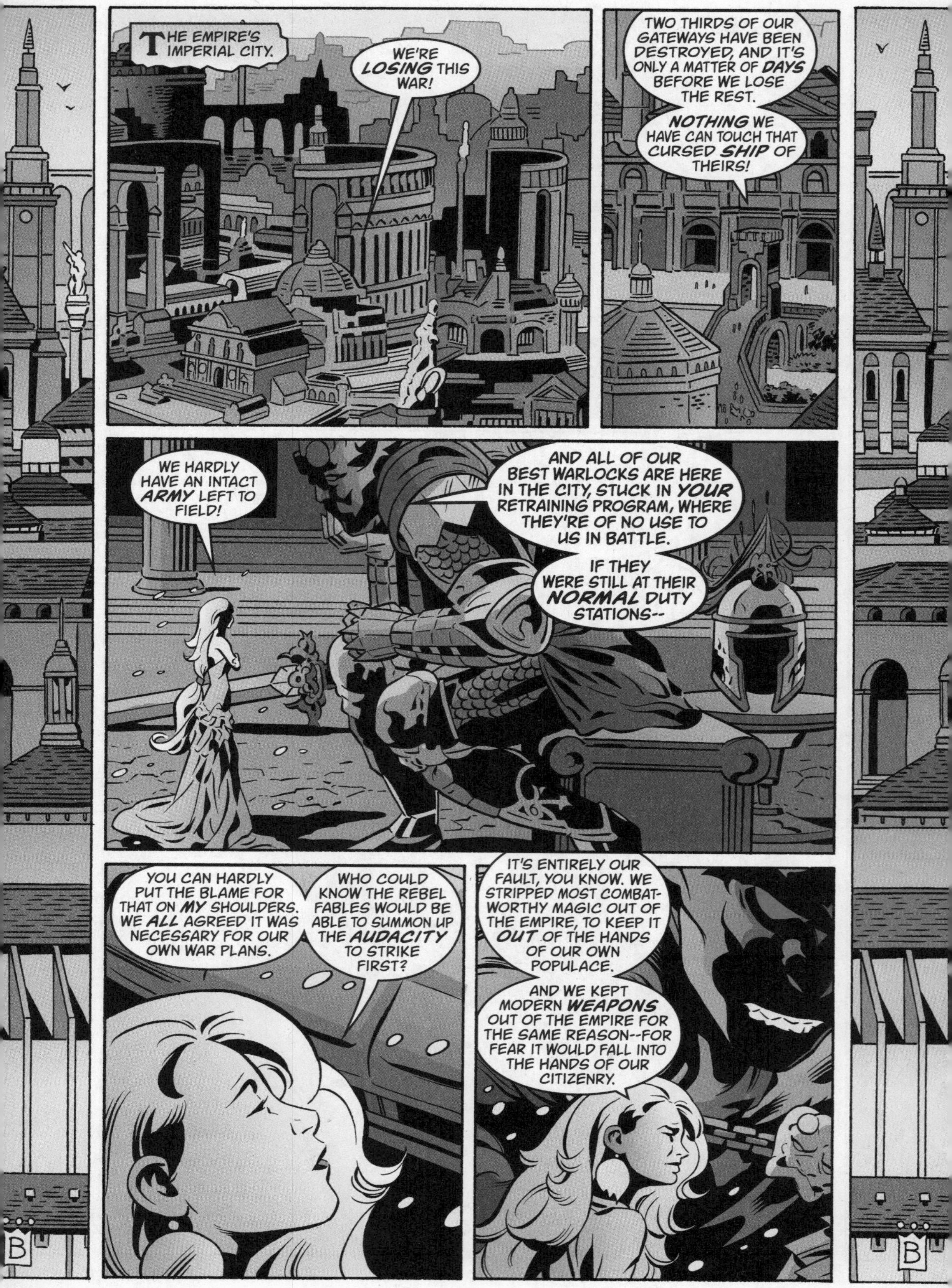

THE EMPIRE'S IMPERIAL CITY.
WE'RE LOSING THIS WAR!
TWO THIRDS OF OUR GATEWAYS HAVE BEEN DESTROYED, AND IT'S ONLY A MATTER OF DAYS BEFORE WE LOSE THE REST.
NOTHING WE HAVE CAN TOUCH THAT CURSED SHIP OF THEIRS!
WE HARDLY HAVE AN INTACT ARMY LEFT TO FIELD!
AND ALL OF OUR BEST WARLOCKS ARE HERE IN THE CITY, STUCK IN YOUR RETRAINING PROGRAM, WHERE THEY'RE OF NO USE TO US IN BATTLE.
IF THEY WERE STILL AT THEIR NORMAL DUTY STATIONS--
YOU CAN HARDLY PUT THE BLAME FOR THAT ON MY SHOULDERS. WE ALL AGREED IT WAS NECESSARY FOR OUR OWN WAR PLANS.
WHO COULD KNOW THE REBEL FABLES WOULD BE ABLE TO SUMMON UP THE AUDACITY TO STRIKE FIRST?
IT'S ENTIRELY OUR FAULT, YOU KNOW. WE STRIPPED MOST COMBAT-WORTHY MAGIC OUT OF THE EMPIRE, TO KEEP IT OUT OF THE HANDS OF OUR OWN POPULACE.
AND WE KEPT MODERN WEAPONS OUT OF THE EMPIRE FOR THE SAME REASON--FOR FEAR IT WOULD FALL INTO THE HANDS OF OUR CITIZENRY.

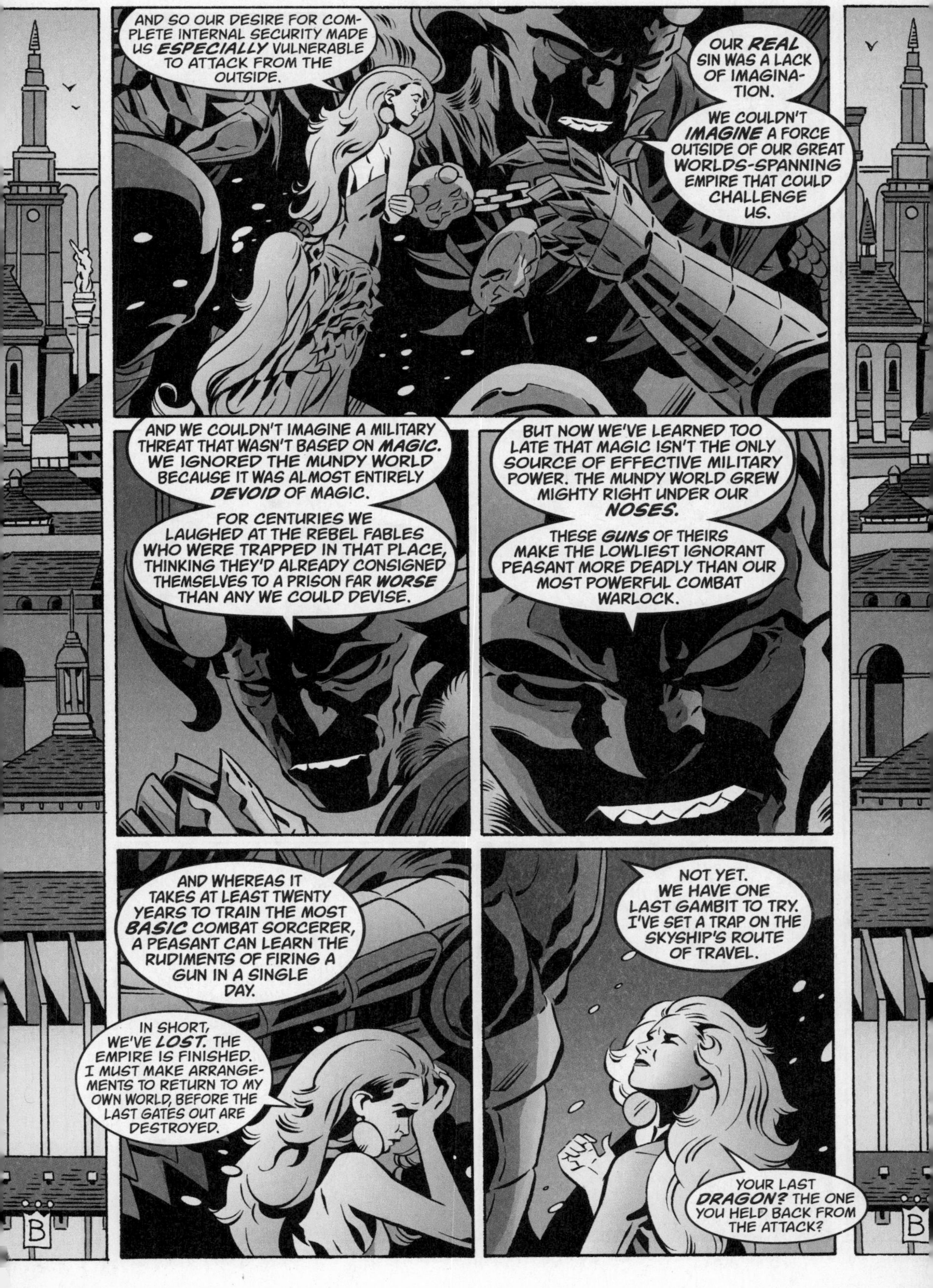
AND SO OUR DESIRE FOR COMPLETE INTERNAL SECURITY MADE US ESPECIALLY VULNERABLE TO ATTACK FROM THE OUTSIDE.
OUR REAL SIN WAS A LACK OF IMAGINATION.
WE COULDN'T IMAGINE A FORCE OUTSIDE OF OUR GREAT WORLDS-SPANNING EMPIRE THAT COULD CHALLENGE US.
AND WE COULDN'T IMAGINE A MILITARY THREAT THAT WASN'T BASED ON MAGIC. WE IGNORED THE MUNDY WORLD BECAUSE IT WAS ALMOST ENTIRELY DEVOID OF MAGIC.
FOR CENTURIES WE LAUGHED AT THE REBEL FABLES WHO WERE TRAPPED IN THAT PLACE, THINKING THEY'D ALREADY CONSIGNED THEMSELVES TO A PRISON FAR WORSE THAN ANY WE COULD DEVISE.
BUT NOW WE'VE LEARNED TOO LATE THAT MAGIC ISN'T THE ONLY SOURCE OF EFFECTIVE MILITARY POWER. THE MUNDY WORLD GREW MIGHTY RIGHT UNDER OUR NOSES.
THESE GUNS OF THEIRS MAKE THE LOWLIEST IGNORANT PEASANT MORE DEADLY THAN OUR MOST POWERFUL COMBAT WARLOCK.
AND WHEREAS IT TAKES AT LEAST TWENTY YEARS TO TRAIN THE MOST BASIC COMBAT SORCERER, A PEASANT CAN LEARN THE RUDIMENTS OF FIRING A GUN IN A SINGLE DAY.
IN SHORT, WE'VE LOST. THE EMPIRE IS FINISHED. I MUST MAKE ARRANGEMENTS TO RETURN TO MY OWN WORLD, BEFORE THE LAST GATES OUT ARE DESTROYED.
NOT YET. WE HAVE ONE LAST GAMBIT TO TRY. I'VE SET A TRAP ON THE SKYSHIP'S ROUTE OF TRAVEL.
YOUR LAST DRAGON? THE ONE YOU HELD BACK FROM THE ATTACK?

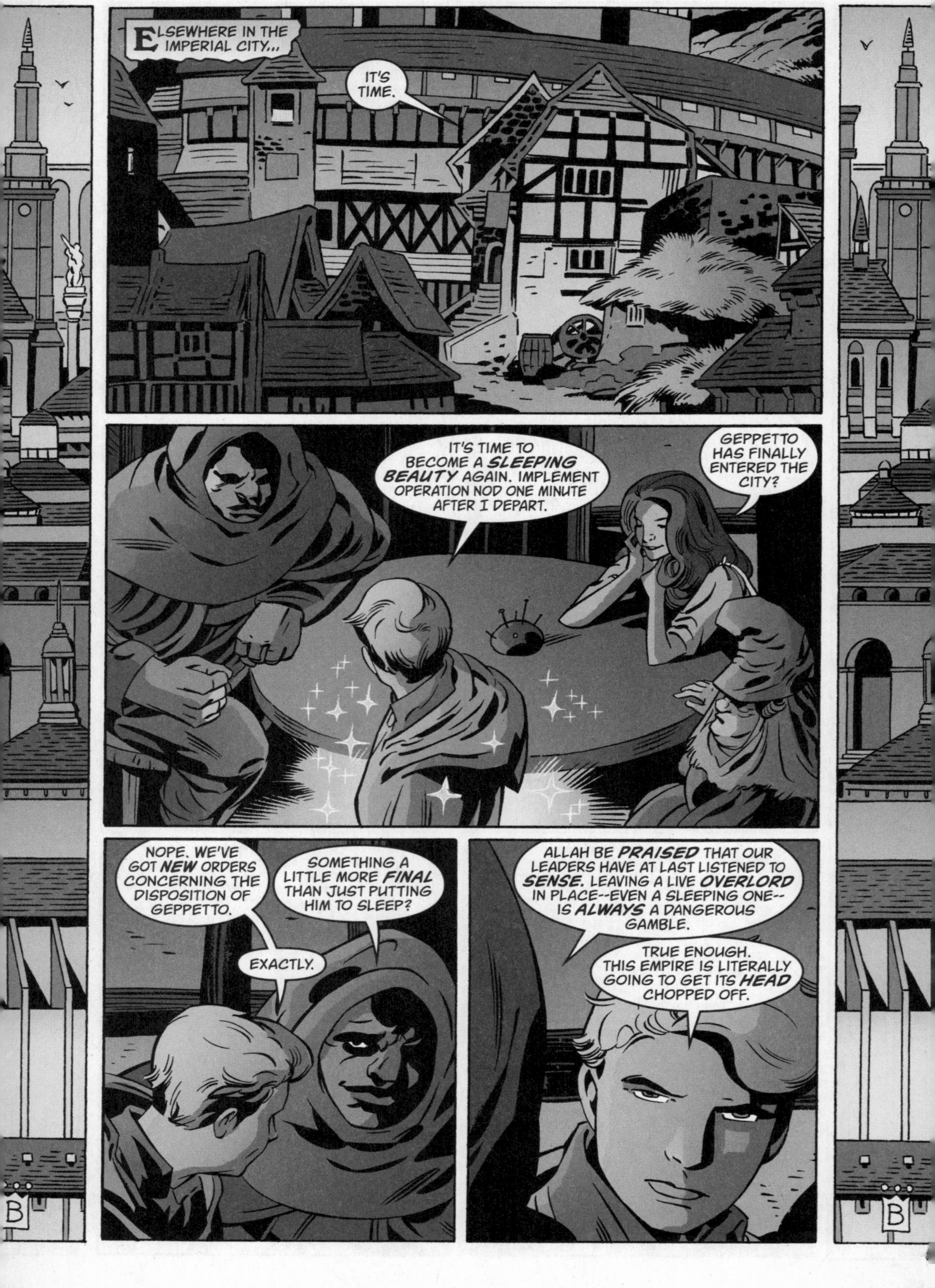

ELSEWHERE IN THE IMPERIAL CITY...
IT'S TIME.
IT'S TIME TO BECOME A **SLEEPING BEAUTY** AGAIN. IMPLEMENT OPERATION NOD ONE MINUTE AFTER I DEPART.
GEPPETTO HAS FINALLY ENTERED THE CITY?
NOPE. WE'VE GOT **NEW** ORDERS CONCERNING THE DISPOSITION OF GEPPETTO.
SOMETHING A LITTLE MORE **FINAL** THAN JUST PUTTING HIM TO SLEEP?
EXACTLY.
ALLAH BE **PRAISED** THAT OUR LEADERS HAVE AT LAST LISTENED TO **SENSE**. LEAVING A LIVE **OVERLORD** IN PLACE--EVEN A SLEEPING ONE--IS **ALWAYS** A DANGEROUS GAMBLE.
TRUE ENOUGH. THIS EMPIRE IS LITERALLY GOING TO GET ITS **HEAD** CHOPPED OFF.

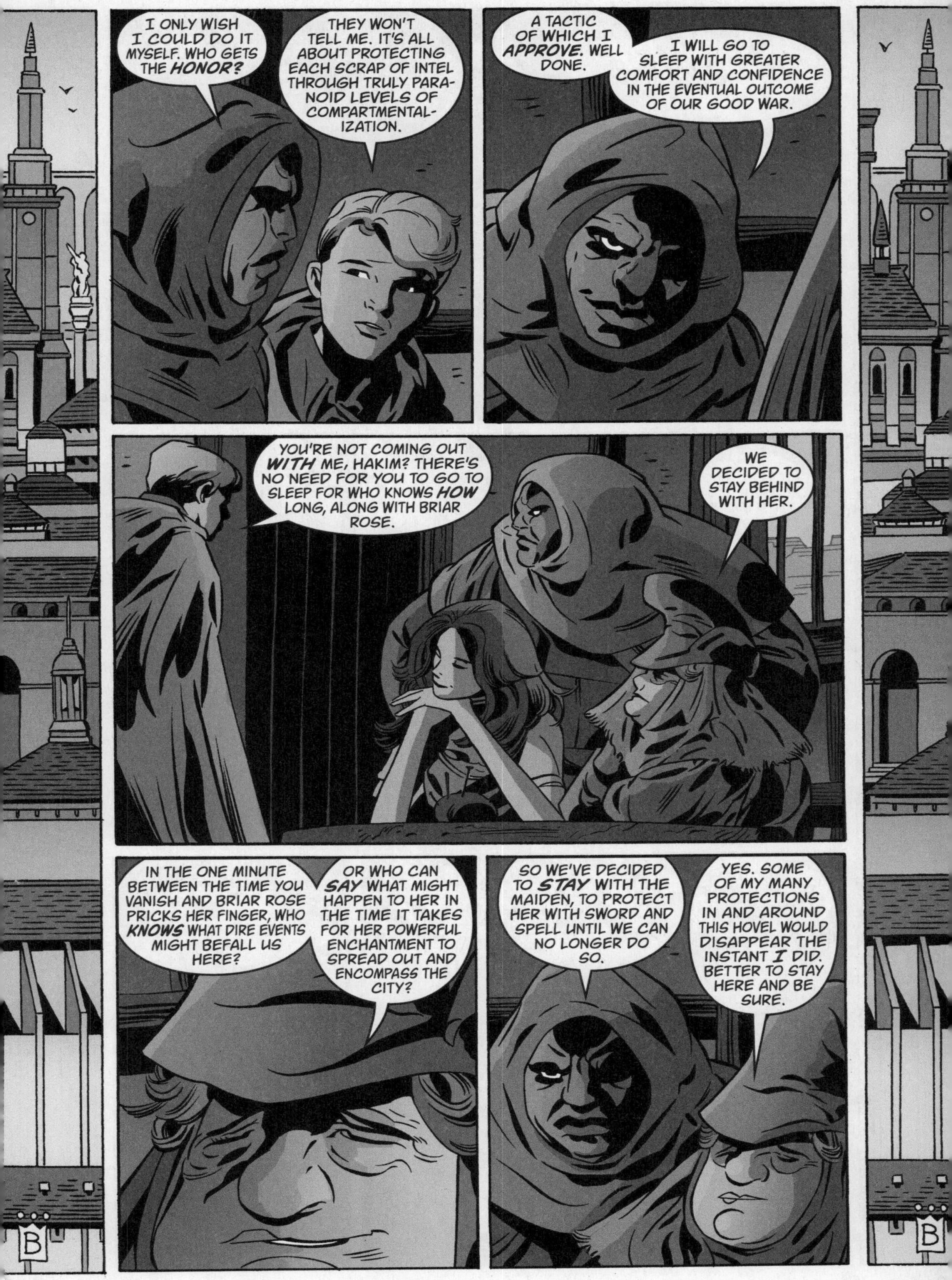
I ONLY WISH I COULD DO IT MYSELF. WHO GETS THE *HONOR?*
THEY WON'T TELL ME. IT'S ALL ABOUT PROTECTING EACH SCRAP OF INTEL THROUGH TRULY PARANOID LEVELS OF COMPARTMENTALIZATION.
A TACTIC OF WHICH I *APPROVE*. WELL DONE.
I WILL GO TO SLEEP WITH GREATER COMFORT AND CONFIDENCE IN THE EVENTUAL OUTCOME OF OUR GOOD WAR.
YOU'RE NOT COMING OUT *WITH* ME, HAKIM? THERE'S NO NEED FOR YOU TO GO TO SLEEP FOR WHO KNOWS *HOW* LONG, ALONG WITH BRIAR ROSE.
WE DECIDED TO STAY BEHIND WITH HER.
IN THE ONE MINUTE BETWEEN THE TIME YOU VANISH AND BRIAR ROSE PRICKS HER FINGER, WHO *KNOWS* WHAT DIRE EVENTS MIGHT BEFALL US HERE?
OR WHO CAN *SAY* WHAT MIGHT HAPPEN TO HER IN THE TIME IT TAKES FOR HER POWERFUL ENCHANTMENT TO SPREAD OUT AND ENCOMPASS THE CITY?
SO WE'VE DECIDED TO *STAY* WITH THE MAIDEN, TO PROTECT HER WITH SWORD AND SPELL UNTIL WE CAN NO LONGER DO SO.
YES. SOME OF MY MANY PROTECTIONS IN AND AROUND THIS HOVEL WOULD DISAPPEAR THE INSTANT *I* DID. BETTER TO STAY HERE AND BE SURE.

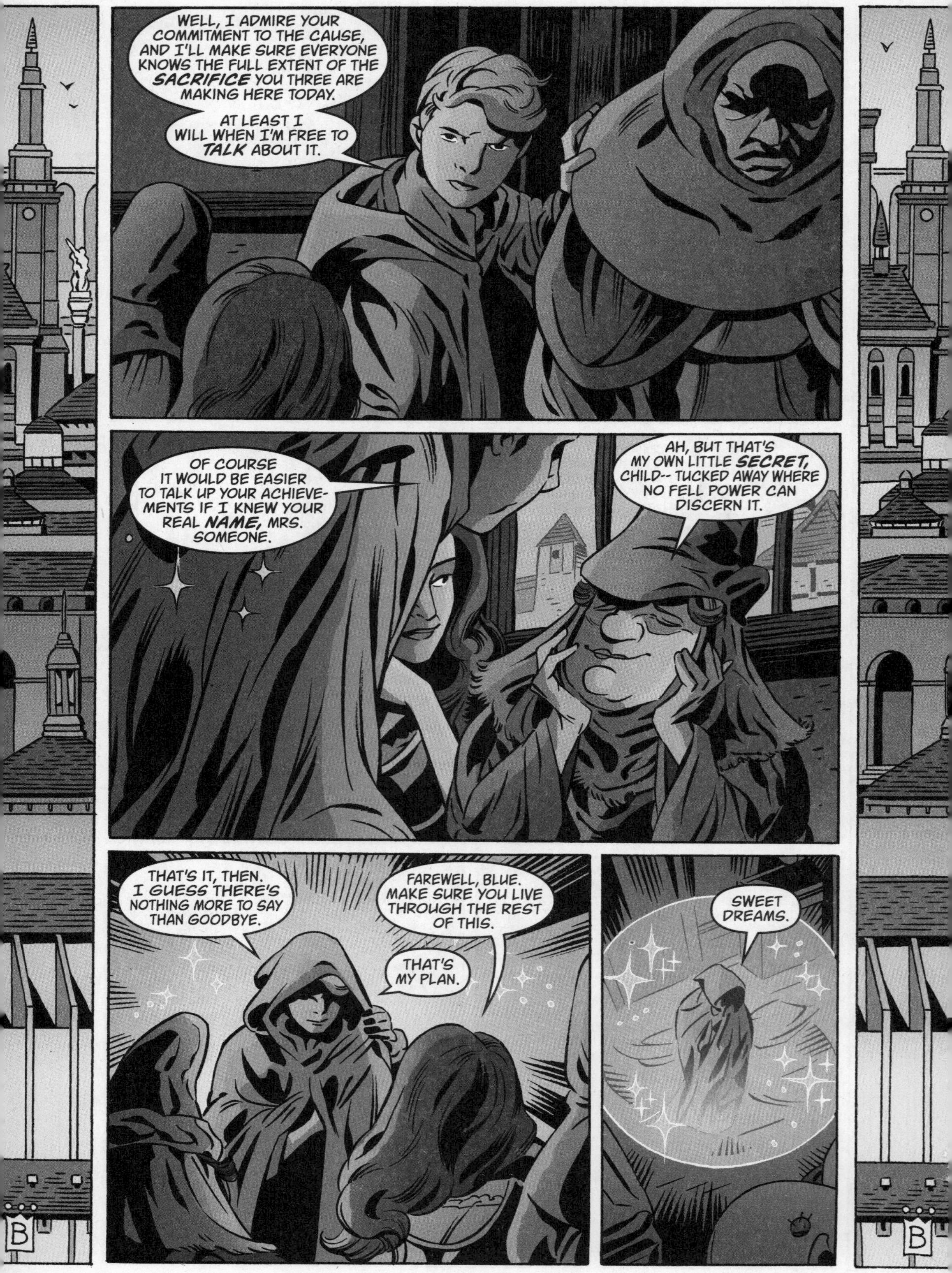
WELL, I ADMIRE YOUR COMMITMENT TO THE CAUSE, AND I'LL MAKE SURE EVERYONE KNOWS THE FULL EXTENT OF THE SACRIFICE YOU THREE ARE MAKING HERE TODAY.
AT LEAST I WILL WHEN I'M FREE TO TALK ABOUT IT.
OF COURSE IT WOULD BE EASIER TO TALK UP YOUR ACHIEVEMENTS IF I KNEW YOUR REAL NAME, MRS. SOMEONE.
AH, BUT THAT'S MY OWN LITTLE SECRET, CHILD-- TUCKED AWAY WHERE NO FELL POWER CAN DISCERN IT.
THAT'S IT, THEN. I GUESS THERE'S NOTHING MORE TO SAY THAN GOODBYE.
FAREWELL, BLUE. MAKE SURE YOU LIVE THROUGH THE REST OF THIS.
THAT'S MY PLAN.
SWEET DREAMS.

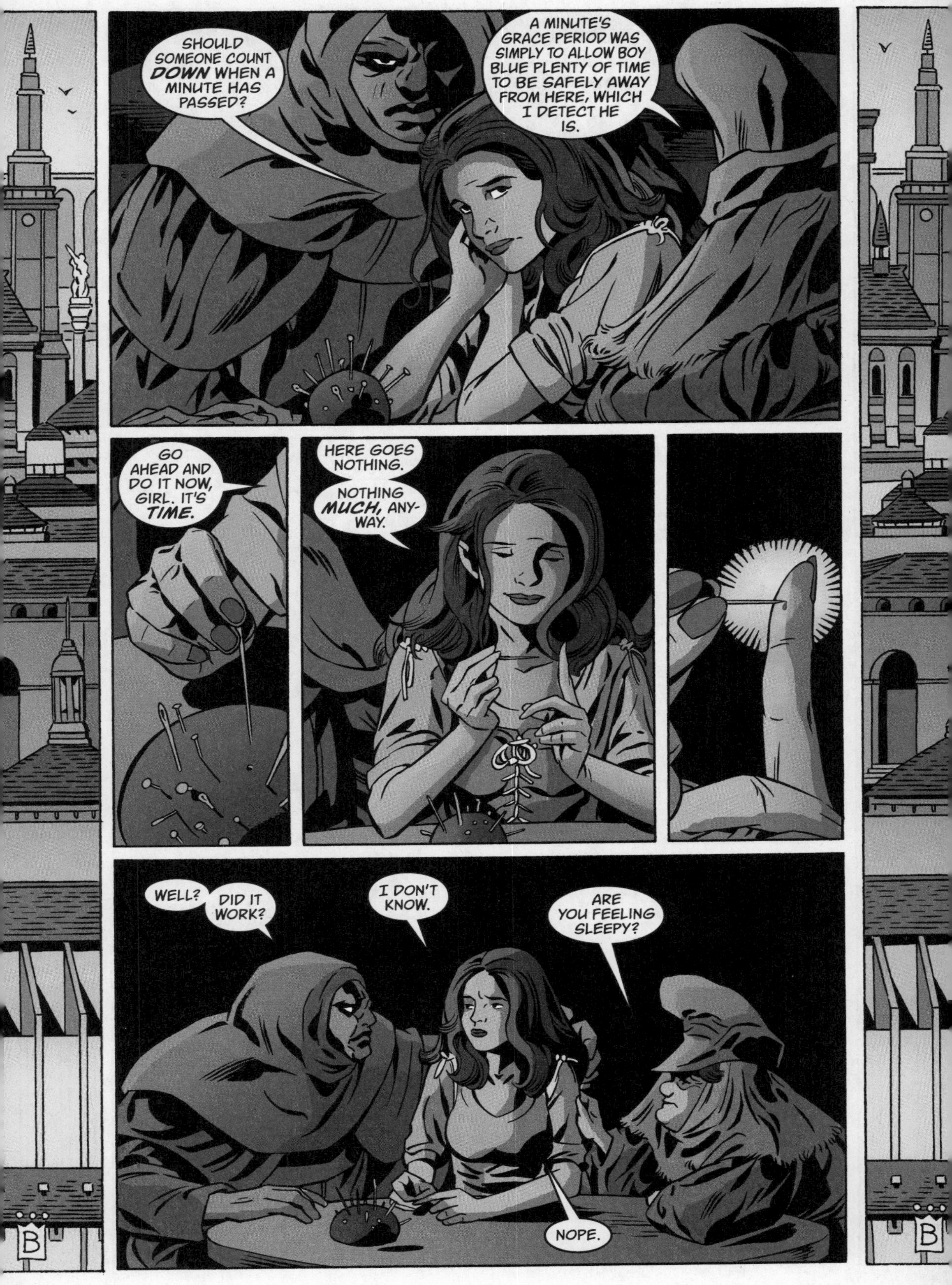
SHOULD SOMEONE COUNT DOWN WHEN A MINUTE HAS PASSED?
A MINUTE'S GRACE PERIOD WAS SIMPLY TO ALLOW BOY BLUE PLENTY OF TIME TO BE SAFELY AWAY FROM HERE, WHICH I DETECT HE IS.
GO AHEAD AND DO IT NOW, GIRL. IT'S TIME.
HERE GOES NOTHING.
NOTHING MUCH, ANYWAY.
WELL?
DID IT WORK?
I DON'T KNOW.
ARE YOU FEELING SLEEPY?
NOPE.

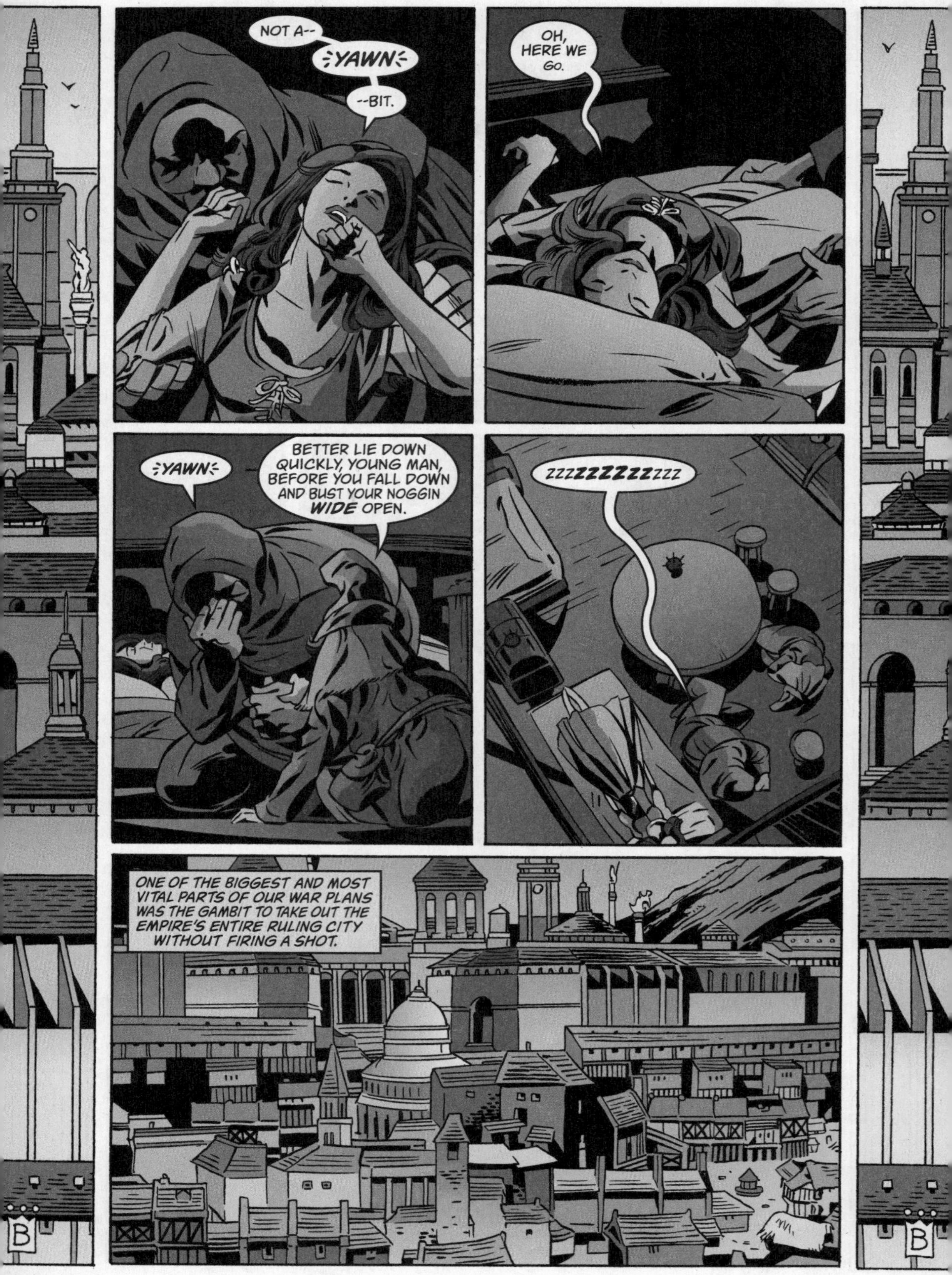
NOT A--
YAWN
--BIT.
OH, HERE WE GO.
YAWN
BETTER LIE DOWN QUICKLY, YOUNG MAN, BEFORE YOU FALL DOWN AND BUST YOUR NOGGIN **WIDE** OPEN.
zzzZZZZZZZzzz
ONE OF THE BIGGEST AND MOST VITAL PARTS OF OUR WAR PLANS WAS THE GAMBIT TO TAKE OUT THE EMPIRE'S ENTIRE RULING CITY WITHOUT FIRING A SHOT.
B
B

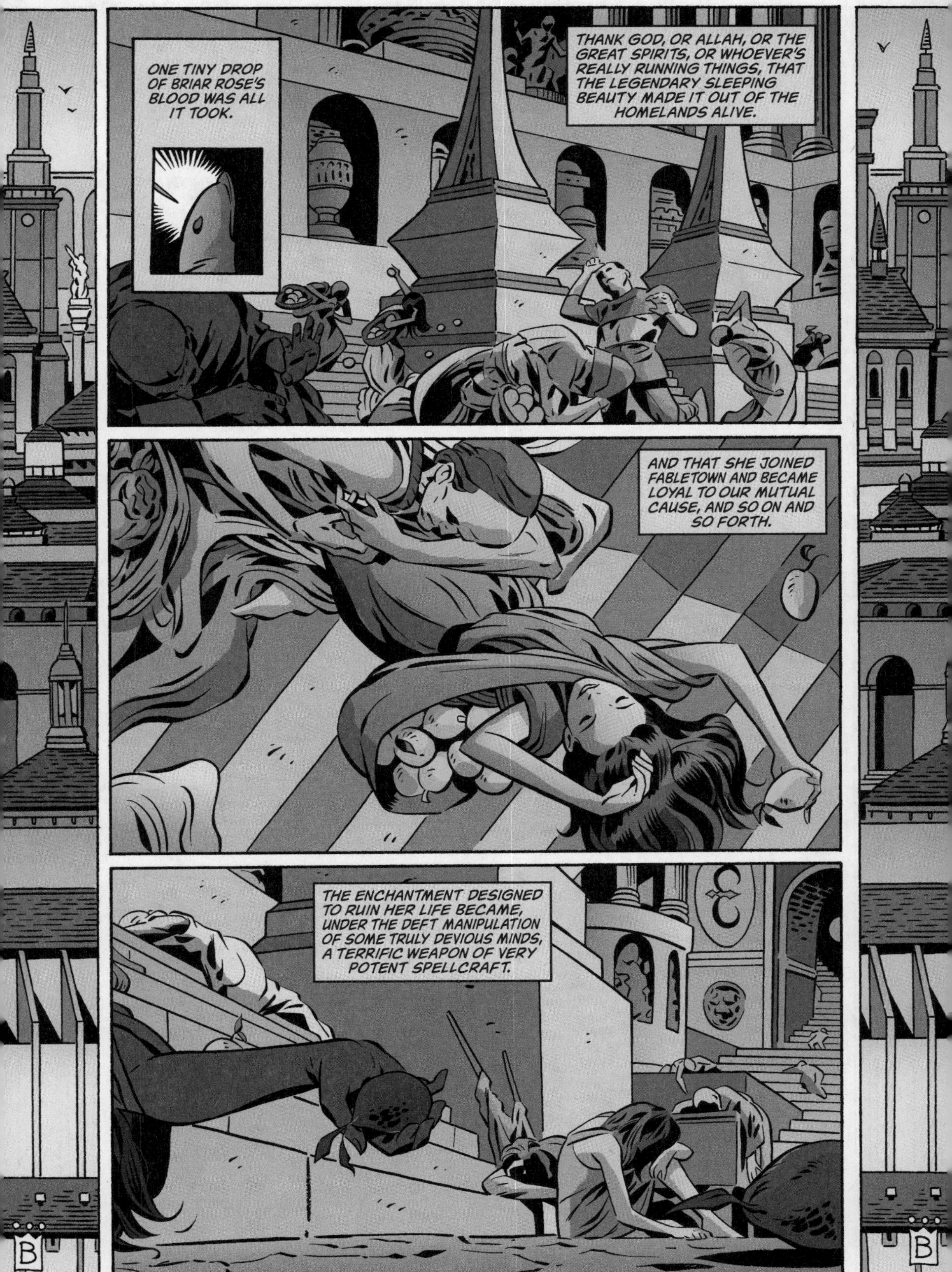
ONE TINY DROP OF BRIAR ROSE'S BLOOD WAS ALL IT TOOK.
THANK GOD, OR ALLAH, OR THE GREAT SPIRITS, OR WHOEVER'S REALLY RUNNING THINGS, THAT THE LEGENDARY SLEEPING BEAUTY MADE IT OUT OF THE HOMELANDS ALIVE.
AND THAT SHE JOINED FABLETOWN AND BECAME LOYAL TO OUR MUTUAL CAUSE, AND SO ON AND SO FORTH.
THE ENCHANTMENT DESIGNED TO RUIN HER LIFE BECAME, UNDER THE DEFT MANIPULATION OF SOME TRULY DEVIOUS MINDS, A TERRIFIC WEAPON OF VERY POTENT SPELLCRAFT.
B
B

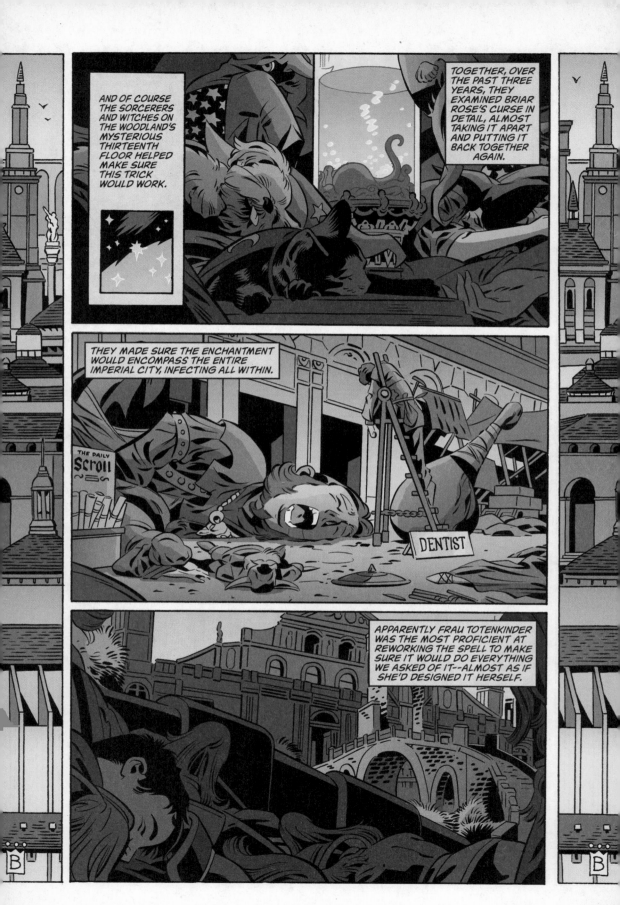

AND OF COURSE THE SORCERERS AND WITCHES ON THE WOODLAND'S MYSTERIOUS THIRTEENTH FLOOR HELPED MAKE SURE THIS TRICK WOULD WORK.

TOGETHER, OVER THE PAST THREE YEARS, THEY EXAMINED BRIAR ROSE'S CURSE IN DETAIL, ALMOST TAKING IT APART AND PUTTING IT BACK TOGETHER AGAIN.

THEY MADE SURE THE ENCHANTMENT WOULD ENCOMPASS THE ENTIRE IMPERIAL CITY, INFECTING ALL WITHIN.

THE DAILY SCROLL

DENTIST

APPARENTLY FRAU TOTENKINDER WAS THE MOST PROFICIENT AT REWORKING THE SPELL TO MAKE SURE IT WOULD DO EVERYTHING WE ASKED OF IT--ALMOST AS IF SHE'D DESIGNED IT HERSELF.

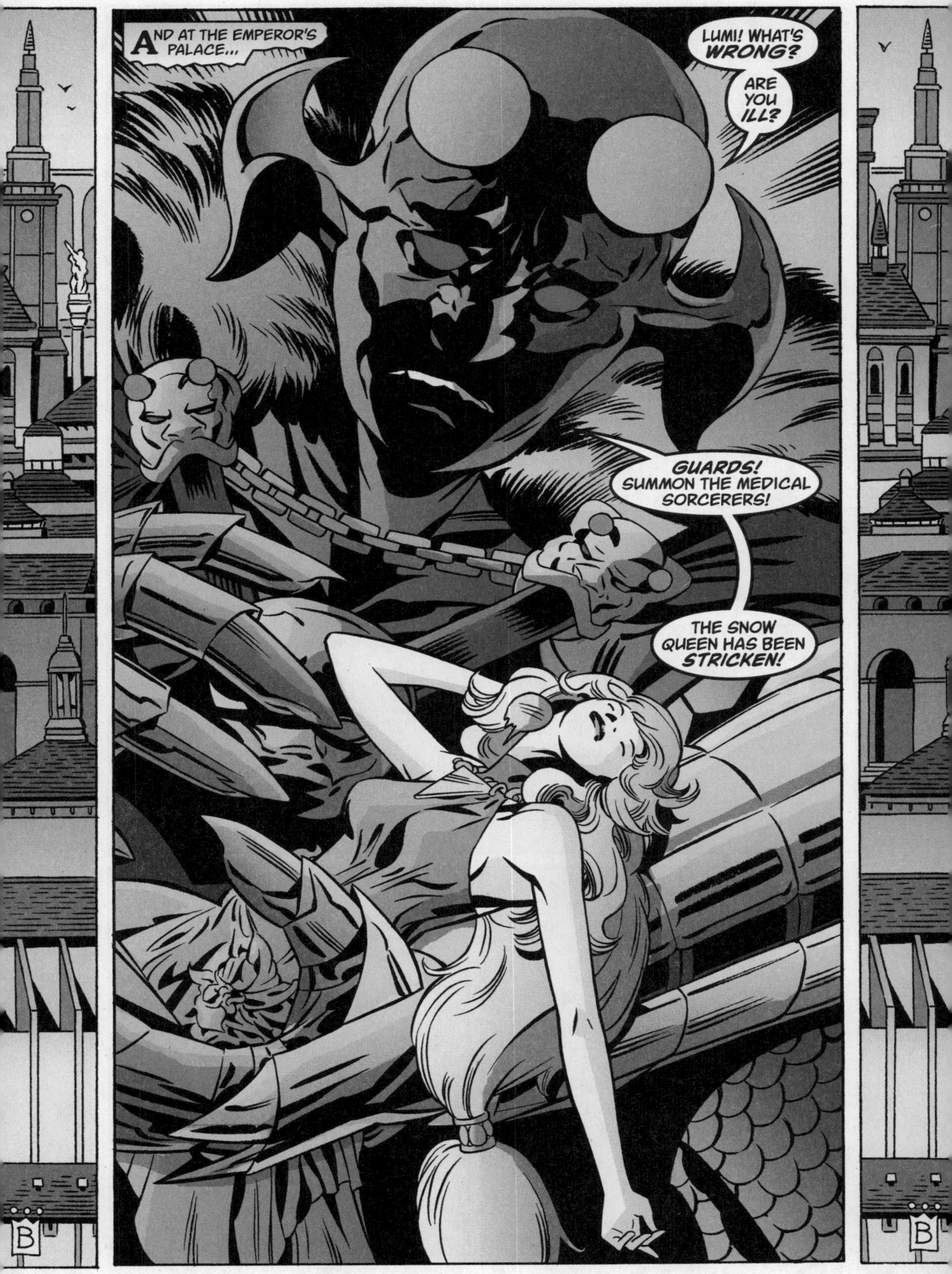
AND AT THE EMPEROR'S PALACE...
LUMI! WHAT'S WRONG?
ARE YOU ILL?
GUARDS! SUMMON THE MEDICAL SORCERERS!
THE SNOW QUEEN HAS BEEN STRICKEN!

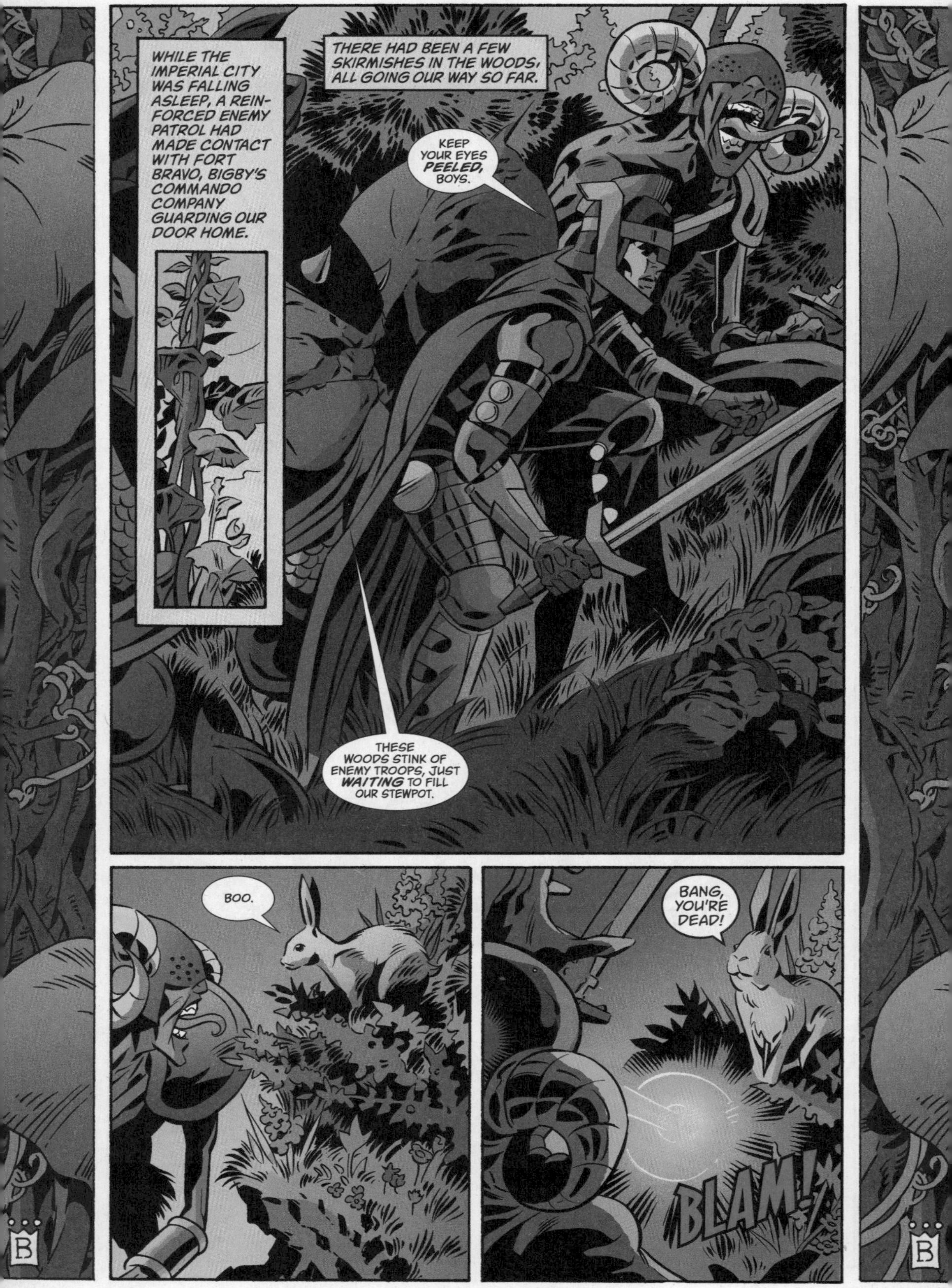
WHILE THE IMPERIAL CITY WAS FALLING ASLEEP, A REIN-FORCED ENEMY PATROL HAD MADE CONTACT WITH FORT BRAVO, BIGBY'S COMMANDO COMPANY GUARDING OUR DOOR HOME.
THERE HAD BEEN A FEW SKIRMISHES IN THE WOODS, ALL GOING OUR WAY SO FAR.
KEEP YOUR EYES PEELED, BOYS.
THESE WOODS STINK OF ENEMY TROOPS, JUST WAITING TO FILL OUR STEWPOT.
BOO.
BANG, YOU'RE DEAD!
BLAM!

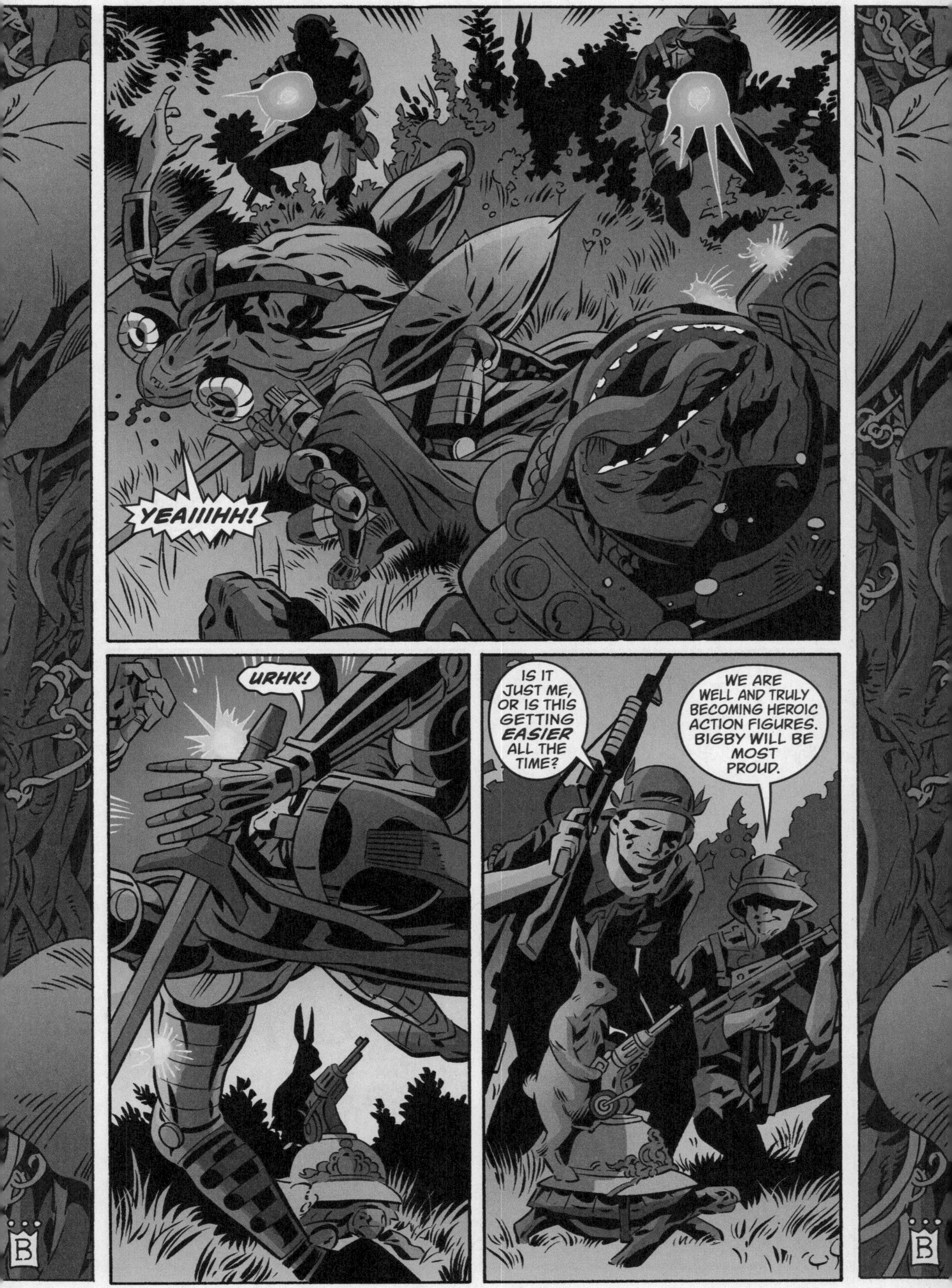
YEAIIIHH!
URHK!
IS IT JUST ME, OR IS THIS GETTING EASIER ALL THE TIME?
WE ARE WELL AND TRULY BECOMING HEROIC ACTION FIGURES. BIGBY WILL BE MOST PROUD.

HELLO?

ANYONE STILL *AWAKE*, RALLY TO YOUR EMPEROR!

HELLO? CAN ANYONE *HEAR* ME?

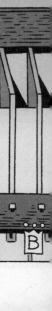

RALLY TO THE SOUND OF MY--

HUH?

BLOOD OF THE GODS!

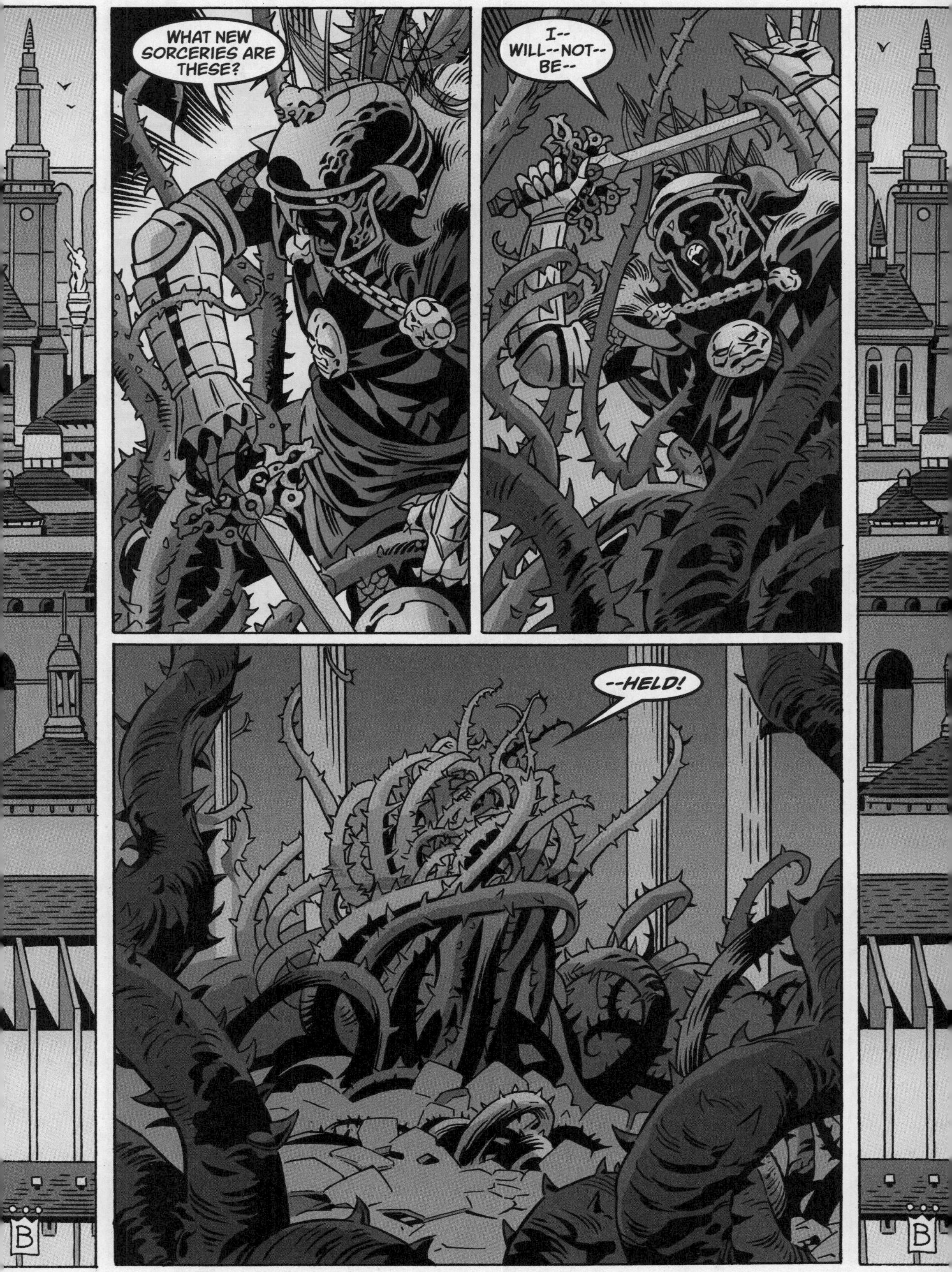
WHAT NEW SORCERIES ARE THESE?
I-- WILL--NOT-- BE--
--HELD!

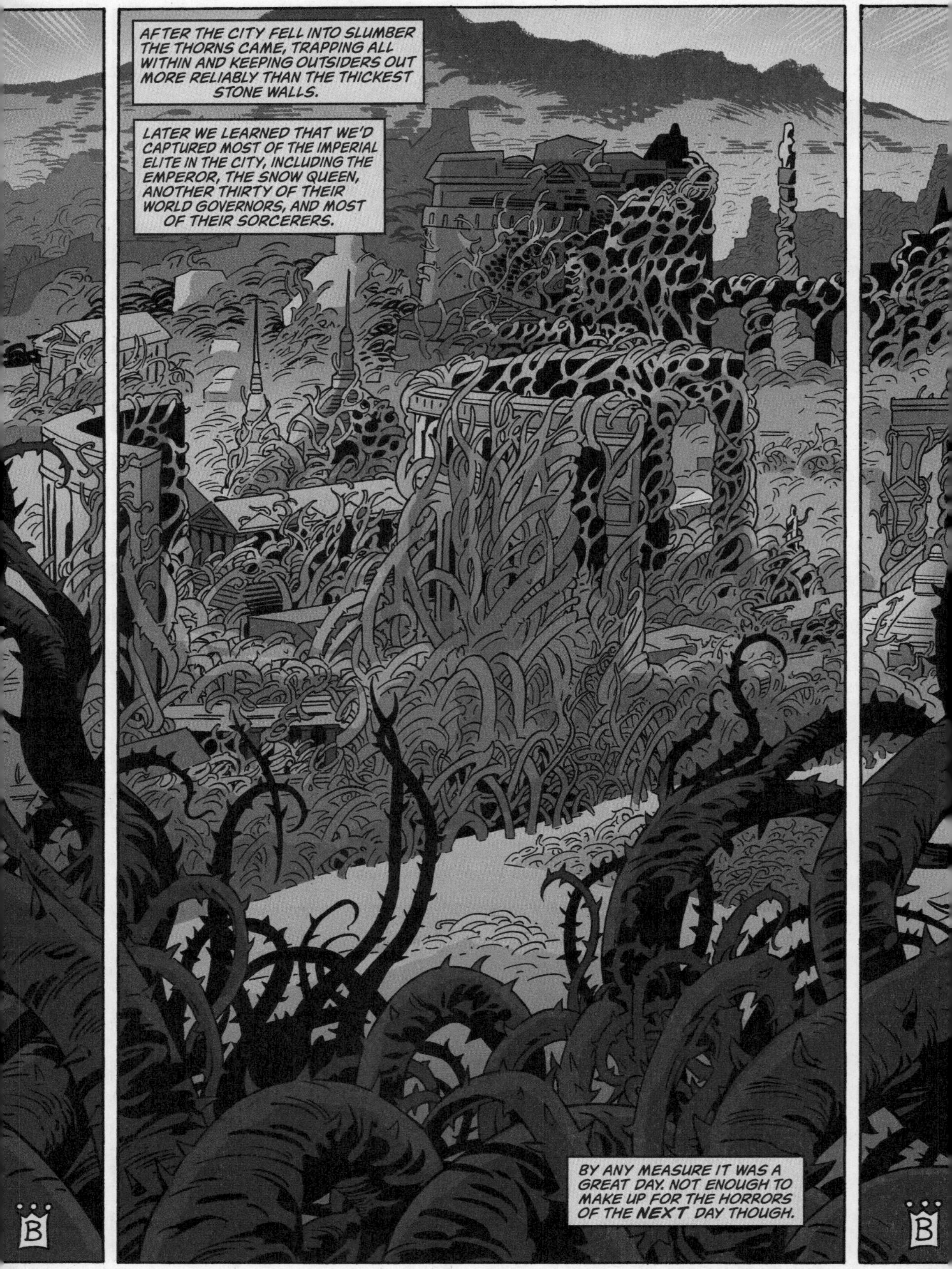
AFTER THE CITY FELL INTO SLUMBER THE THORNS CAME, TRAPPING ALL WITHIN AND KEEPING OUTSIDERS OUT MORE RELIABLY THAN THE THICKEST STONE WALLS.
LATER WE LEARNED THAT WE'D CAPTURED MOST OF THE IMPERIAL ELITE IN THE CITY, INCLUDING THE EMPEROR, THE SNOW QUEEN, ANOTHER THIRTY OF THEIR WORLD GOVERNORS, AND MOST OF THEIR SORCERERS.
BY ANY MEASURE IT WAS A GREAT DAY. NOT ENOUGH TO MAKE UP FOR THE HORRORS OF THE **NEXT** DAY THOUGH.

NEXT: THE NEXT DAY

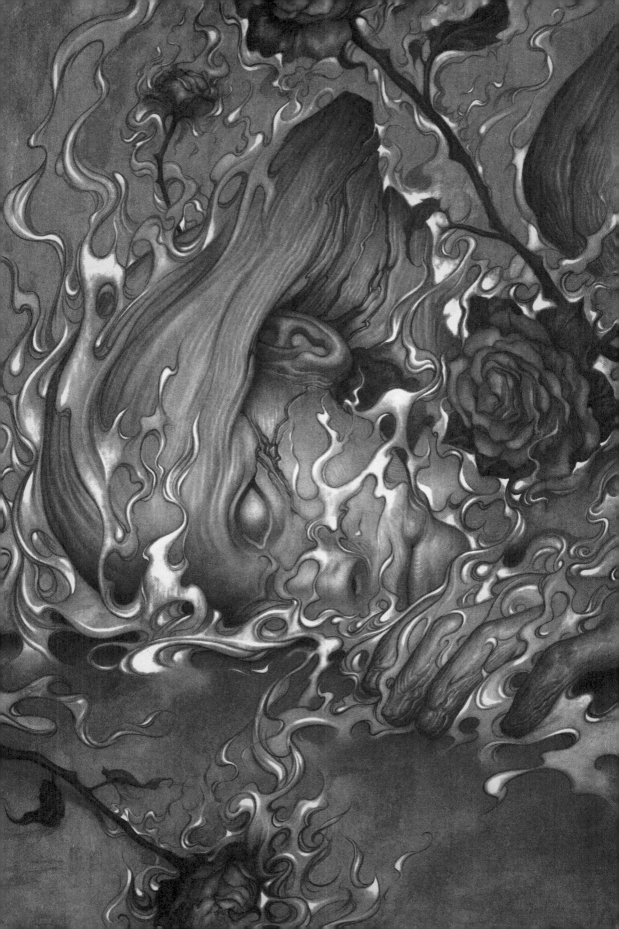

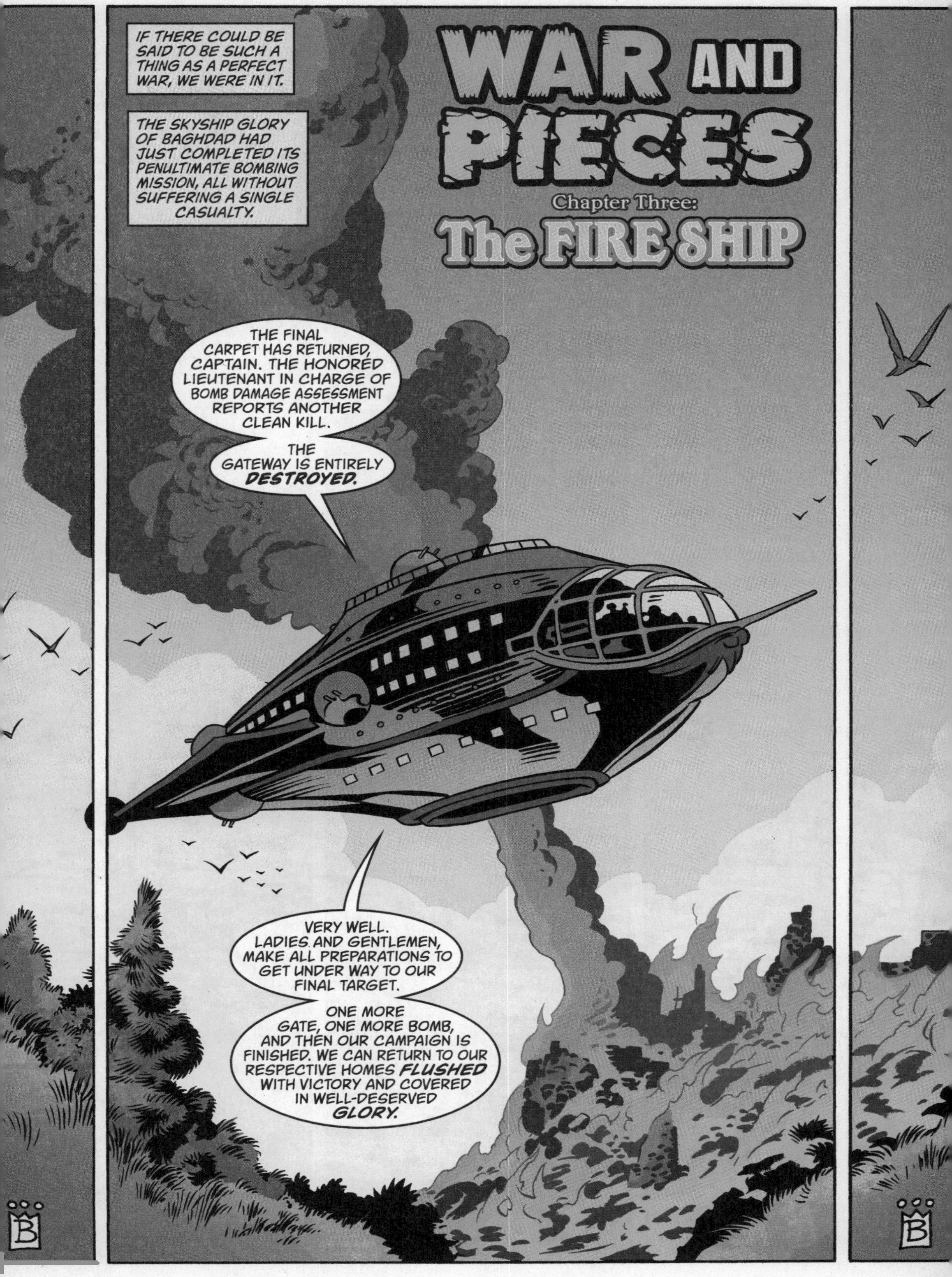
IF THERE COULD BE SAID TO BE SUCH A THING AS A PERFECT WAR, WE WERE IN IT.
THE SKYSHIP GLORY OF BAGHDAD HAD JUST COMPLETED ITS PENULTIMATE BOMBING MISSION, ALL WITHOUT SUFFERING A SINGLE CASUALTY.
WAR AND PIECES
Chapter Three:
The FIRE SHIP
THE FINAL CARPET HAS RETURNED, CAPTAIN. THE HONORED LIEUTENANT IN CHARGE OF BOMB DAMAGE ASSESSMENT REPORTS ANOTHER CLEAN KILL.
THE GATEWAY IS ENTIRELY DESTROYED.
VERY WELL. LADIES AND GENTLEMEN, MAKE ALL PREPARATIONS TO GET UNDER WAY TO OUR FINAL TARGET.
ONE MORE GATE, ONE MORE BOMB, AND THEN OUR CAMPAIGN IS FINISHED. WE CAN RETURN TO OUR RESPECTIVE HOMES FLUSHED WITH VICTORY AND COVERED IN WELL-DESERVED GLORY.

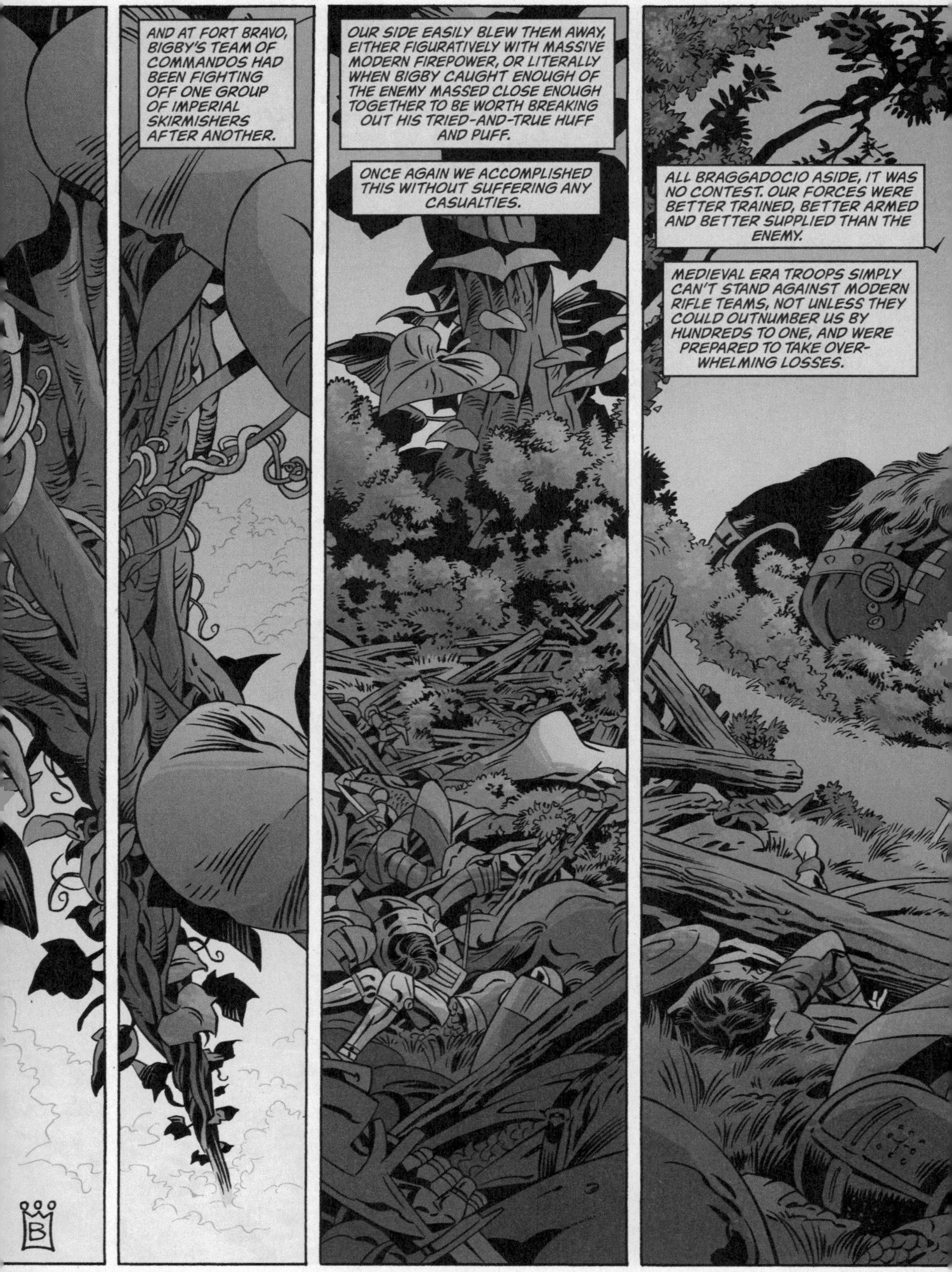
AND AT FORT BRAVO, BIGBY'S TEAM OF COMMANDOS HAD BEEN FIGHTING OFF ONE GROUP OF IMPERIAL SKIRMISHERS AFTER ANOTHER.
OUR SIDE EASILY BLEW THEM AWAY, EITHER FIGURATIVELY WITH MASSIVE MODERN FIREPOWER, OR LITERALLY WHEN BIGBY CAUGHT ENOUGH OF THE ENEMY MASSED CLOSE ENOUGH TOGETHER TO BE WORTH BREAKING OUT HIS TRIED-AND-TRUE HUFF AND PUFF.
ONCE AGAIN WE ACCOMPLISHED THIS WITHOUT SUFFERING ANY CASUALTIES.
ALL BRAGGADOCIO ASIDE, IT WAS NO CONTEST. OUR FORCES WERE BETTER TRAINED, BETTER ARMED AND BETTER SUPPLIED THAN THE ENEMY.
MEDIEVAL ERA TROOPS SIMPLY CAN'T STAND AGAINST MODERN RIFLE TEAMS, NOT UNLESS THEY COULD OUTNUMBER US BY HUNDREDS TO ONE, AND WERE PREPARED TO TAKE OVER-WHELMING LOSSES.

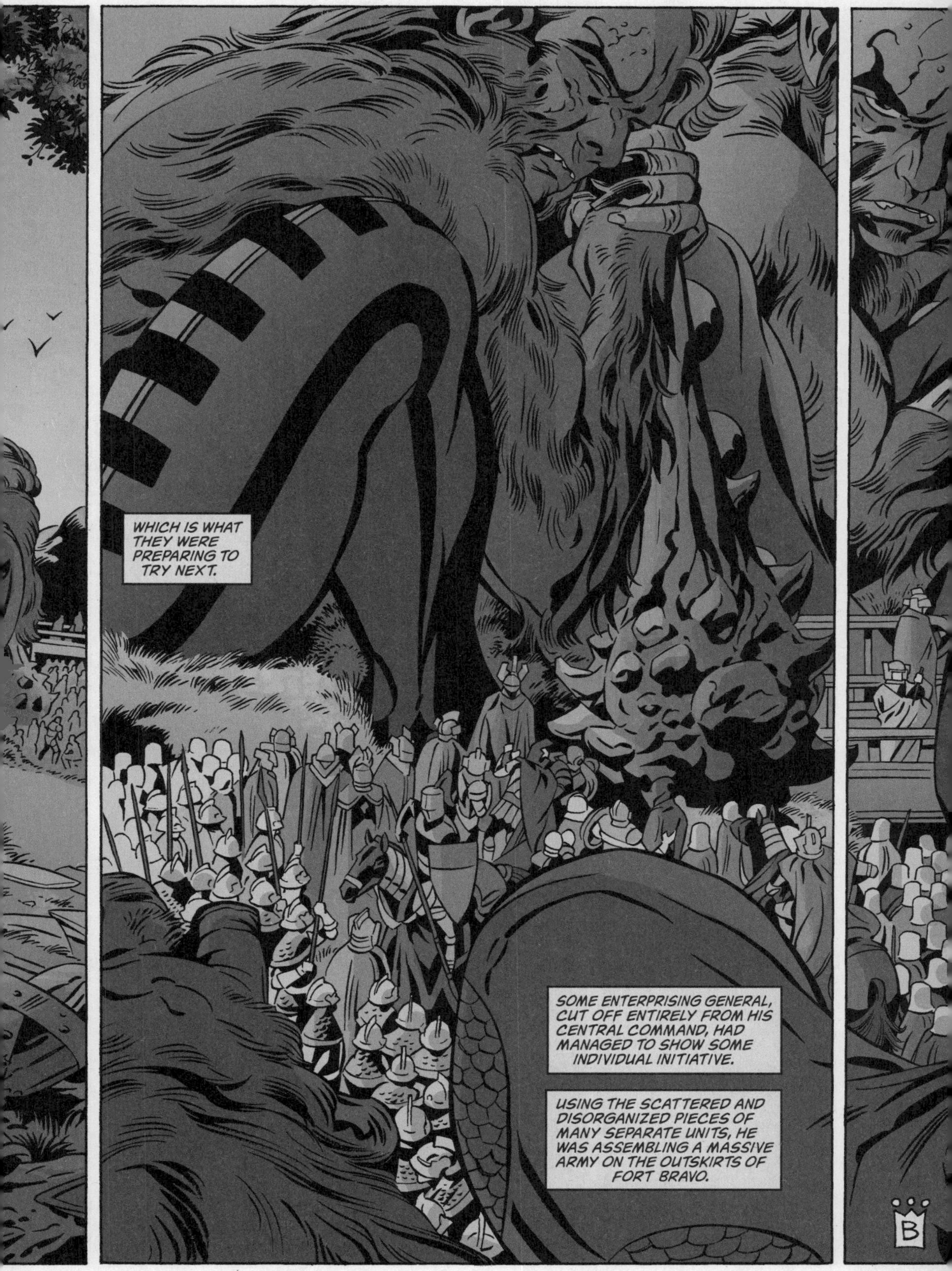
WHICH IS WHAT THEY WERE PREPARING TO TRY NEXT.
SOME ENTERPRISING GENERAL, CUT OFF ENTIRELY FROM HIS CENTRAL COMMAND, HAD MANAGED TO SHOW SOME INDIVIDUAL INITIATIVE.
USING THE SCATTERED AND DISORGANIZED PIECES OF MANY SEPARATE UNITS, HE WAS ASSEMBLING A MASSIVE ARMY ON THE OUTSKIRTS OF FORT BRAVO.

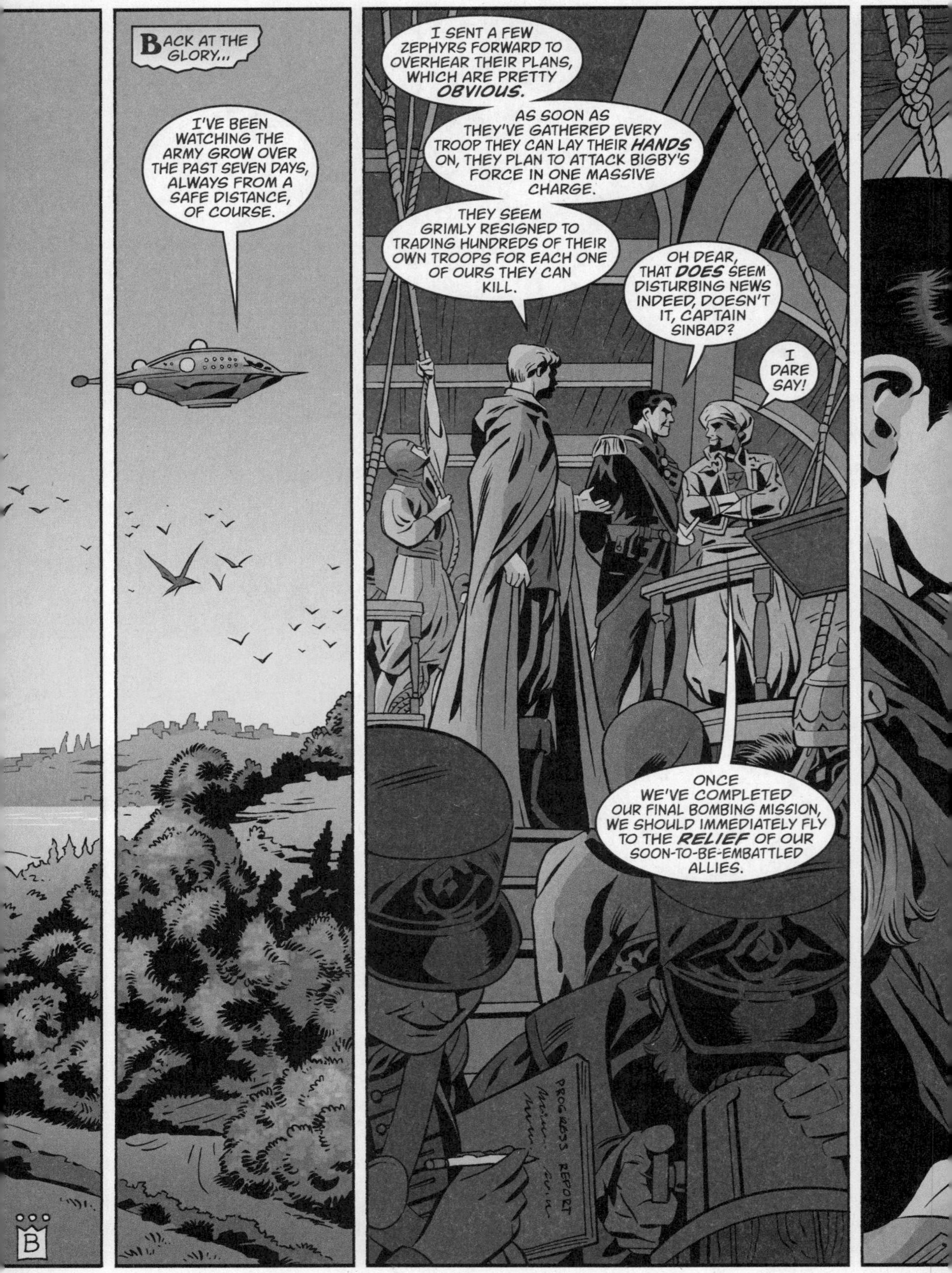
BACK AT THE GLORY...
I'VE BEEN WATCHING THE ARMY GROW OVER THE PAST SEVEN DAYS, ALWAYS FROM A SAFE DISTANCE, OF COURSE.
I SENT A FEW ZEPHYRS FORWARD TO OVERHEAR THEIR PLANS, WHICH ARE PRETTY OBVIOUS.
AS SOON AS THEY'VE GATHERED EVERY TROOP THEY CAN LAY THEIR HANDS ON, THEY PLAN TO ATTACK BIGBY'S FORCE IN ONE MASSIVE CHARGE.
THEY SEEM GRIMLY RESIGNED TO TRADING HUNDREDS OF THEIR OWN TROOPS FOR EACH ONE OF OURS THEY CAN KILL.
OH DEAR, THAT DOES SEEM DISTURBING NEWS INDEED, DOESN'T IT, CAPTAIN SINBAD?
I DARE SAY!
ONCE WE'VE COMPLETED OUR FINAL BOMBING MISSION, WE SHOULD IMMEDIATELY FLY TO THE RELIEF OF OUR SOON-TO-BE-EMBATTLED ALLIES.
PROGRESS REPORT

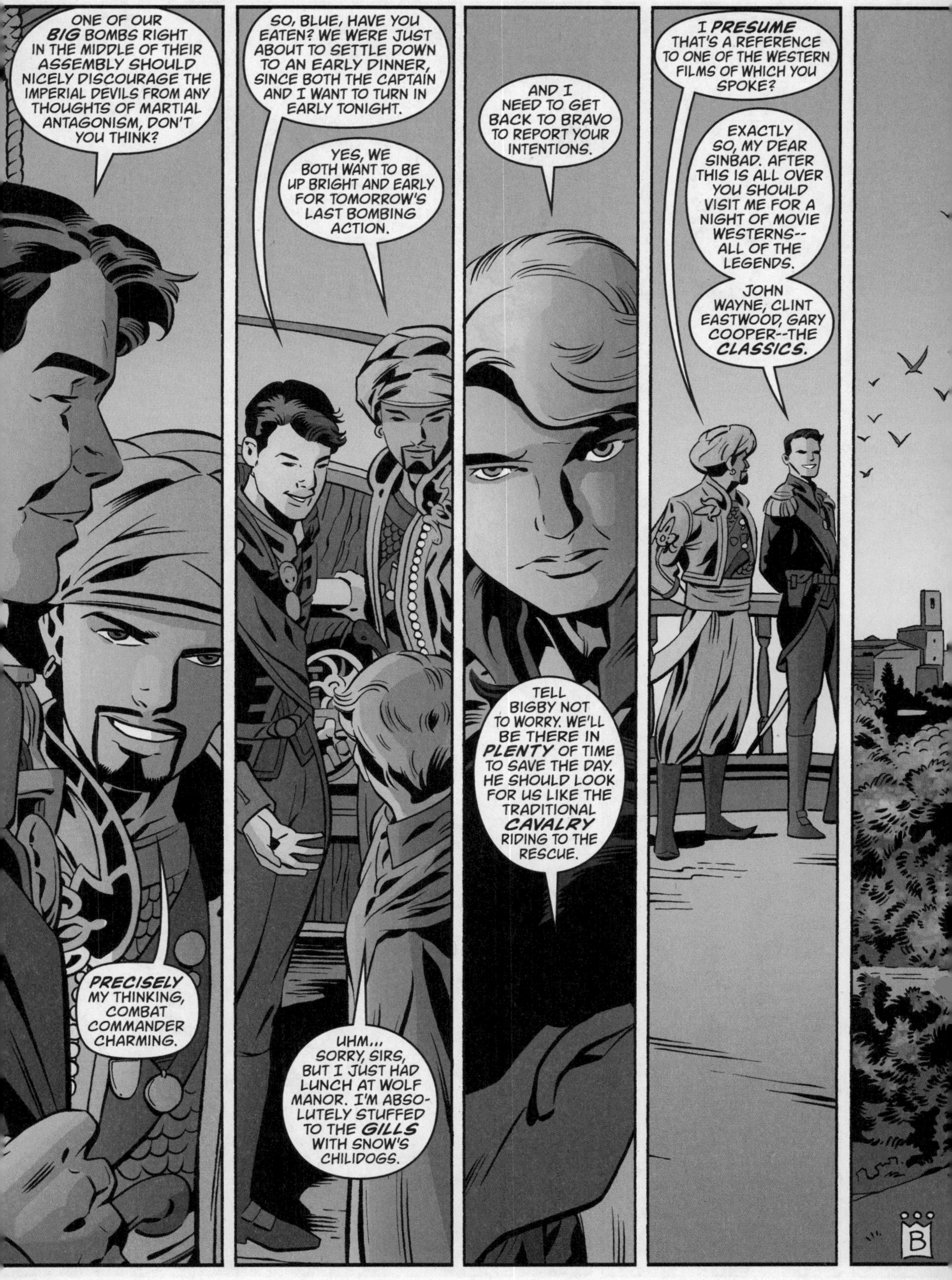
ONE OF OUR BIG BOMBS RIGHT IN THE MIDDLE OF THEIR ASSEMBLY SHOULD NICELY DISCOURAGE THE IMPERIAL DEVILS FROM ANY THOUGHTS OF MARTIAL ANTAGONISM, DON'T YOU THINK?
PRECISELY MY THINKING, COMBAT COMMANDER CHARMING.
SO, BLUE, HAVE YOU EATEN? WE WERE JUST ABOUT TO SETTLE DOWN TO AN EARLY DINNER, SINCE BOTH THE CAPTAIN AND I WANT TO TURN IN EARLY TONIGHT.
YES, WE BOTH WANT TO BE UP BRIGHT AND EARLY FOR TOMORROW'S LAST BOMBING ACTION.
UHM... SORRY, SIRS, BUT I JUST HAD LUNCH AT WOLF MANOR. I'M ABSOLUTELY STUFFED TO THE GILLS WITH SNOW'S CHILIDOGS.
AND I NEED TO GET BACK TO BRAVO TO REPORT YOUR INTENTIONS.
TELL BIGBY NOT TO WORRY. WE'LL BE THERE IN PLENTY OF TIME TO SAVE THE DAY. HE SHOULD LOOK FOR US LIKE THE TRADITIONAL CAVALRY RIDING TO THE RESCUE.
I PRESUME THAT'S A REFERENCE TO ONE OF THE WESTERN FILMS OF WHICH YOU SPOKE?
EXACTLY SO, MY DEAR SINBAD. AFTER THIS IS ALL OVER YOU SHOULD VISIT ME FOR A NIGHT OF MOVIE WESTERNS--ALL OF THE LEGENDS.
JOHN WAYNE, CLINT EASTWOOD, GARY COOPER--THE CLASSICS.

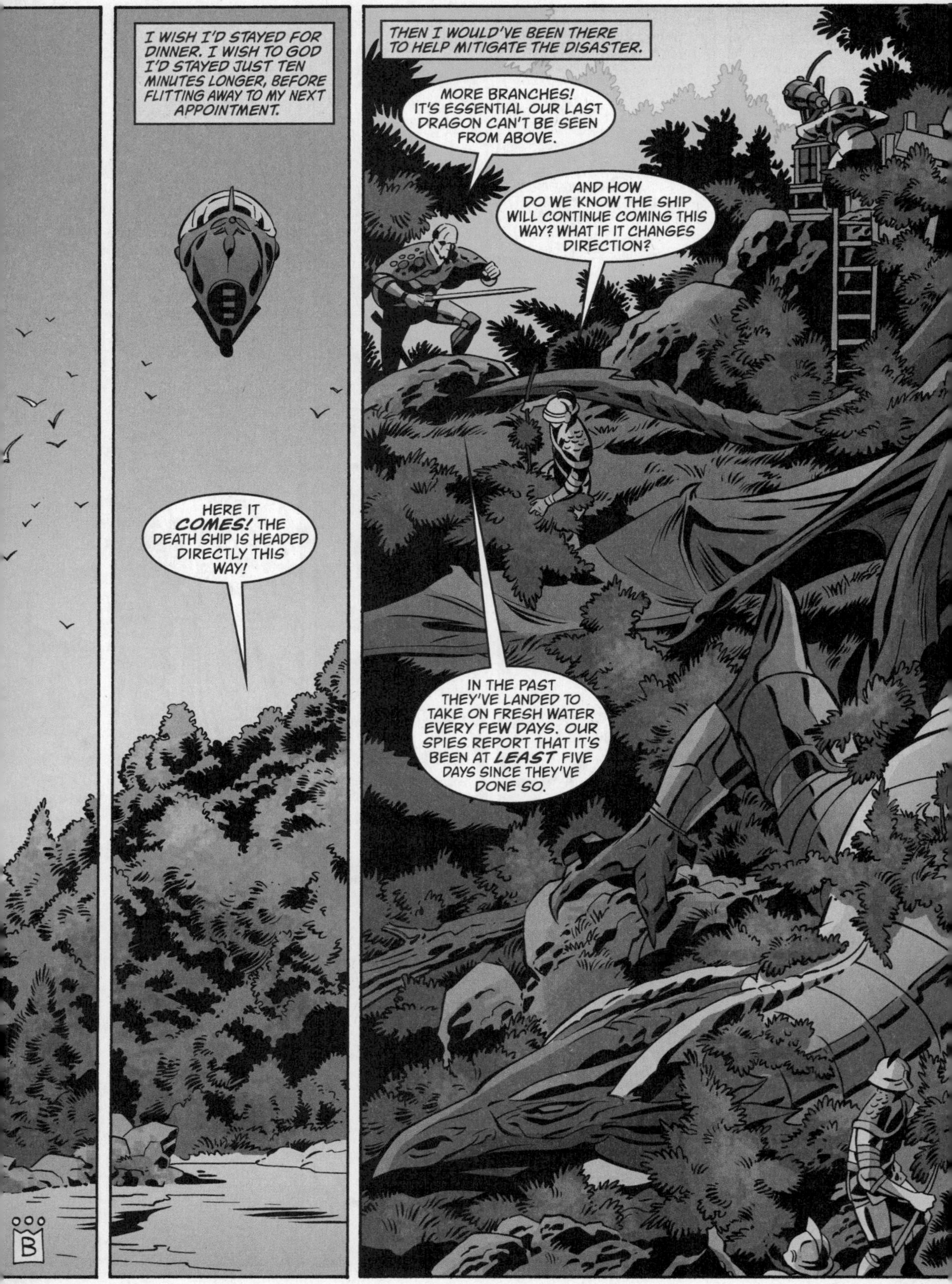
I WISH I'D STAYED FOR DINNER. I WISH TO GOD I'D STAYED JUST TEN MINUTES LONGER, BEFORE FLITTING AWAY TO MY NEXT APPOINTMENT.
HERE IT **COMES!** THE DEATH SHIP IS HEADED DIRECTLY THIS WAY!
THEN I WOULD'VE BEEN THERE TO HELP MITIGATE THE DISASTER.
MORE BRANCHES! IT'S ESSENTIAL OUR LAST DRAGON CAN'T BE SEEN FROM ABOVE.
AND HOW DO WE KNOW THE SHIP WILL CONTINUE COMING THIS WAY? WHAT IF IT CHANGES DIRECTION?
IN THE PAST THEY'VE LANDED TO TAKE ON FRESH WATER EVERY FEW DAYS. OUR SPIES REPORT THAT IT'S BEEN AT **LEAST** FIVE DAYS SINCE THEY'VE DONE SO.

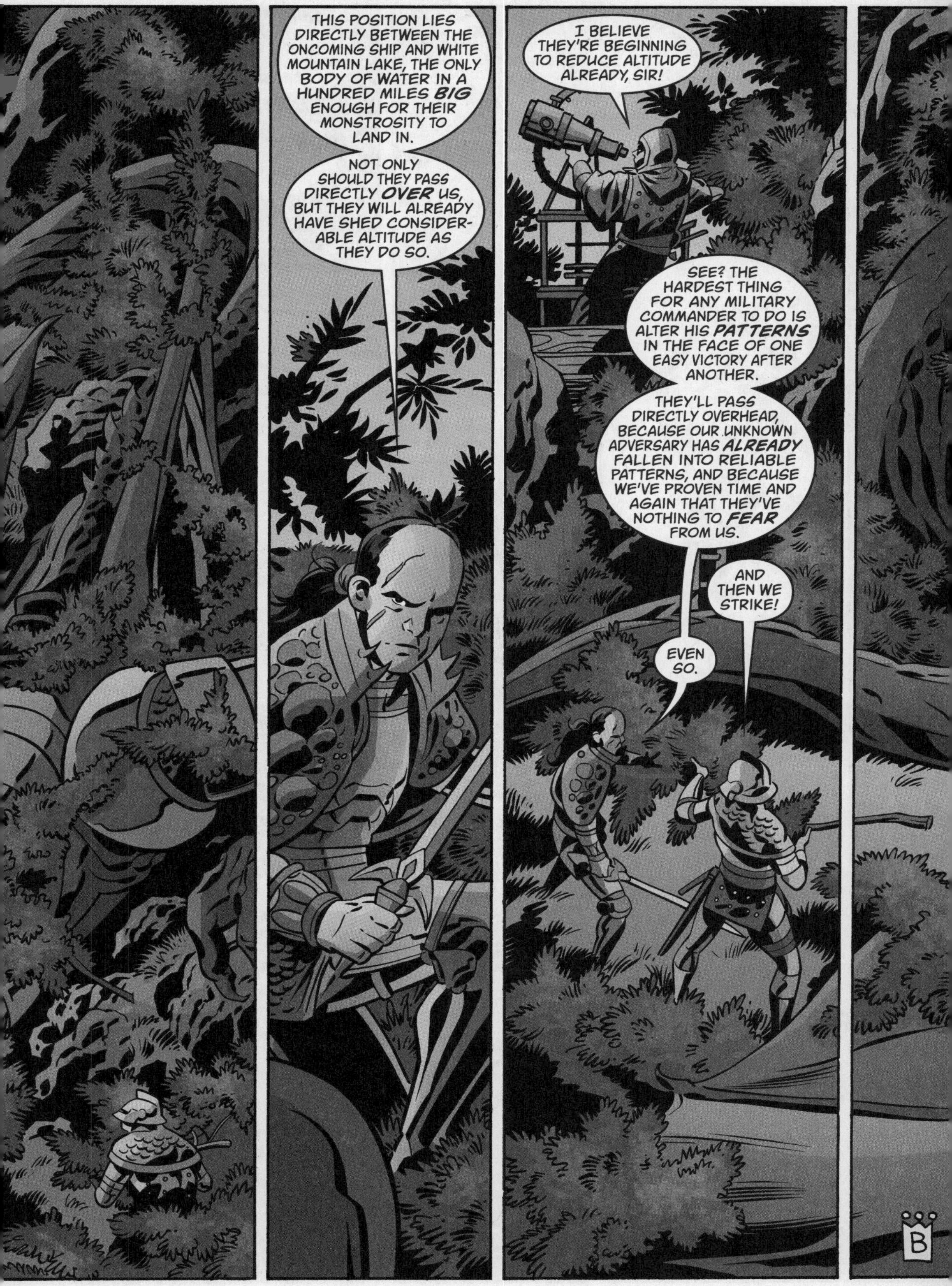
THIS POSITION LIES DIRECTLY BETWEEN THE ONCOMING SHIP AND WHITE MOUNTAIN LAKE, THE ONLY BODY OF WATER IN A HUNDRED MILES BIG ENOUGH FOR THEIR MONSTROSITY TO LAND IN.
NOT ONLY SHOULD THEY PASS DIRECTLY OVER US, BUT THEY WILL ALREADY HAVE SHED CONSIDER-ABLE ALTITUDE AS THEY DO SO.
I BELIEVE THEY'RE BEGINNING TO REDUCE ALTITUDE ALREADY, SIR!
SEE? THE HARDEST THING FOR ANY MILITARY COMMANDER TO DO IS ALTER HIS PATTERNS IN THE FACE OF ONE EASY VICTORY AFTER ANOTHER.
THEY'LL PASS DIRECTLY OVERHEAD, BECAUSE OUR UNKNOWN ADVERSARY HAS ALREADY FALLEN INTO RELIABLE PATTERNS, AND BECAUSE WE'VE PROVEN TIME AND AGAIN THAT THEY'VE NOTHING TO FEAR FROM US.
EVEN SO.
AND THEN WE STRIKE!

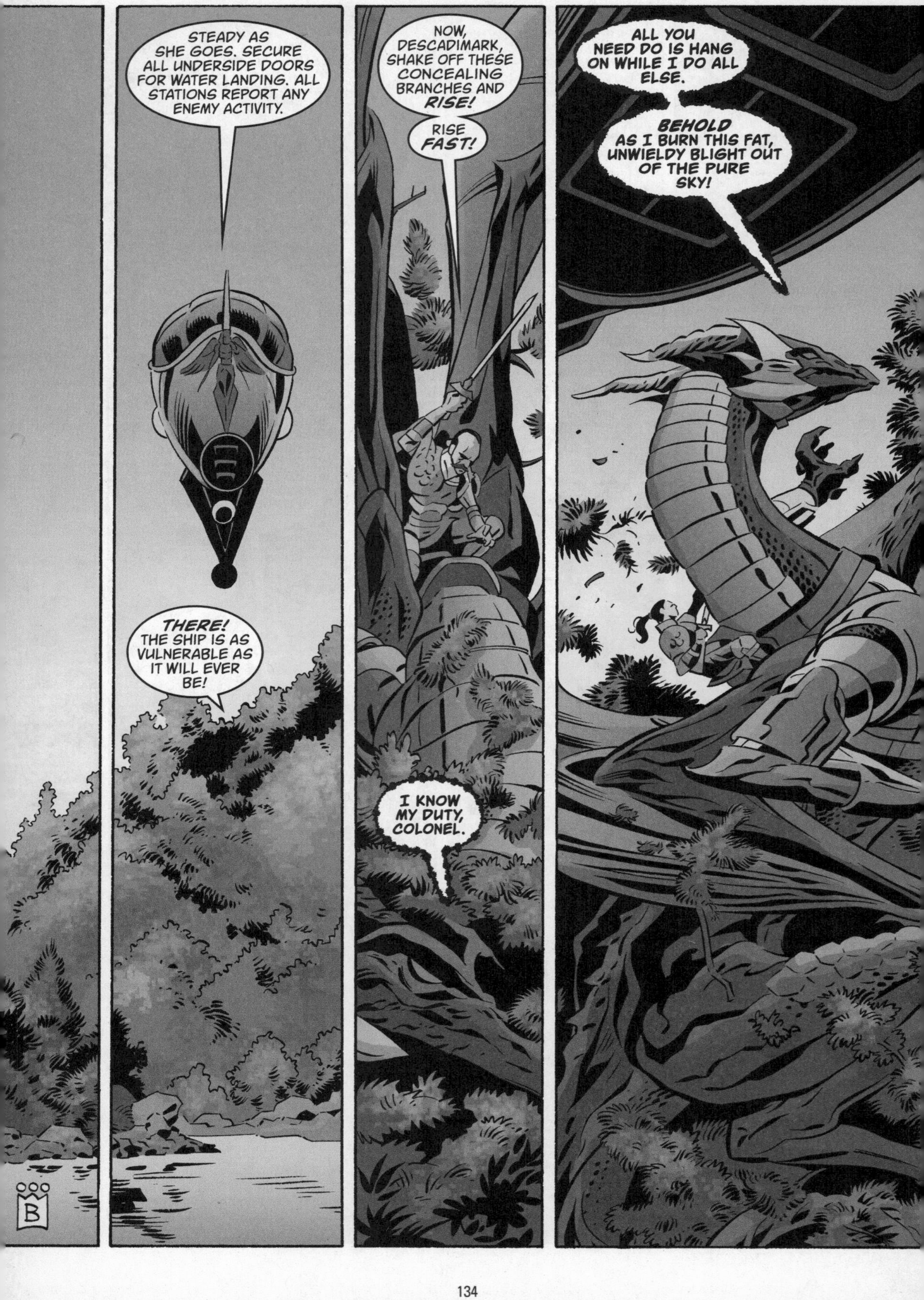
STEADY AS SHE GOES. SECURE ALL UNDERSIDE DOORS FOR WATER LANDING. ALL STATIONS REPORT ANY ENEMY ACTIVITY.
THERE! THE SHIP IS AS VULNERABLE AS IT WILL EVER BE!
NOW, DESCADIMARK, SHAKE OFF THESE CONCEALING BRANCHES AND RISE!
RISE FAST!
I KNOW MY DUTY, COLONEL.
ALL YOU NEED DO IS HANG ON WHILE I DO ALL ELSE.
BEHOLD AS I BURN THIS FAT, UNWIELDY BLIGHT OUT OF THE PURE SKY!

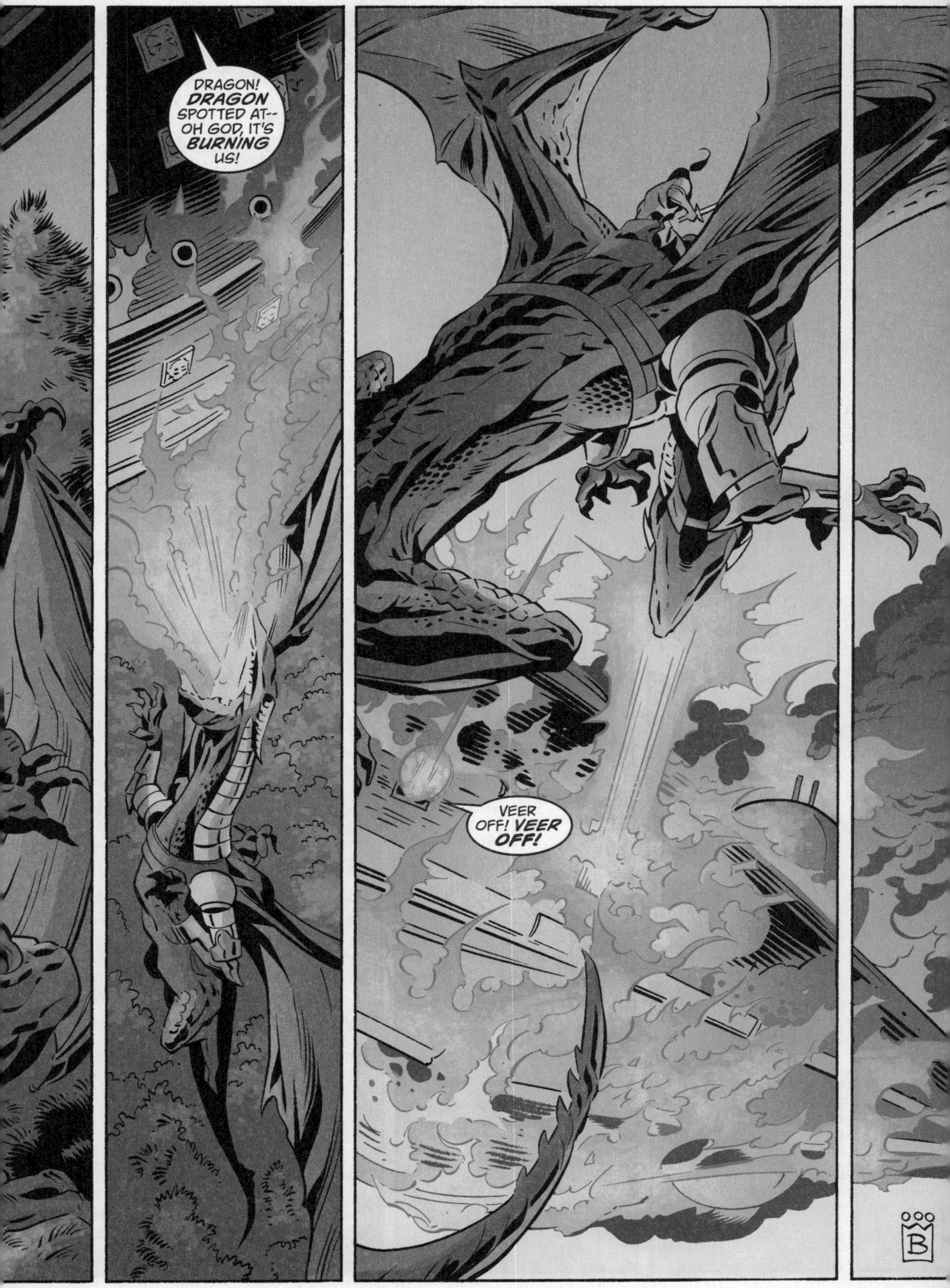
DRAGON! **DRAGON** SPOTTED AT-- OH GOD, IT'S **BURNING** US!
VEER OFF! **VEER OFF!**

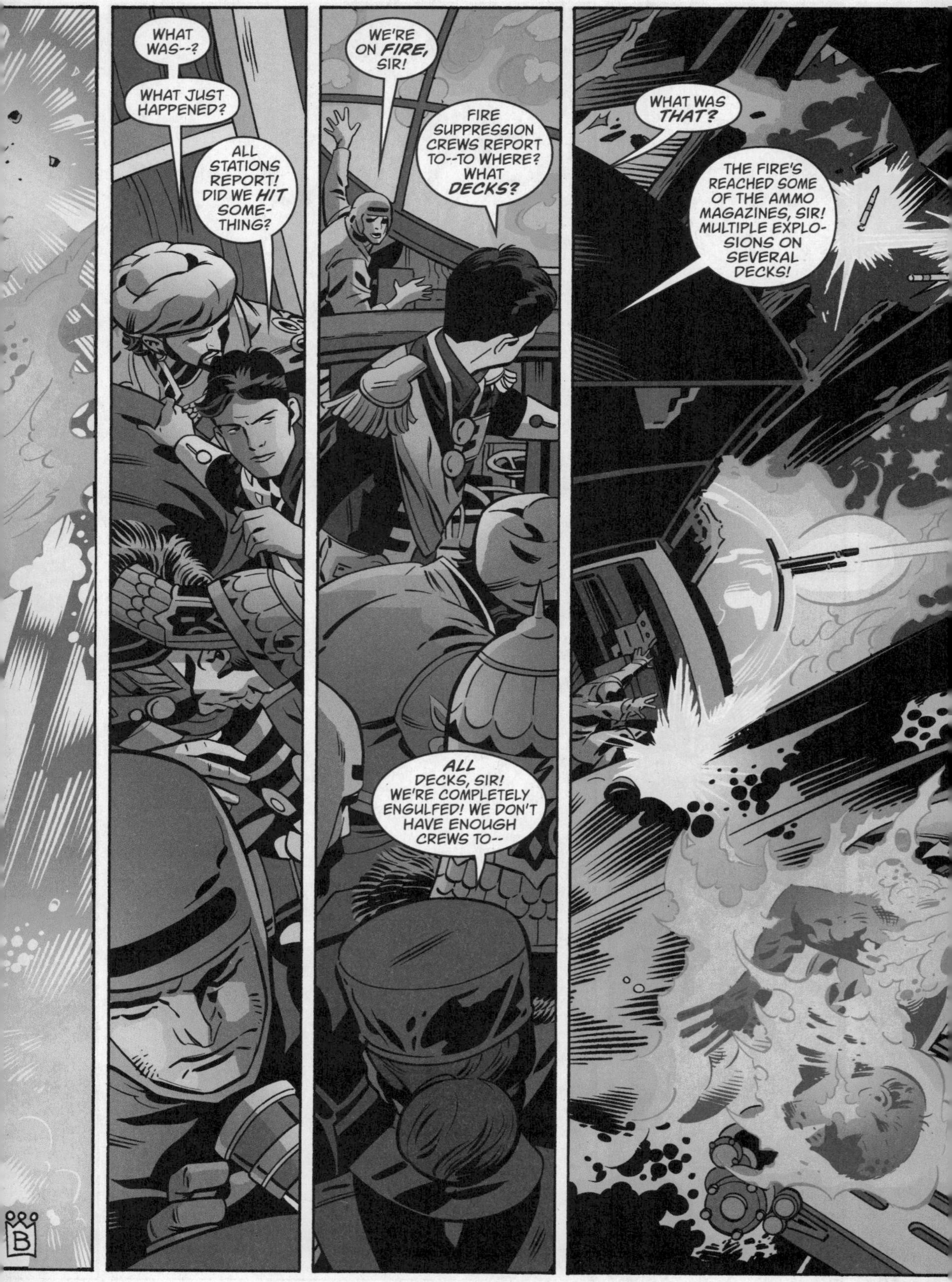
WHAT WAS--?
WHAT JUST HAPPENED?
ALL STATIONS REPORT! DID WE HIT SOME-THING?
WE'RE ON FIRE, SIR!
FIRE SUPPRESSION CREWS REPORT TO--TO WHERE? WHAT DECKS?
ALL DECKS, SIR! WE'RE COMPLETELY ENGULFED! WE DON'T HAVE ENOUGH CREWS TO--
WHAT WAS THAT?
THE FIRE'S REACHED SOME OF THE AMMO MAGAZINES, SIR! MULTIPLE EXPLO-SIONS ON SEVERAL DECKS!

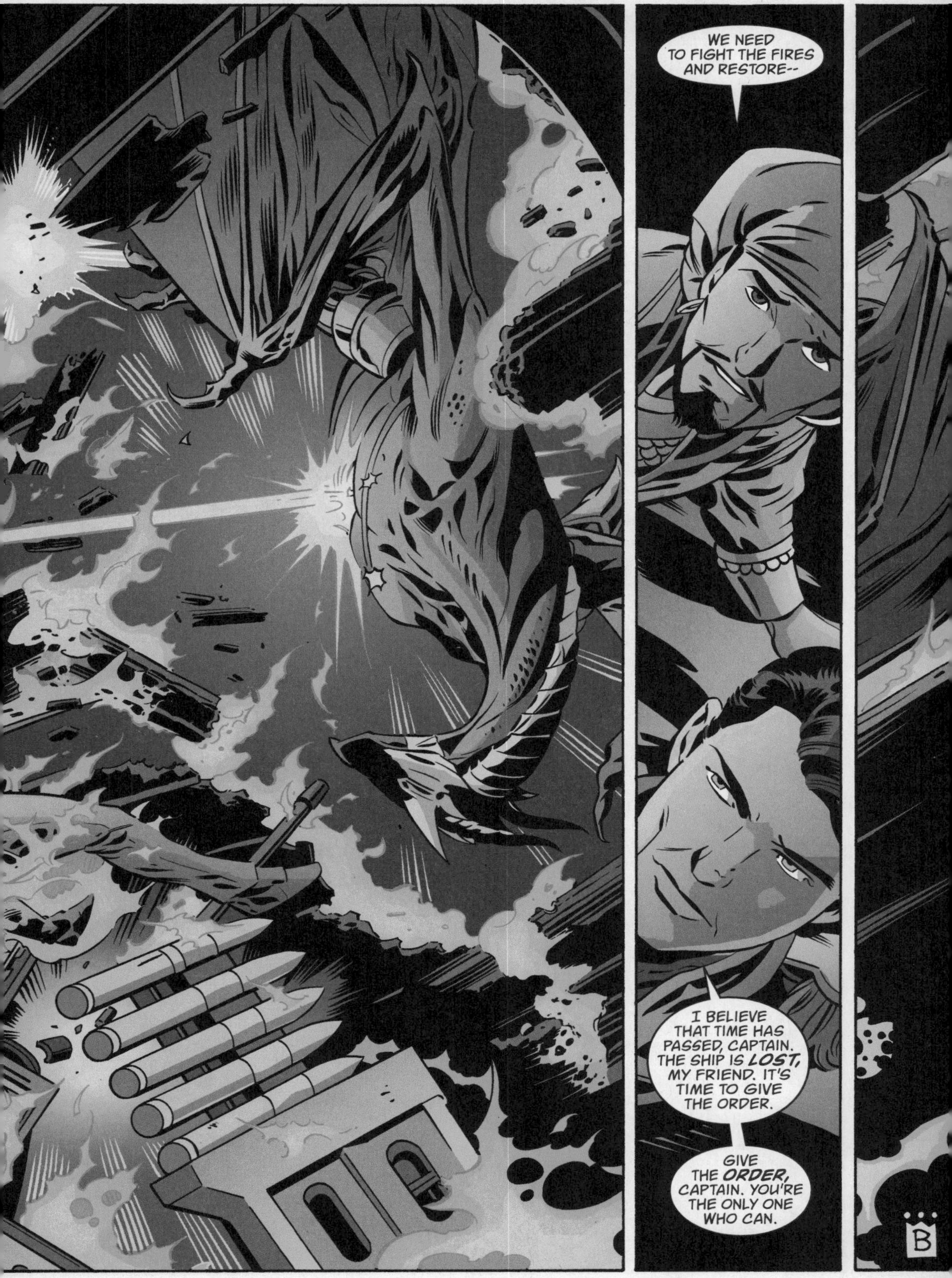
WE NEED TO FIGHT THE FIRES AND RESTORE--
I BELIEVE THAT TIME HAS PASSED, CAPTAIN. THE SHIP IS LOST, MY FRIEND. IT'S TIME TO GIVE THE ORDER.
GIVE THE ORDER, CAPTAIN. YOU'RE THE ONLY ONE WHO CAN.

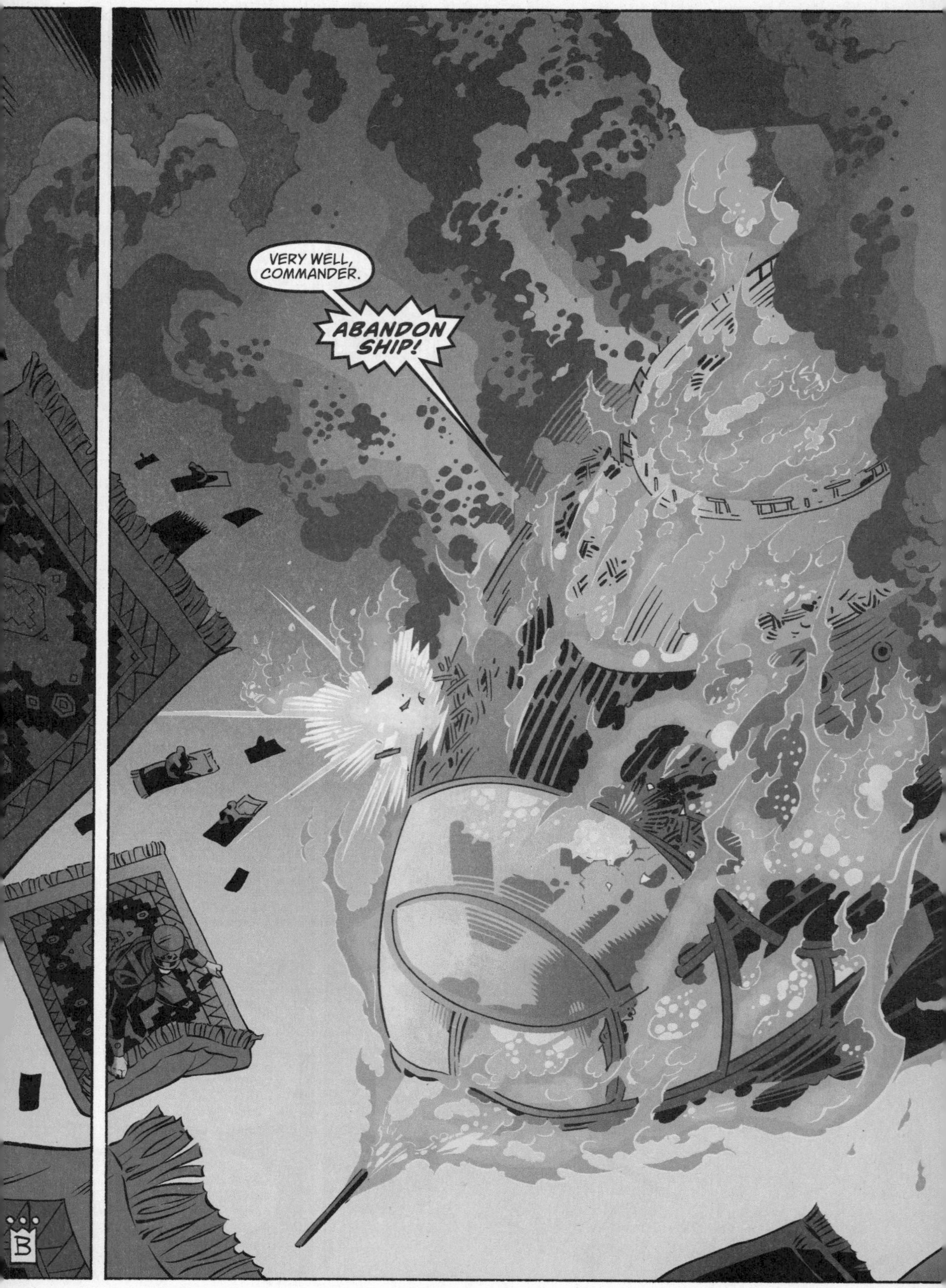
VERY WELL, COMMANDER.
ABANDON SHIP!

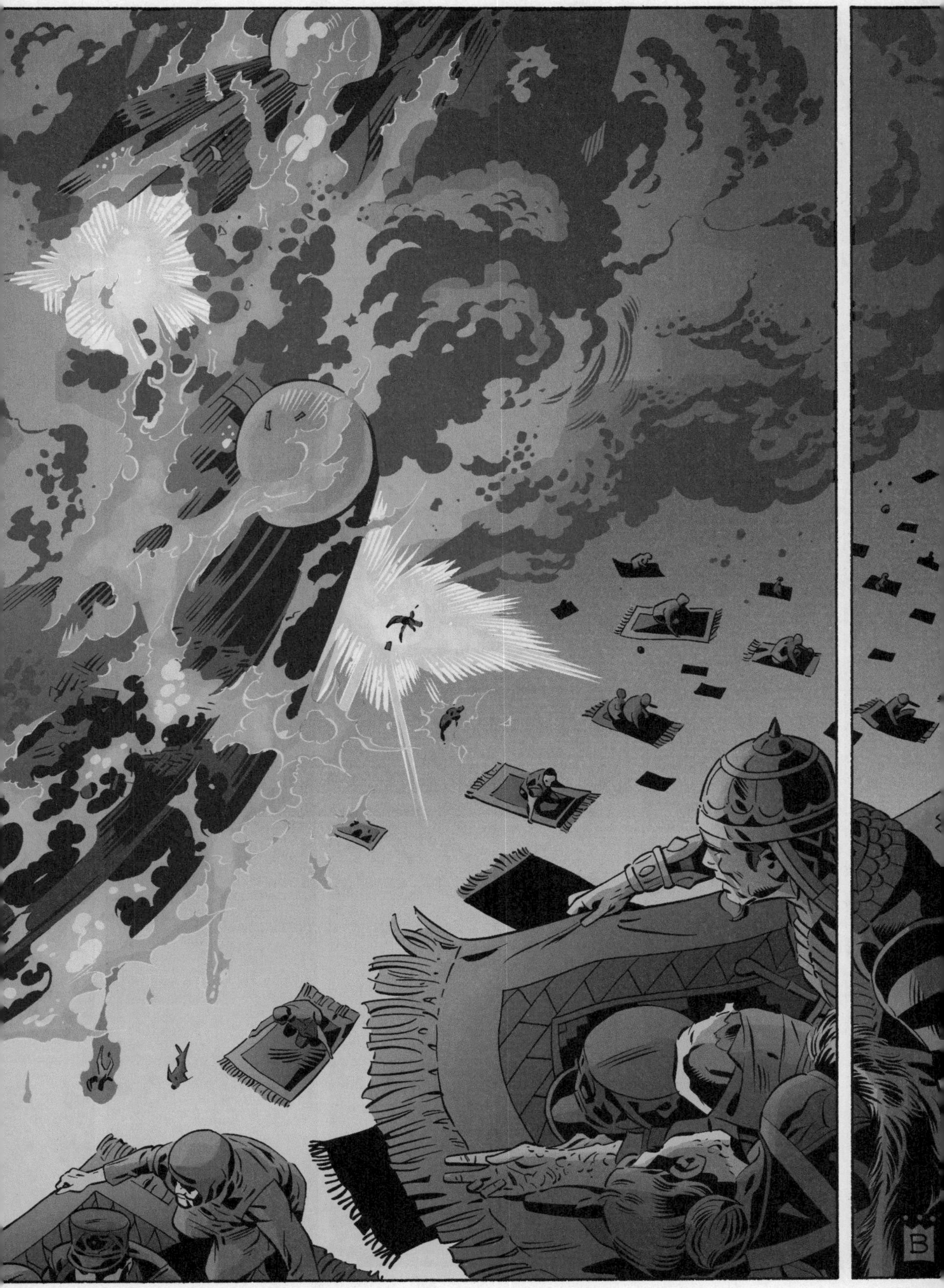

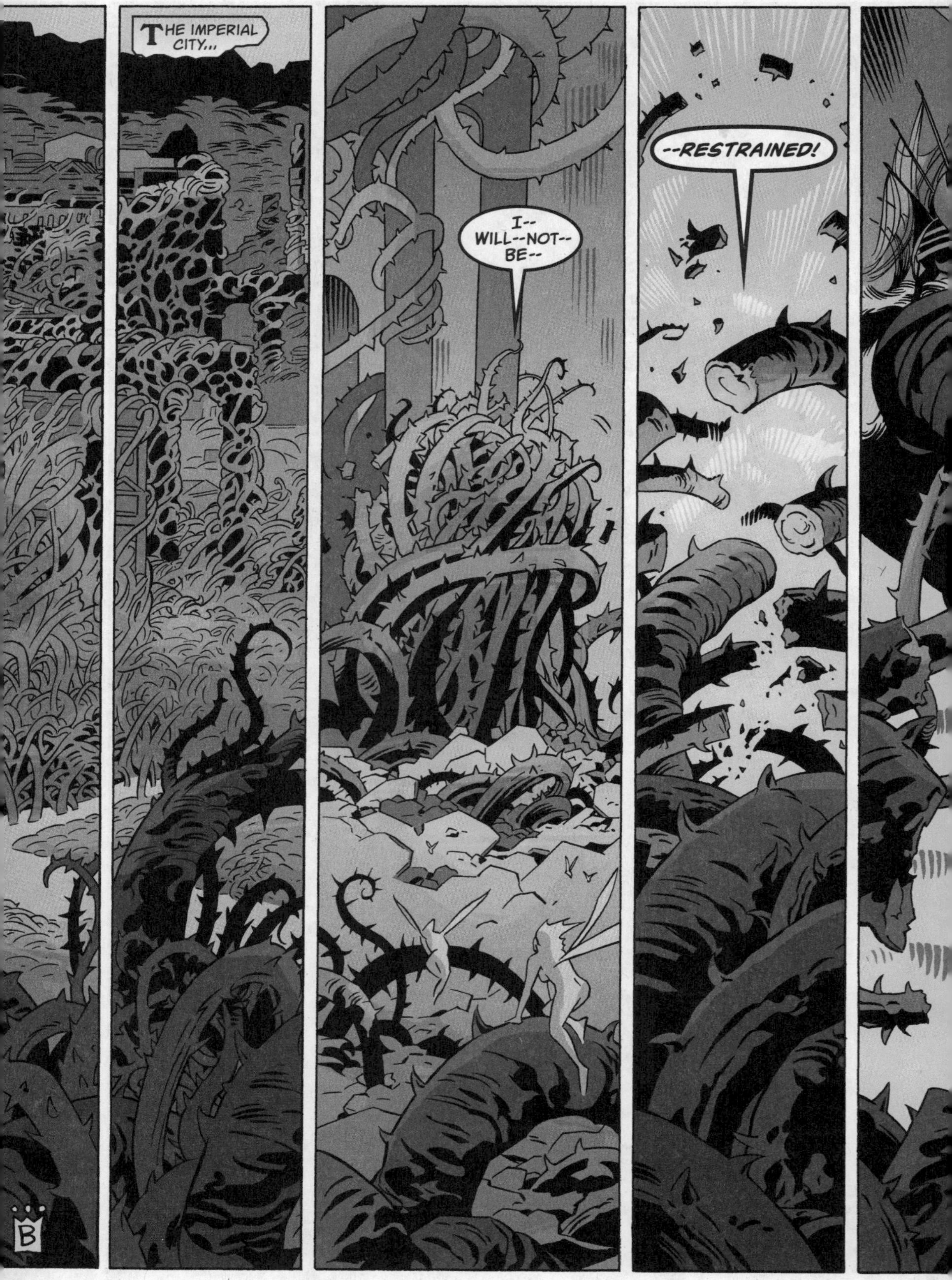
THE IMPERIAL CITY...
I-- WILL--NOT-- BE--
--RESTRAINED!

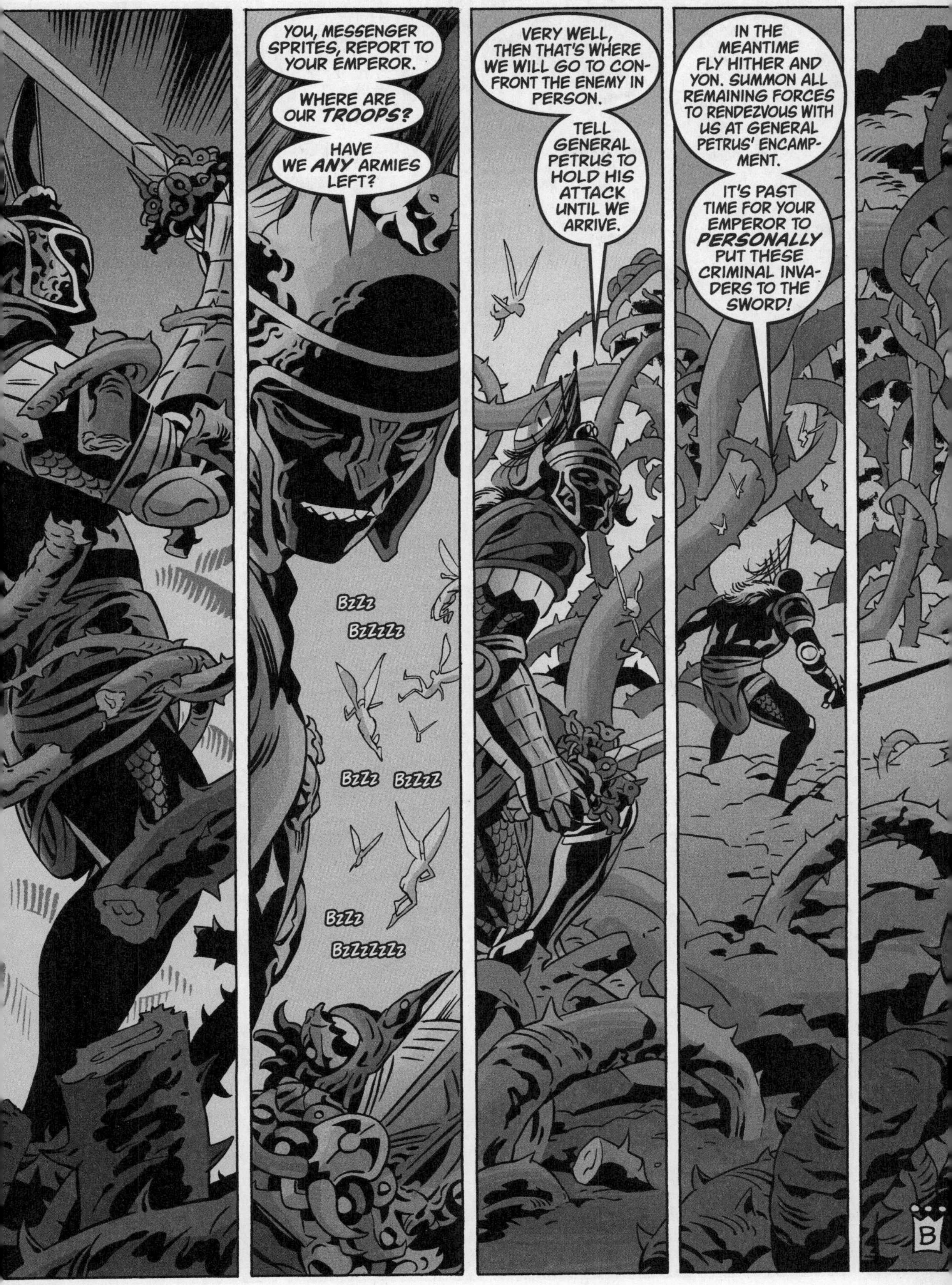
YOU, MESSENGER SPRITES, REPORT TO YOUR EMPEROR.
WHERE ARE OUR TROOPS?
HAVE WE ANY ARMIES LEFT?
BzZz
BzZzZz
BzZz BzZzZ
BzZz
BzZzZzZz
VERY WELL, THEN THAT'S WHERE WE WILL GO TO CON-FRONT THE ENEMY IN PERSON.
TELL GENERAL PETRUS TO HOLD HIS ATTACK UNTIL WE ARRIVE.
IN THE MEANTIME FLY HITHER AND YON. SUMMON ALL REMAINING FORCES TO RENDEZVOUS WITH US AT GENERAL PETRUS' ENCAMP-MENT.
IT'S PAST TIME FOR YOUR EMPEROR TO PERSONALLY PUT THESE CRIMINAL INVA-DERS TO THE SWORD!

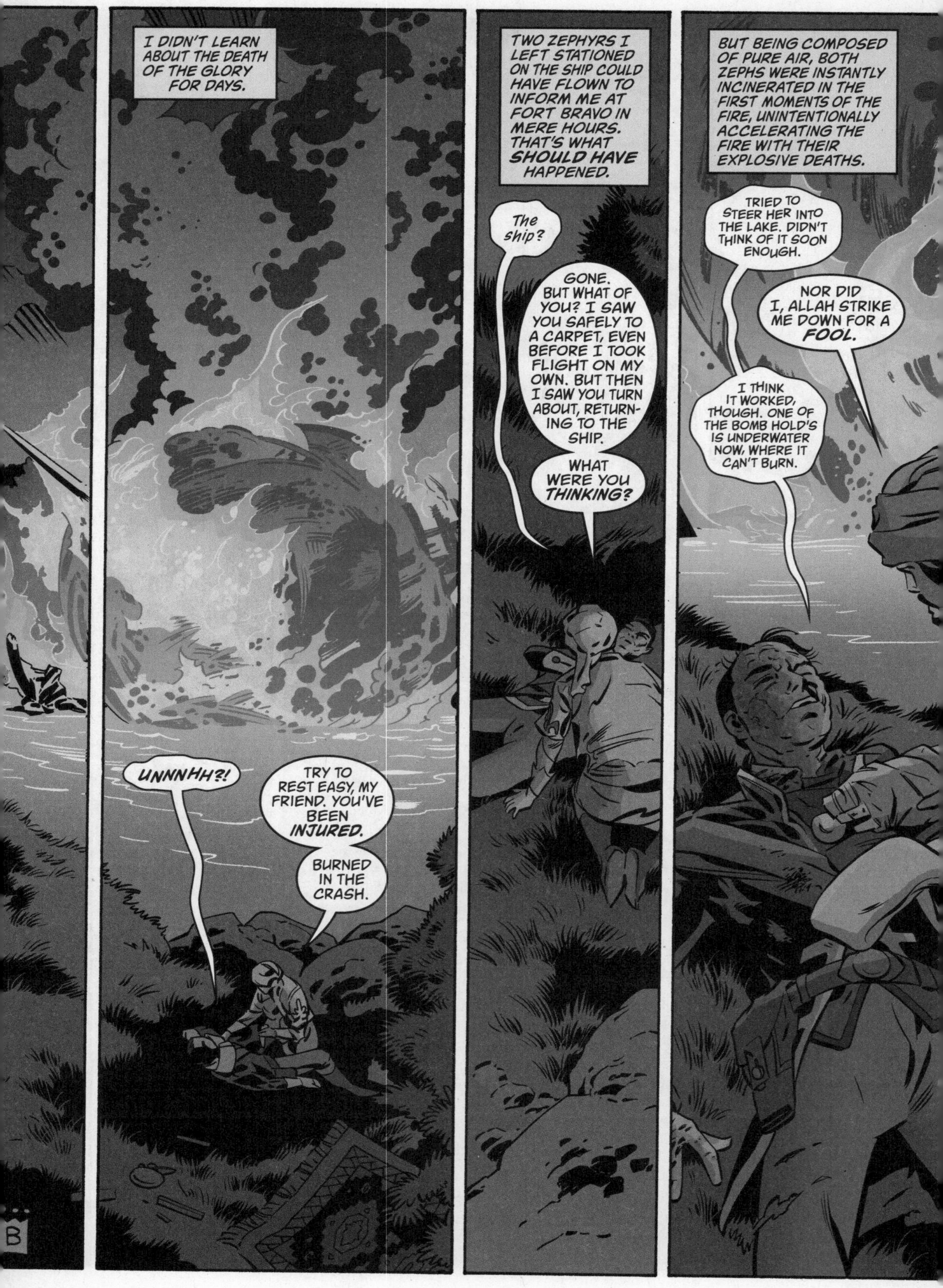

I DIDN'T LEARN ABOUT THE DEATH OF THE GLORY FOR DAYS.
UNNNHH?!
TRY TO REST EASY, MY FRIEND. YOU'VE BEEN INJURED.
BURNED IN THE CRASH.
TWO ZEPHYRS I LEFT STATIONED ON THE SHIP COULD HAVE FLOWN TO INFORM ME AT FORT BRAVO IN MERE HOURS. THAT'S WHAT SHOULD HAVE HAPPENED.
The ship?
GONE. BUT WHAT OF YOU? I SAW YOU SAFELY TO A CARPET, EVEN BEFORE I TOOK FLIGHT ON MY OWN. BUT THEN I SAW YOU TURN ABOUT, RETURNING TO THE SHIP.
WHAT WERE YOU THINKING?
BUT BEING COMPOSED OF PURE AIR, BOTH ZEPHS WERE INSTANTLY INCINERATED IN THE FIRST MOMENTS OF THE FIRE, UNINTENTIONALLY ACCELERATING THE FIRE WITH THEIR EXPLOSIVE DEATHS.
TRIED TO STEER HER INTO THE LAKE. DIDN'T THINK OF IT SOON ENOUGH.
NOR DID I, ALLAH STRIKE ME DOWN FOR A FOOL.
I THINK IT WORKED, THOUGH. ONE OF THE BOMB HOLD'S IS UNDERWATER NOW, WHERE IT CAN'T BURN.
B

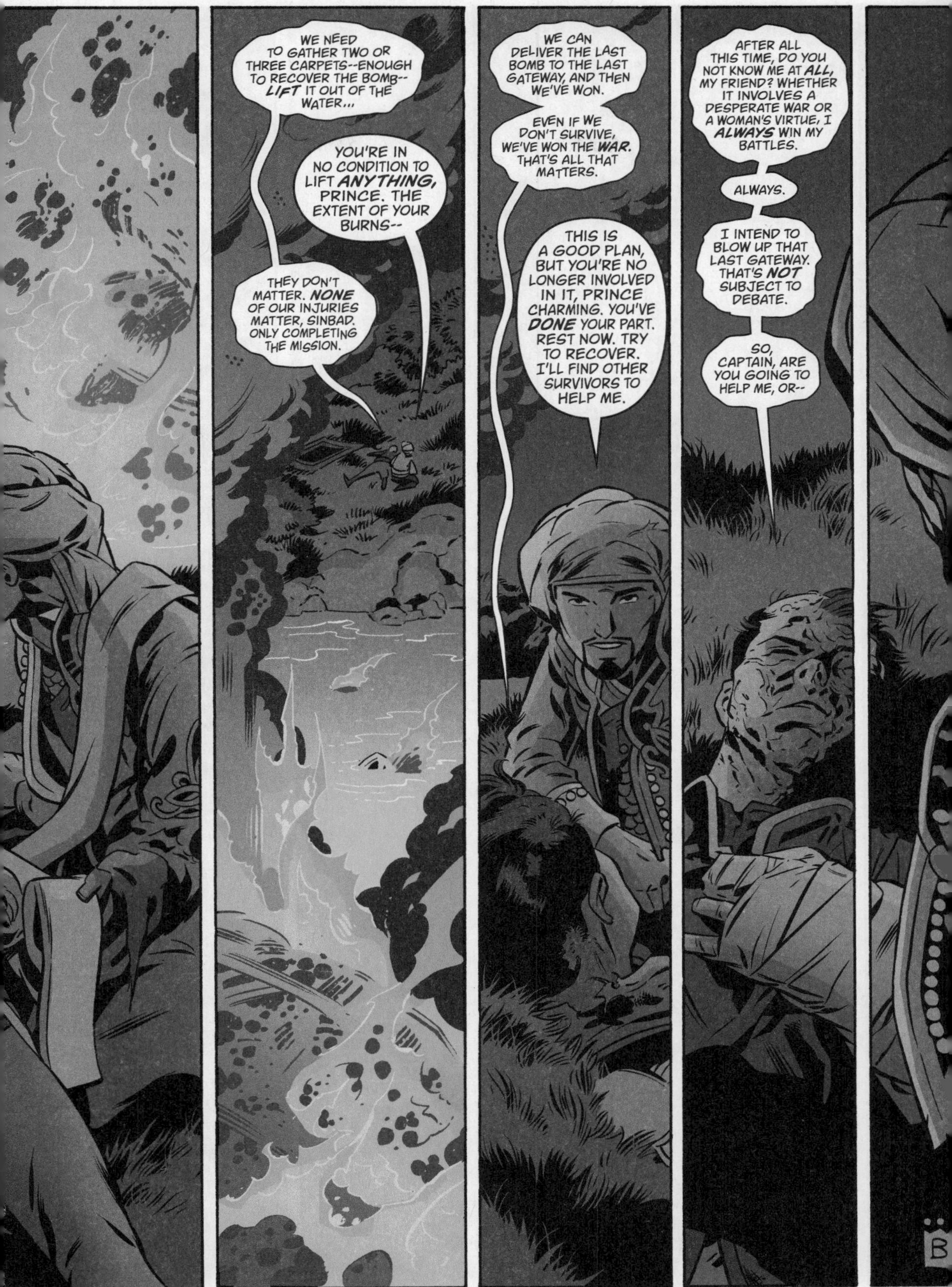

WE NEED TO GATHER TWO OR THREE CARPETS--ENOUGH TO RECOVER THE BOMB--LIFT IT OUT OF THE WATER...
YOU'RE IN NO CONDITION TO LIFT ANYTHING, PRINCE. THE EXTENT OF YOUR BURNS--
THEY DON'T MATTER. NONE OF OUR INJURIES MATTER, SINBAD. ONLY COMPLETING THE MISSION.
WE CAN DELIVER THE LAST BOMB TO THE LAST GATEWAY, AND THEN WE'VE WON.
EVEN IF WE DON'T SURVIVE, WE'VE WON THE WAR. THAT'S ALL THAT MATTERS.
THIS IS A GOOD PLAN, BUT YOU'RE NO LONGER INVOLVED IN IT, PRINCE CHARMING. YOU'VE DONE YOUR PART. REST NOW. TRY TO RECOVER. I'LL FIND OTHER SURVIVORS TO HELP ME.
AFTER ALL THIS TIME, DO YOU NOT KNOW ME AT ALL, MY FRIEND? WHETHER IT INVOLVES A DESPERATE WAR OR A WOMAN'S VIRTUE, I ALWAYS WIN MY BATTLES.
ALWAYS.
I INTEND TO BLOW UP THAT LAST GATEWAY. THAT'S NOT SUBJECT TO DEBATE.
SO, CAPTAIN, ARE YOU GOING TO HELP ME, OR--

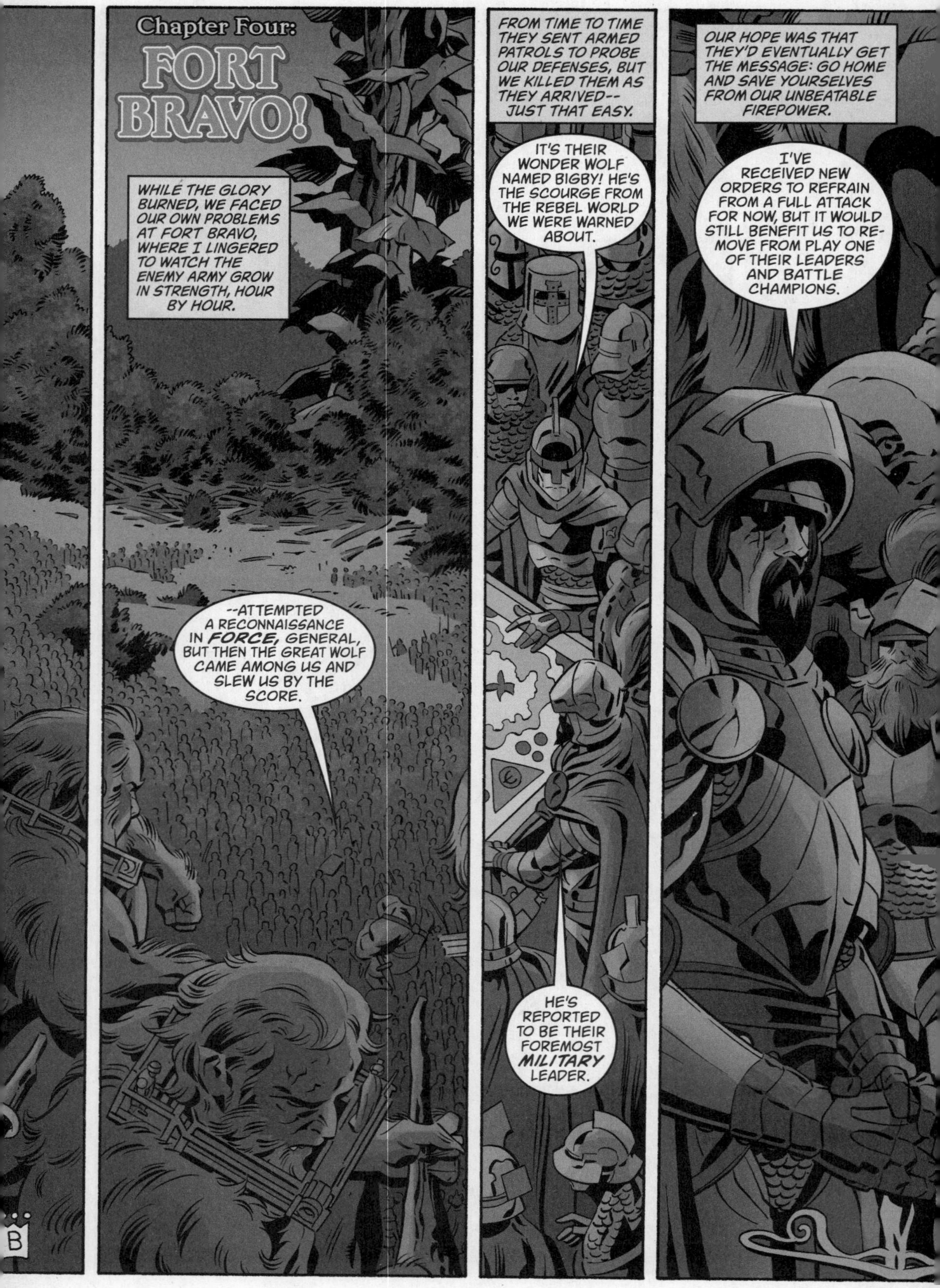
Chapter Four:
FORT BRAVO!
WHILE THE GLORY BURNED, WE FACED OUR OWN PROBLEMS AT FORT BRAVO, WHERE I LINGERED TO WATCH THE ENEMY ARMY GROW IN STRENGTH, HOUR BY HOUR.
--ATTEMPTED A RECONNAISSANCE IN FORCE, GENERAL, BUT THEN THE GREAT WOLF CAME AMONG US AND SLEW US BY THE SCORE.
FROM TIME TO TIME THEY SENT ARMED PATROLS TO PROBE OUR DEFENSES, BUT WE KILLED THEM AS THEY ARRIVED-- JUST THAT EASY.
IT'S THEIR WONDER WOLF NAMED BIGBY! HE'S THE SCOURGE FROM THE REBEL WORLD WE WERE WARNED ABOUT.
HE'S REPORTED TO BE THEIR FOREMOST MILITARY LEADER.
OUR HOPE WAS THAT THEY'D EVENTUALLY GET THE MESSAGE: GO HOME AND SAVE YOURSELVES FROM OUR UNBEATABLE FIREPOWER.
I'VE RECEIVED NEW ORDERS TO REFRAIN FROM A FULL ATTACK FOR NOW, BUT IT WOULD STILL BENEFIT US TO RE-MOVE FROM PLAY ONE OF THEIR LEADERS AND BATTLE CHAMPIONS.

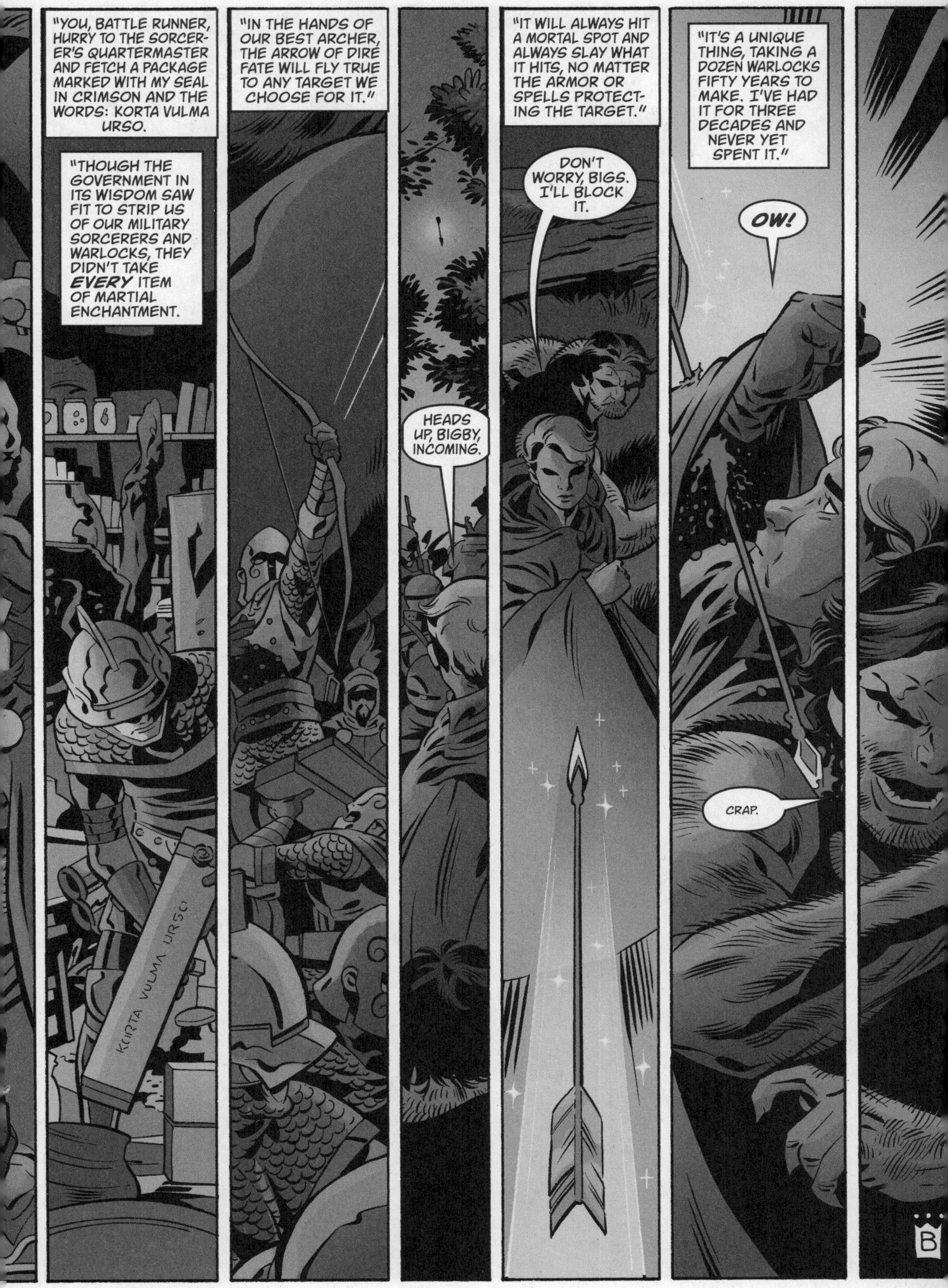
"YOU, BATTLE RUNNER, HURRY TO THE SORCERER'S QUARTERMASTER AND FETCH A PACKAGE MARKED WITH MY SEAL IN CRIMSON AND THE WORDS: KORTA VULMA URSO.
"THOUGH THE GOVERNMENT IN ITS WISDOM SAW FIT TO STRIP US OF OUR MILITARY SORCERERS AND WARLOCKS, THEY DIDN'T TAKE **EVERY** ITEM OF MARTIAL ENCHANTMENT.
KORTA VULMA URSO
"IN THE HANDS OF OUR BEST ARCHER, THE ARROW OF DIRE FATE WILL FLY TRUE TO ANY TARGET WE CHOOSE FOR IT."
HEADS UP, BIGBY, INCOMING.
"IT WILL ALWAYS HIT A MORTAL SPOT AND ALWAYS SLAY WHAT IT HITS, NO MATTER THE ARMOR OR SPELLS PROTECTING THE TARGET."
DON'T WORRY, BIGS. I'LL BLOCK IT.
"IT'S A UNIQUE THING, TAKING A DOZEN WARLOCKS FIFTY YEARS TO MAKE. I'VE HAD IT FOR THREE DECADES AND NEVER YET SPENT IT."
OW!
CRAP.

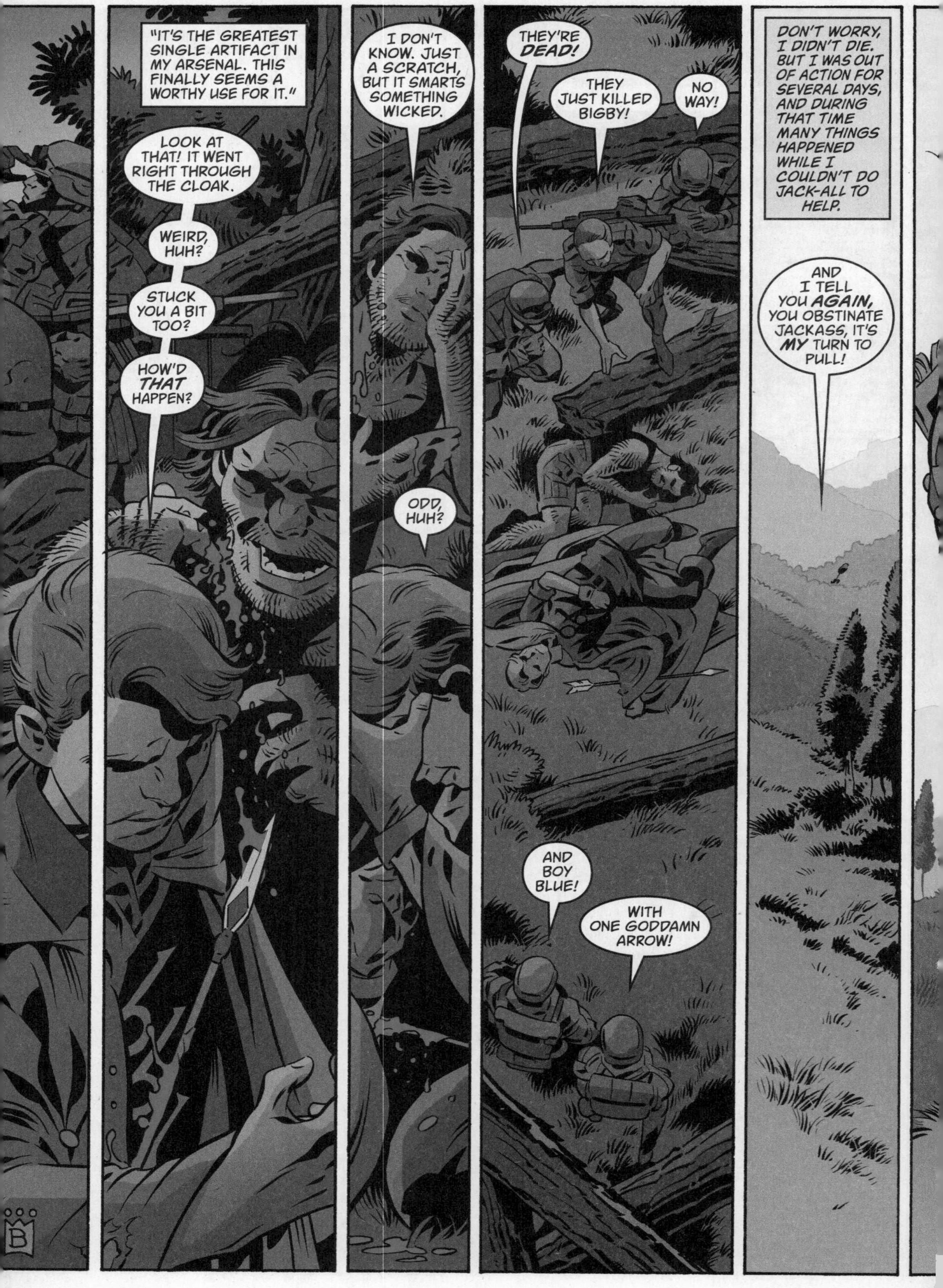
"IT'S THE GREATEST SINGLE ARTIFACT IN MY ARSENAL. THIS FINALLY SEEMS A WORTHY USE FOR IT."
LOOK AT THAT! IT WENT RIGHT THROUGH THE CLOAK.
WEIRD, HUH?
STUCK YOU A BIT TOO?
HOW'D *THAT* HAPPEN?
I DON'T KNOW. JUST A SCRATCH, BUT IT SMARTS SOMETHING WICKED.
ODD, HUH?
THEY'RE *DEAD!*
THEY JUST KILLED BIGBY!
NO WAY!
AND BOY BLUE!
WITH ONE GODDAMN ARROW!
DON'T WORRY, I DIDN'T DIE. BUT I WAS OUT OF ACTION FOR SEVERAL DAYS, AND DURING THAT TIME MANY THINGS HAPPENED WHILE I COULDN'T DO JACK-ALL TO HELP.
AND I TELL YOU *AGAIN,* YOU OBSTINATE JACKASS, IT'S *MY* TURN TO PULL!

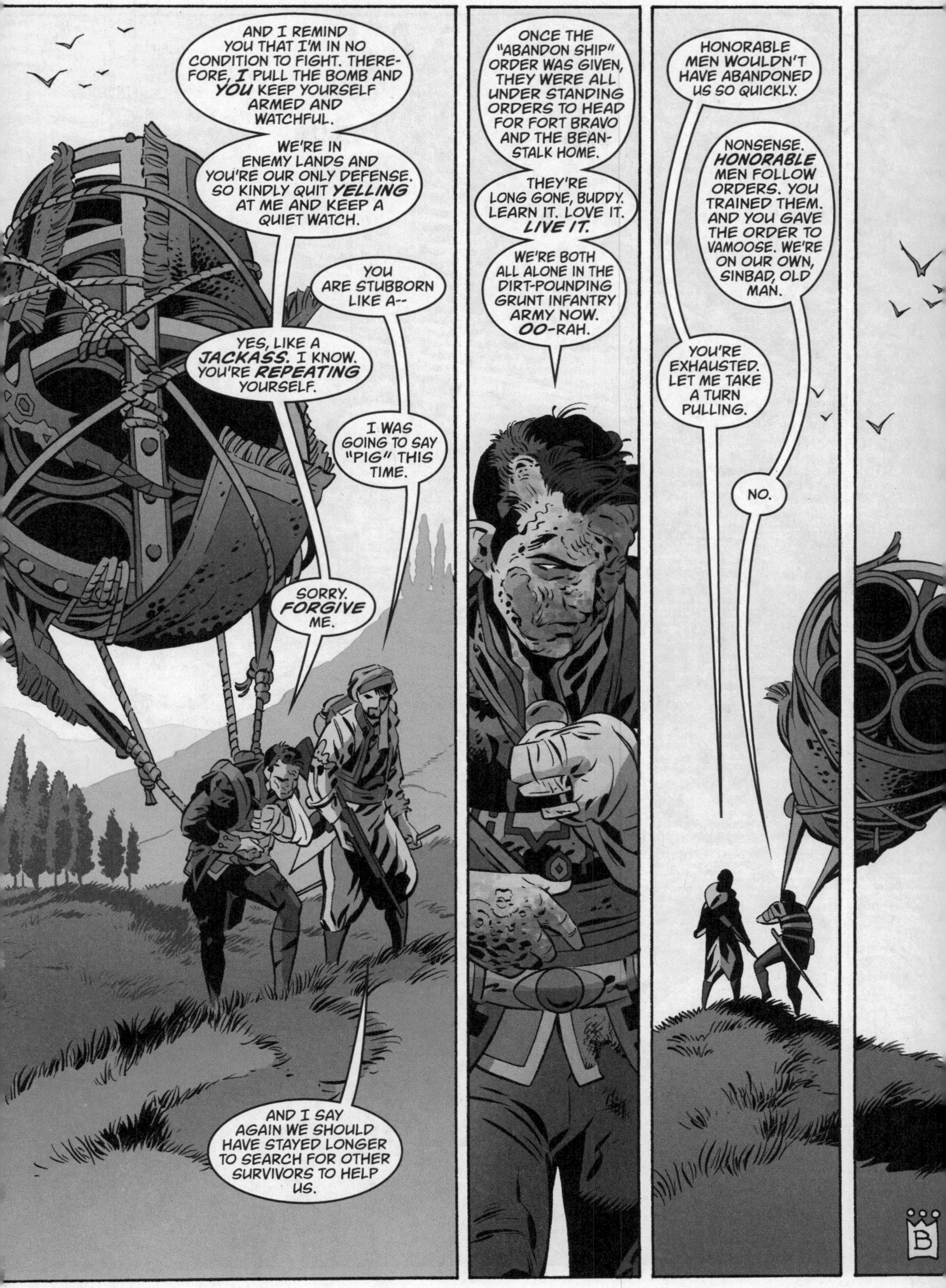

AND I REMIND YOU THAT I'M IN NO CONDITION TO FIGHT. THEREFORE, *I* PULL THE BOMB AND *YOU* KEEP YOURSELF ARMED AND WATCHFUL.
WE'RE IN ENEMY LANDS AND YOU'RE OUR ONLY DEFENSE. SO KINDLY QUIT *YELLING* AT ME AND KEEP A QUIET WATCH.
YOU ARE STUBBORN LIKE A--
YES, LIKE A *JACKASS*. I KNOW. YOU'RE *REPEATING* YOURSELF.
I WAS GOING TO SAY "PIG" THIS TIME.
SORRY. *FORGIVE* ME.
AND I SAY AGAIN WE SHOULD HAVE STAYED LONGER TO SEARCH FOR OTHER SURVIVORS TO HELP US.
ONCE THE "ABANDON SHIP" ORDER WAS GIVEN, THEY *WERE* ALL UNDER STANDING ORDERS TO HEAD FOR FORT BRAVO AND THE BEANSTALK HOME.
THEY'RE LONG GONE, BUDDY. LEARN IT. LOVE IT. *LIVE IT.*
WE'RE BOTH ALL ALONE IN THE DIRT-POUNDING GRUNT INFANTRY ARMY NOW. *OO*-RAH.
HONORABLE MEN *WOULDN'T* HAVE ABANDONED US SO QUICKLY.
NONSENSE. *HONORABLE* MEN FOLLOW ORDERS. YOU TRAINED THEM. AND YOU GAVE THE ORDER TO VAMOOSE. WE'RE ON OUR OWN, SINBAD, OLD MAN.
YOU'RE EXHAUSTED. LET ME TAKE A TURN PULLING.
NO.

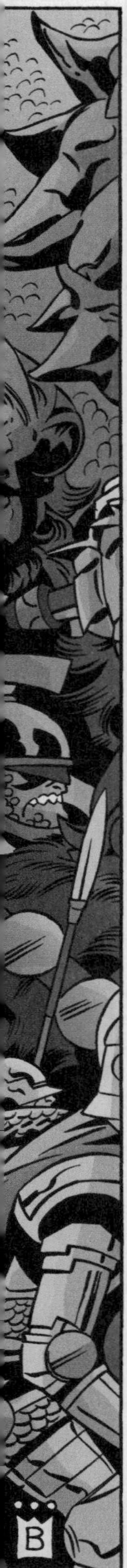

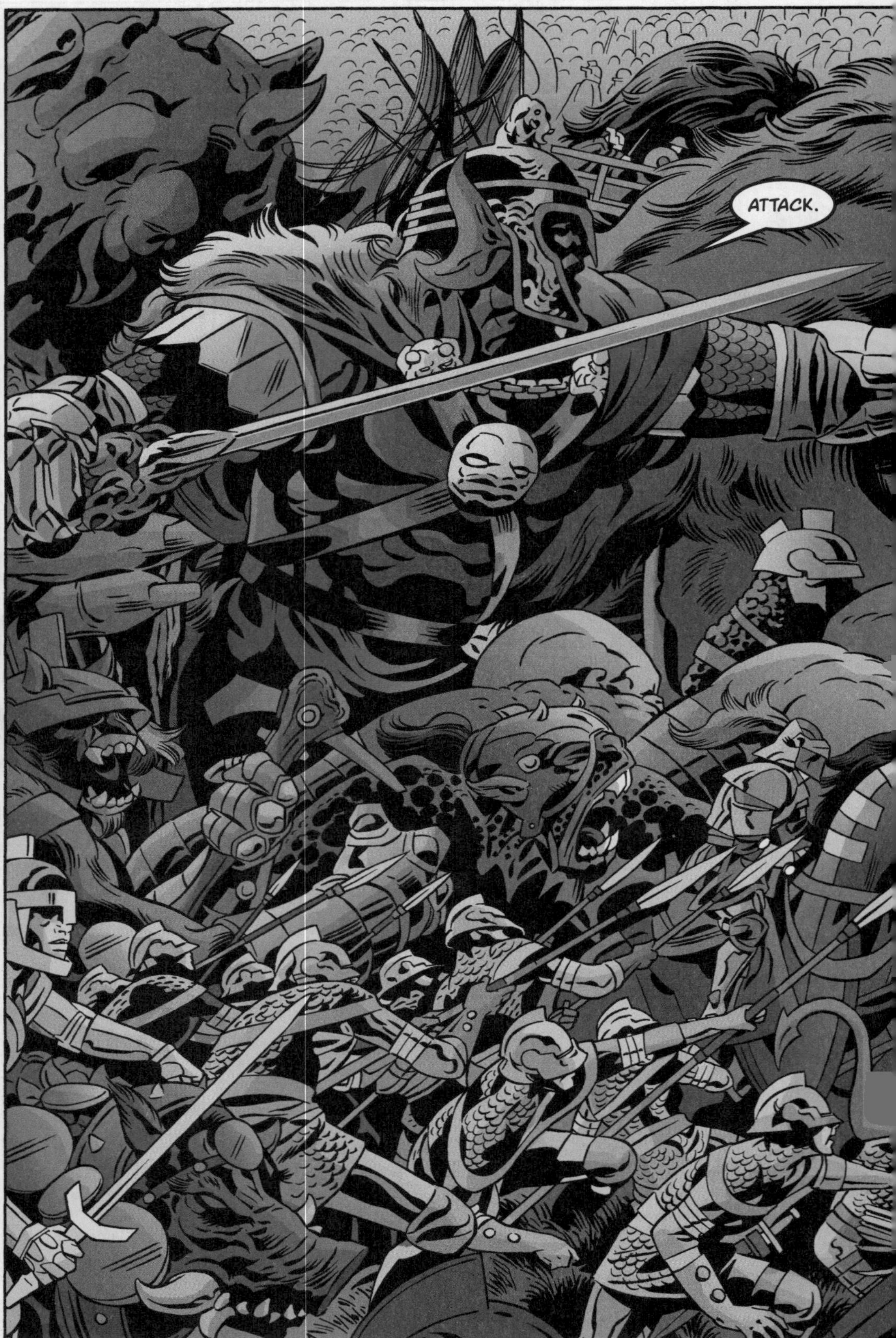
ATTACK.

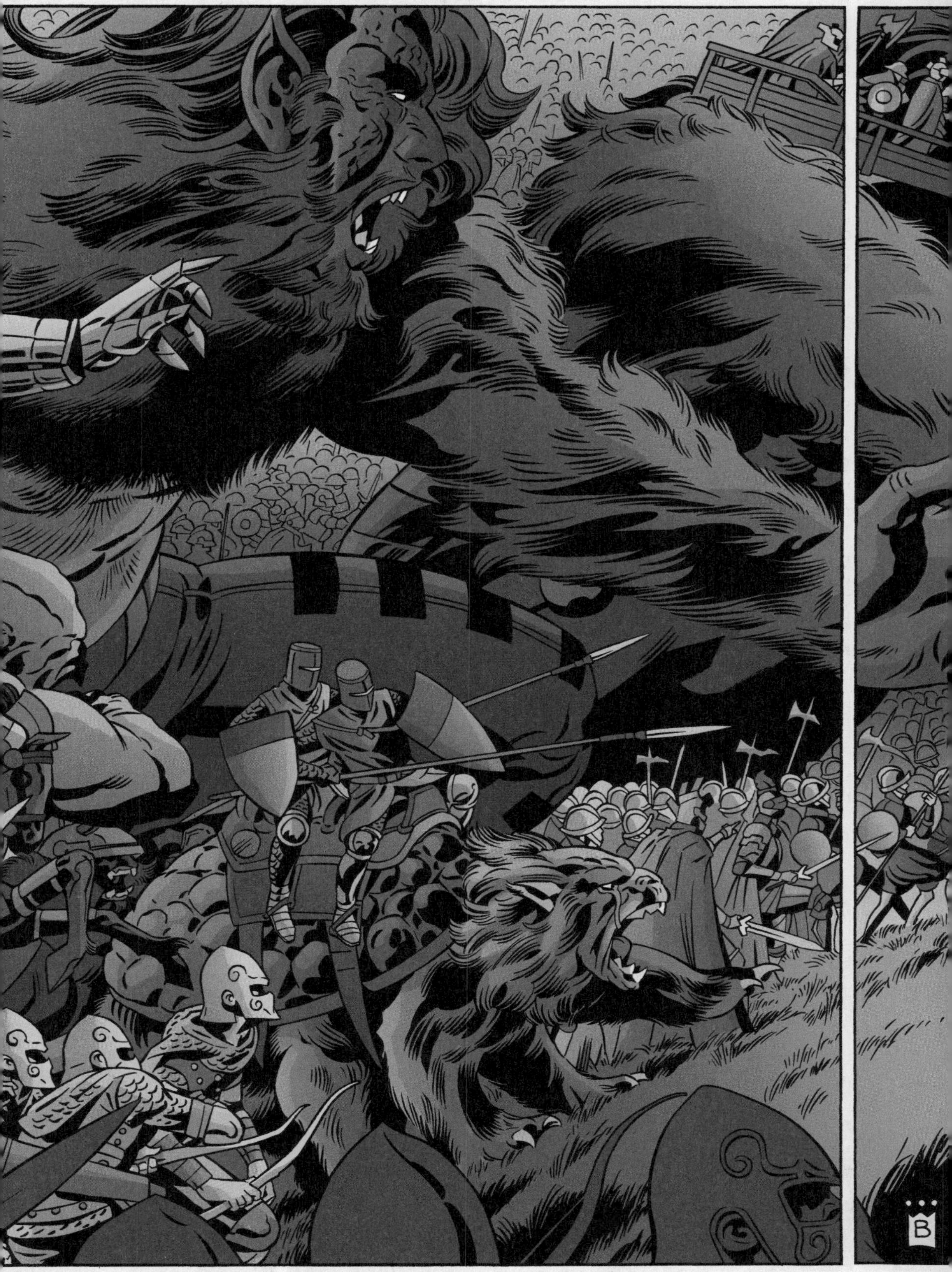

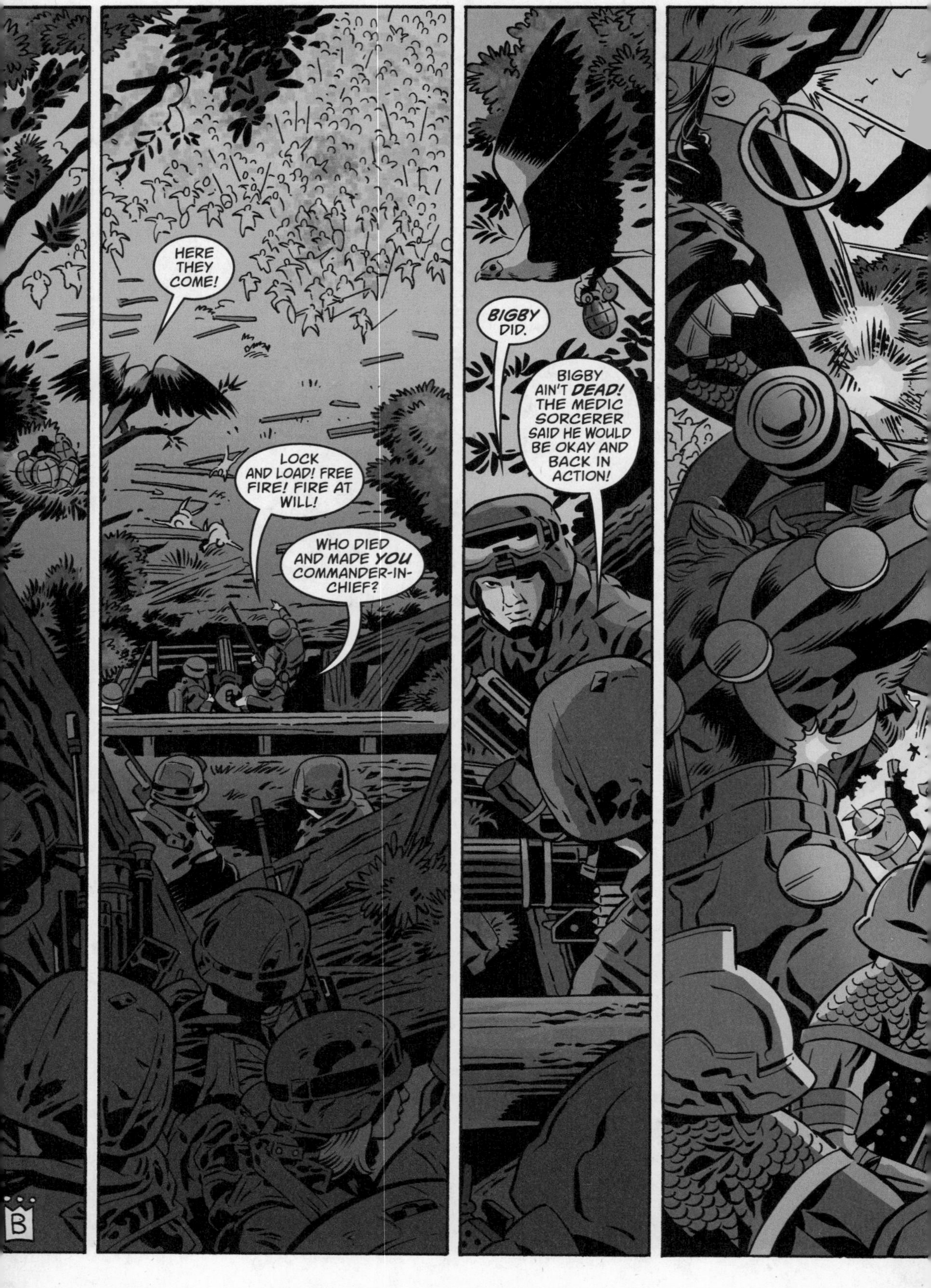

HERE THEY COME!
LOCK AND LOAD! FREE FIRE! FIRE AT WILL!
WHO DIED AND MADE YOU COMMANDER-IN-CHIEF?
BIGBY DID.
BIGBY AIN'T DEAD! THE MEDIC SORCERER SAID HE WOULD BE OKAY AND BACK IN ACTION!

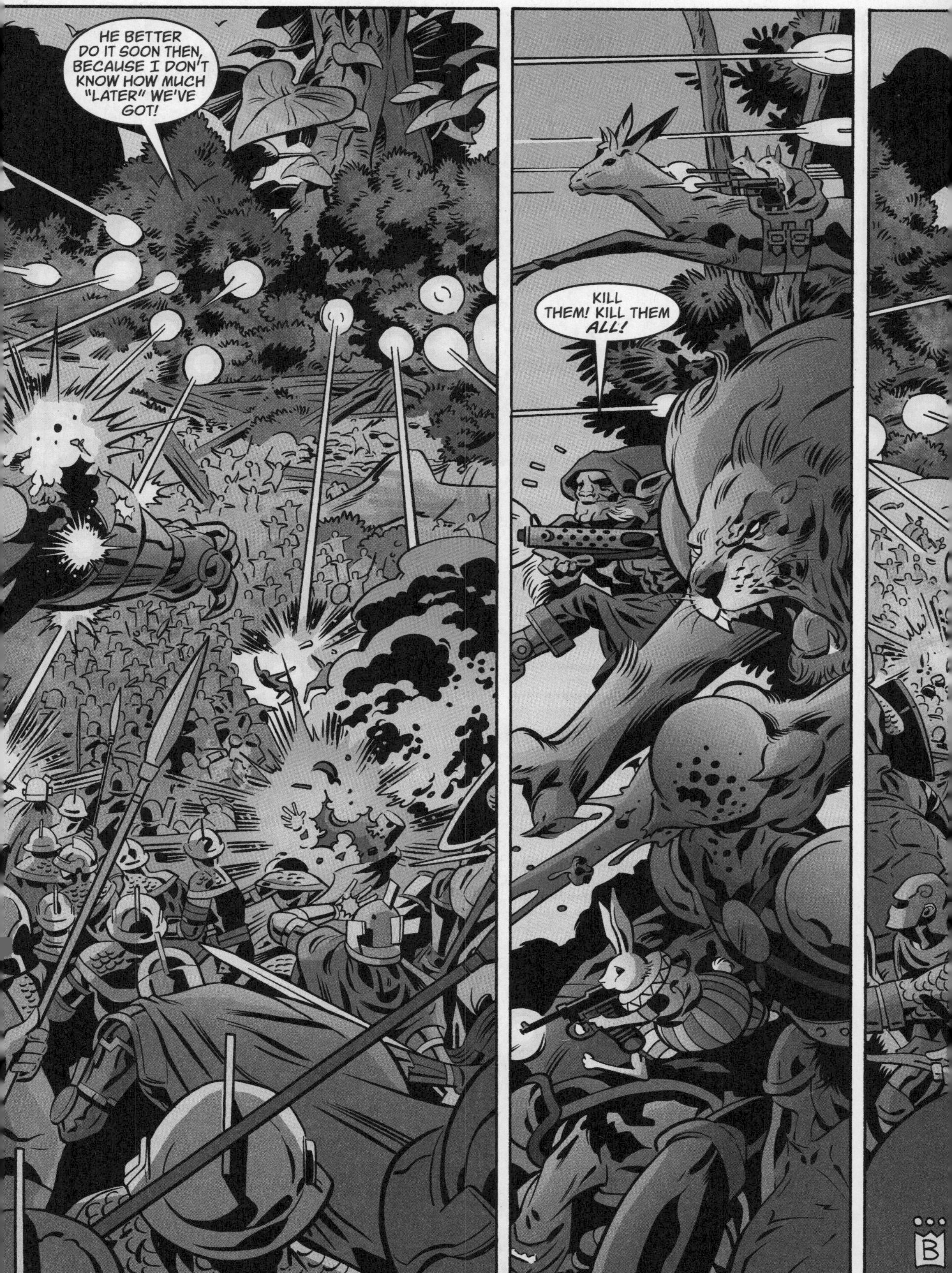
HE BETTER DO IT SOON THEN, BECAUSE I DON'T KNOW HOW MUCH "LATER" WE'VE GOT!
KILL THEM! KILL THEM ALL!

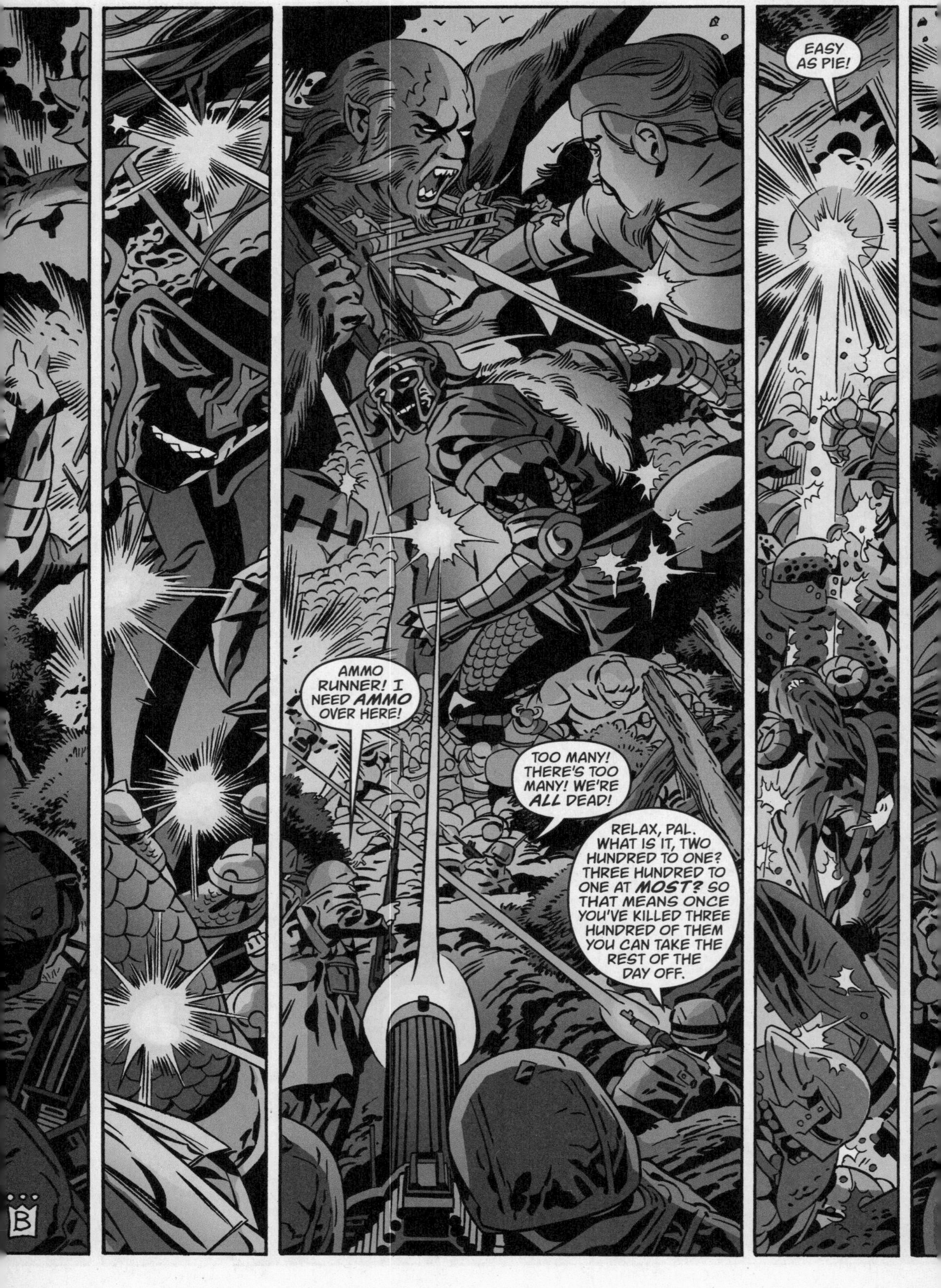
AMMO RUNNER! I NEED AMMO OVER HERE!
TOO MANY! THERE'S TOO MANY! WE'RE ALL DEAD!
RELAX, PAL. WHAT IS IT, TWO HUNDRED TO ONE? THREE HUNDRED TO ONE AT MOST? SO THAT MEANS ONCE YOU'VE KILLED THREE HUNDRED OF THEM YOU CAN TAKE THE REST OF THE DAY OFF.
EASY AS PIE!

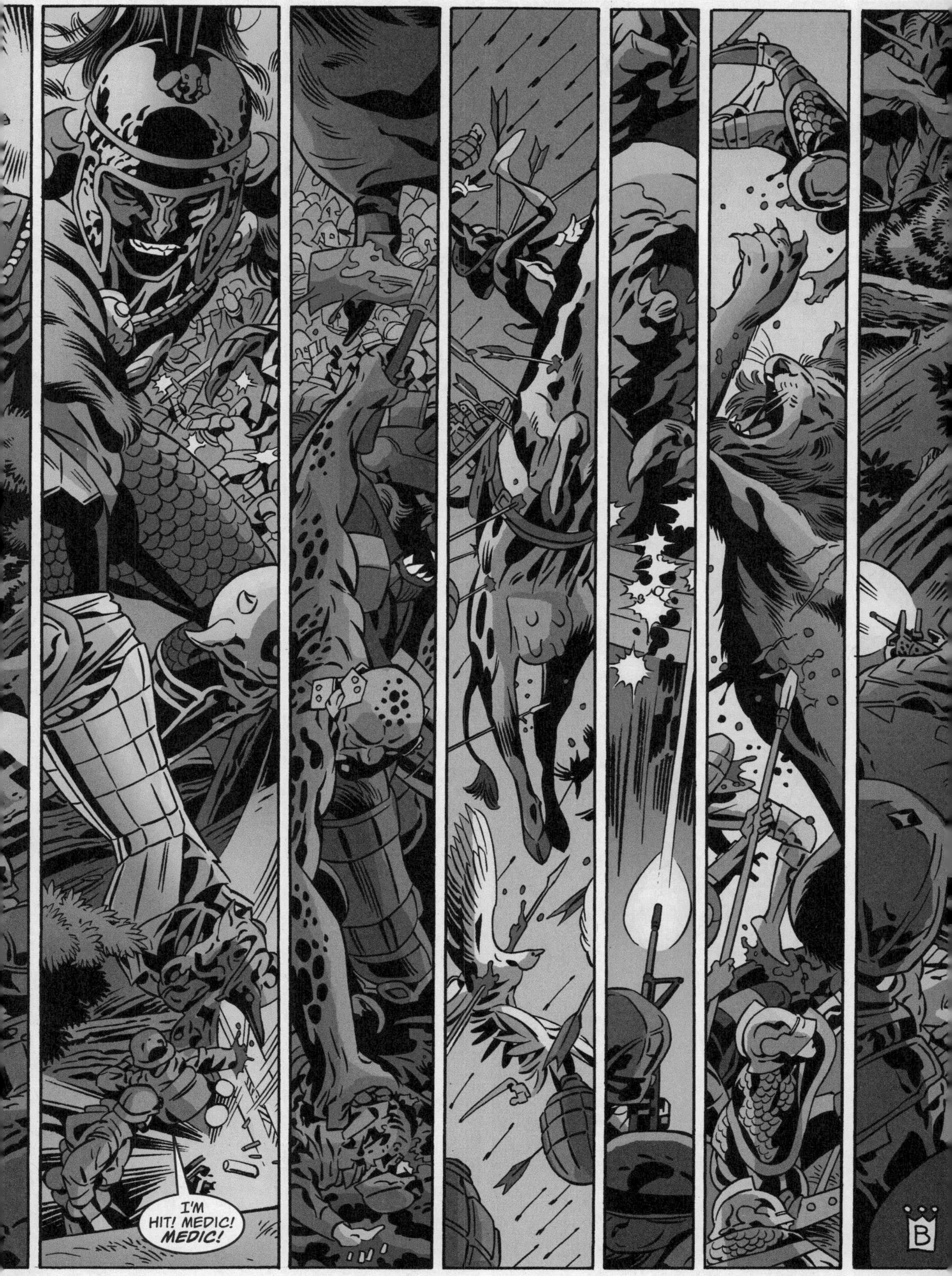
I'M HIT! MEDIC! MEDIC!

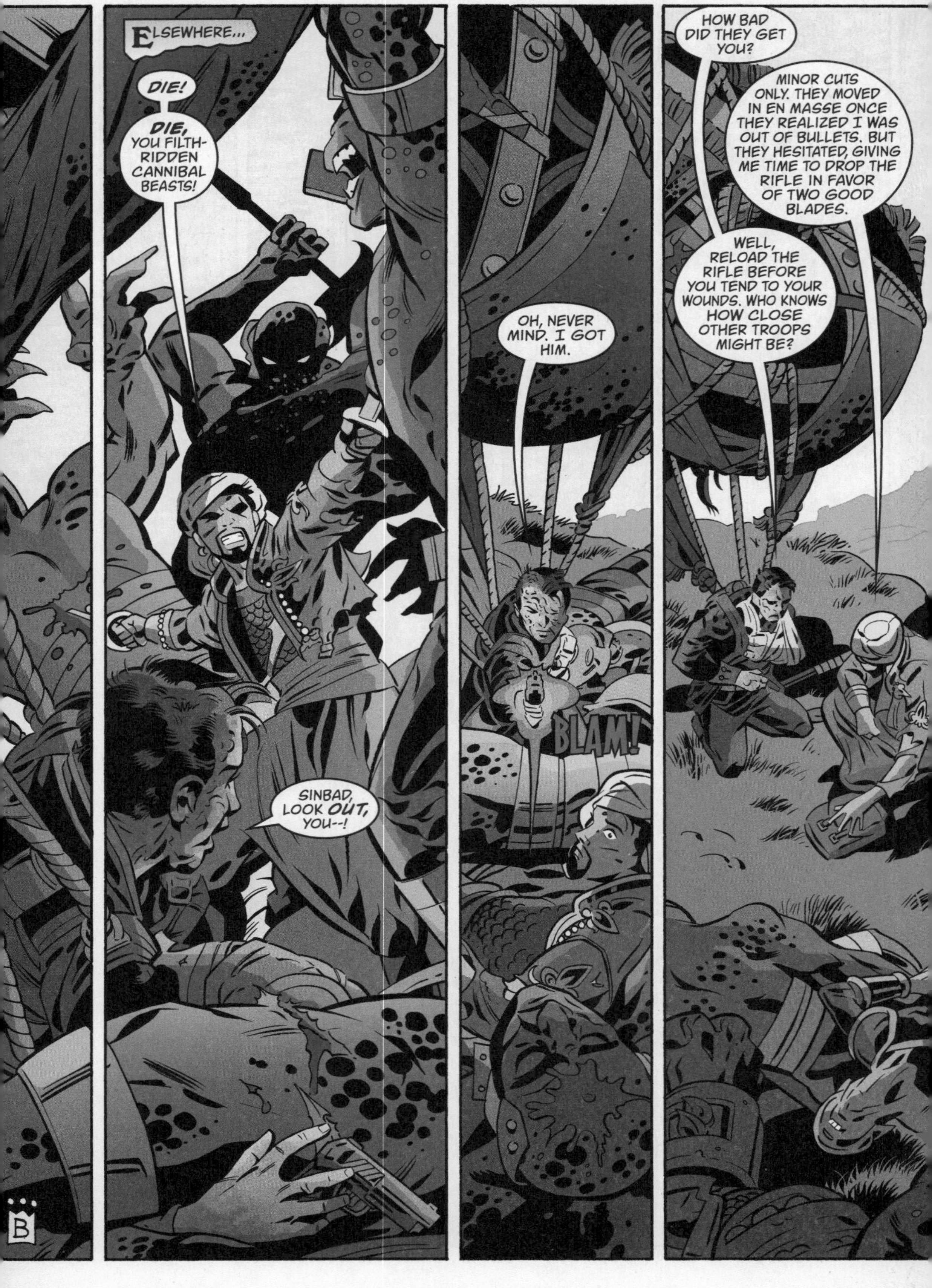
ELSEWHERE...
DIE!
DIE, YOU FILTH-RIDDEN CANNIBAL BEASTS!
SINBAD, LOOK OUT, YOU--!
OH, NEVER MIND. I GOT HIM.
BLAM!
HOW BAD DID THEY GET YOU?
MINOR CUTS ONLY. THEY MOVED IN EN MASSE ONCE THEY REALIZED I WAS OUT OF BULLETS. BUT THEY HESITATED, GIVING ME TIME TO DROP THE RIFLE IN FAVOR OF TWO GOOD BLADES.
WELL, RELOAD THE RIFLE BEFORE YOU TEND TO YOUR WOUNDS. WHO KNOWS HOW CLOSE OTHER TROOPS MIGHT BE?

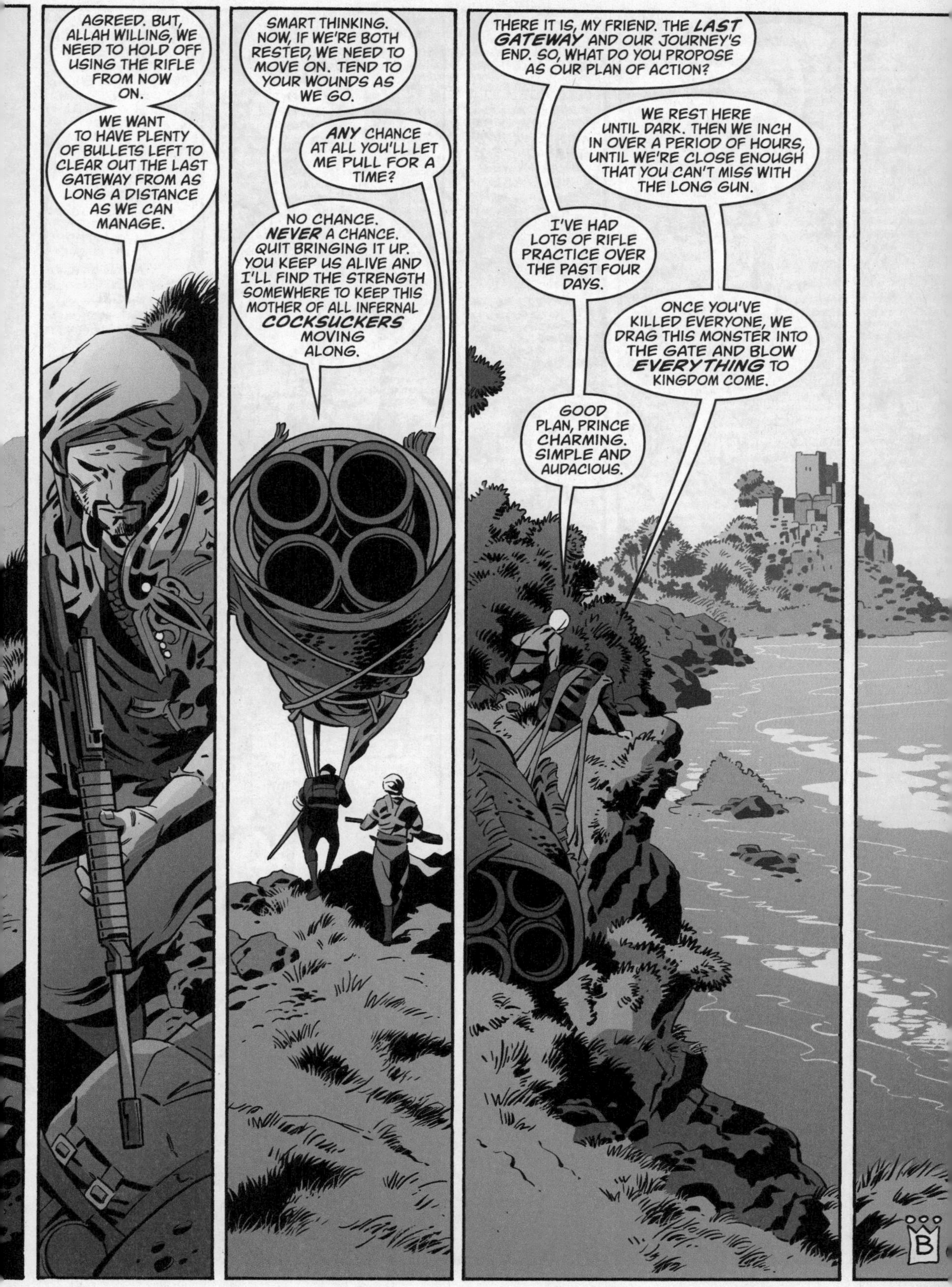
AGREED. BUT, ALLAH WILLING, WE NEED TO HOLD OFF USING THE RIFLE FROM NOW ON.
WE WANT TO HAVE PLENTY OF BULLETS LEFT TO CLEAR OUT THE LAST GATEWAY FROM AS LONG A DISTANCE AS WE CAN MANAGE.
SMART THINKING. NOW, IF WE'RE BOTH RESTED, WE NEED TO MOVE ON. TEND TO YOUR WOUNDS AS WE GO.
ANY CHANCE AT ALL YOU'LL LET ME PULL FOR A TIME?
NO CHANCE. NEVER A CHANCE. QUIT BRINGING IT UP. YOU KEEP US ALIVE AND I'LL FIND THE STRENGTH SOMEWHERE TO KEEP THIS MOTHER OF ALL INFERNAL COCKSUCKERS MOVING ALONG.
THERE IT IS, MY FRIEND. THE LAST GATEWAY AND OUR JOURNEY'S END. SO, WHAT DO YOU PROPOSE AS OUR PLAN OF ACTION?
WE REST HERE UNTIL DARK. THEN WE INCH IN OVER A PERIOD OF HOURS, UNTIL WE'RE CLOSE ENOUGH THAT YOU CAN'T MISS WITH THE LONG GUN.
I'VE HAD LOTS OF RIFLE PRACTICE OVER THE PAST FOUR DAYS.
ONCE YOU'VE KILLED EVERYONE, WE DRAG THIS MONSTER INTO THE GATE AND BLOW EVERYTHING TO KINGDOM COME.
GOOD PLAN, PRINCE CHARMING. SIMPLE AND AUDACIOUS.

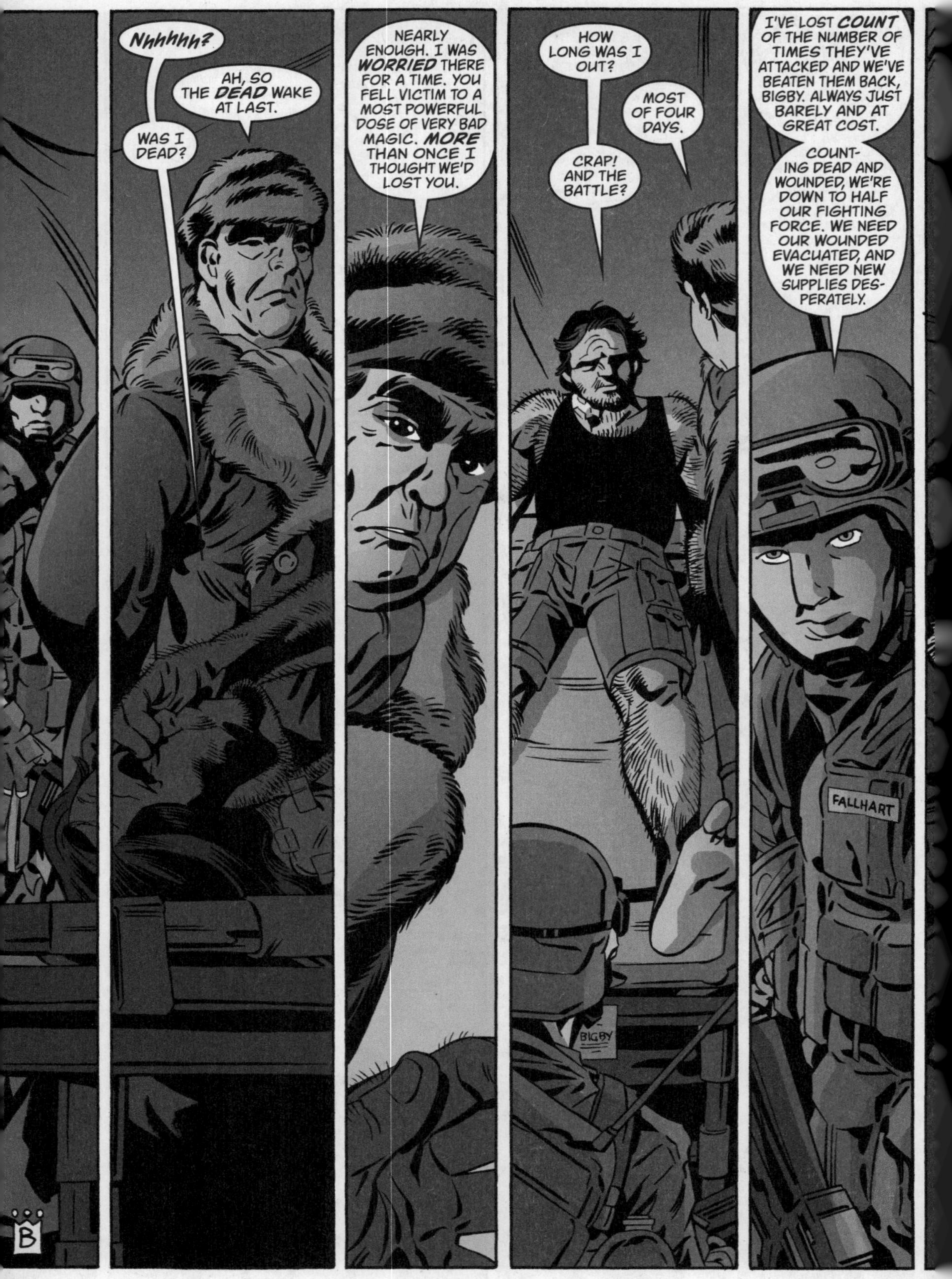
Nhhhhh?
AH, SO THE DEAD WAKE AT LAST.
WAS I DEAD?
NEARLY ENOUGH. I WAS WORRIED THERE FOR A TIME. YOU FELL VICTIM TO A MOST POWERFUL DOSE OF VERY BAD MAGIC. MORE THAN ONCE I THOUGHT WE'D LOST YOU.
HOW LONG WAS I OUT?
MOST OF FOUR DAYS.
CRAP! AND THE BATTLE?
BIGBY
I'VE LOST COUNT OF THE NUMBER OF TIMES THEY'VE ATTACKED AND WE'VE BEATEN THEM BACK, BIGBY. ALWAYS JUST BARELY AND AT GREAT COST.
COUNTING DEAD AND WOUNDED, WE'RE DOWN TO HALF OUR FIGHTING FORCE. WE NEED OUR WOUNDED EVACUATED, AND WE NEED NEW SUPPLIES DESPERATELY.
FALLHART

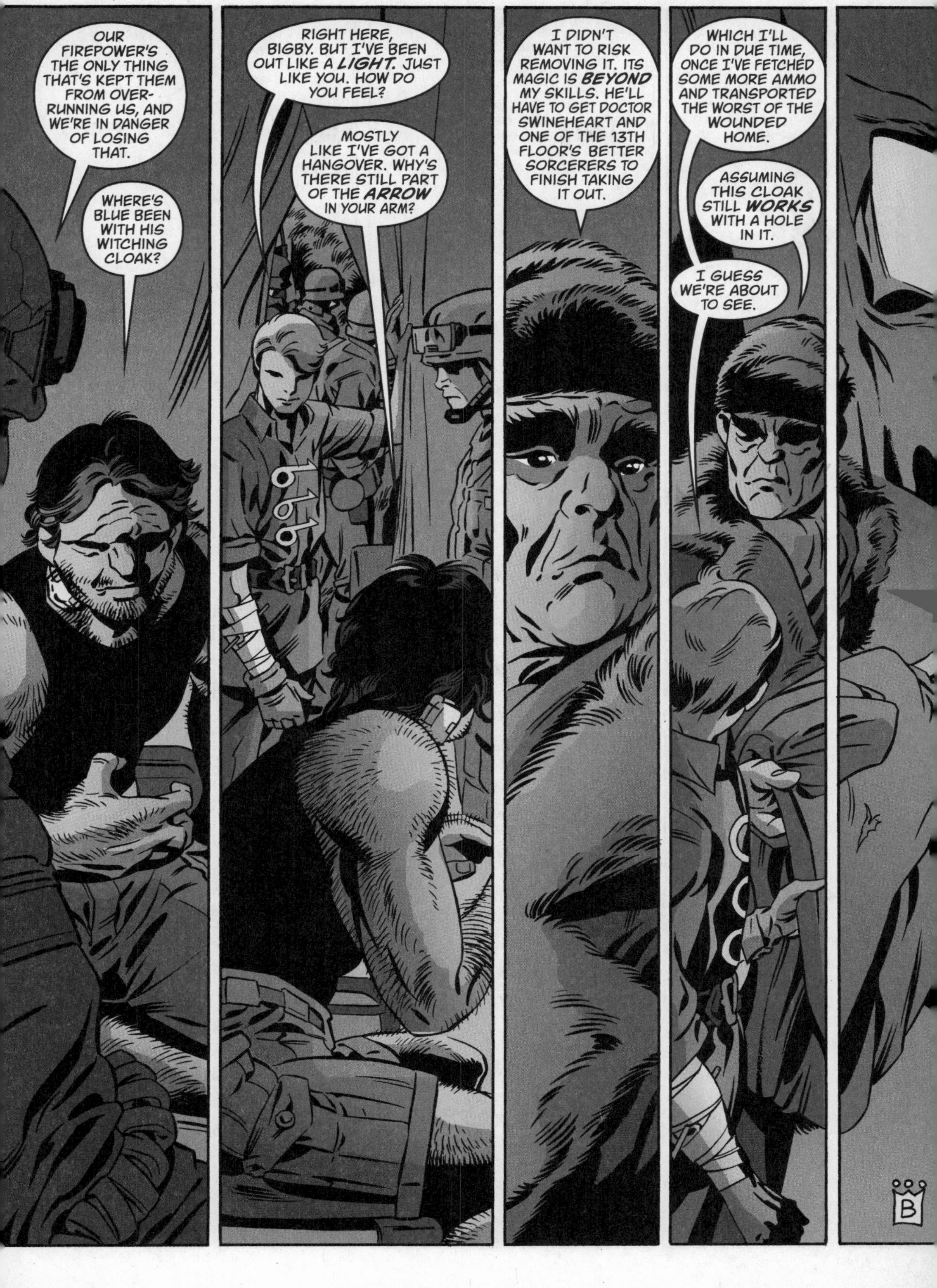
OUR FIREPOWER'S THE ONLY THING THAT'S KEPT THEM FROM OVER-RUNNING US, AND WE'RE IN DANGER OF LOSING THAT.
WHERE'S BLUE BEEN WITH HIS WITCHING CLOAK?
RIGHT HERE, BIGBY. BUT I'VE BEEN OUT LIKE A LIGHT. JUST LIKE YOU. HOW DO YOU FEEL?
MOSTLY LIKE I'VE GOT A HANGOVER. WHY'S THERE STILL PART OF THE ARROW IN YOUR ARM?
I DIDN'T WANT TO RISK REMOVING IT. ITS MAGIC IS BEYOND MY SKILLS. HE'LL HAVE TO GET DOCTOR SWINEHEART AND ONE OF THE 13TH FLOOR'S BETTER SORCERERS TO FINISH TAKING IT OUT.
WHICH I'LL DO IN DUE TIME, ONCE I'VE FETCHED SOME MORE AMMO AND TRANSPORTED THE WORST OF THE WOUNDED HOME.
ASSUMING THIS CLOAK STILL WORKS WITH A HOLE IN IT.
I GUESS WE'RE ABOUT TO SEE.
B

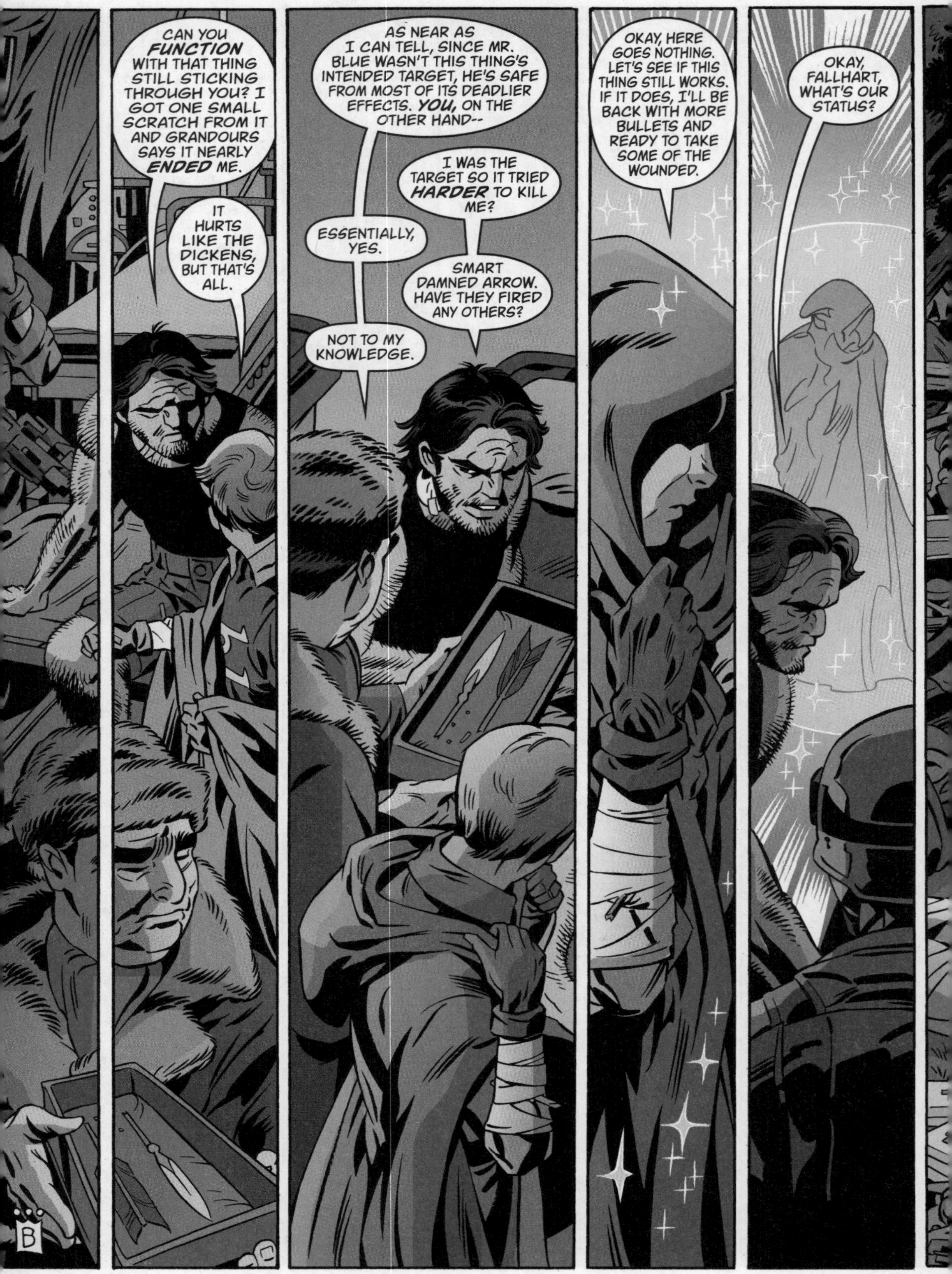

CAN YOU FUNCTION WITH THAT THING STILL STICKING THROUGH YOU? I GOT ONE SMALL SCRATCH FROM IT AND GRANDOURS SAYS IT NEARLY ENDED ME.
IT HURTS LIKE THE DICKENS, BUT THAT'S ALL.
AS NEAR AS I CAN TELL, SINCE MR. BLUE WASN'T THIS THING'S INTENDED TARGET, HE'S SAFE FROM MOST OF ITS DEADLIER EFFECTS. YOU, ON THE OTHER HAND--
I WAS THE TARGET SO IT TRIED HARDER TO KILL ME?
ESSENTIALLY, YES.
SMART DAMNED ARROW. HAVE THEY FIRED ANY OTHERS?
NOT TO MY KNOWLEDGE.
OKAY, HERE GOES NOTHING. LET'S SEE IF THIS THING STILL WORKS. IF IT DOES, I'LL BE BACK WITH MORE BULLETS AND READY TO TAKE SOME OF THE WOUNDED.
OKAY, FALLHART, WHAT'S OUR STATUS?

WE'VE TAKEN OUT ALL OF THEIR BIGGER ASSETS, AT THE COST OF *OUR* BIGGER ASSETS--ONLY THEY'VE STILL GOT THE EMPEROR HIMSELF.

HE'S HERE?

YEAH, AND NOTHING WE DO CAN *TOUCH* HIM. IT'S LIKE HE'S GOT SOME SORT OF FORCE FIELD AGAINST EVERY POSSIBLE KIND OF WEAPON.

YEAH, HE'S SUPPOSED TO BE IMMUNE TO EVERYTHING EXCEPT THE BIGGEST, BADDEST SORT OF MAGIC. AND THAT'S *ME* IN A NUTSHELL.

GET READY TO FALL BACK TO THE BASE OF THE BEANSTALK. I'M GOING TO TAKE OUT THE EMPEROR MYSELF.

FALL BACK, PEOPLE! FALL BACK TO THE LAST REDOUBT AROUND THE BEANSTALK!

AFTER THAT WE'LL *MOP UP* WHOEVER'S LEFT.

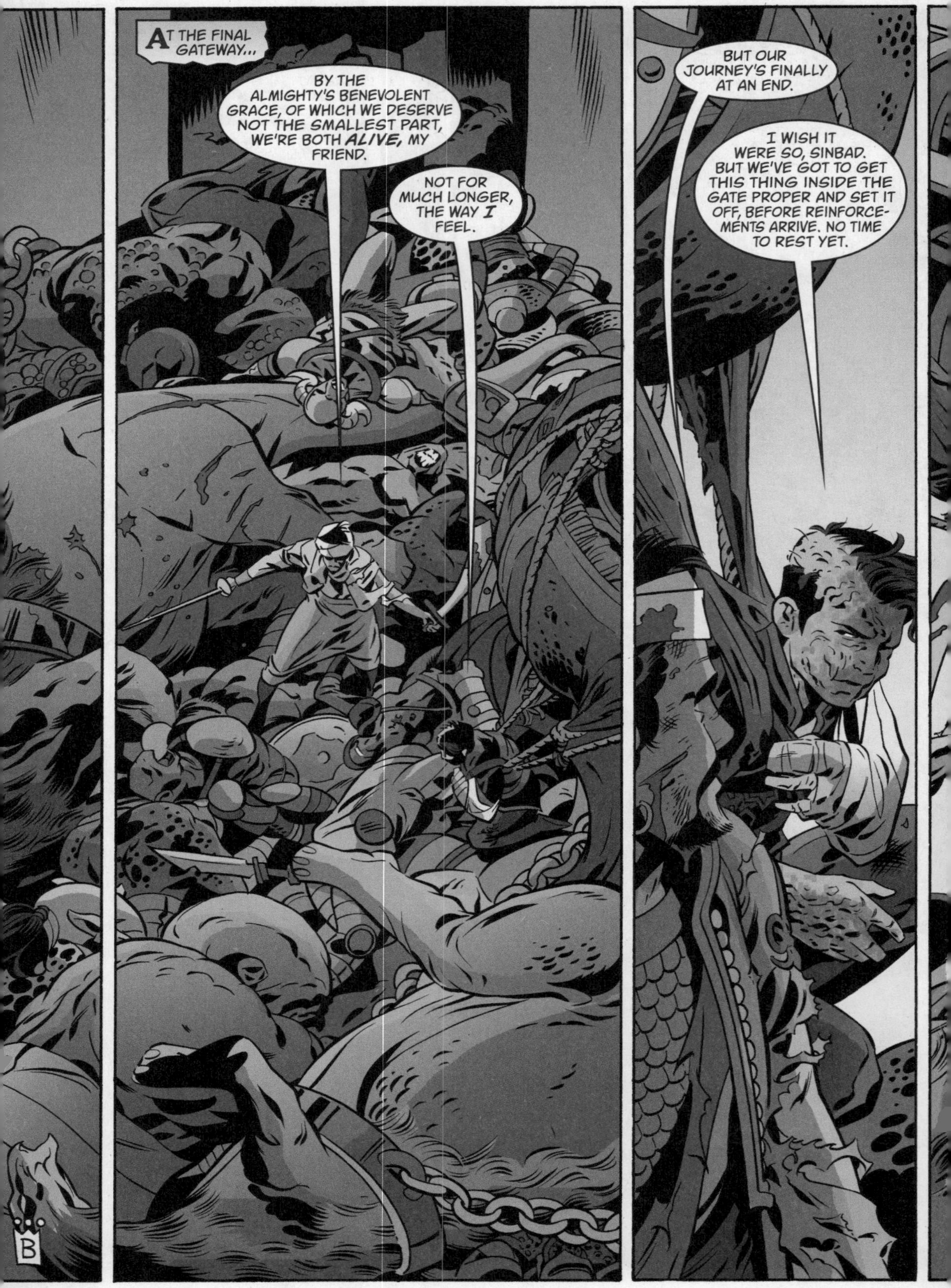

AT THE FINAL GATEWAY...
BY THE ALMIGHTY'S BENEVOLENT GRACE, OF WHICH WE DESERVE NOT THE SMALLEST PART, WE'RE BOTH ALIVE, MY FRIEND.
NOT FOR MUCH LONGER, THE WAY I FEEL.
BUT OUR JOURNEY'S FINALLY AT AN END.
I WISH IT WERE SO, SINBAD. BUT WE'VE GOT TO GET THIS THING INSIDE THE GATE PROPER AND SET IT OFF, BEFORE REINFORCEMENTS ARRIVE. NO TIME TO REST YET.

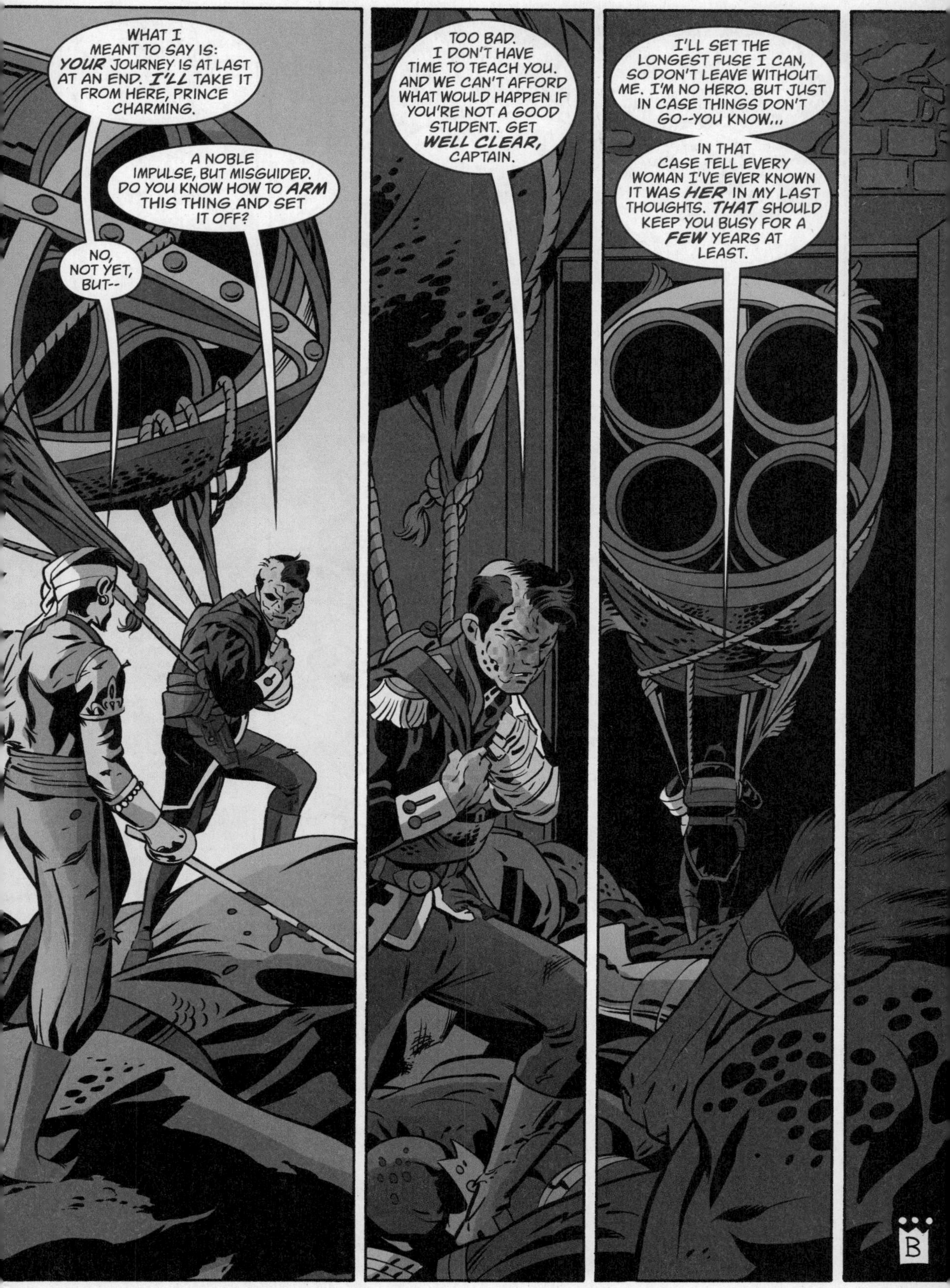
WHAT I MEANT TO SAY IS: YOUR JOURNEY IS AT LAST AT AN END. I'LL TAKE IT FROM HERE, PRINCE CHARMING.
A NOBLE IMPULSE, BUT MISGUIDED. DO YOU KNOW HOW TO ARM THIS THING AND SET IT OFF?
NO, NOT YET, BUT--
TOO BAD. I DON'T HAVE TIME TO TEACH YOU. AND WE CAN'T AFFORD WHAT WOULD HAPPEN IF YOU'RE NOT A GOOD STUDENT. GET WELL CLEAR, CAPTAIN.
I'LL SET THE LONGEST FUSE I CAN, SO DON'T LEAVE WITHOUT ME. I'M NO HERO. BUT JUST IN CASE THINGS DON'T GO--YOU KNOW...
IN THAT CASE TELL EVERY WOMAN I'VE EVER KNOWN IT WAS HER IN MY LAST THOUGHTS. THAT SHOULD KEEP YOU BUSY FOR A FEW YEARS AT LEAST.

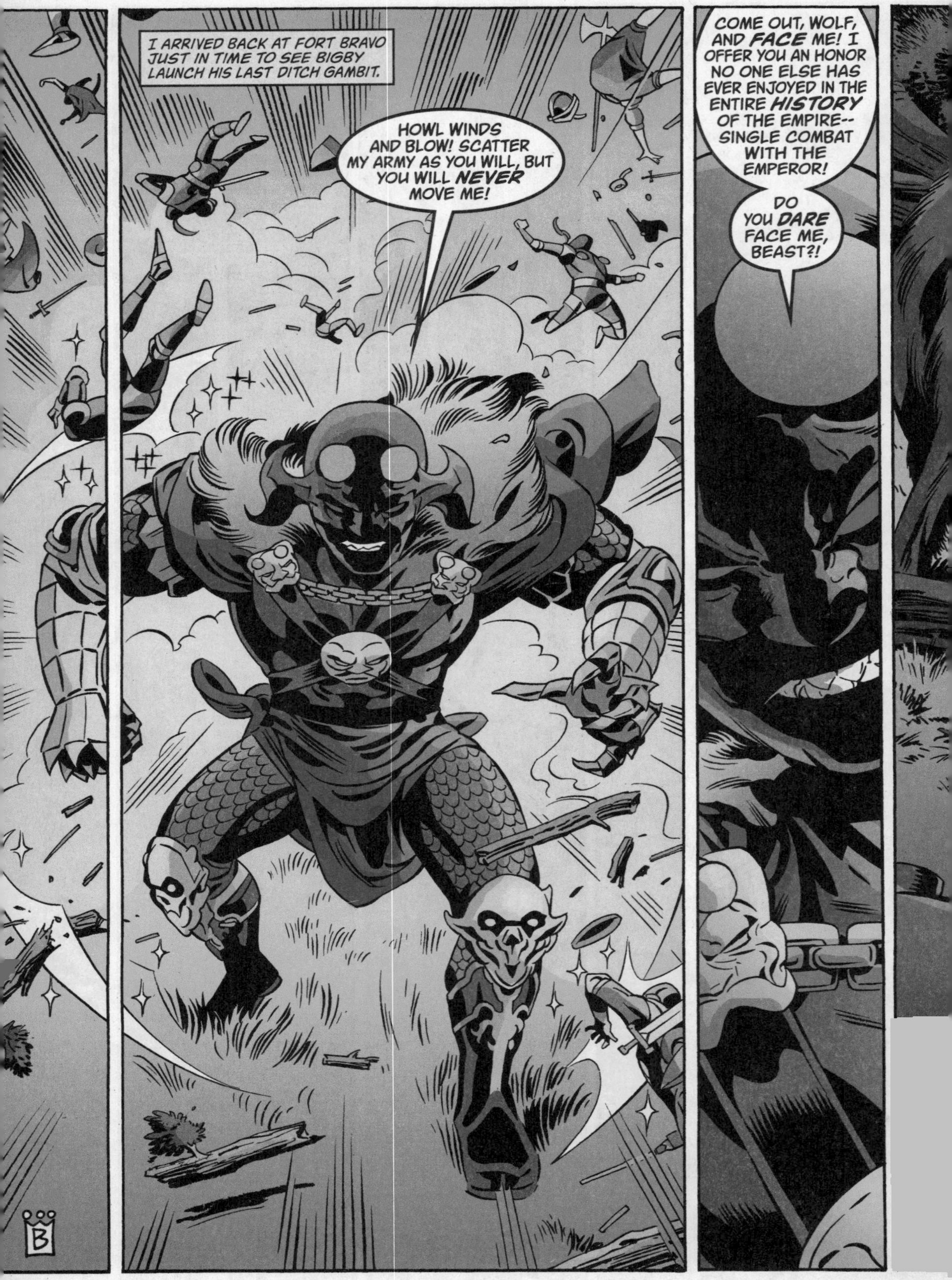
I ARRIVED BACK AT FORT BRAVO JUST IN TIME TO SEE BIGBY LAUNCH HIS LAST DITCH GAMBIT.
HOWL WINDS AND BLOW! SCATTER MY ARMY AS YOU WILL, BUT YOU WILL NEVER MOVE ME!
COME OUT, WOLF, AND FACE ME! I OFFER YOU AN HONOR NO ONE ELSE HAS EVER ENJOYED IN THE ENTIRE HISTORY OF THE EMPIRE-- SINGLE COMBAT WITH THE EMPEROR!
DO YOU DARE FACE ME, BEAST?!

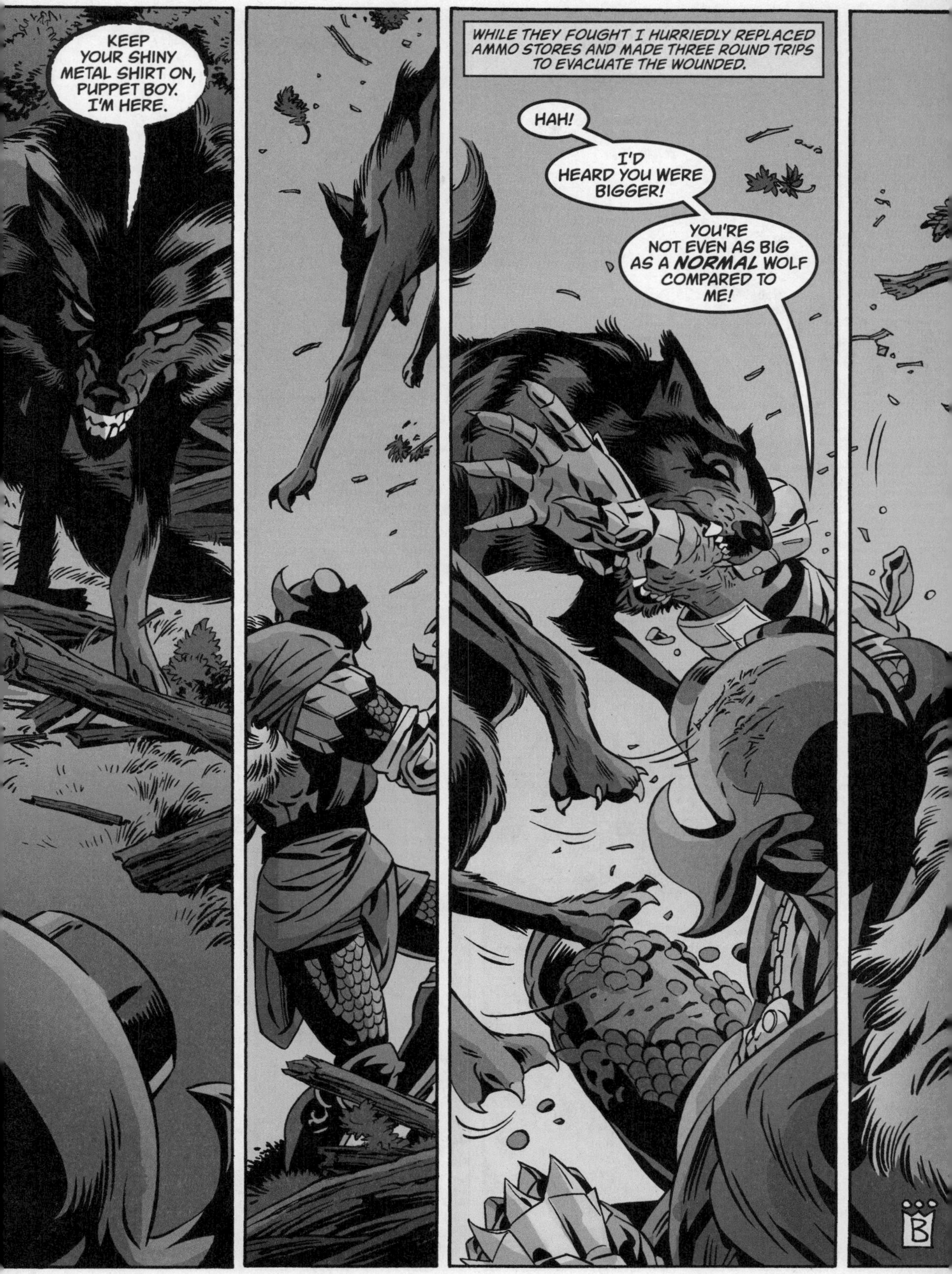
KEEP YOUR SHINY METAL SHIRT ON, PUPPET BOY. I'M HERE.
WHILE THEY FOUGHT I HURRIEDLY REPLACED AMMO STORES AND MADE THREE ROUND TRIPS TO EVACUATE THE WOUNDED.
HAH!
I'D HEARD YOU WERE BIGGER!
YOU'RE NOT EVEN AS BIG AS A NORMAL WOLF COMPARED TO ME!

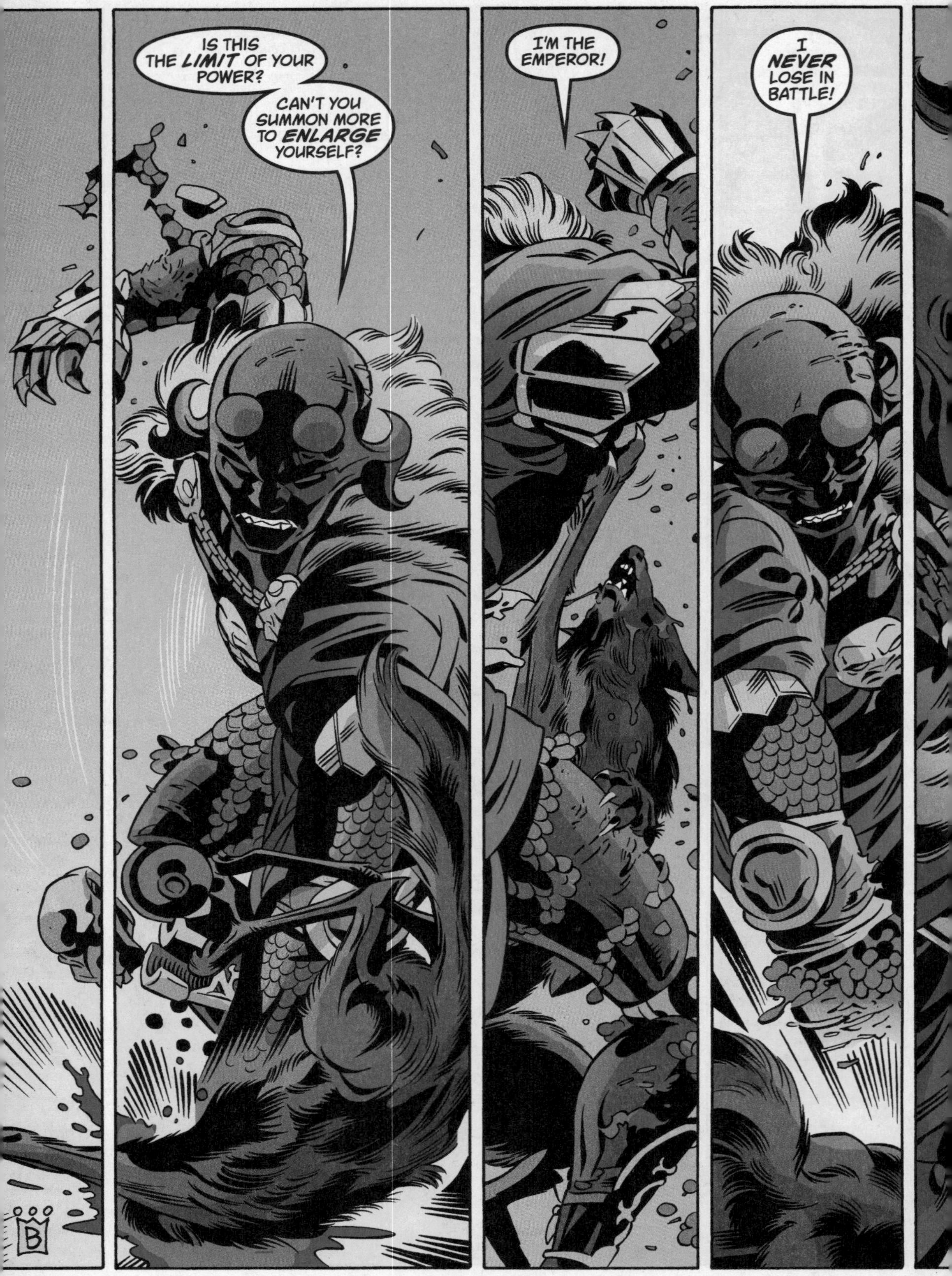
IS THIS THE LIMIT OF YOUR POWER?
CAN'T YOU SUMMON MORE TO ENLARGE YOURSELF?
I'M THE EMPEROR!
I NEVER LOSE IN BATTLE!

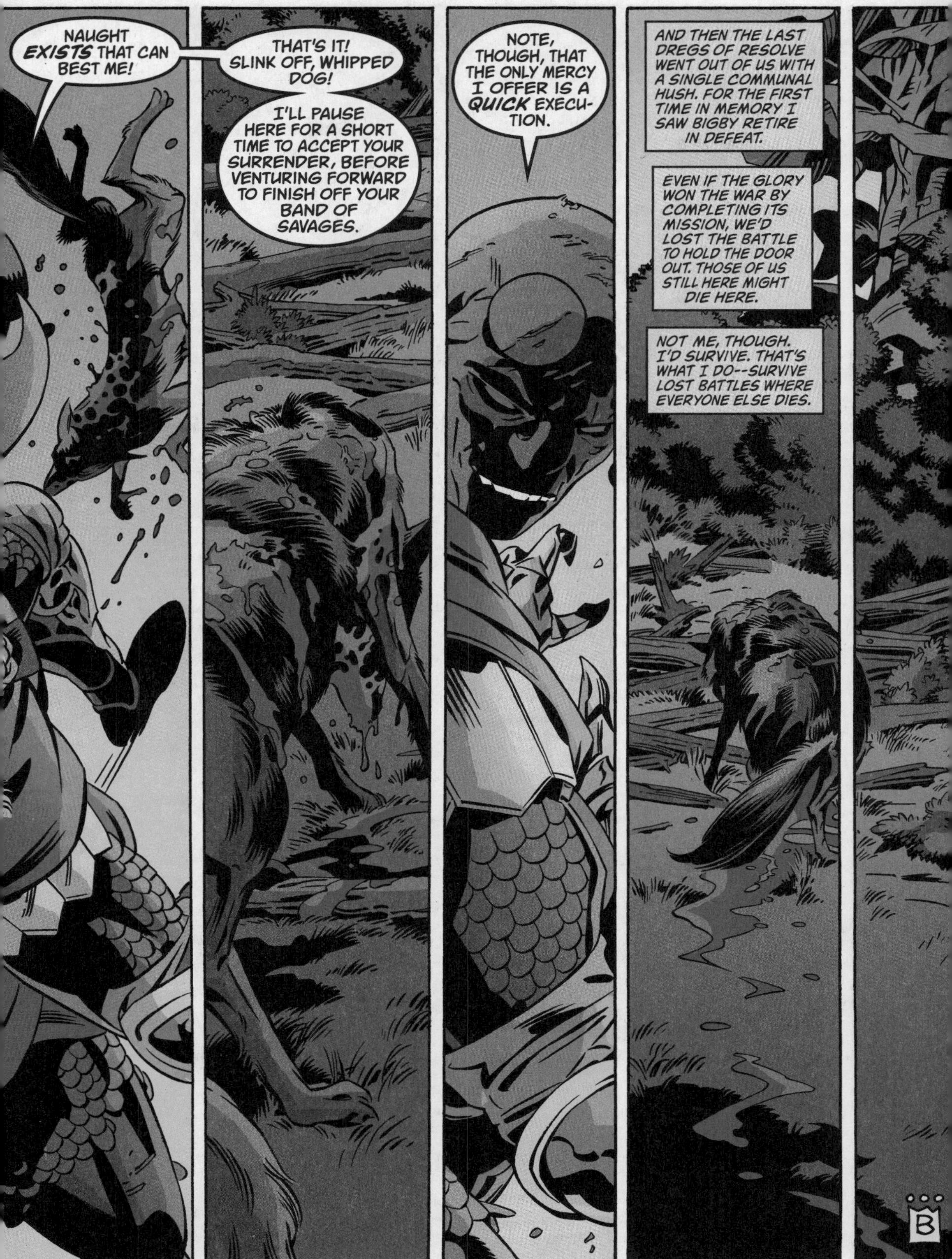
NAUGHT EXISTS THAT CAN BEST ME!
THAT'S IT! SLINK OFF, WHIPPED DOG!
I'LL PAUSE HERE FOR A SHORT TIME TO ACCEPT YOUR SURRENDER, BEFORE VENTURING FORWARD TO FINISH OFF YOUR BAND OF SAVAGES.
NOTE, THOUGH, THAT THE ONLY MERCY I OFFER IS A QUICK EXECUTION.
AND THEN THE LAST DREGS OF RESOLVE WENT OUT OF US WITH A SINGLE COMMUNAL HUSH. FOR THE FIRST TIME IN MEMORY I SAW BIGBY RETIRE IN DEFEAT.
EVEN IF THE GLORY WON THE WAR BY COMPLETING ITS MISSION, WE'D LOST THE BATTLE TO HOLD THE DOOR OUT. THOSE OF US STILL HERE MIGHT DIE HERE.
NOT ME, THOUGH. I'D SURVIVE. THAT'S WHAT I DO--SURVIVE LOST BATTLES WHERE EVERYONE ELSE DIES.

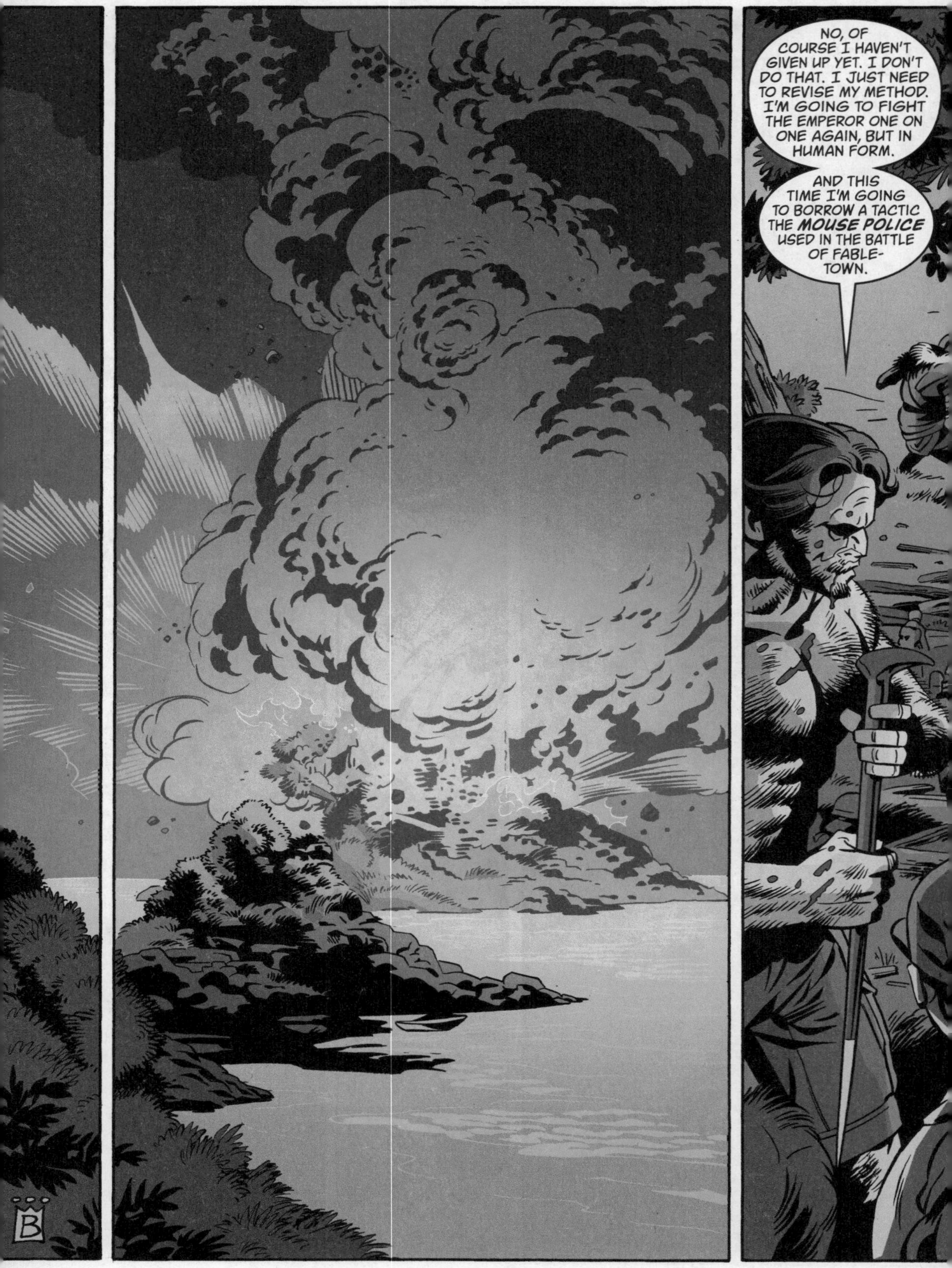
NO, OF COURSE I HAVEN'T GIVEN UP YET. I DON'T DO THAT. I JUST NEED TO REVISE MY METHOD. I'M GOING TO FIGHT THE EMPEROR ONE ON ONE AGAIN, BUT IN HUMAN FORM.
AND THIS TIME I'M GOING TO BORROW A TACTIC THE MOUSE POLICE USED IN THE BATTLE OF FABLE-TOWN.

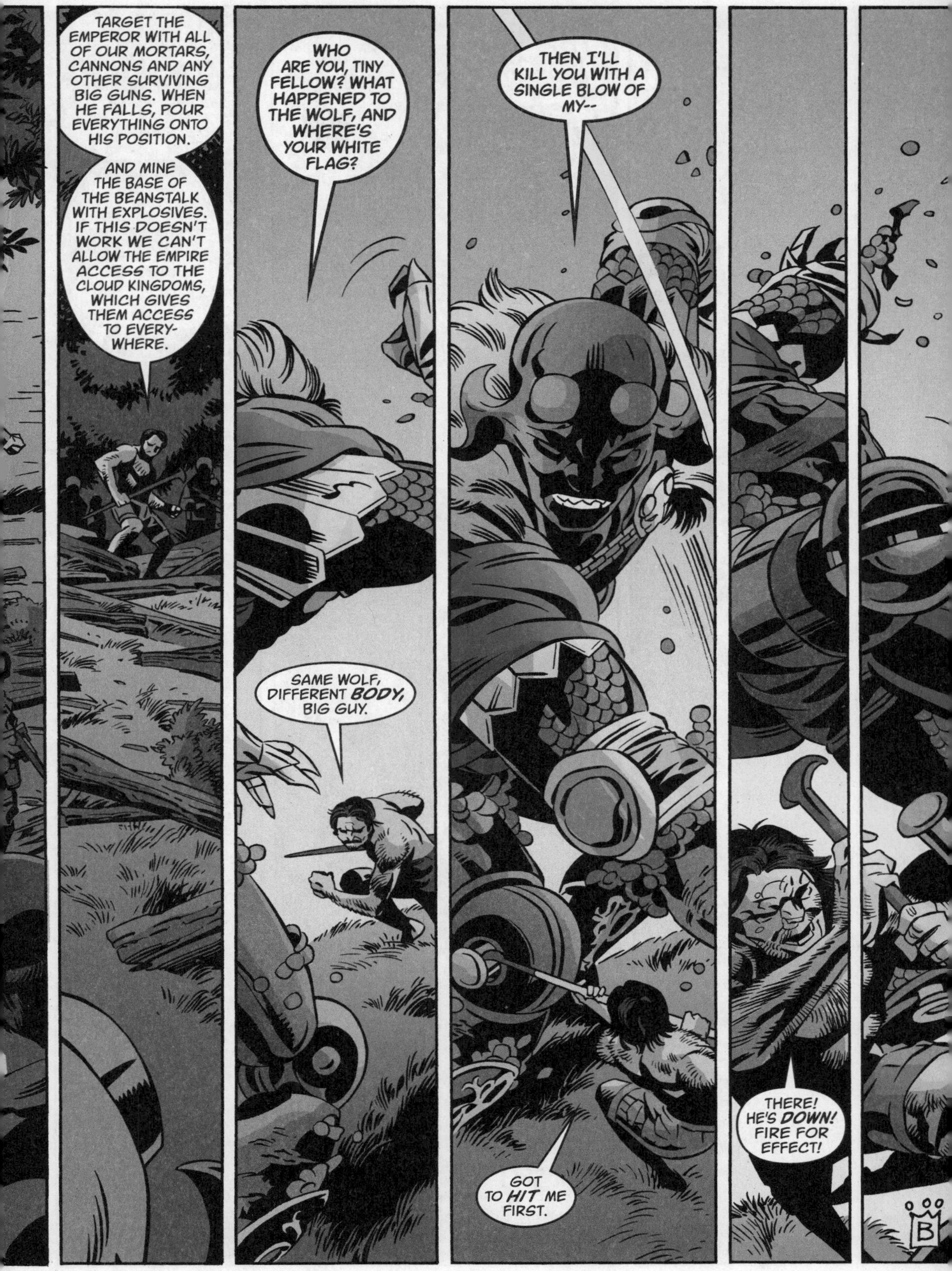
TARGET THE EMPEROR WITH ALL OF OUR MORTARS, CANNONS AND ANY OTHER SURVIVING BIG GUNS. WHEN HE FALLS, POUR EVERYTHING ONTO HIS POSITION.
AND MINE THE BASE OF THE BEANSTALK WITH EXPLOSIVES. IF THIS DOESN'T WORK WE CAN'T ALLOW THE EMPIRE ACCESS TO THE CLOUD KINGDOMS, WHICH GIVES THEM ACCESS TO EVERY-WHERE.
WHO ARE YOU, TINY FELLOW? WHAT HAPPENED TO THE WOLF, AND WHERE'S YOUR WHITE FLAG?
SAME WOLF, DIFFERENT BODY, BIG GUY.
THEN I'LL KILL YOU WITH A SINGLE BLOW OF MY--
GOT TO HIT ME FIRST.
THERE! HE'S DOWN! FIRE FOR EFFECT!

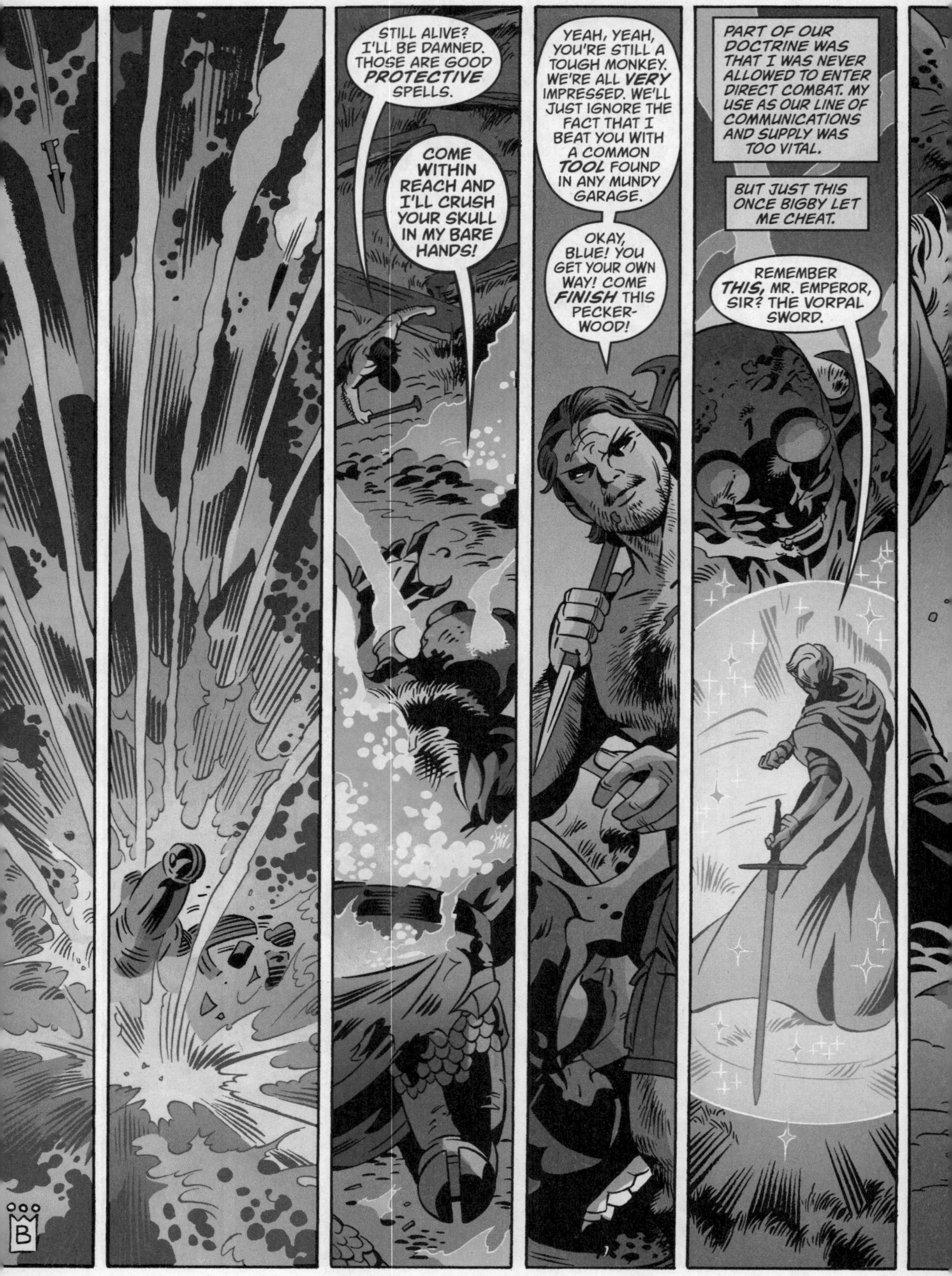
STILL ALIVE? I'LL BE DAMNED. THOSE ARE GOOD PROTECTIVE SPELLS.
COME WITHIN REACH AND I'LL CRUSH YOUR SKULL IN MY BARE HANDS!
YEAH, YEAH, YOU'RE STILL A TOUGH MONKEY. WE'RE ALL VERY IMPRESSED. WE'LL JUST IGNORE THE FACT THAT I BEAT YOU WITH A COMMON TOOL FOUND IN ANY MUNDY GARAGE.
OKAY, BLUE! YOU GET YOUR OWN WAY! COME FINISH THIS PECKER-WOOD!
PART OF OUR DOCTRINE WAS THAT I WAS NEVER ALLOWED TO ENTER DIRECT COMBAT. MY USE AS OUR LINE OF COMMUNICATIONS AND SUPPLY WAS TOO VITAL.
BUT JUST THIS ONCE BIGBY LET ME CHEAT.
REMEMBER THIS, MR. EMPEROR, SIR? THE VORPAL SWORD.

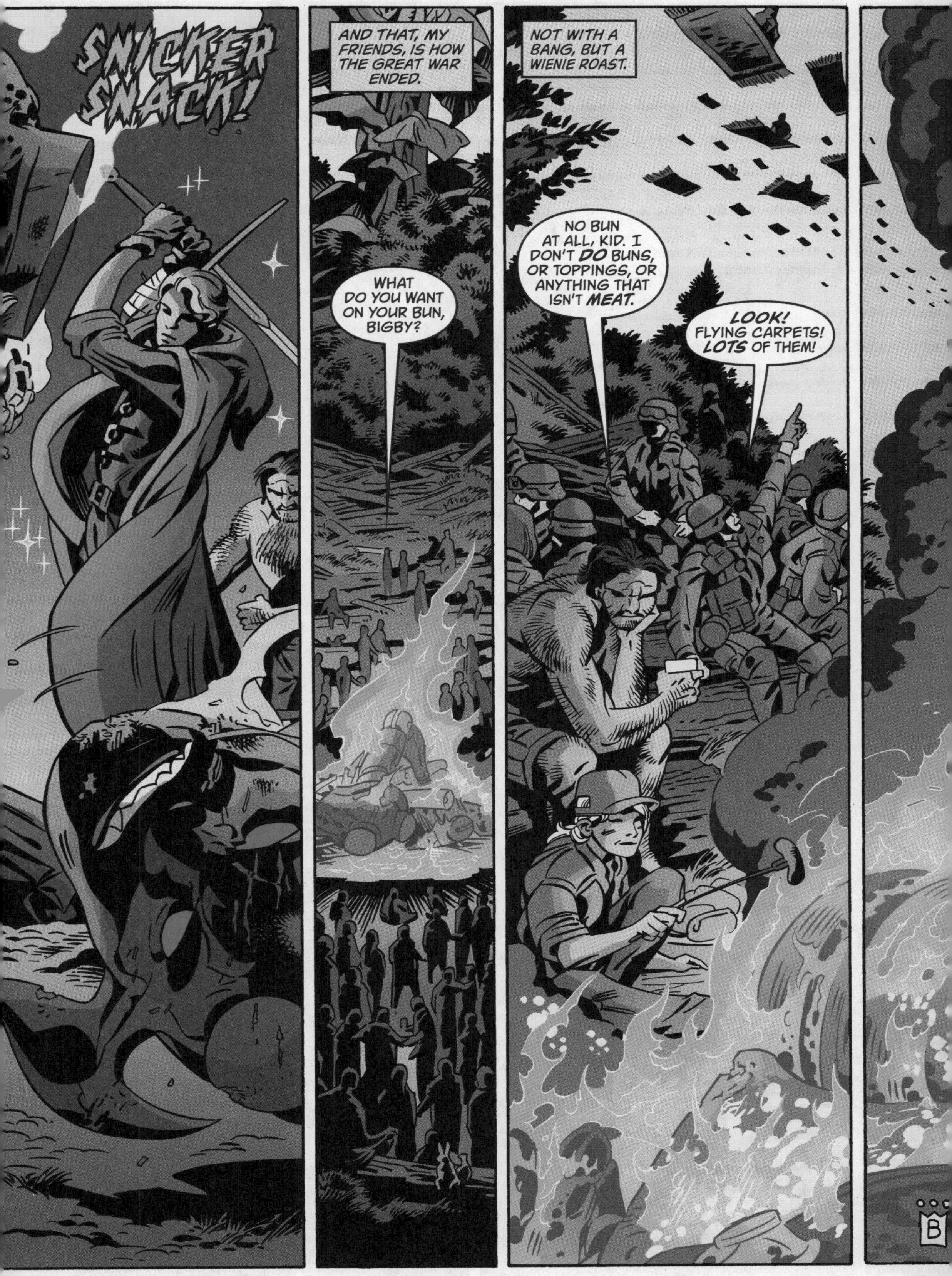

SNICKER SNACK!
AND THAT, MY FRIENDS, IS HOW THE GREAT WAR ENDED.
WHAT DO YOU WANT ON YOUR BUN, BIGBY?
NOT WITH A BANG, BUT A WIENIE ROAST.
NO BUN AT ALL, KID. I DON'T *DO* BUNS, OR TOPPINGS, OR ANYTHING THAT ISN'T *MEAT*.
LOOK! FLYING CARPETS! *LOTS* OF THEM!

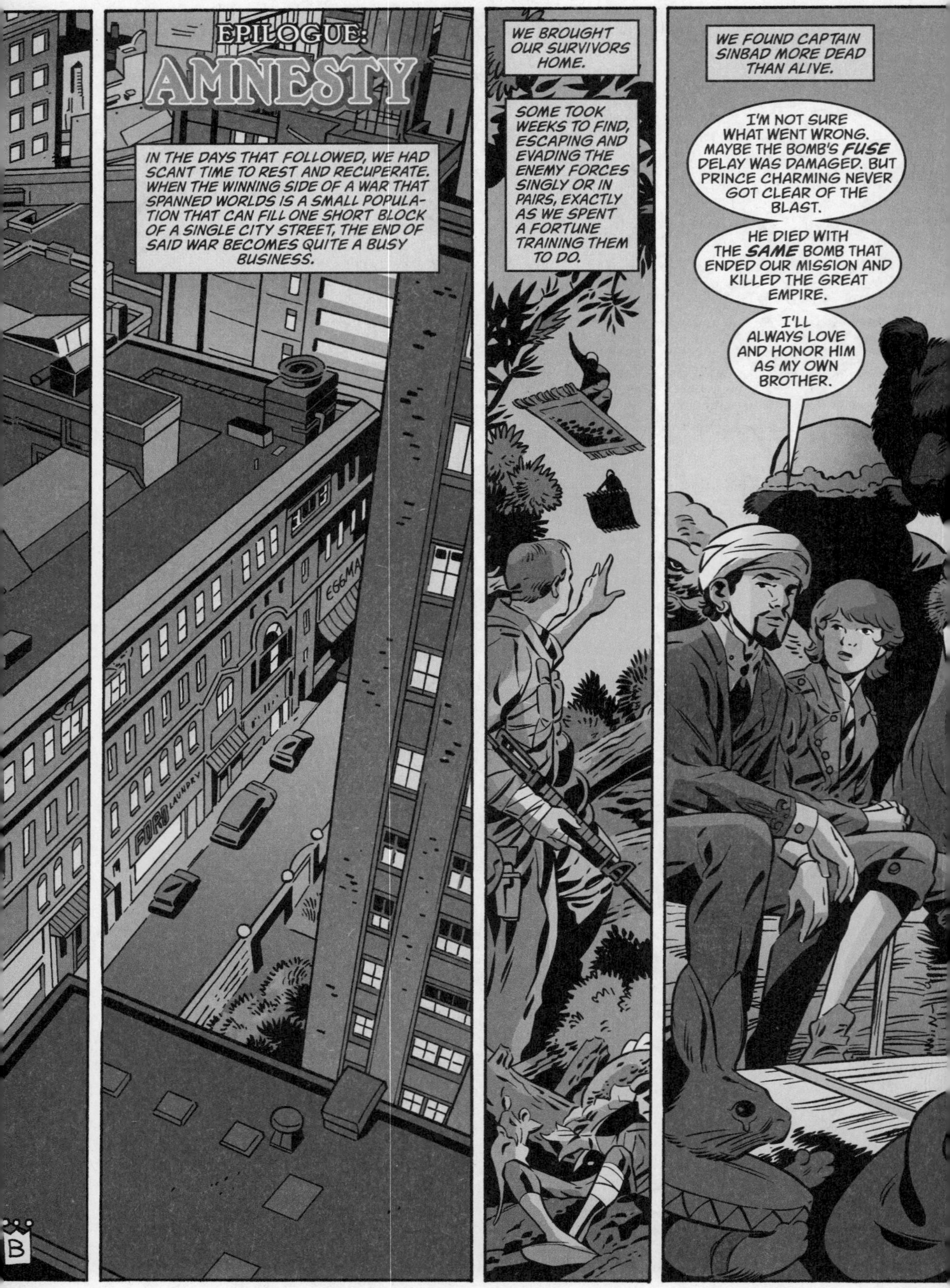
EPILOGUE:
AMNESTY
IN THE DAYS THAT FOLLOWED, WE HAD SCANT TIME TO REST AND RECUPERATE. WHEN THE WINNING SIDE OF A WAR THAT SPANNED WORLDS IS A SMALL POPULATION THAT CAN FILL ONE SHORT BLOCK OF A SINGLE CITY STREET, THE END OF SAID WAR BECOMES QUITE A BUSY BUSINESS.
WE BROUGHT OUR SURVIVORS HOME.
SOME TOOK WEEKS TO FIND, ESCAPING AND EVADING THE ENEMY FORCES SINGLY OR IN PAIRS, EXACTLY AS WE SPENT A FORTUNE TRAINING THEM TO DO.
WE FOUND CAPTAIN SINBAD MORE DEAD THAN ALIVE.
I'M NOT SURE WHAT WENT WRONG. MAYBE THE BOMB'S FUSE DELAY WAS DAMAGED. BUT PRINCE CHARMING NEVER GOT CLEAR OF THE BLAST.
HE DIED WITH THE SAME BOMB THAT ENDED OUR MISSION AND KILLED THE GREAT EMPIRE.
I'LL ALWAYS LOVE AND HONOR HIM AS MY OWN BROTHER.

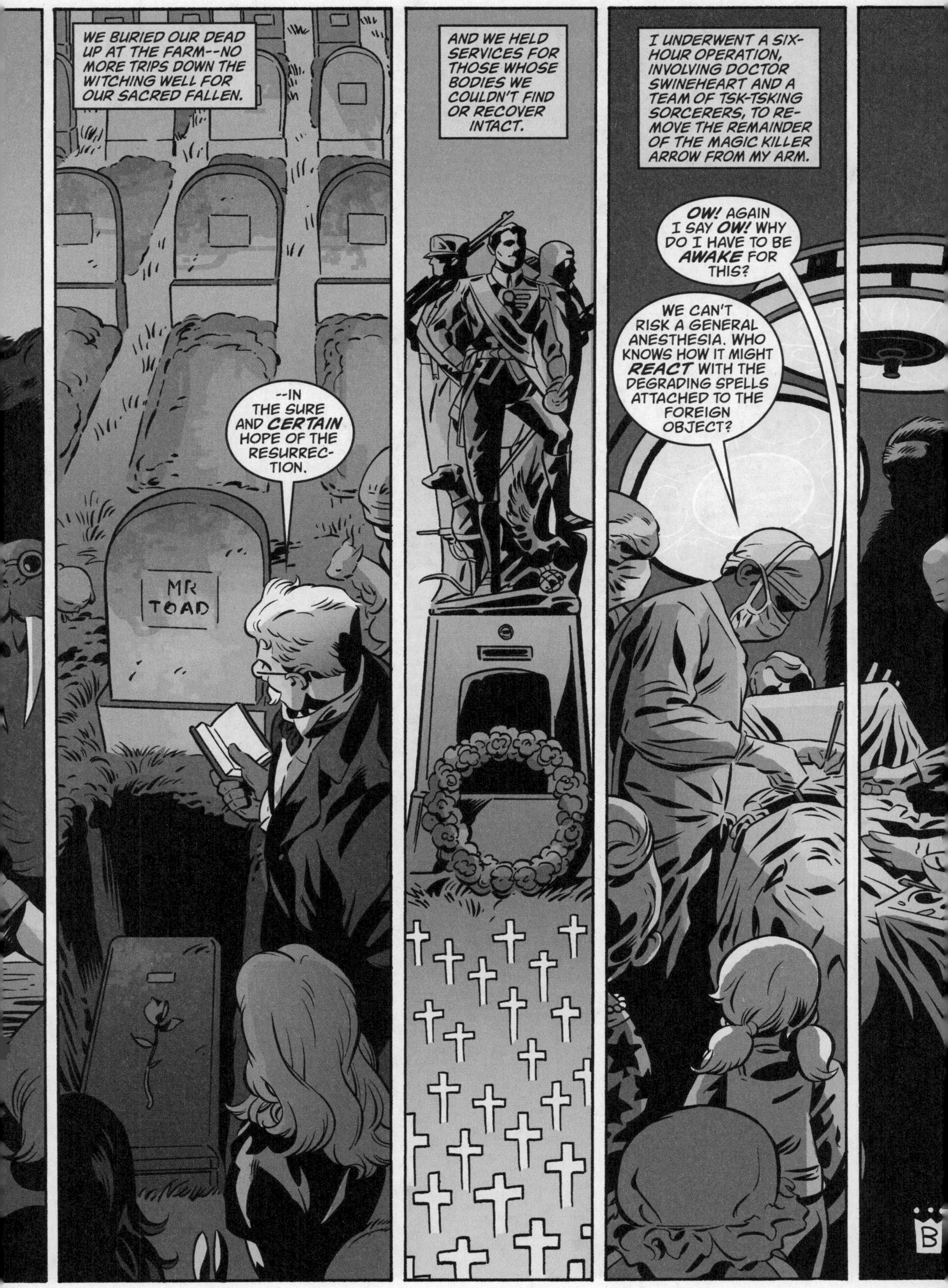
WE BURIED OUR DEAD UP AT THE FARM--NO MORE TRIPS DOWN THE WITCHING WELL FOR OUR SACRED FALLEN.
MR TOAD
--IN THE SURE AND CERTAIN HOPE OF THE RESURREC-TION.
AND WE HELD SERVICES FOR THOSE WHOSE BODIES WE COULDN'T FIND OR RECOVER INTACT.
I UNDERWENT A SIX-HOUR OPERATION, INVOLVING DOCTOR SWINEHEART AND A TEAM OF TSK-TSKING SORCERERS, TO RE-MOVE THE REMAINDER OF THE MAGIC KILLER ARROW FROM MY ARM.
OW! AGAIN I SAY OW! WHY DO I HAVE TO BE AWAKE FOR THIS?
WE CAN'T RISK A GENERAL ANESTHESIA. WHO KNOWS HOW IT MIGHT REACT WITH THE DEGRADING SPELLS ATTACHED TO THE FOREIGN OBJECT?

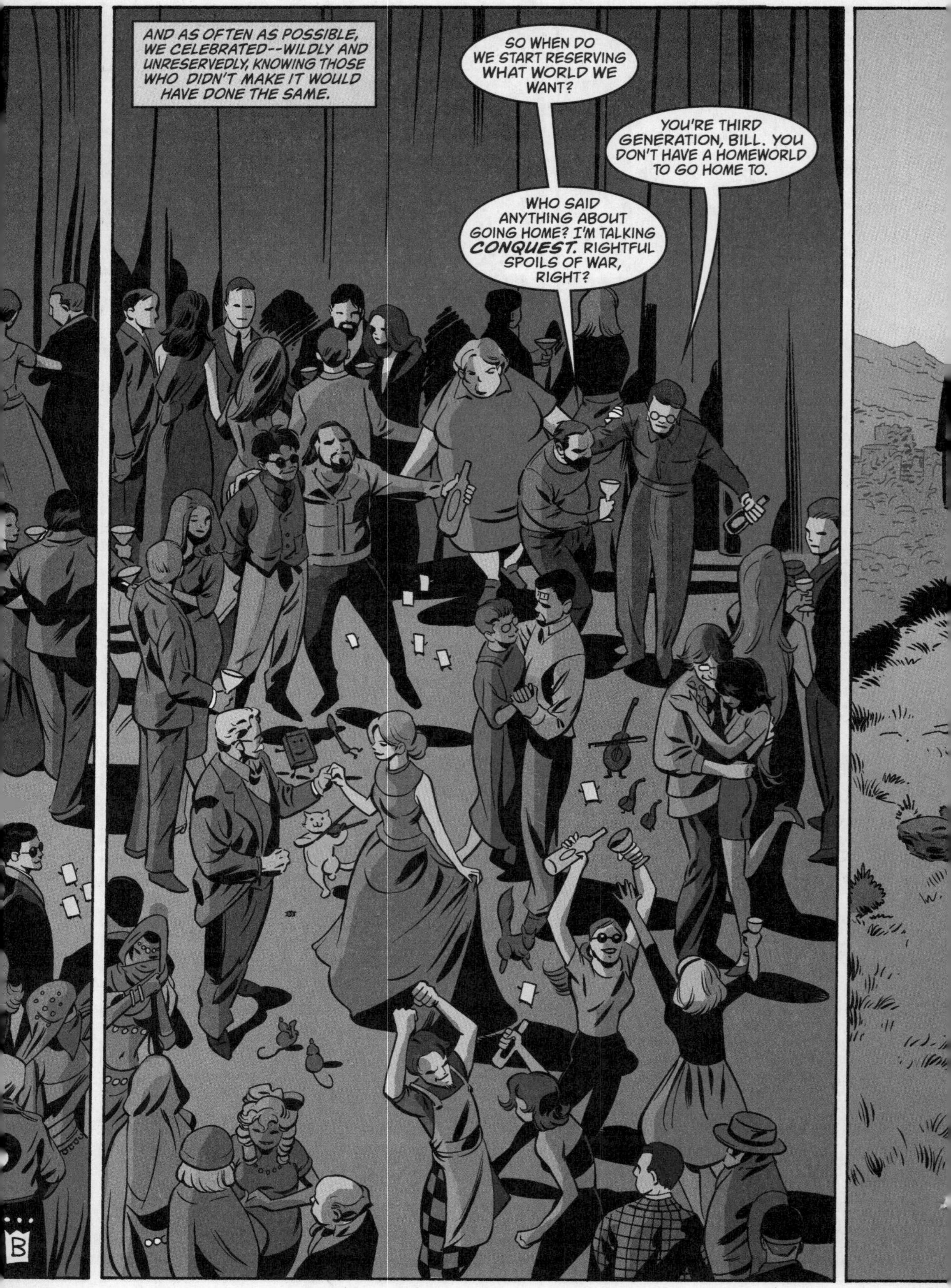
AND AS OFTEN AS POSSIBLE, WE CELEBRATED--WILDLY AND UNRESERVEDLY, KNOWING THOSE WHO DIDN'T MAKE IT WOULD HAVE DONE THE SAME.
SO WHEN DO WE START RESERVING WHAT WORLD WE WANT?
YOU'RE THIRD GENERATION, BILL. YOU DON'T HAVE A HOMEWORLD TO GO HOME TO.
WHO SAID ANYTHING ABOUT GOING HOME? I'M TALKING **CONQUEST.** RIGHTFUL SPOILS OF WAR, RIGHT?

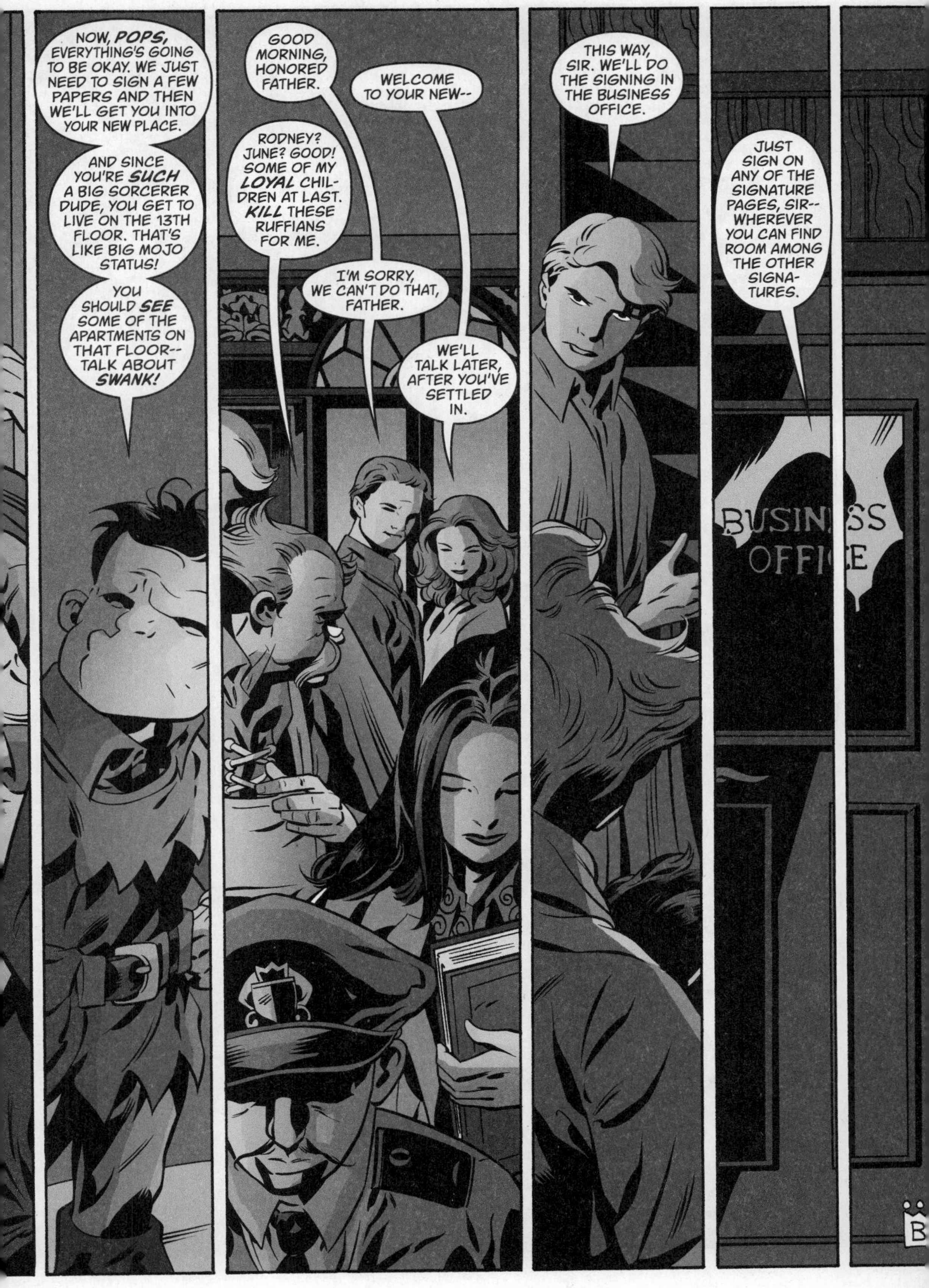
NOW, POPS, EVERYTHING'S GOING TO BE OKAY. WE JUST NEED TO SIGN A FEW PAPERS AND THEN WE'LL GET YOU INTO YOUR NEW PLACE.
AND SINCE YOU'RE SUCH A BIG SORCERER DUDE, YOU GET TO LIVE ON THE 13TH FLOOR. THAT'S LIKE BIG MOJO STATUS!
YOU SHOULD SEE SOME OF THE APARTMENTS ON THAT FLOOR--TALK ABOUT SWANK!
GOOD MORNING, HONORED FATHER.
WELCOME TO YOUR NEW--
RODNEY? JUNE? GOOD! SOME OF MY LOYAL CHILDREN AT LAST. KILL THESE RUFFIANS FOR ME.
I'M SORRY, WE CAN'T DO THAT, FATHER.
WE'LL TALK LATER, AFTER YOU'VE SETTLED IN.
THIS WAY, SIR. WE'LL DO THE SIGNING IN THE BUSINESS OFFICE.
JUST SIGN ON ANY OF THE SIGNATURE PAGES, SIR--WHEREVER YOU CAN FIND ROOM AMONG THE OTHER SIGNATURES.
BUSIN SS
OFFI E

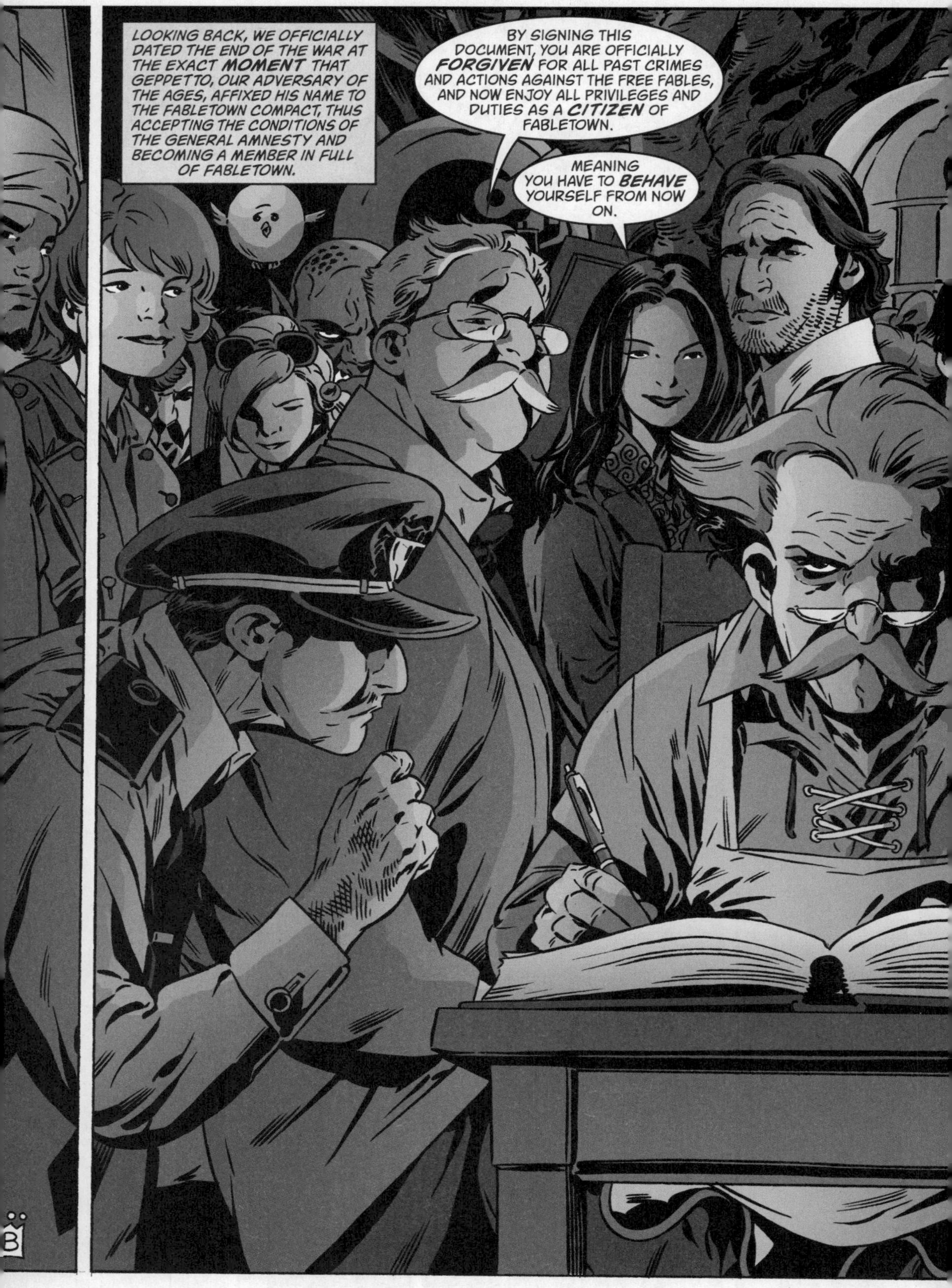

LOOKING BACK, WE OFFICIALLY DATED THE END OF THE WAR AT THE EXACT **MOMENT** THAT GEPPETTO, OUR ADVERSARY OF THE AGES, AFFIXED HIS NAME TO THE FABLETOWN COMPACT, THUS ACCEPTING THE CONDITIONS OF THE GENERAL AMNESTY AND BECOMING A MEMBER IN FULL OF FABLETOWN.
BY SIGNING THIS DOCUMENT, YOU ARE OFFICIALLY **FORGIVEN** FOR ALL PAST CRIMES AND ACTIONS AGAINST THE FREE FABLES, AND NOW ENJOY ALL PRIVILEGES AND DUTIES AS A **CITIZEN** OF FABLETOWN.
MEANING YOU HAVE TO **BEHAVE** YOURSELF FROM NOW ON.

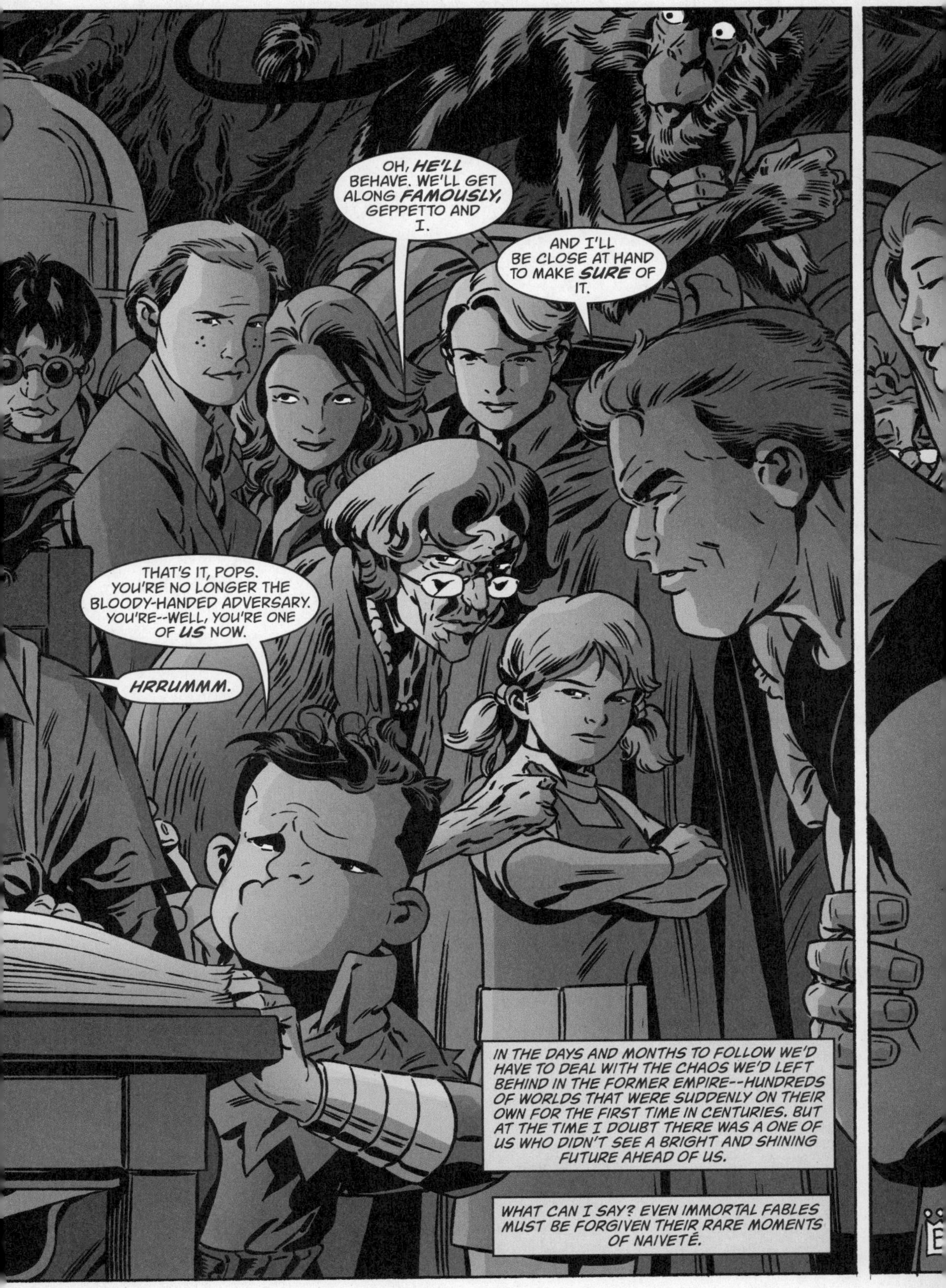
OH, HE'LL BEHAVE. WE'LL GET ALONG FAMOUSLY, GEPPETTO AND I.
AND I'LL BE CLOSE AT HAND TO MAKE SURE OF IT.
THAT'S IT, POPS. YOU'RE NO LONGER THE BLOODY-HANDED ADVERSARY. YOU'RE--WELL, YOU'RE ONE OF US NOW.
HRRUMMM.
IN THE DAYS AND MONTHS TO FOLLOW WE'D HAVE TO DEAL WITH THE CHAOS WE'D LEFT BEHIND IN THE FORMER EMPIRE--HUNDREDS OF WORLDS THAT WERE SUDDENLY ON THEIR OWN FOR THE FIRST TIME IN CENTURIES. BUT AT THE TIME I DOUBT THERE WAS A ONE OF US WHO DIDN'T SEE A BRIGHT AND SHINING FUTURE AHEAD OF US.
WHAT CAN I SAY? EVEN IMMORTAL FABLES MUST BE FORGIVEN THEIR RARE MOMENTS OF NAIVETÉ.

The Fables Road

An Afterword by Bill Willingham

In Germany there's a road of stories. It's called, in a very loose translation (I'm no scholar of languages), the Fairytale Road. It recreates the path (as best the historical records allow, given the caveat that even the most learned historians seldom completely agree with each other) taken by the original wanderings of the Brothers Grimm on their journeys to collect and document the folktales for which they are justly famous. Sometimes the delightfully meandering Fairytale Road travels along existing roads, while at other times, in places where the original pathways no longer exist, one section of the road is connected to another by nothing more than imagination and some lines on a map. And always there are many interesting and rewarding diversions along the way.

You can walk the Fairytale Road today. The German people are quite justifiably proud of it, and a goodly chunk of their tourist industry is dedicated to helping you enjoy it to whatever extent you desire. I was privileged to walk parts of the Road during my all-too-brief years in Germany — only parts, though. Having just two or three days at a time when I was free to visit it, I had to pick and choose small sections of the greater path. To travel it in its entirety, as many do each year, can take months. But that was just fine. The few steps I was able to take along the famous Fairytale Road were often glorious ones, and never less than completely worth it.

And this brings us, finally, to the point of my afterword. I would like to propose, by virtue of the storyteller's long-established right of extended metaphor, that the FABLES series is a road similar to Germany's Fairytale Road, equal in intent and ambition, if not in stature. It's a journey of connected stories that began a bit more than six years ago, when a breathless Jack Horner ran into the Woodland Building to report a terrible crime. Now, seventy-five issues later, we've reached one of the important milestones along our route. With the exception of a few (one hopes) interesting diversions along the way, every episode of the series to date was leading up to the events chronicled in these pages. That's worth pausing briefly on our travels to take note and remark upon it; hence these paragraphs.

But the journey doesn't end here. Far from it. Like the wanderings of the Brothers Grimm, FABLES is a journey of years — perhaps even a lifetime (we'll see). We've got a long way to go yet before our great Fairytale Road — carved in bits and pieces out of their scholarship — is complete. And, like our distinguished predecessors, we would like nothing more than to fill the coming years with many fellow travelers.

Some of you reading these words have been with us for all six-plus years of the road so far, strolling right along with us as we blaze the path. Thank you. Your company is always enjoyable, making the hard parts of the road easier and making the fun and exciting parts all the better for having someone along to share the delights as we first notice them. Others have walked the Fables Road only once in a while (as I did back in Germany), sampling specific stories that happened to catch your eye. Thank you, too. Your visits, brief though they might be, are always welcome. And some of you, to run this extended metaphor completely into the ground, have only recently discovered the Fables Road, and are walking different sections of it, either following us at your own pace or hurrying to catch up to the first of us. Thank you, and welcome. We hope you enjoy our road, and its many diversions and side trips, as much as we've enjoyed (and continue to enjoy) building it for you.

So here we are at issue seventy-five. We've paused to catch our breath, but now it's time to continue on. We've got a long way to go yet. To quote a favorite minstrel of mine, "The long road is a rainbow, and the pot of gold lies out there somewhere." Care to walk along with us for a bit longer?

War Plans

Designs and sketches by Mark Buckingham

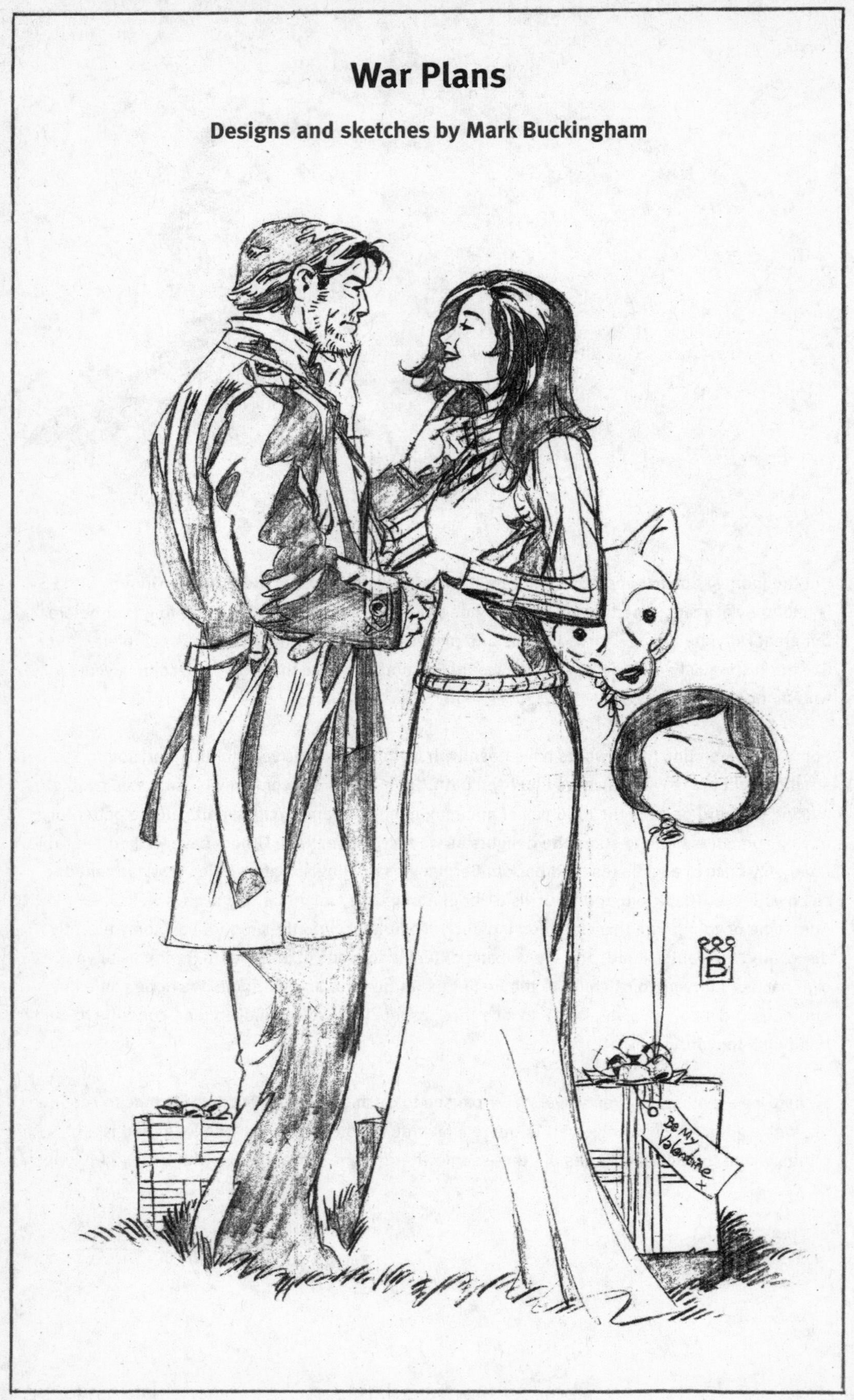
Be My Valentine x

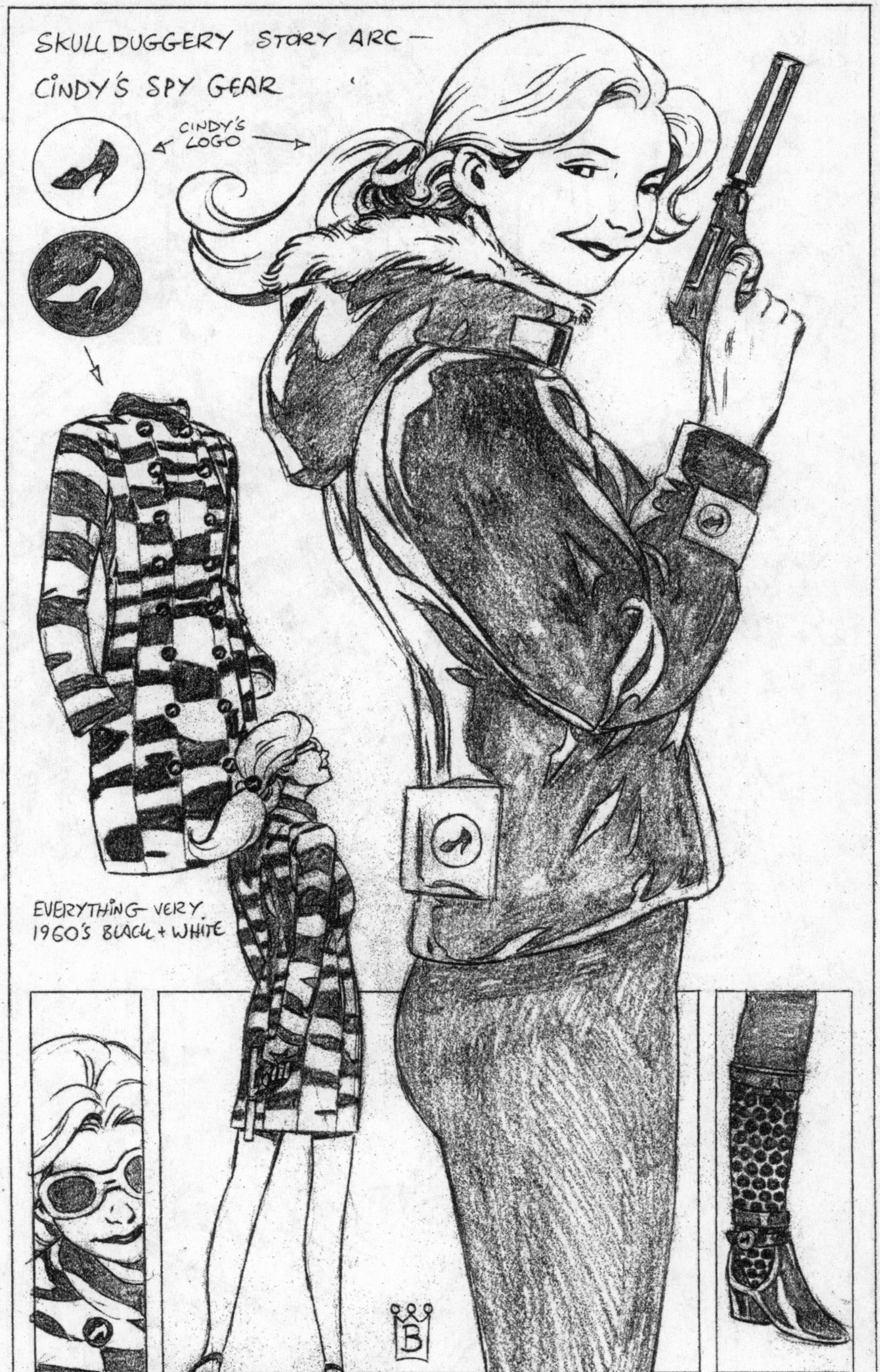
SKULLDUGGERY STORY ARC —
CINDY'S SPY GEAR
CINDY'S LOGO
EVERYTHING VERY 1960'S BLACK + WHITE

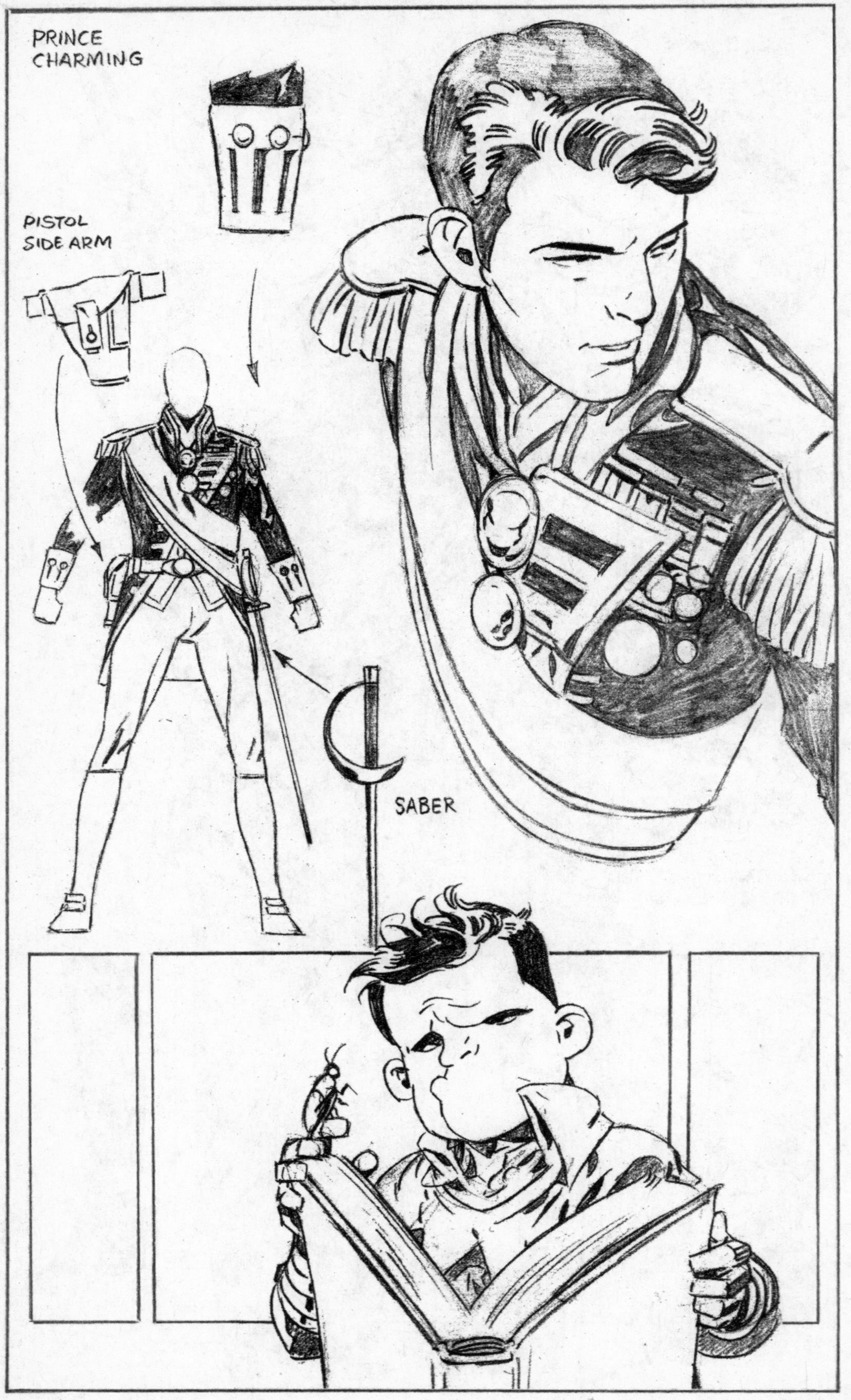
PRINCE
CHARMING
PISTOL
SIDE ARM
SABER

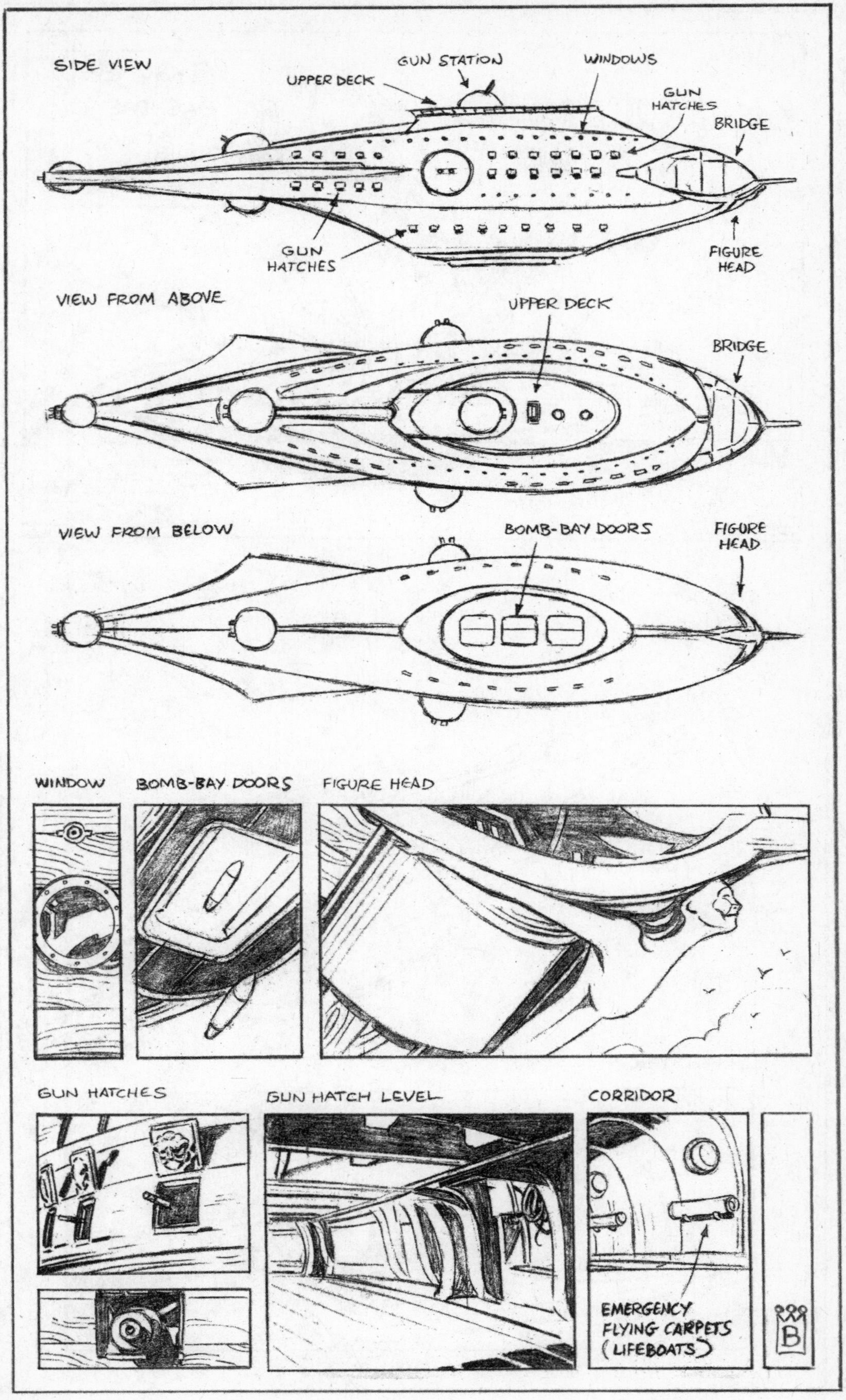
SIDE VIEW
GUN STATION
WINDOWS
UPPER DECK
GUN HATCHES
BRIDGE
GUN HATCHES
FIGURE HEAD
VIEW FROM ABOVE
UPPER DECK
BRIDGE
VIEW FROM BELOW
BOMB-BAY DOORS
FIGURE HEAD
WINDOW
BOMB-BAY DOORS
FIGURE HEAD
GUN HATCHES
GUN HATCH LEVEL
CORRIDOR
EMERGENCY FLYING CARPETS (LIFEBOATS)
B

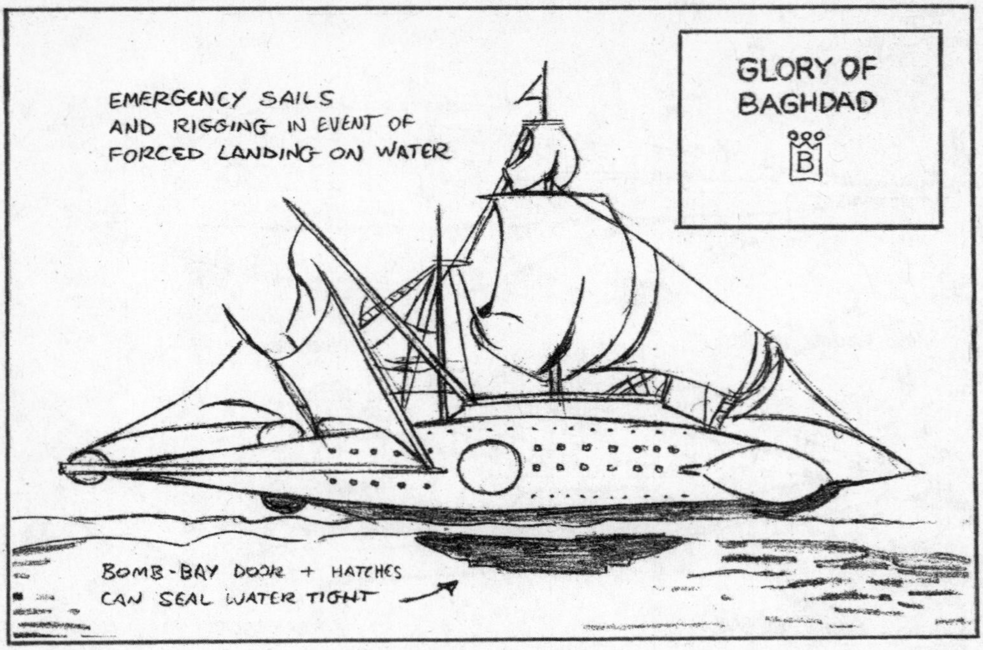
EMERGENCY SAILS
AND RIGGING IN EVENT OF
FORCED LANDING ON WATER
GLORY OF
BAGHDAD
B
BOMB-BAY DOOR + HATCHES
CAN SEAL WATER TIGHT

SKY SHIP
IN FLIGHT

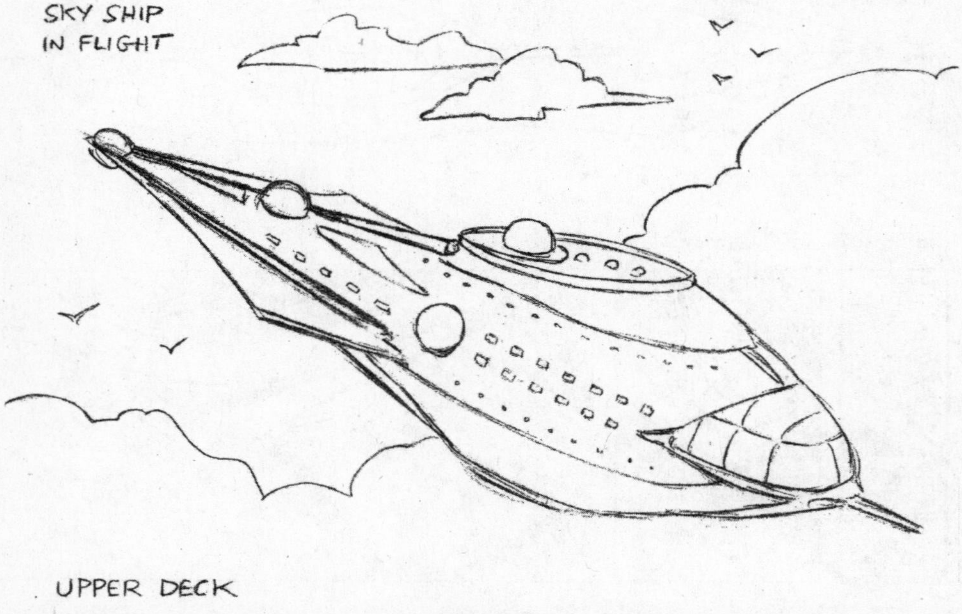

UPPER DECK

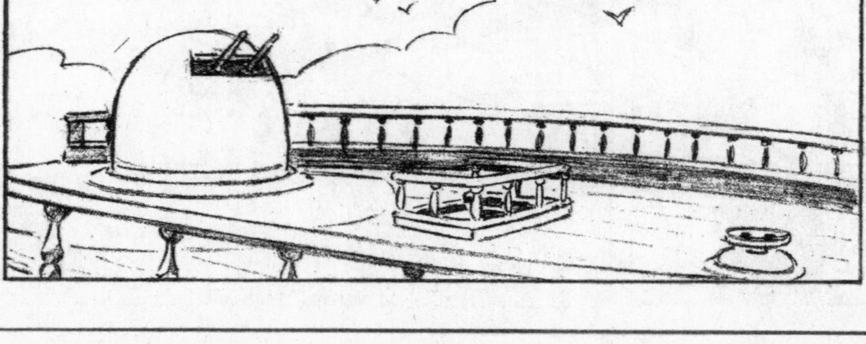

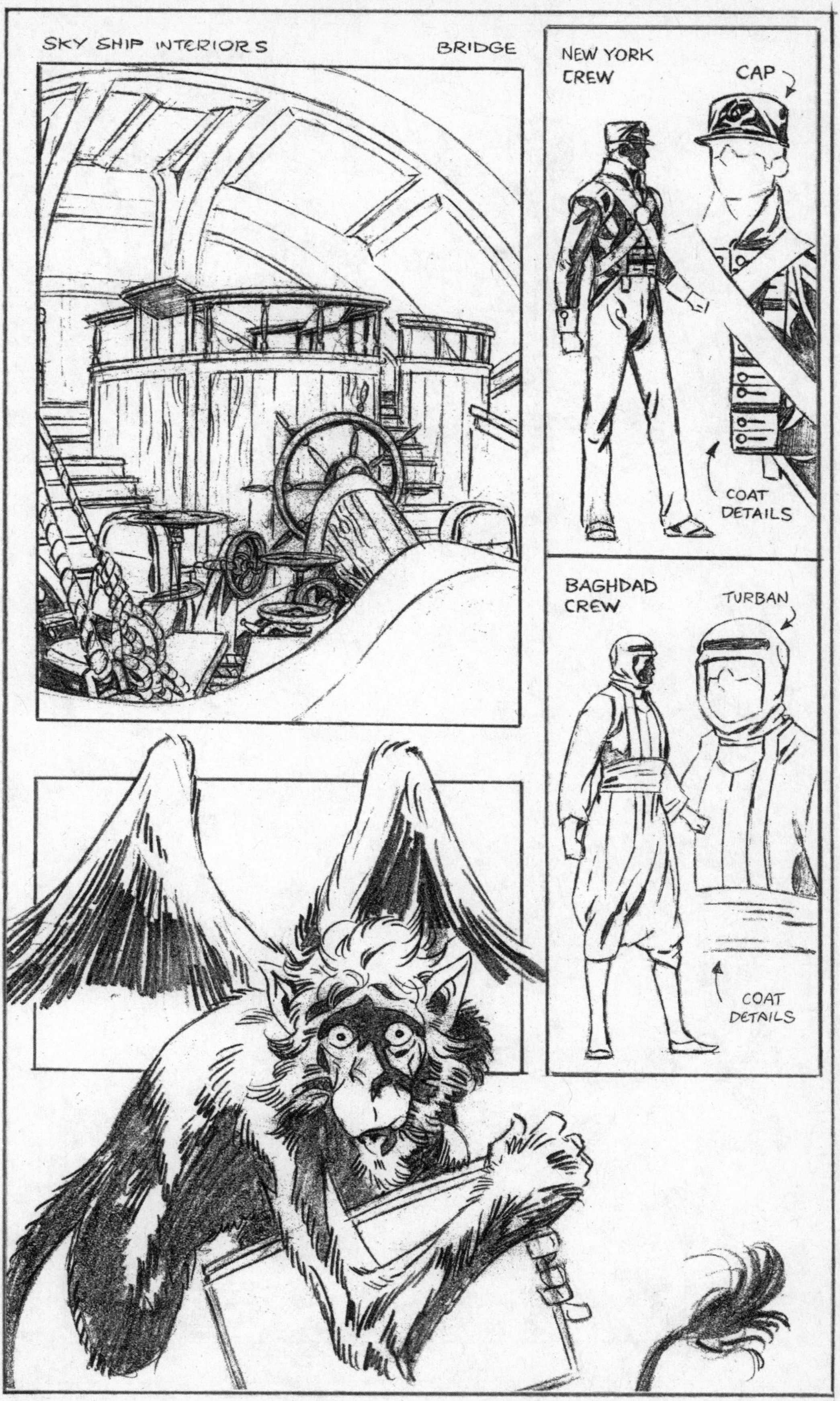
SKY SHIP INTERIORS
BRIDGE
NEW YORK CREW
CAP
COAT DETAILS
BAGHDAD CREW
TURBAN
COAT DETAILS

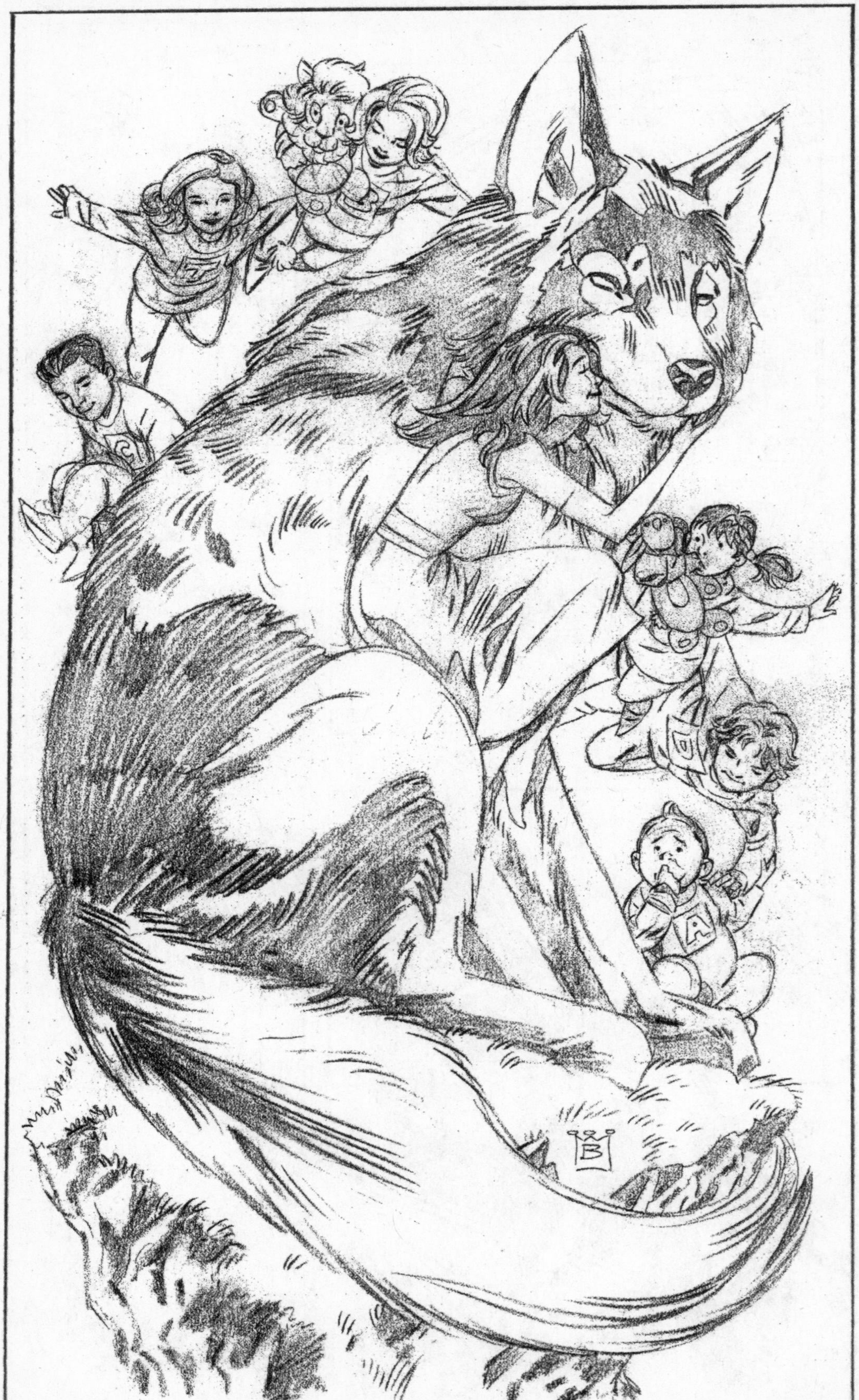

- A FABLES GALLERY -

ADVERSARY
WARRIORS
BY
ERIC POWELL

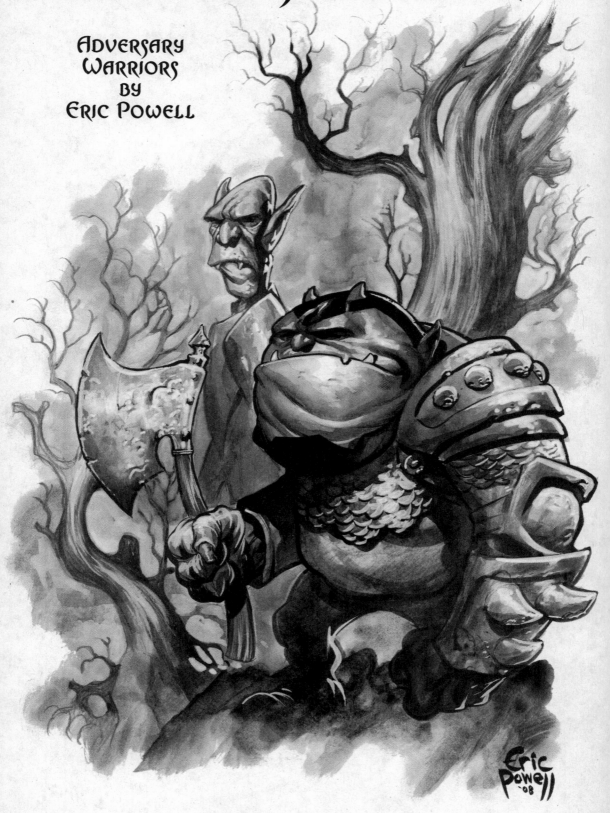

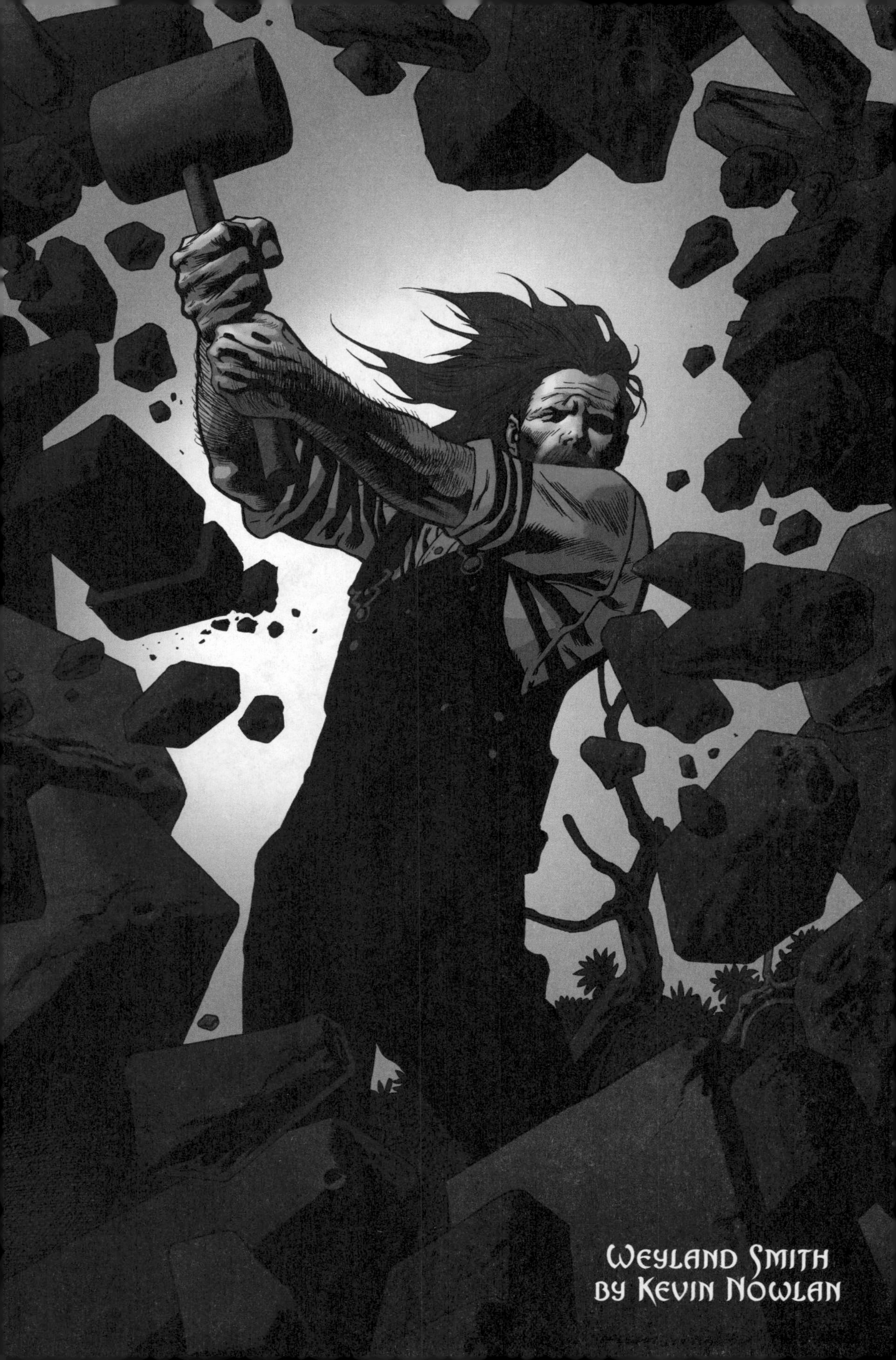
Weyland Smith
by Kevin Nowlan

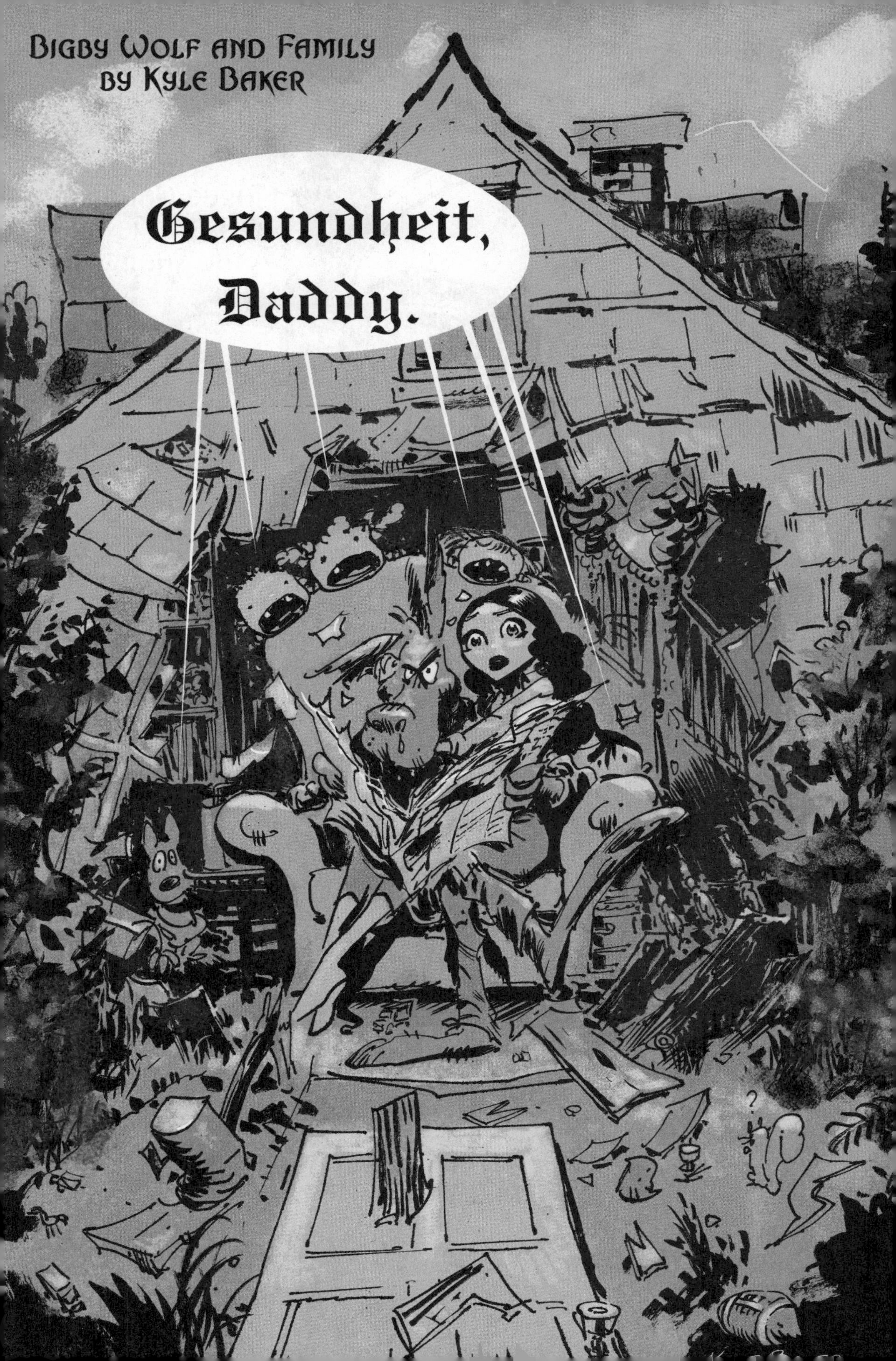
Bigby Wolf and Family
by Kyle Baker
Gesundheit, Daddy.

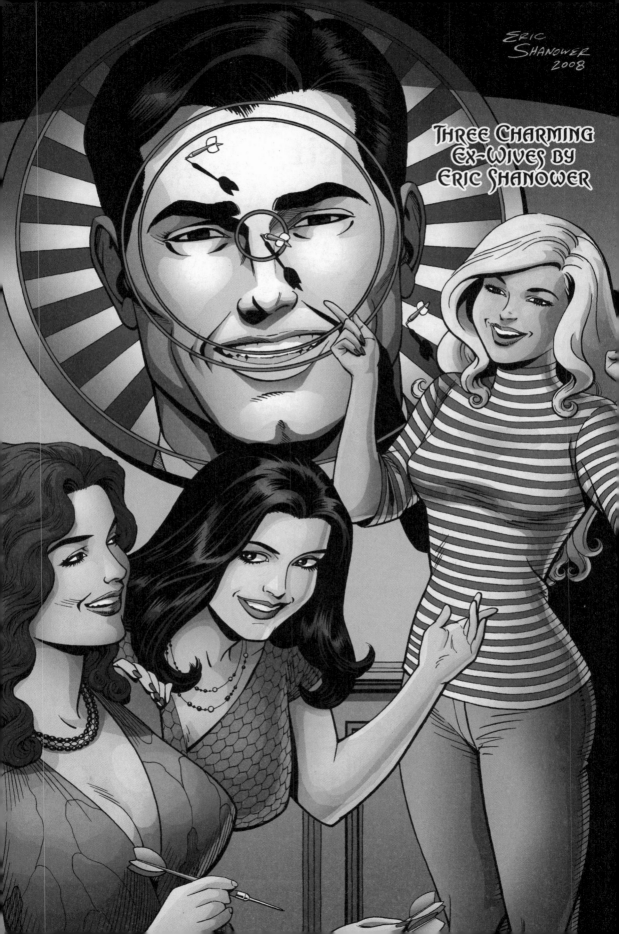

THREE CHARMING
EX-WIVES BY
ERIC SHANOWER

Red Riding Hood and Friend
by Darwyn Cooke

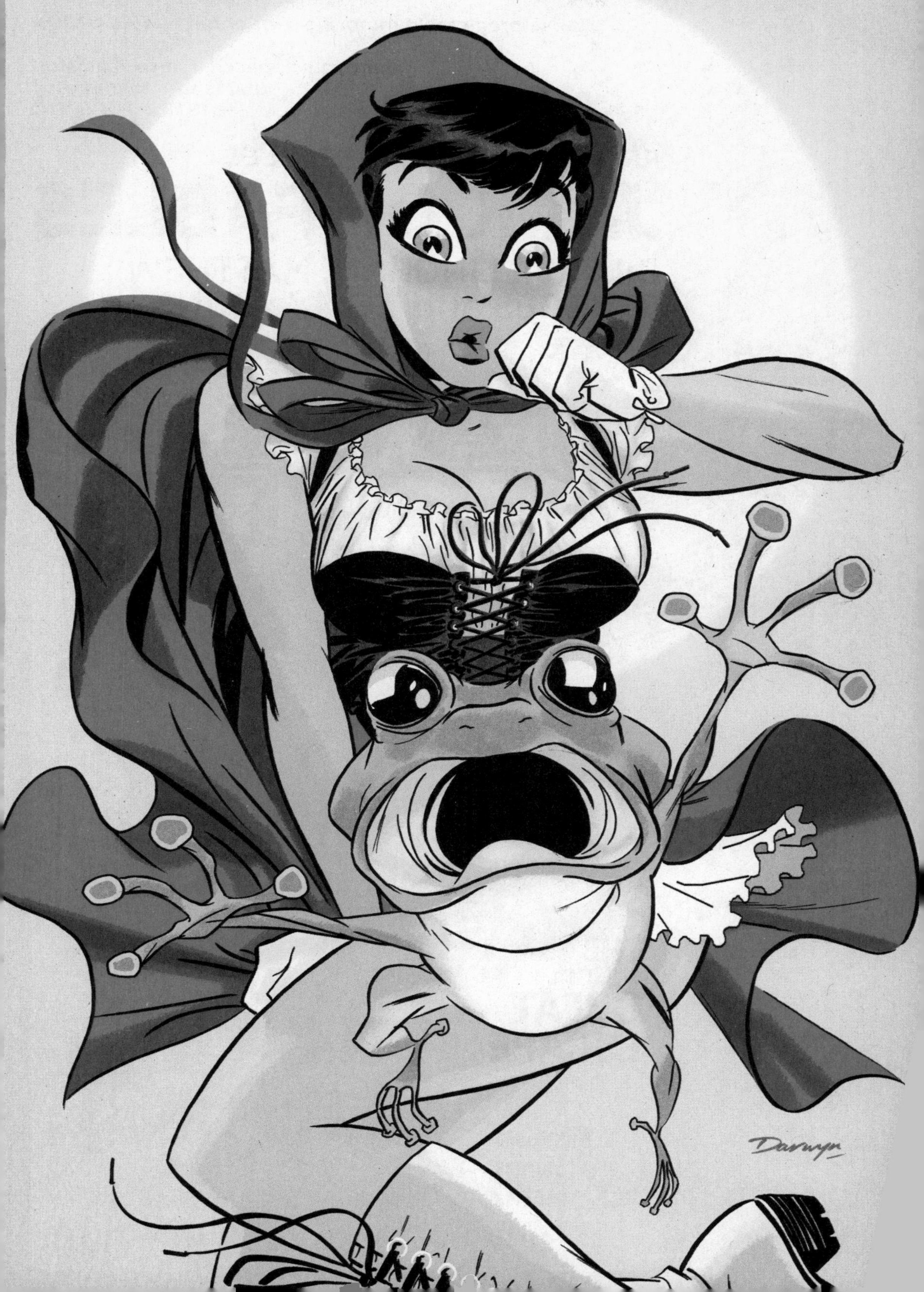
Darwyn

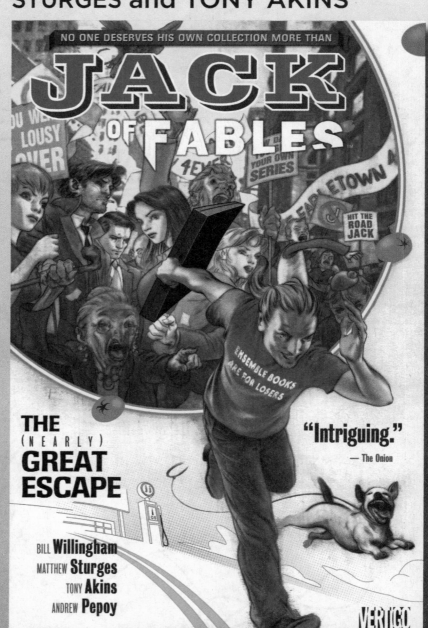